K. Nagdi
Rubber as an Engineering Material:
Guideline for Users

Khairi Nagdi

Rubber as
an Engineering Material:
Guideline for Users

106 Figures and 71 Tables

Hanser Publishers, Munich Vienna New York Barcelona

The Author: Dr. Khairi Nagdi, D-7015 Korntal-Münchingen

Die Deutsche Bibliothek – CIP-Einheitsaufnahme

Nagdi, Khairi:
Rubber as an engineering material : guideline for users ; 71 tables
/ Khairi Nagdi. – Munich ; Vienna ; New York ; Barcelona :
Hanser Publ., 1993
    ISBN 3-446-16282-8

Typesetting: Fertigsatz, München

Printed and bound in Germany by PDC Paderborner Druckcentrum GmbH

To my wife,
Julia,
for her patience
and encouragement

Preface

Rubber as an Engineering Material is a general guide intended primarily for users of rubber parts and materials. It has no equivalent on the international book market, being the most comprehensive, concise and easily understandable book that describes those rubber properties required by the engineer for his or her designs. Other innumerable publications on rubber materials, intended mainly for chemists and rubber technologists, deal primarily with compounding and processing but do not provide the user with adequate essential information. The information provided in this book is indispensable for selecting the rubber materials of critical parts for all kinds of applications (including automotive and hydraulic industries, offshore engineering and aerospace technology).

This book is addressed to the following:
– designers and technicians;
– rubber maintenance and sales engineers;
– materials scientists and testers;
– specification writers;
– lubricants sales engineers;
– sales personnel and buyers;
– high school students and engineering faculty; and
– participants of training seminars and courses on rubber applications.

Furthermore, young chemists in the rubber industry will find in this book the fundamentals of rubber chemistry.

The terminology in *Rubber as an Engineering Material* is greatly simplified, and the topics are ordered systematically. Those readers who are not familiar with rubber materials are advised to follow the given sequence. An Appendix is offered for those users who are not trained in chemistry, to help them understand the meanings of common chemical names; it is recommended that such users first study the Appendix before reading the rest of the book.

I would like to thank Dr. W. Glenz, of Hanser Publishers, for the excellent cooperation during the production of this book.

Khairi Nagdi

Contents

CHAPTER 1

Basic Principles of Rubber Chemistry

1.1 Basic Terms

The term "rubber" originally meant the material obtained from the rubber tree *Hevea brasiliensis*. Today, a distinction is made between **crude** rubbers and **vulcanized** rubbers, or **elastomers**. (*Elastomer* is the preferred term for vulcanized rubber. Other terms that are less frequently used include **vulcanizate** and **cross-linked** rubber).

For over a century, all rubber goods were manufactured from natural crude rubber, which is generated in the rubber tree as a milky liquid (**emulsion**) known as **natural latex.** The latter is coagulated and the solid material separated, washed and dried to obtain a solid natural crude rubber. Later, man-made **synthetic** crude rubbers were developed and became available in commercial quantities. They are prepared by reacting certain low-molecular-weight substances called **monomers** to form long-chain molecules called **polymers**. They are usually obtained as a water emulsion known as **synthetic latex**, which is similarly coagulated and the solid material separated, washed and dried to obtain solid synthetic crude rubbers.

Crude rubbers, whether natural or synthetic, are plastic-like materials that can be deformed at high temperatures. They are generally not suitable for use in the form in which they are supplied. The **elastic** properties have to be developed by further **compounding** (i.e., incorporating certain additives in the crude rubber). By heating the rubber mixture, a chemical reaction called **vulcanization** or **cure** takes place. In this process the chain molecules are fastened together at various points along their lengths by cross-links. These cross-links prevent slippage of chains past each other.

Unlike crude rubber, elastomers are elastic materials, that is, they have the ability to deform substantially under the application of force and then snap back to almost their original shape when the force is removed. The term *elastomer* is derived from *elastic polymers*.

One important group of elastomers, which do not require vulcanization, are the **thermoplastic elastomers (TPEs)**. These are polymers that combine **thermoplasticity** and elasticity. They have elastic properties (like conventional elastomers) within a certain range of temperature, but they melt at elevated temperatures.

Synthetic elastomers are used either because they perform better than vulcanized natural rubbers or because they are lower in price or for both reasons.

1.2 Macromolecules, Polymers and Monomers

Materials such as fibers, plastics, crude rubbers and elastomers are all composed of **macromolecules**, which are many thousands of times larger than molecules of ordinary chemical substances like benzene (C_6H_6), methanol (CH_3-OH) and acetone (CH_3-CO-CH_3). It should be noted, however, that these "giant" long chain molecules are not visible even under the best microscopes available.

Macromolecules are generally made up of a large number of simple repeating units attached to each other in long chains. For this reason, they have been named **polymers** from the Greek *poly* (= many) and *meros* (= parts). As mentioned before, the molecular units that are used to synthesize polymers are called monomers, low-molecular-weight substances the molecules of which are capable of reacting with like or unlike molecules to form a polymer. The chemical reactions in which monomers are joined together to form a polymer are called **polymerization** reactions.

1.3 The Synthesis of Polymers

There are many polymers that occur ready-made in nature (biopolymers), but it is not known how these natural chain molecules are made. However, chemists have been able to produce synthetic polymers by polymerizing a wide variety of monomers. There are two main types of polymerization:
– addition polymerization; and
– condensation polymerization.

Addition polymerization involves a simple addition of monomer molecules to each other, without the loss of any atoms from the original molecule. A typical example of addition polymerization is the formation of the flexible plastic polyethylene from ethylene gas as shown in **Fig. 1.1**. Ethylene is an unsaturated hydrocarbon because of the presence of a double bond between the two carbon atoms. One of these two bonds opens and becomes available as two bonds, ready to unite with similarly available bonds from adjacent ethylene molecules. In this way it is possible to produce a **saturated** long-chain polymer from **unsaturated** monomer.

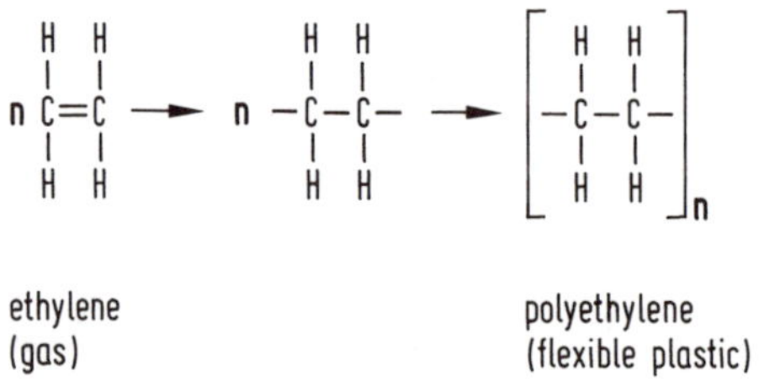

ethylene
(gas)

polyethylene
(flexible plastic)

Fig. 1.1: Synthesis of Polyethylene

A somewhat more complex form of addition polymerization occurs with unsaturated monomers of the **diene** type. These differ from the ethylene monomers in possessing two conjugated double bonds (i.e., double bonds alternating with single bonds). An important and typical diene is **butadiene**. The structural formulas of the monomer and polymer are shown in **Fig. 1.2**. It can be seen that when a diene is polymerized, the polymer obtained differs in one important aspect from polyethylene: it still contains a double bond in each unit of the chain. This is a natural outcome of the the monomer having two double bonds at the start.

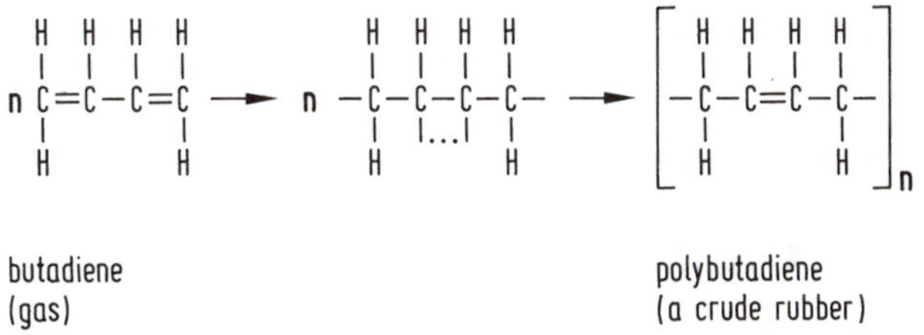

butadiene
(gas)

polybutadiene
(a crude rubber)

Fig. 1.2: Synthesis of Polybutadiene

Condensation polymerization involves a reaction between bifunctional reactants in which a small molecule is eliminated during each step of the polymer- building reaction. A typical example of condensation polymerization is the formation of polyamide polymers (e.g., nylon). According to the equation shown in **Fig. 1.3** they are produced by condensing diamines (H_2N-R-NH_2) and dicarboxylic acids HOOC-R'-COOH. The resulting product contains reactive groups, which can continue to react to produce high-molecular-weight polymers. Water is eliminated at each step of the polymer building.

1) $H_2N-R-N-$ ┃ H + HO ┃ $OC-R'-COOH$ ⟶

diamine   dicarboxylic acid

$H_2N-R-NH-OC-R'-COOH$ + H_2O

2)   n $H_2N-R-NH-OC-R'-COOH$ ⟶

H_2N┤R-NH-OC-R'├ₙCOOH + n H_2O

polyamide polymer

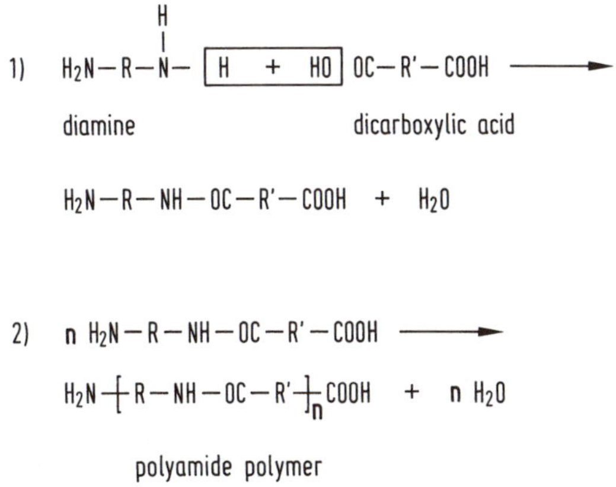

Fig. 1.3: Synthesis of Polyamides

1.4 Molecular Weight of Polymers

The molecular weight of one single macromolecule is equal to the molecular weight of the repeating unit multiplied by the number of repeating units (n) in the molecule. The molecular weight of polyethylene, for example, can be calculated from the formula (C_2H_4)n. This is equal to 28 n. If n is equal to 1000, for example, the molecular weight of the polyethylene in question will be 28000. The molecular weight of polyethylene can vary from below 2000 (waxy products) to above one million (very tough materials) according to the polymerization reaction conditions.

Some natural polymers (biopolymers) as specific proteins consist of macromolecules with identical molecular weight. However, most synthetic polymers and many natural polymers such as cellulose and crude natural rubber consist of macromolecules with different molecular weight. Accordingly, it is customary to use the term **average molecular weight** when describing the molecular weight of polymers.

1.5 Homopolymers, Copolymers and Terpolymers

Polymers consisting of multiples of the same repeating units, as polyethylene, are called **homopolymers**. If two different monomers (e.g., A and B) are polymerized, the resulting product is called a **copolymer**. The arrangement of A and B could be either **random** or **alternating**, as shown in **Fig. 1.4a** and **1.4b**, respectively. Copolymers may also consist of sequences of the repeating units in the chain and these are called **block copolymers (Fig. 1.4c)**. When these sequences are present as branches, the copolymer is said to be a **graft copolymer (Fig. 1.4d)**. Polymers obtained from three different monomers (e.g., A, B and C) are called **terpolymers** with the general formula (A) (B) (C).

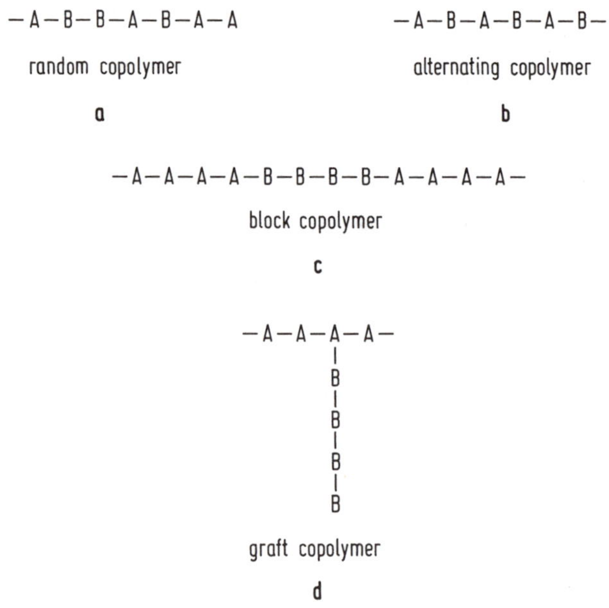

```
 − A − B − B − A − B − A − A              − A − B − A − B − A − B −

      random  copolymer                      alternating  copolymer

             a                                       b


         − A − A − A − A − B − B − B − B − A − A − A − A −

                       block  copolymer

                             c


               − A − A − A − A −
                       |
                       B
                       |
                       B
                       |
                       B
                       |
                       B

                  graft  copolymer

                       d
```

Fig. 1.4: Configurations of Copolymers

The polymer chains may be linear, branched or cross-linked, as shown in **Fig. 1.5**. The properties of a polymer depend mainly on the length and configuration of the macromolecules, the extent of interaction among them and the presence or absence of functional groups.

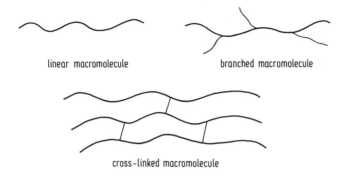

linear macromolecule   branched macromolecule

cross-linked macromolecule

Fig. 1.5: Configurations of Macromolecules

1.6 Plastomers, Elastomers, Thermoplastic Elastomers and Thermosets

Polymers can be divided into four groups according to their deformation properties in the solid state:
– plastomers (thermoplastics);
– elastomers (vulcanized rubbers);
– thermoplastic elastomers; and
– thermosets (duromers).

Plastomers, such as polyethylene, polystyrene and PVC, consist of entangled linear or branched macromolecules, held together by intermolecular forces. In the solid state they deform permanently and do not recover after complete release of the force producing the deformation. This is because their macromolecules are loose **(Fig. 1.6a)** and can slip past each other on the application of pressure.

Plastomers are usually supplied in granular or pelleted form and can be repeatedly softened by heating and hardened by cooling, within a temperature range characteristic of each plastic. In the softened state, they can be shaped into articles by molding or extrusion. The change upon heating is substantially physical. Therefore, scrap or reject parts can be reprocessed. Furthermore, plastomers can be dissolved in suitable solvents and regain their properties when the solvent is evaporated.

As mentioned earlier, **elastomers** are elastic materials that recover to almost their original shape after complete release of the applied force. Furthermore, they are insoluble and infusible, that is, they can swell only in solvents such as benzene and methyl ethyl ketone and decompose when heated far beyond the maximum service temperature. These unique properties occur because the macromolecules of elastomers, in contrast to those of plastomers, are cross-linked by chemical bonds **(Fig. 1.6b)**. These cross-links prevent the long-chain molecules from slipping past each other on the application of force and from dissolving in solvents or melting by heating. The number of cross-links can be increased until a rigid network results, as in the case of hard rubber (ebonite).

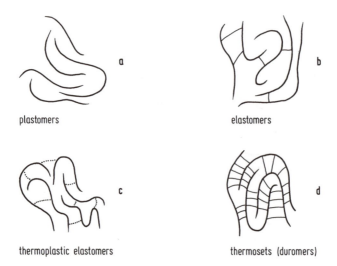

plastomers   elastomers

thermoplastic elastomers   thermosets (duromers)

Fig. 1.6: Configurations of Polymer Types

As mentioned in section 1.1, elastomers are produced from crude rubbers, in which a variety of compounding ingredients are incorporated. The obtained rubber mixtures are usually tacky, thermoplastic and soluble in strong solvents. During the vulcanization (cure) the chain molecules of the crude rubber are joined by widely spaced cross-links.

After having been cross-linked, the soft plastic-like material exhibits a high degree of elastic recovery, loses its tackiness, becomes insoluble in solvents and infusible when heated and is more resistant to deterioration caused by aging factors.

Scrap or reject parts cannot be reprocessed unless the cross-links have been destroyed by chemical and mechanical processes. The "devulcanized" product is called **reclaim** or **reclaimed rubber**. (See chapter 8 for a further discussion of elastomers.)

Thermoplastic elastomers are block copolymers **(Fig. 1.6c)** that possess elastic properties within a certain range of temperature, typically from room temperature to about 70°C. The elastic properties are due to "physical" cross-links resulting from secondary intermolecular forces such as hydrogen bonding. These cross-links (shown as points in **Fig. 1.6c**) disappear when heated above a certain temperature and reform immediately on cooling to develop elastic properties. (Thermoplastic elastomers will be discussed in more detail in chapter 9.)

Thermoplastic elastomers fill a gap between the noncross-linked plastomers and the chemically cross-linked elastomers. They can be processed and even reprocessed in the manner of thermoplastic materials without vulcanization. Some thermoplastic elastomers can be dissolved in common solvents and regain their properties when the solvent is evaporated.

Thermosets (duromers) such as phenolic resins, urea and melamine plastics, are rigid materials that are produced from certain reactants. By heating, they undergo a chemical change in which space network molecules are formed. This process is similar to the vulcanization of rubber mixtures. However, the macromolecules of thermosets are much more tightly cross-linked than are those of elastomers **(Fig. 1.6d)**. After having been cross-linked, thermosets are infusible and insoluble. Consequently, scrap or reject parts cannot be reprocessed.

1.7 Crystalline and Amorphous Structure of Polymers

Some polymers are almost completely amorphous under normal conditions, but may become crystalline when stretched or when conditioned in certain low temperature ranges (section 4.15). The term **crystalline** is commonly used to describe a polymer possessing both crystalline and amorphous regions. These regions are not mechanically separable phases, because the same macromolecule may at the same time have part of its length in a crystalline and the remainder in an amorphous region **(Fig. 1.7)**. Therefore, it has been suggested to use the term **semicrystalline** for polymers. Some elastomers, particularly cross-linked natural rubbers, have the ability to undergo this kind of crystallization when stretched. Under the extension force, the chain molecules are oriented in the direction of pull.

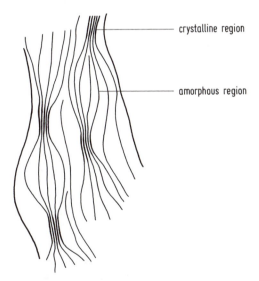

crystalline region

amorphous region

Fig. 1.7: Crystallization of Polymers on Stretching

Many properties of polymers, such as hardness, modulus, tensile strength and solubility, are affected by the degree of crystallinity in the polymer. Those polymers which do not have the ability to crystallize on stretching exhibit inferior tensile strength.

CHAPTER 2

Fundamentals of Compounding, Forming, Vulcanizing and Finishing of Elastomeric Products

2.1 Introduction

Some confusion may arise because terms such as **rubber compound** and **compounding** are used where strictly the terms **rubber mixture** and **mixing**, respectively, should be used. By rubber compounding is meant the way of making useful products from crude rubbers. There are about 35 commercially available types of crude rubbers, which will be discussed in detail in chapter 8. It is sufficient to note here that crude rubbers are essentially noncross-linked polymers and that they are the basic component for manufacturing all elastomeric products.

The first step of rubber compounding is usually to soften the crude rubber by mechanical working. This can be done on **two-roll mills** or in **internal mixers**. In this soft condition the rubber is easily blended with a variety of compounding ingredients that are normally given in parts per weight, based on 100 parts of crude rubber **(phr)**. A generalized rubber formula is given in **Table 2.1**. Rubber formulas are almost never publicized by manufacturers.

Table 2.1: A Generalized Rubber Formula

	Parts per weight
Crude rubber	100
Filler	50
Softener	5
Antioxidant	1
Stearic acid	1
Zinc oxide	5
Accelerator	1
Sulphur	2
Total	*165*

Each ingredient has a specific function, either in processing, vulcanization or end use of the product. The various ingredients may be classified according to their specific function in the following groups:
- fillers (carbon blacks and nonblack fillers);
- plasticizers or softeners (extenders, processing aids, special plasticizers);
- age resistors or antidegradants (antioxidants, antiozonants, special age resistors, protective waxes);
- vulcanizing or curing ingredients (vulcanizing agents, accelerators, activators); and

– special-purpose ingredients (coloring pigments, blowing agents, flame retardants, odorants, antistatic agents, retarders, peptizers).

However, many ingredients are capable of functioning in more than one manner. A typical example is zinc oxide, which may function as an activator, vulcanizing agent, filler or coloring pigment, depending on which it is selected for.

After all components have been properly mixed, the compounded **green stock** is
tacky and thermoplastic. In this plastic condition, the stock can be shaped by the
application of force. This can be accomplished, for example, by squeezing it between rolls **(calendering)** or pushing it through an orifice having the desired shape
(tubing or **extruding)**.

After the green stock has been formed to the desired shape, it needs to be
converted to an elastic material. This is achieved by the vulcanization process
usually under pressure at elevated temperature using different techniques such as
press vulcanization, open vulcanization and continuous vulcanization. Chemically,
the process involves insertion of cross-links between the polymer macromolecules
through the action of vulcanizing ingredients. Without these chemical bonds no
improvement in the physical properties of the rubber mix can occur. It is quite
probable that the cross-bonds tie the macromolecules together in such a way that
the whole mass becomes a single molecule. (The cross-linking of rubber is also
referred to as **curing**, because it is a process whereby a raw material is converted
into a useful product.)

The thermoplastic elastomers (section 1.6) do not require vulcanization. They
can be shaped more easily using plastic industry techniques such as injection molding and extrusion.

2.2 Fillers

Fillers are compounding ingredients, usually in powder form, added to crude rubber in relatively large proportions (typically 50 phr). They include two major
groups: carbon blacks and nonblack fillers.

Carbon blacks consist mainly of finely divided carbon manufactured by incom-
plete combustion of natural gas or petroleum using different processes. A standard
classification system for carbon blacks used in the rubber industry is described in
ASTM (American Society for Testing and Materials) D 1765. The designation
consists of a letter followed by three digits. The letter indicates the effect of the
carbon black on the cure rate. The letter N is used to indicate a normal curing rate
and S indicates slow-curing blacks. The first digit following the letter indicates the
particle size range as determined by electron microscope measurement. The particle size range has been divided into 10 arbitrary groups (from 0 to 9). Lower
numbers indicate smaller-particle-size blacks. The last two digits are arbitrarily
assigned by ASTM. Examples of commercially available carbon blacks include,
among others, S 212, N 110, N 550, N 762 and N 990. Before the ASTM classification was adopted, three-letter designations were used to indicate the function of
the carbon black; examples: SAF (super abrasion furnace), HAF (high abrasion
furnace), GPF (general purpose furnace).

The **nonblack fillers** include, for example, clays, calcium carbonate, silicates and precipitated and fumed (anhydrous) silicas. Special items such as packings may also contain cotton or other fibers to impart specific properties.

Fillers are added for economic or technical purposes. Some are incorporated primarily to extend and therefore make the final product less expensive and others mainly to reinforce it. By **reinforcement** is meant enhancement of properties such as tensile strength, tear and abrasion resistance. Consequently, fillers may be classified into two broad groups: **reinforcing** and **nonreinforcing**, or **active** and **inactive**. However, the distinction between the two groups is not clear-cut because many fillers exhibit intermediate properties. Examples of reinforcing fillers include, among others, smaller-particle-size blacks and precipitated silica. Nonreinforcing fillers include, for example, larger-particle-size blacks, soft clays and calcium carbonates.

2.3 Plasticizers

Plasticizers or softeners can be liquids, semisolids or solids. They must be completely compatible with the crude rubber and other compounding ingredients because incompatibility will result in poor processing,"bleeding" or both.

Plasticizers are incorporated for various purposes:
- as an extender to make the final product less expensive;
- as a processing aid to facilitate the manufacturing operations of the compounded rubber; and
- as a modifier of certain vulcanizate properties.

Petroleum oils are the most widely used extenders and processing aids, depending on the amount added. A large amount (above 20 phr) may act as an extender and a small amount (ca. 2−5 phr) as a processing aid. Other frequently used processing aids include, for example, low-molecular-weight polyethylene, natural fats and oils, certain waxes, soaps, resins and factices.

Factices are rubbery products made from unsaturated vegetable oils by heating them with sulphur (brown factice) or by reaction with sulphur chloride (white factice). They are added primarily to facilitate the extrusion and calendering processes and to prevent deformation of shaped stocks during the free vulcanization.

Special plasticizers based on **synthetic esters** and **ethers** are added primarily to specialty rubbers to improve the low temperature properties, but they are too expensive for general applications.

2.4 Age Resistors

Age resistors or antidegradants are organic substances usually added in small amounts (about 1−4 phr) to retard deterioration caused by aging, thus extending the service life of the elastomeric product involved. They protect elastomers against such agents as oxygen, ozone, heat, sunlight, high energy radiation and high humidity. **Antioxidants** primarily protect the elastomer against oxidation and heat. **Antiozonants** retard or prevent the appearance of surface cracks caused by ozone when the elastomeric part is exposed under tension to air containing ozone. **Antiflex-cracking** agents retard cracking caused by cyclic deformation. **Antirads** protect against high energy radiations. **Antihydrolysing** agents retard deterioration caused by high humidity and water (hydrolysis).

Age resistors may be divided into two main groups: staining and nonstaining. The **staining** age resistors, usually secondary amines, are strong protective agents but discolor and stain to various degrees. Consequently, they are used only where color is not important. The **nonstaining** protectants, normally phenolics, are less effective but are nondiscoloring and nonstaining. They are used in white or light-colored goods.

Besides the above-mentioned chemical protectants, there are certain waxes that provide physical protection. Such waxes tend to migrate (bloom) to the surface after vulcanization. The resulting film protects the elastomeric parts from the effects of oxygen and ozone. Physical protectants are effective only in applications where little or no movement is involved and so long as the protective film remains intact. In dynamic applications the film can break and the elastomer becomes susceptible to attack. Normally, protective waxes are used along with chemical protectants.

Another method of increasing the ozone resistance of a nonresistant compound is to blend it with an ozone-resistant rubber. Compared with chemical antiozonants, the amount required is considerably higher, usually 20−30 phr.

2.5 Vulcanizing Ingredients

As the name implies, vulcanizing ingredients are those chemicals which are incorporated in order to insert cross-linking between the polymer chains when the compounded stock is heated to an appropriate temperature.

Sulphur is the main vulcanizing agent for most crude rubbers that contain enough double bonds in their macromolecules. In order to increase the rate of vulcanization, it is necessary to add **accelerators** and **activators**. The combination of vulcanizing agent, accelerators and activators is frequently called the **vulcanizing system**.

Accelerators are compounding ingredients added in small amounts with a curing agent to increase the speed of vulcanization. Without accelerators, a vulcanization with sulphur usually requires several hours. By adding accelerators, the vulcanization time can be cut to minutes or seconds and in most cases the physical properties of the vulcanizates are also improved.

At one time, basic oxides such as lime, litharge and magnesia were widely used as accelerators. Today, accelerators are almost always organic compounds containing either nitrogen or sulphur or both. Very few accelerators, known as **sulphur donors**, such as tetramethylthiuram disulphide, can be used as vulcanizing agents without the addition of elemental sulphur.

According to speed of action, accelerators are sometimes described as slow, moderately fast, fast and ultra accelerators.

Activators are substances added in small proportions that increase the effectiveness of accelerators. The most widely used activators are zinc oxide and stearic acid.

Elemental sulphur has a cyclic structure consisting of rings composed of eight sulphur atoms (S_8). It is generally accepted that vulcanization with elemental sulphur leads to cross-links of the type R-S_x-R, where R is the polymer macromolecule and x denotes the number of sulphur atoms in the cross-link. The resulting cross-links can have a **monosulphide** or a **polysulphide** structure, or both types, depending on the curing system used. However, not all the sulphur in the vulcanizing ingredient combines with the base rubber to form cross-links. Usually, a very small portion of sulphur, known as **free sulphur**, remains uncombined in the vulcanizate. It is extractable by acetone, whereas the **combined sulphur** in the cross-links cannot be removed by acetone extraction.

Conventional sulphur vulcanizing systems for soft rubber products consist of relatively high amounts of elemental sulphur (about 1−3 phr) combined with a low concentration of accelerator(s). If the amount of sulphur is increased to 25−45 phr, a hard rubber, or **ebonite**, is formed **(Fig. 2.1)**.

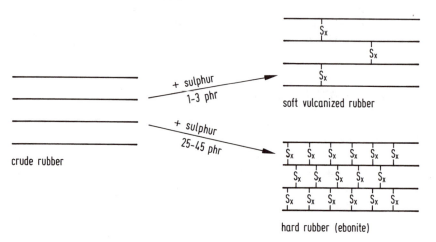

Fig. 2.1: Sulphur Cross-linking of Highly Unsaturated Rubbers

Low sulphur vulcanizing systems comprise a low concentration of elemental sulphur (usually 0.2−0.5 phr) and a high concentration of accelerator(s). **Nonelemental sulphur vulcanizing systems** consist mainly of sulphur donors that release atomic sulphur during the vulcanization. Both low sulphur and nonelemental sulphur vulcanization systems are frequently called **efficient vulcanizing** (EV) systems because they produce vulcanizates that resist aging at elevated temperatures, much more effectively than those cured by conventional sulphur vulcanizing systems.

It is generally accepted that the EV systems produce at optimum cure a network containing predominantly thermally stable **monosulphide** cross-links (x = 1 in **Fig. 2.1**). Once the vulcanization is complete, no sulphur is available for further cross-linking.

In contrast to EV systems, the conventional sulphur vulcanizing systems produce vulcanizates in which the combined sulphur exists predominantly in **polysulphide** cross-links. Such vulcanizates tend to harden excessively at elevated temperatures, possibly because sulphur is released from the polysulphide cross-links to form additional cross-links.

EV systems are much more expensive than the conventional sulphur vulcanizing systems because of the large amounts of sulphur donors used. Therefore, they are applied only when a maximum of heat resistance of the end product is required.

Saturated rubbers cannot be cross-linked by sulphur and accelerators because of the absence of double bonds in the polymer chains. They are usually vulcanized by **organic peroxides**, either alone or in the presence of other compounding ingredients known as **co-agents** or **promotors**. These substances, if used, are added to increase the efficiency of the organic peroxide.

Organic peroxides decompose at the vulcanization temperature and form **free radicals (R')**. These free radicals extract hydrogen atoms from the polymer chains **(PH)**, forming **RH** and leaving polymer radicals **(P')**. Adjacent polymer radicals combine to form carbon to carbon cross-links **(P-P)**. The mechanism can be illustrated as follows:

1) R' +   PH $\longrightarrow$ RH   + P'

   free radical   polymer chain   by-product   polymer radical

2) P' +   'P $\longrightarrow$ P–P

   2 polymer radicals   cross-linked polymer

In contrast to sulphur, organic peroxides do not enter into the polymer network. Cross-links of this type are also formed by high-energy radiation using either gamma radiation or electron beams. Organic peroxides are also used for cross-linking of some unsaturated crude rubbers in applications that require good heat aging properties. Other sulphurless vulcanizing agents used for certain rubber types include, for instance, metal oxides, diamines, bisphenols and special resins. All these vulcanizing agents insert cross-linking between the polymer chains involved.

2.6 Special-Purpose Ingredients

Certain ingredients are added for specific purposes, but these ingredients are not normally required in the majority of rubber compounds. Examples include coloring pigments, blowing agents, flame retardants, odorants, antistatic agents, retarders and peptizers.

Coloring pigments are substances added for coloring nonblack rubber goods. It is important to note that only the nonstaining grades of crude rubbers, age resistors, accelerators and other ingredients should be used for colored compounds.

Coloring pigments are usually divided into two groups:
– inorganic or mineral pigments; and
– organic dyes.

The **inorganic pigments** (such as titanium dioxide, lithopone and red and yellow iron oxides) are stable to heat and light, show little or no tendency to bloom or chalk and cannot be extracted by solvents. However, they do not produce bright colors, and usually large amounts are needed to achieve a given intensity. Furthermore, some of these inorganic pigments react with acids and alkalis.

Organic pigments (such as azo compounds) produce bright colors, and intense coloration is normally achieved with small amounts. The disadvantages include: limited stability to heat and light, tendency to bloom and chalk, reactivity to many chemicals and solubility in many organic solvents and liquids. Consequently, the color can change as a result of a chemical reaction or the dye itself may be partially or completely extracted by contacting fluids. Therefore, it is necessary to consider the stability of the organic dye to the service conditions before using a colored elastomeric part.

Blowing agents are gas-generating chemicals that are necessary for manufacturing sponge and microporous rubber products. Suitable agents that are capable of releasing gas during the vulcanization period include sodium bicarbonate, ammonium carbonate and certain nitrogen-bearing compounds. The released gas brings about a cellular or spongelike structure.

Flame retardants are chemicals added to reduce the flammability of the end product. Materials used extensively for this purpose include, for example, chlorinated hydrocarbons, certain phosphates and antimony compounds.

Odorants or odor improvers are strongly scented substances added in very small amounts (about 0.1 phr) that are capable of masking the characteristic odor of some rubber compounds or imparting a pleasant scent. Vanillin is frequently used for this purpose.

Antistatic agents are sometimes added to reduce the accumulation of dust or dirt on the surface of the elastomeric part during service and also to minimize the possibility of sparking resulting from the discharge of accumulated static electricity. Typical antistatic agents include certain esters, fatty amines and amides.

Retarders are substances used to reduce the tendency of a rubber mix to scorch, that is, to avoid premature vulcanization during factory processing.

Peptizers are compounding ingredients used in small proportions to accelerate the softening of crude rubber under the influence of mechanical action, generally induced on open mills or in internal mixers.

2.7 Mixing Equipment and Procedures

Rubber compounding is generally carried out on open mills or in internal mixers. An **open mill** consists of two adjacent, smooth, hardened-steel rolls set horizontally. They rotate in opposite directions (i.e., toward each other) **(Fig. 2.2)**. The back roll rotates faster than the front one in order to produce a friction or grinding action between them. The ratio between the operating speed of the front and back roll is referred to as the **friction ratio**. Mixing is achieved by the shearing action induced in the space between the rolls, which is adjustable. The mill rolls are hollow and are equipped for internal cooling with water.

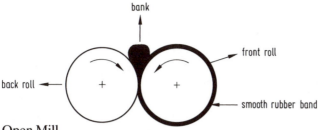

Fig. 2.2: Open Mill

The mixing process on an open mill involves masticating or breaking down the crude rubber until an even and smooth band is formed around the front roll. Some crude rubbers, such as natural rubbers, require special chemicals (peptizers) to help the breakdown. Most synthetic crude rubbers do not require a peptizer.

When the crude rubber becomes soft and plastic, the fillers and other ingredients are added and worked in, following a definite time, temperature range and sequence schedule. The space between the rolls is increased at intervals to maintain a constant bank. Powders that drop into the mill tray are swept to the front by the operator and added back to the mix. During the mixing operation, cutting and blending is carried out in order to obtain a thorough and uniform dispersion of the ingredients in the rubber mix.

An **internal mixer** consists of an enclosed chamber and two rotors with small clearance between them and the enclosing wall **(Fig. 2.3)**. As with the open mill, the rotors rotate in opposite directions. The mixing chambers can be cooled by circulating water or heated by steam, as required.

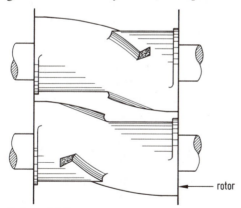

Fig. 2.3: Internal Mixer

Internal mixers are widely used for masticating crude rubbers and incorporating other ingredients. The mixed batch is dropped from the bottom of the internal mixer onto a sheeting mill and then taken off for storage until further processing.

The so-called upside-down mixing involves first adding the compounding ingredients to the mixer, followed by the crude rubber at the end. The advantages of this procedure are good dispersion and remarkable reduction of the mixing time.

2.8 Forming Operations

After mixing, the green stock generally requires forming (shaping) into blanks of suitable dimensions. At this stage the stock will retain the shape imposed on it because it is predominantly plastic. The basic processing machines used for forming rubber stocks are the calenders and extruders.

The **calender** is a machine equipped with two, three or more heavy internally heated or cooled rolls, which are usually placed above each other **(Fig. 2.4)**. The rolls rotate in opposite directions and operate at even or uneven speeds as the application requires.

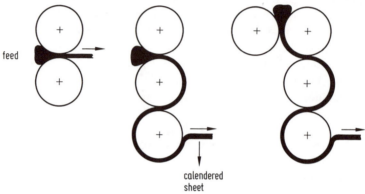

Fig. 2.4: Calender Types

The calender is used essentially for producing rubber sheets of various lengths and thicknesses. It is also widely used for **frictioning** or **skim coating** of fabrics. Frictioned fabric is produced by passing both fabric and rubber stock between calender rolls rotating at different speeds. The induced friction pushes the rubber stock into the pores of the fabric. By using even-speed rolls, the fabric receives a coat of the rubber compound and is referred to as **coated** fabric. Coating of fabrics may also be achieved by spreading, dipping and painting. In this case, the rubber stock is used in combination with a solvent, the mixture being commonly known as a **dough**.

An **extruder** (also called tubing machine or, simply, tuber) is used for continuous shaping of a material by passage through an orifice called a **die**. It consists basically of a driven screw turning in a cylinder or barrel. The stock is fed in at one end and transferred along the cylinder by the rotating screw. The material becomes hot and plastic as it moves to the exit end of the extruder. It is then pushed through a die having the desired shape. The shaped uncured product (**extrudate**) is either cured directly (continuous vulcanization) or laid on pans for steam autoclave curing (batch curing).

Extrusion is normally used for manufacturing products such as rubber tubes, insulated cables and weather-sealing strips.

Another extruder-type machine, known as a **strainer**, is designed to force a crude rubber or mix through a sieve (or sieves) to remove solid foreign materials.

2.9 Vulcanization Techniques

After the green stock has been formed to the desired shape, the material needs to be converted to a predominantly elastic final product. This is accomplished by the process of vulcanization, which usually takes place under pressure at elevated temperature, using different techniques. The most important vulcanization methods are:
- press vulcanization;
- open vulcanization;
- continuous vulcanization; and
- cold vulcanization.

2.9.1 Press Vulcanization

As the name implies, press vulcanization takes place in presses that supply heat and pressure. A vulcanizing press consists essentially of two or more plates that can be brought together and separated by hydraulic pressure. The plates are usually heated by steam or electricity. The rubber articles are vulcanized in various molds between the heated plates under pressure. In its simplest form, a mold consists of two metal plates with cavities conforming to the outside shape of the desired finished part.

The molded parts shrink when they cool to room temperature after removal from the mold to a size smaller than the cavities. This **mold shrinkage** is due to the thermal contraction of elastomers, which is considerably higher than that of metals. The coefficient of thermal expansion of elastomers is roughly 10 times that of steel (section 4.12). The coefficient of thermal expansion of a rubber compound depends largely on the type and amount of fillers incorporated in the crude rubber. In general, the addition of fillers lowers the coefficient. Because of these variations, test molds are used to precisely measure the thermal coefficient of each compound. For the production of precision sizes, the mold dimensions are correspondingly made larger to compensate for the mold shrinkage.

Many rubber compounds have similar mold shrinkage and when molded in the same mold the finished parts will have similar dimensions. Other compounds, particularly those based on fluorocarbon rubbers (FPM) and silicone rubbers (Q), shrink more and when molded in standard molds the finished parts will be smaller than those of standard compounds. In order to hold close tolerances in such cases, special molds must be used. However, it is generally difficult and expensive to hold close dimensional tolerances of elastomeric parts.

Molding processes can be classified under three broad headings:
- compression molding;
- transfer molding;
- injection molding.

Compression molding involves placing a properly shaped blank from the unvulcanized stock in each cavity of the mold. The mold is then closed and placed in a hydraulic press. Under the applied pressure and heat, the stock will flow and completely fill the mold cavity. The slight excess flows out through special grooves. This excess is known as **mold flash**.

The mold is maintained closed under pressure for the prescribed time at the particular molding temperature. The mold is then removed from the press and opened to remove the molded part. A simple mold of this type is shown in **Fig. 2.5a**.

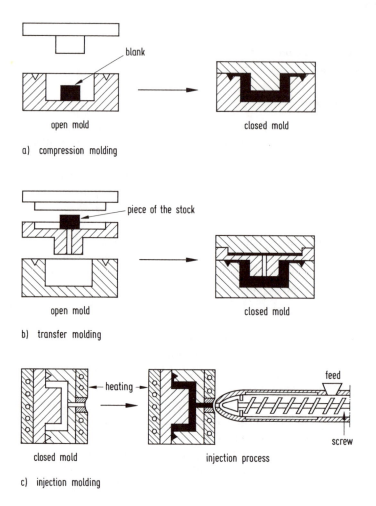

a) compression molding

b) transfer molding

c) injection molding

Fig. 2.5: Methods of Press Vulcanization

The disadvantage of this method is that it is necessary to accurately cut or weigh just enough stock for each cavity. Too much stock or wrong placement of the blank in the cavity can cause defects such as flow lines, blisters or unfilled parts. Excessive use of material is not only wasteful but causes heavy flash, which is more difficult to remove. Other disadvantages are longer curing cycles and more labor needed to load and unload the mold.

Transfer molding differs from compression molding in that the stock is transferred through a hole into the mold cavity. In its simplest form a transfer mold consists of three parts: a piston, a cylinder (pot) and the mold cavity, as shown in **Fig. 2.5b**. A piece of the unvulcanized stock is placed in the pot and covered by the piston. When the press is closed the piston forces the stock through a hole into the actual mold cavity. This allows shorter cure times because of the heat generated as the stock is forced to flow through the hole. After the compound has been cured, the mold is disassembled, the residual cured rubber is removed from the pot and the cavities are unloaded.

All transfer molds leave pads of cured rubber in the pot, which are thrown away. This additional cost is offset to some degree by shorter cure times and reduced stock preparation costs, since several cavities can be filled from a single piece of the stock placed in one pot.

Injection molding is similar to transfer molding in that the rubber stock is forced into a closed mold cavity through a nozzle. A strip of the stock is fed into a heated cylinder and masticated by a screw, which then moves forward like a ram and forces this preheated stock through a nozzle into the mold cavities (**Fig. 2.5c**). As a result, rubber items can be vulcanized in very short times, usually reported in seconds (typical time is 30−60 seconds). Other advantages of injection molding are reduced stock preparation costs and low cured scrap. However, both the molds and the equipment are much more expensive than those used for compression and transfer molding.

2.9.2 Open Vulcanization

Open vulcanization can take place in hot air or in steam. Vulcanization in hot-air ovens is not very efficient because of the poor heat transfer of hot air. Consequently, longer vulcanization times at lower temperatures are necessary to prevent aging caused by oxygen.

Open steam vulcanization takes place in large containers called **autoclaves** with a heated jacket and a closed chamber in which the articles are placed and the steam is introduced. Unlike hot air, saturated steam has better heat transfer and acts as an inert gas. Consequently, shorter cure times at higher temperatures are possible. Open steam curing is used in the production of extruded articles such as hoses, cables and strips.

2.9.3 Continuous Vulcanization

In this process the rubber stock is shaped and cured in a single-line operation. While there are several methods of continuous vulcanization, they have the same principle: the shaped uncured product is transferred along a curing medium. Curing media include, for example, liquid, hot air, steam, microwaves and infrared and high-energy radiation. Continuous vulcanization is usually used for producing extruded goods, coated wiring, conveyor belts and flooring.

The continuous vulcanization in liquid baths is called **LCM** (**liquid curing method**). In this process, the extrudate is run through a suitable hot bath immediately after leaving the extruder. The bath temperature is in the range of 200–300°C. Suitable heating media include, for example, salt mixtures, polyglycols, silicone oil and metal alloys. The most frequently used salt mixture consists of 53% potassium nitrate, 40% sodium nitrite and 7% sodium nitrate.

Hot-air tunnels can be used for continuous curing of thin articles. An alternative form of hot air curing involves the use of **fluidized beds** consisting of small glass beads suspended in a stream of hot air. The heat transfer is considerably greater than with hot air alone.

Continuous vulcanization in **steam tubes** is used mainly in the cable industry. After extrusion of the rubber cover onto the wire, the cable is drawn rapidly through a jacketed tube containing steam under pressure.

Flat rubber goods such as conveyor belts and floor coverings are vulcanized continuously by the **Rotocure** method. This process involves the use of a wide steel band that presses the article against large, slowly rotating heated drums.

Microwave energy, or UHF (ultrahigh frequency fields), can be used to warm up or vulcanize rubber parts with large or uneven cross sections. Frequently, microwaves are used first to heat the extrudate rapidly to the vulcanization temperature; then the cure is completed by passing the hot product through a short length of one of the other vulcanization media, such as hot air. However, it should be noted that the process requires polar rubber mixtures, since nonpolar materials will not absorb the microwave energy. Unlike other heating media such as hot air or steam, the heating action of the microwave energy is based on the rapid heating from within the material. The atoms or molecules are excited by the microwave energy and heat is instantaneously developed through the whole thickness of the article.

Infrared is also used in continuous curing in which infrared bulbs supply the heat. Continuous vulcanization by **high-energy radiation** is achieved by using gamma radiation from cobalt 60 or electron beams. Curing takes place at room temperature without chemical curing agents. The high-energy radiation creates polymer free radicals that combine with each other to form C-C cross-linking, similar to peroxide curing (section 2.5).

2.9.4 Cold Vulcanization

Thin articles may be vulcanized at room temperature by exposure to sulphur monochloride (S_2Cl_2) vapors. However, this curing agent has been essentially replaced by ultra accelerators that can cause the vulcanization at room temperature.

2.10 Postcure

Some elastomer types require two curing steps: a primary vulcanization in the press followed by a **postcure** in circulating hot-air ovens with a constant fresh air supply. The postcure process usually lasts several hours (up to 24 hours) at a considerably higher temperature than the vulcanization temperature in the press.

Postcure is carried out to improve one or more properties of the vulcanizate. Furthermore, the decomposition products of the compounding ingredients are removed during this process.

2.11 Finishing Operations

Many rubber articles require finishing operations after vulcanization. For example, the flash attached to molded parts must be removed before the parts are ready for use. This is sometimes carried out by hand trimming using scissors or knives. Several trimming machines have been designed to abrade the flash away with power-driven circular knives.

A widely used method of deflashing involves exposing the rubber parts to low temperature (using liquid nitrogen or carbon dioxide) until the flash is frozen, while the thick sections remain unfrozen. The frozen flash will then break by mechanical action while the parts are being tumbled. Another deflashing method uses a water-filled drum in which molded parts are turned with stones.

Some rubber parts are painted either to give them an attractive finish or, more often, to protect against ozone, oils, acids, chemicals and the like. The paints are usually rubber-based.

Items such as seals and windshield wiper blades may require surface treatment with chlorine, bromine or fluorine in water. The halogenated surface will have lower friction than the untreated surface, while the bulk will be unaffected.

The finishing operations of extruded articles include, for example, coiling, cutting to specific length and washing. Some rubber parts are cut from flat sheets using cutting machines.

2.12 Quality Control

Quality control is necessary to ensure the quality of the final products. During various stages, checking will be performed on incoming materials, in-process materials and finished products. The rubber manufacturer usually tests the raw materials (i.e., the crude rubbers and compounding ingredients) to make sure that they are uniform and of adequate quality.

Control tests are applied to various steps in the manufacturing process. The most important of these are run on batches after the mixing operation, in order to make certain that no errors have been made. The tests employed are sensitive to any change in the rubber compound resulting from errors, such as faulty compounding ingredients, poor dispersion, improper temperature control, wrong sequence addition and too-short or too-long mixing cycles.

The control schemes utilize mostly standardized physical tests on both unvulcanized and vulcanized rubber compounds. The tests made on unvulcanized compounds include, for example, measurement of the viscosity, scorch time and cure rate. Standard tests that may be run on vulcanizates include, for instance, measurement of the density, hardness, tensile modulus, tensile strength and elongation at break.

Quality control of finished products involves visual inspection for defects, dimensional control as well as physical tests according to specifications such as hardness, compression set and density.

CHAPTER 3

Nomenclature and Classification of Elastomers

3.1 Introduction

As stated in the previous chapters, all elastomers are manufactured from a combination of ingredients. The most important ingredient is the crude rubber because it provides the basic vulcanizate properties such as ozone and oil resistance, low-temperature flexibility, flammability and so on. However, other ingredients, such as fillers, plasticizers, vulcanizing systems and age resistors, also have a great influence on the properties of the final product. Because of the enormous number of possible combinations of crude rubbers with other ingredients, rubber compounds can be developed with improved or specific properties required for certain applications.

The crude rubbers used for producing elastomeric materials are identified by abbreviations of their chemical composition in accordance with ISO standard 1629 (1987) or ASTM standard D 1418−90.

3.2 Nomenclature of Crude Rubbers According to ISO 1629

The basic, or crude, rubbers (in both dry and latex forms) are classified and designated on the basis of the chemical composition of the polymer chain in accordance with international standard 1629 in the following manner:

M Rubbers having a saturated chain of the polymethylene type
N Rubbers having nitrogen (but not oxygen or phosphorus) in the polymer chain
O Rubbers having oxygen in the polymer chain
Q Rubbers having silicon and oxygen in the polymer chain
R Rubbers having an unsaturated carbon chain
T Rubbers having sulphur in the polymer chain
U Rubbers having carbon, oxygen and nitrogen in the polymer chain
Z Rubbers having phosphorus and nitrogen in the polymer chain

Each group includes many rubber types that are identified by inserting other letters in front of the group designation; for example, ACM, ECO, VMQ, NBR, EOT, AU and FZ.

Rubbers of the **R** class having carboxylic acid groups ($-COOH$) in the polymer chain are identified by the prefix **X**. For example:

XSBR = carboxylic styrene-butadiene rubber
XNBR= carboxylic acrylonitrile-butadiene rubber.

Isobutene-isoprene rubbers (IIR) containing halogen in the polymer chains are identified as follows:

BIIR = bromo-isobutene-isoprene rubbers (usually known as bromobutyl rubbers)
CIIR = chloro-isobutene-isoprene rubbers (usually known as chlorobutyl rubbers)

Thermoplastic elastomers are identified by inserting the letter **Y** in front of the rubber designation; for example:

YSBR = a block copolymer of styrene and butadiene

YXSBR = a block copolymer of styrene and butadiene containing carboxylic acid groups in the polymer chain

The designations and chemical names of most common types of crude rubbers, as well as examples of trademarks, are listed in **Table 3.1**. These types and others are described in chapters 8 and 9.

Table 3.1: Designations, Chemical Names and Selected Trademarks of Typical Crude Rubbers

Designation (ISO 1629: 1987 E)	Chemical Name	Selected Trademarks
BR	Butadiene rubbers (usually as a blend)	Buna CB, Budene
CR	Chloroprene rubbers	Neoprene, Baypren
IIR	Isobutene-isoprene rubbers (butyl rubbers)	Exxon Butyl
IR	Isoprene rubbers, synthetic	Natsyn
NBR	Acrylonitrile-butadiene rubbers (nitrile rubbers)	Perbunan, Chemigum
HNBR*	Hydrogenated nitrile rubbers	Therban, Zetpol
NR	Isoprene rubbers, natural (natural rubbers)	
SBR	Styrene-butadiene rubbers	Buna Hüls, Cariflex S
ACM	Polyacrylate rubbers	Cyanacryl, Europrene AR
AEM*	Ethylene-acrylic rubbers	Vamac
CSM	Chlorosulphonated polyethylene rubbers	Hypalon
EPDM	Ethylene-propylene-diene rubbers	Keltan, Nordel
EPM	Ethylene-propylene rubbers	Vistalon, Dutral
FPM	Fluorocarbon rubbers	Viton, Fluorel
FFKM*	Perfluorocarbon rubbers	Kalrez
VMQ	Vinyl-methyl silicone rubbers	Silopren
FMQ	Fluorosilicone rubbers	Silastic
ECO	Epichlorohydrin rubbers	Hydrin, Epichlomer
AU	Polyester urethanes	Urepan, Pellethane
EU	Polyether urethanes	Adiprene
YBPO*	Thermoplastic polyether-esters	Hytrel

*designation in accordance with ASTM D 1418

3.3 Nomenclature of Crude Rubbers According to ASTM D 1418

Standard D 1418 of the American Society for Testing and Materials is very similar to ISO standard 1629 but differs from it on four points:

1) The ASTM designation for fluorocarbon rubbers is FKM instead of FPM.
2) The ASTM standard includes more rubber types. These are:
   AEM = ethylene-acrylic rubbers
   FFKM = perfluorocarbon rubbers
   HNBR = hydrogenated acrylonitrile-butadiene rubbers
   GECO = epichlorhydrin-ethylene oxide-allylglycidylether terpolymer
   YBPO = thermoplastic polyether-esters
3) ASTM D 1418 does not include IM (polyisobutene) and FMQ (silicone rubber having both methyl and fluorine substituent groups in the polymer chain).
4) The ASTM standard also establishes designations for rubber blends. If the composition is known, the major component is listed first; for example, a 60/40 blend of NR and BR is designated NR/BR. If the rubbers are present in equal amounts or if the proportion is unknown, the rubbers are designated in alphabetical order; for example, BR/NR is used for a 50/50 ratio and BR-NR is used for an unknown composition.

3.4 Generic Names of Elastomers

Elastomers are designated according to the chemical composition of the basic (crude) rubbers described in ISO standard 1629 or ASTM standard D 1418. Trade names should not be used on drawings or specifications. Only the chemical names, the designations or both should be used. It should be noted, however, that these names are generic; that is, a variety of different compounds exists under one name (e.g., NBR), all of which may have certain general properties but also specific properties that differ according to the degree of compounding. As mentioned before, various compounding ingredients are incorporated into the basic rubber to tailor the required properties of the elastomeric part.

It should also be noted that many (but not all) of the basic rubbers listed in **Table 3.1** are often used in blends in order to combine properties of two or more rubbers into one vulcanizate. Such combinations are used, for example, to improve the ozone resistance of a general-purpose rubber or to improve the low-temperature flexibility of an oil-resistant elastomer.

3.5 Classification of Elastomers

Elastomers may be classified in groups according to different aspects including the following:
- chemical saturation of the polymer chain;
- oil resistance;
- flame resistance; and
- service performance.

3.5.1 Chemical Saturation of the Polymer Chain

Elastomers may be classified according to the chemical saturation of the polymer chain of the basic rubber in three groups, as shown in **Table 3.2**.

Table 3.2: Classification of Elastomers According to Chemical Saturation of the Polymer Chain

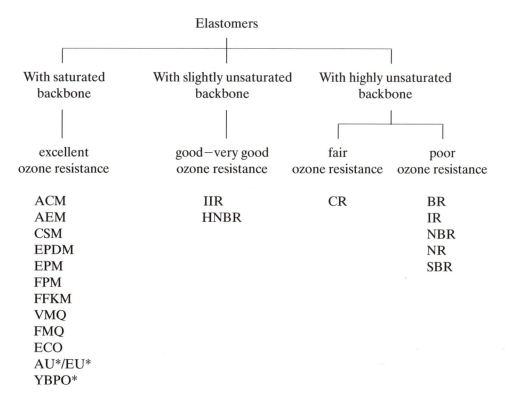

*susceptible to hydrolysis (i. e., deterioration from water or high humidity)

Elastomers that exhibit high resistance to ozone and weatherability are characterized by a saturated backbone (i.e., without double bonds). It should be noted, however, that saturated backbones having few double bonds in side groups (e.g., to enable a sulphur cure) belong to the group of saturated elastomers, although strictly speaking they are unsaturated. Nevertheless, such elastomers retain excellent ozone resistance because the saturation of the backbone is the controlling factor for high resistance. A typical example of an elastomer type having few double bonds in side groups is EPDM.

Elastomers with highly unsaturated backbones are not inherently ozone resistant. Therefore, antiozonants and protective waxes are added to the compound to achieve a desired degree of ozone resistance (section 2.4). CR elastomers, although highly unsaturated, show fair ozone resistance in contrast to other poly-diene elastomers such as IR, NBR, NR and SBR. This is because the chlorine atoms reduce the reactivity of the double bonds to oxidizing agents, including oxygen and ozone.

Elastomers with a low level of unsaturation in the backbone, such as IIR and HNBR, show greatly improved resistance to ozone compared with polydiene elastomers. For maximum ozone and aging resistance, the least unsaturated types are the best to use.

3.5.2 Oil Resistance

Elastomers that are resistant to mineral oils contain polar groups in the polymer chain, which give them the necessary resistance to swelling. The nonoil-resistant elastomers are based on hydrocarbon polymer chains without polar groups.

The most common elastomers are grouped in **Table 3.3** according to their oil and ozone resistance.

Table 3.3: Classification of Elastomers According to Oil and Ozone Resistance

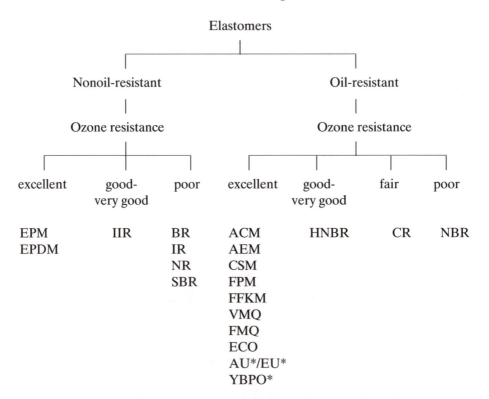

*susceptible to hydrolysis (i. e., deterioration from water or high humidity)

3.5.3 Flame Resistance

Elastomers that are inherently flame resistant are based on halogen-containing polymers. Examples include FFKM, FPM, CR, CSM, CO and ECO. The flame resistance is improved as the polymer halogen content increases. Further improvement can be achieved by incorporating a flame retardant (section 2.6). Halogen-free polymers are not flame resistant unless they contain a high concentration of flame retardants.

3.5.4 Service Performance

Elastomers may be classified according to their service performance in three groups:
- general-purpose elastomers;
- high-performance elastomers; and
- specialty elastomers.

General-purpose elastomers, such as NR and SBR, deteriorate in hostile environments such as heat, mineral oils, fuels, oxidizing chemicals, ozone and weather. The main advantages are the lower prices and the good low-temperature properties.

High-performance elastomers, such as CR, NBR and EPDM, provide substantially better resistance to certain hostile environments at only a reasonable price increase over NR and SBR.

Specialty elastomers, such as FFKM, FPM, FMQ and VMQ, usually provide truly outstanding properties such as heat and fluid resistance or low-temperature flexibility. However, these specialties are extremely expensive compared with general-purpose and high-performance elastomers.

3.6 Prices of Elastomers

The price of any elastomeric part includes the prices of the raw materials plus the costs of mixing, forming, vulcanizing, finishing and quality control. The prices of uncured stocks vary enormously, depending on the types and concentrations of the crude rubbers and compounding ingredients. Many ingredients such as carbon blacks, nonblack fillers and conventional plasticizers usually cost far less than the polymer. Therefore, the stock price will be reduced as the concentration of cheaper additives increases.

The price index of various unvulcanized rubber stocks given in chapter 8 **(Table 8.20)** is a general guideline for average prices and should be regarded as approximate. The stock prices may be higher or lower than those given in the table, depending on the formulation of the compound in question. Furthermore, it should be remembered that the prices of crude rubbers are subject to considerable fluctuations and that the price of the rubber stock is only one factor in the cost of the finished product.

CHAPTER 4

Unique Properties of Elastomers

4.1 Introduction

Elastomers are complex materials that exhibit unique combinations of useful properties. The first and foremost property is **elasticity** (the opposite of **plasticity**). All elastomers have the ability to deform substantially by stretching, compression or torsion and then snap back to almost their original shape after removal of the force causing the deformation.

Besides elastic recovery, the majority of elastomers possess other useful properties, including:
– low permeability to air, several gases, water and steam;
– good electrical and thermal insulation;
– good mechanical properties; and
– the capability of adhering to various fibers, metals and rigid plastics.

Also, by proper selection of compounding ingredients, products with improved or specific properties can be designed to meet a wide variety of service conditions.

This remarkable combination of useful properties is the reason that elastomers serve an enormous number of engineering needs in fields dealing with sealing, shock absorbing, vibration damping, electrical and thermal insulation and so on. Furthermore, elastomers are used in such widely varying items as tires, mats, shoe soles, belts, toys, balloons, medical goods, household products, sponge rubber, raincoats, hoses and thousands of other elastomeric products essential to modern civilization.

The aim of this chapter is to survey the most important properties of elastomeric materials. The methods of measuring these properties are described in chapter 10.

4.2 Hardness

Hardness as applied to elastomers is defined as the resistance of the surface to penetration by an indentor of specified dimensions under specified load. The hardness testers have the same indicating scale (on which hardness can be read directly) but different types of indentors and loads (section 10.4). The scale is arbitrary, ranging from 0 (infinitely soft) to 100 (bone hard). The load may be applied by means of a deadweight or a spring.

The hardness is quoted in either **IRHDs** (International Rubber Hardness Degrees) or **Shore hardness degrees**. The IRHD test is based on measuring the penetration of a specified rigid ball into the test specimen under specified dead load. The Shore hardness testers are called **durometers**, types A and D. In both Shore devices a calibrated spring forces a specified indentor into the test specimen. The type-A durometer has a blunt conical indentor and is used for measuring hardness of soft rubber compounds up to a reading of about 90 Shore A. The D type, having a pointed conical indentor and a different spring, is recommended for testing harder materials (above 90 Shore A).

The Shore A degrees are approximately the same as IRHDs. However, a direct conversion to IRHDs should be avoided because large differences can occur. For most applications of elastomeric components the hardness can vary between 40 and 90 IRHDs. Hardness below 40 can be obtained by incorporating large amounts of plasticizers in the rubber compound.

4.3 Tensile Properties

Tensile properties include tensile strength, elongation and tensile modulus. These properties are determined by stretching standard test pieces at a constant rate using a tensile machine (section 10.5).

Tensile strength is the force, or stress, expressed in MPa or N/mm^2, required to rupture a standard test piece by stretching at a constant rate. The tensile strength of different elastomers can vary from below 7 N/mm^2 to above 45 N/mm^2, depending on the basic rubber and compounding ingredients used.

Elongation, or strain, is defined as the extension produced by a tension force applied to a standard specimen and is expressed as a percentage of the original length. An elongation of 300%, for example, means that the specimen has been stretched to four times its original length. **Ultimate elongation**, or **elongation at break**, is the elongation at the time of rupture and is determined simultaneously with the tensile strength test. The elongation at break of different rubber compounds can vary from below 100% to above 1,000%, depending on the formulation of the compound.

Tensile modulus as applied to elastomers is defined as the force, expressed in N/mm^2, required to produce a certain elongation. The test elongation is typically 100% or 300%. Thus, if 5 N/mm^2 are required to produce 100% elongation, the elastomer is said to have 100% modulus of 5 N/mm^2. Tensile modulus is a measure of the stiffness and vulcanization degree of a rubber compound. It is normally determined during the course of tensile strength testing. The 100% modulus of different elastomeric materials can vary from below 1 N/mm^2 to above 13 N/mm^2, depending on the chemical composition of the rubber compound.

4.4 Tear Resistance

Elastomeric parts may fail in service because of the generation and propagation of a special type of rupture called **tear**. It is more likely to occur where there is high stress concentration at a nick or sharp angle. Tear resistance as applied to elastomers is defined as the maximum force per unit of thickness required to tear a specified test piece into two parts (section 10.6). It is commonly expressed in N/mm.

Tear resistance is strongly affected by degree of vulcanization. Low vulcanization temperatures and short cure times give high tear resistance. In general, low modulus, high ultimate elongation and high compression set are allied to high tear values. Elastomers with low tear resistance, such as silicone elastomers, need particular care in handling and fitting to avoid the possibility of damage during service.

4.5 Friction and Abrasion

Friction and abrasion are interrelated subjects, as abrasion is a process of wearing away the material surface by friction (section 10.7). If there is no friction, abrasion will not occur. However, the two topics are most often considered separately.

Friction and abrasion are two properties of major importance when considering elastomeric components for dynamic applications. Dynamic seals, for example, can undergo abrasion when sliding over a dry surface where friction is correspondingly high.

The friction coefficient of an elastomer depends on a number of factors, such as its geometric shape and composition, temperature, pressure, rubbing speed and surface finish of both the elastomeric part and the material with which it is in contact.

High friction can be harmful because it generates heat, which can cause degradation of the elastomer. The friction can be markedly decreased by using a suitable lubricant or by chemical treatment of the elastomer surface (section 2.11). Rubber compounds with "self-contained" lubricants may also be used where continuous presence of a lubricant is suspect and where minimal friction is essential.

4.6 Set, Stress Relaxation and Creep

Elastomers are not perfectly elastic. They are **viscoelastic** materials behaving partially as a viscous liquid and partially as an elastic solid. Prolonged deformation leads to some degree of permanent deformation, which means that part of the deformation is recovered and part is permanently retained. Set, stress relaxation and creep are progressive property changes resulting from prolonged application of stress or strain.

Set is defined as the amount of deformation remaining after removing the deforming force. If the elastomer is stretched under specified conditions and allowed to retract, the extension remaining after retraction, expressed as a percentage of the original length, is called **tension set**. If the elastomer is compressed under specified conditions, the residual decrease in its thickness after complete release of the compressive force is known as **compression set**. It is usually expressed as a percentage of the deflection employed (section 10.9). A 100% compression set means complete deformation; 0% means no deformation. The extent of compression set depends on the temperature and the amount and duration of deformation.

A low-compression set at service temperature is an essential requirement for seal materials. The compression set should not be 100% even after long periods of time. It is the remaining tendency to resume the original shape that maintains the necessary sealing force between the surfaces.

Stress relaxation of an elastomeric part is the loss in stress when it is held at a constant strain (deformation) over a period of time. The most important rubber products in which stress relaxation is a critical parameter are seals and gaskets. The measurement of stress relaxation in compression (section 10.8) is used to evaluate the sealing efficiency.

Creep is the converse of stress relaxation. It is the progressive increase in deformation when a constant load is applied to the elastomer over a period of time.

4.7 Rebound Resilience

Resilience as applied to elastomers is essentially the ability of an elastomeric part to return quickly to its original shape after a temporary deflection. In other words, it indicates the speed of recovery, unlike compression set, which indicates the degree of recovery. When an elastomer is deformed, an energy input is involved, part of which is not returned when the elastomer returns to its original shape. That part of energy which is not returned is dissipated as heat in the elastomer. The ratio of energy returned to energy applied to produce the deformation is the material's resilience.

When the deformation results from a single impact, the ratio between the returned and applied impact energy is called **rebound resilience** (section 10.10). The rebound resilience of most elastomers varies widely with temperature (section 4.15). At room temperature, the rebound resilience of different elastomers can vary between below 5% and above 75%, depending on the basic rubber and compounding ingredients.

4.8 Hysteresis and Heat Buildup

As mentioned in section 4.7, when an elastomer is temporarily deformed and released, part of the energy is not recovered but is converted to heat. This energy lost per cycle of deformation is called **hysteresis**. It is equal to 100% minus the resilience percentage.

Heat buildup is the temperature rise in an elastomeric part due to hysteresis. It occurs as a result of rapid cyclic deformations. When the elastomer is repeatedly deformed, heat is generated throughout the bulk of the material because elastomers are poor conductors of heat (section 4.11). For example, elastomeric components of considerable thickness may reach temperatures above 150 °C in the thickest part if the cyclic deformation is at a high frequency. This not only affects the properties of the compound but may actually cause complete deterioration of the material. Heat buildup can be reduced by using a more resilient compound, by altering the shape of the component or by both methods.

4.9 Permeability to Gases and Vapors

The permeability to gases and vapors is a property of great importance when considering such elastomeric items as inner tubes and diaphragms. All elastomers are permeable to gases and vapors, but the permeability rate varies considerably with different elastomers. In general, silicone elastomers have the highest permeability to gases, followed by NR, EPDM, SBR, CR, NBR, FPM, ECO and IIR. However, different compounds belonging to the same elastomer type can differ considerably in permeability rate because of different compounding ingredients. Therefore, the permeability of a given compound cannot be predicted merely from the knowledge of the basic rubber it contains. The incorporation of certain fillers, for instance, lowers the gas permeability to a certain extent depending on the concentration. Conversely, large amounts of plasticizers usually increase the gas permeability.

The process of permeation of a gas through an elastomer appears to take place in two steps: the gas dissolves on one side of the elastomer and the dissolved gas diffuses to the opposite side, where evaporation takes place. Consequently, the permeability rate of various gases through different elastomeric materials varies in an unpredictable way depending on the size of the gas molecules and the solubility of the gas in the rubber compound in question.

Permeability is temperature-dependent, increasing with higher temperatures. Although the permeability coefficient should theoretically be independent of the applied pressure, considerable deviations have been observed at high pressures.

4.10 Resistance to Explosive Decompression

If an elastomer is subjected to a gas under high pressure, a certain amount of the gas will dissolve and permeate into the elastomer. The higher the pressure, the larger the quantity of gas forced into the material. If the gas pressure is released slowly after a soak period, the trapped gas inside the elastomer will expand and may escape harmlessly into the atmosphere. However, if a rapid depressurization occurs, the trapped gas will expand violently and try to escape to the lower, external pressure.

The explosive expansion of the gas within the elastomeric material can cause swelling, blisters, cracks or even total destruction of the rubber component. This phenomenon is known as **explosive decompression** (section 10.12). (It is the same type of phenomenon as the formation of bubbles in fizzy drinks when the bottle is opened.)

The severity of the damage caused by explosive decompression varies with the pressure applied, the rate of pressure drop, temperature, nature of the gas or gas mixture, other contacting fluids, mechanical properties and cross section of the elastomeric component. Components with smaller cross sections usually have better resistance to explosive decompression than do those with large cross sections.

4.11 Thermal Conductivity

Although the thermal conductivity of elastomers varies with the amount and conductivity of each ingredient in the compound, elastomers are generally poor heat conductors. This property is of practical importance to the designer when using elastomeric components in which heat is generated by vibration, flexing or friction (sections 4.5 and 4.8); that is, the designer must provide for heat dissipation.

4.12 Coefficient of Thermal Expansion

As mentioned in section 2.9.1, the coefficient of thermal expansion of elastomers is much higher than that of metals, roughly 10 times that of steel. This important factor must be considered when, for example, the operating temperature of a seal differs substantially from normal room temperature. At elevated temperatures, the thermal expansion of the seal is substantially greater than that of its surrounding material, and this may be further increased by swelling after contact with a fluid. At low temperatures, the thermal contraction of the seal is much higher than that of its surrounding material. Under certain circumstances, leakage can occur even if the seal is still flexible.

4.13 Joule Effect

The Joule effect is a phenomenon of practical importance that must be considered by machine designers. The simplest way of demonstrating this effect is to suspend a weight on a rubber band sufficient to elongate it at least 50%. When the stretched rubber band is warmed up by an infrared lamp, it does not elongate because of thermal expansion, as may be expected, but it retracts and lifts the weight.

Alternatively, the rubber band may be held at a constant elongation and the load required to maintain it at that elongation determined while the temperature is increasing. Under these conditions the load will increase, indicating that the material has a higher modulus (increase in stiffness) when the temperature is raised. This can be confusing since the standard stress-strain measurements made in the laboratories show that the tensile modulus becomes lower as the temperature increases (section 4.14). However, it is generally accepted that this is not a contradiction because, at higher test temperatures, another effect, the "plastic flow," overrides the Joule effect when the elongation is made at the standard speed (500 mm/min). If the tension tests are run at high speed, the plastic flow will be eliminated and the stress-strain curves will show that the tensile modulus increases as the temperature increases (1).

It should be kept in mind that an unstrained elastomer will expand when heated in accordance with its coefficient of expansion and that the Joule effect occurs only if the elastomer is under tensile stress. The extent of the Joule effect depends on the amount of stretch. There is usually no evidence of this effect at low elongations, say, 10%.

Laboratory tests show that VMQ and FMQ do not exhibit the Joule effect (2). Both of these elastomers are characterized by inferior tensile strength because of their low tendency to crystallize on stretching (section 1.7). On the other hand, elastomers that do exhibit the Joule effect are those types with relatively high tensile strength (because of their ability to undergo crystallization when stretched), including NR, CR, NBR, FPM and EPDM. Accordingly, there appears to be a connection between the Joule effect and strain crystallization. Presumably, heat will melt the crystalline regions of strain-crystallizing elastomers. This means that the orientation of the molecular segments in the direction of pull will be destroyed, resulting in retraction of the polymer chains to their amorphous state, as they were before stretching.

4.14 Property Changes at Elevated Temperatures

The physical properties of elastomers are very dependent on temperature. Normally, the tests are carried out at $23(\pm2)\,°C$. However, there is an increasing interest in making tests at temperatures other than room temperature. Generally speaking, the tensile strength, modulus and hardness decrease as the test temperature is raised above room temperature. The ultimate elongation increases over a certain temperature range and then decreases at still higher temperatures. The rebound resilience increases to a maximum value.

In this connection, distinction should be made between the short- and long-term effects of high temperatures. Short-term effects are almost physical and reversible when the temperature is returned to ambient. The long-term effects, however, bring about major changes in the elastomeric material and are permanent. Such changes are caused by chemical reactions, normally leading to progressive increase or decrease in hardness and modulus with loss in tensile strength, elongation and elastic properties. The extent of these changes is a function mainly of the polymer type and vulcanization system.

4.15 Property Changes at Low Temperatures

Some of the property changes induced by low temperatures occur immediately after thermal equilibrium is reached and others occur after prolonged exposure.

As the temperature decreases, the hardness, modulus, tensile strength and compression set increase, whereas the elongation decreases. The rebound resilience decreases, reaching a minimum (leathery state) and then increases again, showing steel resilience. In the end, the elastomer becomes glasslike and brittle. The temperature at this stage is called **glass transition temperature (Tg)**.

The low temperature graphs given in chapter 8 **(Fig. 8.44–8.55)** illustrate the changes in hardness, compression set and rebound resilience of selected rubber compounds with decreasing temperature. These examples are believed to be representative of many elastomer types. It is notable that silicone and fluorosilicone elastomers retain these properties over a wide range of temperatures.

Long periods of exposure can produce two other kinds of property changes: crystallization of the polymer and partial separation of the plasticizer. **Crystallization** of a polymer refers to orientation of molecular segments, which is evident only after prolonged exposure. It may require days, weeks or even months, depending upon the exposure temperature and the composition of the elastomeric material. In particular, NR and CR crystallize readily. For each elastomer there is a characteristic temperature at which crystallization takes place most rapidly. For unstrained elastomers, this temperature is near $-10\,^{\circ}$C for CR, $-25\,^{\circ}$C for NR, $-35\,^{\circ}$C for IIR, $-10\,^{\circ}$C for AU and $-55\,^{\circ}$C for MQ (3). Both above and below these temperatures, crystallization is slower. However, application of stress usually increases the crystallization rate. As mentioned in section 1.7, many elastomers have the ability to crystallize when stretched. While low-temperature crystallization results in an in crease in stiffness and loss in elasticity, it does not necessarily result in brittleness.

Low-temperature crystallization is not a problem if the elastomeric component is subject to frequent movements, since the heat generated during these movements will melt the crystals. However, strain-crystallizing elastomers in static applications will crystallize if exposed to low temperatures for long periods.

Upon prolonged exposure to very low temperatures, such as $-40\,^{\circ}$C, some plasticized rubbers become stiff and in some cases brittle at temperatures somewhat higher than their normal brittleness point. This **plasticizer-time effect** is generally noted in compounds containing substantial quantities of special plasticizers and may be due to limited solubility of the plasticizer in the rubber compound. Under ordinary temperatures such plasticizers are soluble in the elastomer. Upon prolonged exposure to low temperatures, however, the compatibility of the plasticizer is reduced and a portion of it is separated from the compound. This portion is no longer effective.

Many elastomers with good oil resistance are less flexible at low temperatures than are their nonoil-resistant counterparts. Frequently, the low-temperature behavior of some oil-resistant elastomers can be improved to some extent by incorporating a low-temperature plasticizer in the rubber compound. However, it should be kept in mind that improving the low-temperature flexibility with plasticizers is accompanied by the risk that plasticizers may be volatilized at elevated temperatures or leached out by service fluids, resulting in a shrinkage of the elastomeric component. In certain liquids, such as fuels and organic solvents, the loss of plasticizer is compensated for by the fluid.

4.16 Temperature Limits of Elastomers

The low-temperature limits of elastomers given in chapter 8 **(Table 8.19)** are only approximate values based on laboratory tests. In order to make sure of the suitability of the selected material, functional tests should be carried out under the working conditions because there are other factors that can favor or impair the service performance of an elastomeric part at low temperatures (section 10.14.1).

The upper temperatures given in the table should also be considered as a general guide because the maximum service temperature of a given rubber compound will vary according to the working conditions and the service period required. For example, the maximum temperature recommended for a standard

NBR compound is 100°C, based on a long-term service in standard mineral oils. This means that temperatures below 100°C will extend service life and those above 100°C will reduce it. The same compound may perform well for 100 h at 150°C and possibly for few minutes at 300°C. Another example is FPM, which may be considered suitable for some applications at 300°C for about 24 h, at 280°C for about 100 h, at 250°C for about 1,000 h, at 230°C for about 3,000 h and almost indefinitely in the range of ambient temperature to 200°C. Consequently, the maximum temperatures given in Table 8.19 may be exceeded in short-term applications. Conversely, if aggressive media are used, the given maximum temperatures may be considerably reduced.

4.17 Electrical and Electrostatic Properties

Elastomers are normally good insulators with relatively high electrical resistivity, the nonpolar (nonoil-resistant) elastomers being better than the polar (oil-resistant) ones. However, the electrical properties of rubber compounds are more dependent on the compounding ingredients than on the basic rubber. Compounds containing carbon black must be avoided if very high resistance is required. In this case, silicone elastomers are the best to use.

It is possible to make elastomers antistatic and even conductive by incorporating sufficient quantities of graphite, special types of carbon black, certain metal powders or polar products into the rubber mix. However, conductivity achieved by these means does not approach the conductivity of metals.

It is not possible to make a clear-cut distinction between insulating, antistatic and conducting elastomers. Generally, elastomers having resistances below 10^4 ohms are considered conductive; between 10^4 and 10^8 ohms, antistatic; and above this, insulating. The upper limit is usually about 10^{16} ohms.

Many elastomeric products, such as belts, hoses, footwear and other items used in hospital operating rooms, require sufficient electrical conductivity to prevent buildup of electrical charges caused by the accumulation of static electricity.

Besides serving as an insulator or a conductor, the elastomer must possess good retention of the electrical properties. For this reason, resistance to other factors, including heat, high humidity and outdoor weather, must be considered in conjunction with electrical properties.

4.18 Chemical Properties

The physical properties of elastomers are not permanent properties. Sunlight, oxygen, ozone, heat, high humidity, radiation and the like may quickly rob a rubber compound of its original good properties.

Another deteriorating factor for elastomeric products is exposure to various liquids, such as fuels, oils, solvents, refrigerants, acids and alkalis. The response to these deteriorating influences varies widely with the kind of basic rubber and compounding ingredients. Under severe conditions the elastomer may become unserviceable after a short time. Therefore, it should be ensured that resistant elastomeric materials are used.

(The effects of environmental factors and contiguous materials on the properties of elastomers will be discussed in chapters 5 and 6, respectively.)

References

1. I. Williams, "Language of Rubber," Du Pont De Nemours, 1963.
2. K. Nagdi, unpublished work.
3. ASTM D 832–87, "Rubber Conditioning for Low-Temperature Testing."

CHAPTER 5

Environmental Aging of Elastomers

5.1 Introduction

Aging of elastomers involves a progressive change in their physical and chemical properties, usually marked by deterioration. Factors that contribute to the deterioration of elastomers include ozone, heat, oxygen, sunlight, certain metal ions, high humidity, high-energy radiation, microorganisms and atmospheric pollutants, particularly in industrial areas. Under severe conditions, the elastomer may become unserviceable after a short time.

Deterioration of elastomers can take place in three ways:
1) additional cross-linking resulting in higher molecular weight;
2) chain scission resulting in a reduction in chain length and average molecular weight; or
3) chemical alteration of the molecule by formation of polar groups such as aldehyde, ketone, hydroxyl and ether groups (which affects the electrical insulation properties).

Generally, the greater the amount of unsaturation in the polymer chain, the more susceptible it is to aging.

5.2 Deterioration by Ozone under Tension

Ozone gas (O_3) is a form of oxygen (O_2) with a characteristic odor. It is known to be a very powerful oxidizing agent. It reacts with all organic substances, the rate of reaction being considerably faster with unsaturated compounds than with saturated materials.

Ozone is produced by the action of electrical discharges or certain ultraviolet wavelengths of light on oxygen. It exists in the atmosphere, usually at a concentration of only a few parts per hundred million (pphm) parts of air. However, the concentration varies quite widely, not only geographically but also seasonally and even from day to day in the same locality. The level can also increase to a large extent with atmospheric pollution. In some areas, particularly big cities, the ozone concentration can reach 100 pphm and even more during periods of smog.

Ozone is a serious deteriorating factor for many elastomers if they are in a stretched condition. Even at concentrations of less than 1 pphm, it can severely attack the surface of nonresistant elastomers, causing clearly visible cracks perpendicular to the direction of stretch.

Ozone resistance is controlled primarily by the backbone unsaturation level, since ozone attacks the double bonds. With the exception of CR (section 3.5.1), all elastomers with many double bonds in the backbone (such as NR, SBR and NBR) have inherently poor resistance to ozone cracking. However, their ozone resistance can be improved to some extent by incorporating antiozonants and special waxes (section 2.4), which bloom and protect the surface from ozone attack.

Ozone resistance improves considerably with the decrease of the number of double bonds in the backbone, as in the case of IIR and HNBR. Elastomers with a fully saturated backbone (such as FPM, ACM, AEM, EPM, EPDM and VMQ) show excellent resistance to atmospheric ozone. AU, EU and YBPO are also saturated and consequently ozone resistant, but they are susceptible to deterioration by water and high humidity in hot regions.

For all applications requiring good outdoor resistance, the more expensive saturated elastomers should be used whenever possible. The "protected" unsaturated general-purpose elastomers frequently fail in service because the protective additives could be leached by solvents, oils and the like. In addition, high temperatures increase the solubility of the wax in the rubber, so that eventually it becomes completely soluble and no further blooming takes place.

The mechanism of deterioration of elastomers by ozone is not clearly understood. However, it is generally accepted that ozone reacts with the polymer double bonds to form ozonides on the surface. These are unstable segments that tend to rupture because of constant tension, thus exposing further material to ozone attack. As this reaction is repeated, the cracks become deeper and deeper.

Antiozonant protection may occur either by prevention of the initial formation of the ozonides or by prevention of the decomposition of the ozonides into fragments by forming stable complexes.

The initiation of ozone cracks is favored by high strains, high ozone concentrations and high temperatures. At high strains innumerable minute cracks are formed. Conversely, at low strains only a small number of cracks are developed, but they tend to be deep. The effect is thus more severe in slightly strained elastomeric parts. The critical strain at which cracking occurs depends on the composition and state of cure of the elastomer. It can vary between approximately 10% and 50% for various rubber compounds. No cracking occurs below the critical strain of each compound.

5.3 Deterioration by Corona

Corona is the electric discharge that occurs in the atmosphere around high-voltage cables. It causes the formation of ozone in high concentrations, which in turn can severely attack nonresistant elastomers.

Resistance to deterioration caused by corona is a very important requirement in high-voltage applications. As mentioned in section 5.2, elastomers with low levels of unsaturation (e.g., IIR) or with fully saturated backbones (e.g., EPDM and VMQ) should be used.

5.4 Deterioration by Ozone in Warm Humid Air (Frosting)

Another type of surface degradation caused by ozone is known as **frosting**. It is defined as the dulling of a smooth shiny surface of vulcanized natural and some synthetic rubbers, usually appearing within a few hours or days after vulcanization. It occurs normally in light-colored compounds and cannot be removed by solvents (in contrast to bloom).

Frosting is caused by ozone in warm humid air and produces innumerable minute cracks on the surface. It can be artifically produced within a few hours by exposing a vulcanized rubber specimen without tension to warm, humid, ozonized air.

5.5 Deterioration by Ozone Under Dynamic Strain (Fatigue)

Certain elastomeric products (such as tires, belts, footwear and various molded goods) subjected to flexing during their service life may fail because of the appearance and growth of cracks. This phenomenon is known as **fatigue**. It is defined as the formation and growth of surface cracks resulting from prolonged deformation cycles by bending, extension or compression or combinations of these processes.

The mechanism of fatigue is not clearly understood. However, it is believed that the main factors contributing to flex cracking and crack growth may include oxidation and attack by ozone.

5.6 Deterioration by Heat and Oxygen

Elastomers are usually more resistant to heat in the absence of oxygen (e.g., in a vacuum or in inert gases such as nitrogen). However, in actual practice, the effects of heat and oxygen can hardly be separated.

The oxidation process is controlled mainly by two factors: first, the diffusion rate of oxygen in the elastomer, and second, the temperature. The oxidation rate increases considerably in a hot environment.

The oxidative heat aging of elastomers may involve formation of new cross-links, chain scission or formation of polar groups. These changes occur more rapidly with unsaturated elastomers than with saturated ones.

Most elastomers become hard and brittle after oxidative heat aging because of the formation of new cross-links. Only few elastomer types (such as NR, IIR and ECO) tend to become soft and sticky because of chain scission, usually coupled with the formation of polar groups.

Appropriate choice of antioxidants (section 2.4) can protect many elastomers against oxidation for long periods of time. The vulcanization system can also have a great influence on the oxidative heat aging (section 2.5). In the case of unsaturated elastomers such as NR, SBR and NBR, peroxide cures (which give carbon-carbon cross-links) and efficient vulcanization systems (which yield stable monosulphidic cross-links) are the best to use.

5.7 Deterioration by Sunlight and Oxygen

Exposure of elastomers to sunlight causes another kind of surface crack, called **crazing** or **alligatoring**, which is different from ozone cracks (section 5.2). Crazing occurs whether or not the elastomer is elongated. Furthermore, the resulting cracks do not occur in a uniform direction but extend in all directions. This effect is believed to be due to surface oxidation catalyzed by sunlight (photooxidation) and subsequent leaching of water-soluble oxidation products by rain. On drying, the oxidized layer contracts to produce crazing cracks. If the oxidized layer is washed away, the exposed filler can be rubbed off, creating the condition known as **chalking**.

The sunlight-catalyzed oxidation is more pronounced with unsaturated elastomers and becomes more severe in light-colored articles, which may also undergo discoloration. In contrast, saturated elastomers have some inherent resistance to aging caused by sunlight and may, therefore, be used where colored items are required.

5.8 Deterioration by Metal-Catalyzed Oxidation

A number of heavy metal ions (such as manganese, copper, nickel, iron and cobalt) are capable of increasing the susceptibility of elastomers to deterioration by oxygen attack. These metals are termed **pro-oxidants** because they are effective oxidation catalysts in some elastomers, particularly NR.

Metal-catalyzed oxidation of elastomers can be minimized or prevented by incorporating some antioxidants, notably the aromatic amines (section 2.4). These will react with the metal ions, forming stable complexes that are not capable of acting as catalysts.

5.9 Deterioration by Hydrolysis

Hydrolysis usually refers to a chemical reaction between water and materials whose molecules have certain polar groups, typically ester and amide groups. When such groups are in the backbone of a polymer, the hydrolysis will result in chain scission and molecular weight reduction. The hydrolysis rate increases considerably under acid or alkaline conditions.

Elastomer types that tend to deteriorate when exposed to hot water or high humidity in tropical regions include AU, EU and YBPO. Special ingredients are frequently added to these elastomers to improve their resistance to hydrolysis.

Generally speaking, the hydrolysis resistance of thermoplastic polyurethanes and YBPO increases with the increase of the polymer molecular weight. However, the high-molecular-weight polymers are hard materials (above 95 Shore A).

5.10 Deterioration by Atomic Radiation

Atomic or high-energy radiation involves gamma rays, electrons or beta rays, neutrons and mixtures of these (such as reactor radiation). Exposure of elastomers to high-energy radiation results in extensive changes in the molecular structure. These changes are very similar to those caused by heat aging. The polymer chains may be cross-linked to form a three-dimensional network or may be cleaved into smaller molecules.

Most elastomers become hard and stiff after exposure to high-energy radiation because of the formation of new cross-links. Under compressive deformation, the compression set resistance is most severely affected. The chain scission reaction occurs in few elastomers, such as IIR and ECO. The chain breakdown results in a soft sticky material.

The changes in the molecular structure of elastomeric materials caused by radiation depend on the amount of energy absorbed. The preferred unit is the **rad** (radiation absorbed dose), which is defined as 100 ergs of absorbed energy.

The exact mechanism of radiation effect has not been clarified. However, it is generally accepted that high-energy electrons or gamma rays strike the polymer chains, producing ions and free radicals. The subsequent reactions of these ions and free radicals cause the deterioration by cross-linking or chain scission. The following reaction may be expected to predominate.

$$PH \xrightarrow{\text{radiation}} P^{\cdot} \quad + \quad H^{\cdot}$$

PH		$P^{\cdot}$		$H^{\cdot}$
polymer hydrocarbon chain		polymer free radical		hydrogen atom

$$H^{\cdot} + PH \longrightarrow P^{\cdot} \quad + \quad H_2$$

hydrogen molecule

$$2\,P^{\cdot} \longrightarrow P - P$$

cross-linking

Hydrogen gas and volatile products are formed during cross-linking. These may cause voids or blisters in the compound at high radiation doses. Apparently, it is the radiation dose (not the radiation rate) that is the controlling factor of deterioration. In other words, it makes no difference whether the elastomer absorbs the whole radiation dose in a short time or in small portions over prolonged periods. In both cases the damage is of the same type and approximately to the same extent, as long as the elastomer is not simultaneously exposed to other environments such as oxygen, ozone or heat or other chemically active agents.

Elastomeric materials are frequently used in radiation environments for such applications as seals, hoses and electrical insulation. In general, the type of the base rubber is the controlling factor of the radiation resistance of an elastomer. However, additional protection can be achieved by incorporating selected compounding ingredients, particularly antirads (section 2.4), which are aromatic amines that are also used as antioxidants and antiozonants. In addition, radiation resistance is influenced by the state of cure. It improves with increasingly tighter cross-linking as measured by compression set. In general, the better the initial compression set resistance, the longer the elastomer can be expected to resist radiation.

At 10^6 rads the effects on most elastomers are minor, while at 10^7 rads there are significant differences between elastomer types. At 10^8 rads most elastomers will be deteriorated.

Elastomers that usually have good resistance to 10^7 rads or slightly above include selected compounds based on NBR, HNBR, EPDM, SBR, AU and YBPO.

Elastomers that are usually not suitable to radiation conditions above 10^6 rads include ACM, IIR, ECO and fluorinated elastomers (e.g., FPM and FMQ)(1).

It should be noted, however, that in most applications the elastomer must withstand conditions other than radiation. In a reactor, for example, seals are often exposed to hot water, steam, hot air, silicone fluids or other environments in addition to radiation. Therefore, it is likely that compounds having high radiation resistance cannot be used in certain applications. Polyurethanes, for example, are not resistant to hot water, steam and temperatures above 100°C. NBR compounds, having double bonds in the backbone, tend to embrittle or case harden when exposed to permanent temperature above 120°C. Furthermore, they are susceptible to extraction by the commonly used silicone fluids, resulting in shrinkage and earlier failure in service.

These examples show that it is very important to consider factors other than radiation when selecting elastomeric materials for use in radiation environments. The combined effects of radiation, temperature and fluid can be greater than a simple addition of the individual effects. Therefore, it is recommended to test the elastomers under conditions similar to those in service. The selected compound, not merely the type of elastomer, should then be specified.

5.11 Deterioration by Microorganisms

Biological degradation of elastomeric products caused by microorganisms (bacteria and fungi) is comparatively rare, but for some applications it is a serious problem. Since elastomers are complex mixtures (including, in addition to the basic rubber, many compounding ingredients), the susceptibility of the various constituents to biological attack must be considered separately.

Natural rubber appears to be consumed by microorganisms, whereas most synthetic rubbers are not consumed (2). Organic additives (particularly those based on natural products such as cellulose fibers, wood flour, fatty acids, vegetable oils and animal fats) are also susceptible to attack.

It is to be expected that elastomers containing ingredients that are known to act as food sources for microorganisms would show deterioration in properties when exposed to environments suitable for fungal or bacterial growth. Rubberized cotton fabrics, in particular, may show considerable microbiological deterioration when exposed to certain conditions.

Environments that favor the growth of microorganisms include:
– tropical temperatures (30°C being very favorable);
– high humidities (relative humidities of 95% to 100% are very favorable for fungi, whereas bacteria frequently need the presence of water for growth);
– the soil, where there is an enormous variety of both fungal and bacterial species; and
– underground areas, such as coal mines, where humidity is high.

Microorganisms may cause deterioration of elastomers in a number of ways, such as in the following:

– actual decomposition of the material may be caused by enzymes produced by the microorganism;
– during organisms' growth, undesirable substances may be produced that can discolor the material;
– physical properties, such as tensile strength and elasticity, may be affected if part of the material is consumed;
– the insulating properties of the material may be reduced by holding moisture; and
– the presence of fungi may make the material too unsightly to be used in certain applications.

Elastomeric products requiring high resistance to fungal and bacterial attack can be protected by the incorporation of certain **fungicides** (substances that kill fungi) or **bactericides** (substances that kill bacteria) in the rubber compound.

5.12 Damage from Insects

Whereas the deterioration of elastomers by microorganisms involves chemical reactions, the damage caused by insects is mechanical. The greatest damage is caused by termites and red ants (destructive insects that eat wood, textile, leather, paper, elastomers and plastomers, practically everything except stones, glass and metals). Some species can even penetrate lead sheathing on cables and attack the rubber insulation.

Termites generally live underground. Therefore, the risk of damage to elastomeric items (cables in particular) is greatest when they are in contact with the ground. Aboveground, damage usually results from close contact with woodwork that has become infested with subterranean termites or with certain species that inhabit dead wood, known as the drywood type.

Red ants live and nest in crevices and under stones. They search for food aboveground in daylight. All their attacks are encountered in or on houses or at the tops of line poles. Damage can also be caused by small red ants known as sugar ants, small brown ants, boring beetles and even by wood worms (3).

5.12.1 Prevention of Damage from Insects

There are three methods for preventing (or at least minimizing) attack by termites and other insects:
1) using insecticides to kill the attacking insects;
2) using repellents to prevent attack; and
3) adding barriers such as steel tape or increasing the hardness of the elastomeric material.

Using **insecticides** involves several problems. First, true insecticides do not prevent initial attack but are effective only after some of the "protected" article has already been consumed. Thus, where a large number of attacking insects is involved (and this is usually the case), it is only a matter of time until a significant part of the article is destroyed even though many of the attackers are killed in the process.

Another problem is the incorporation of insecticides in the rubber compound. The high volatility and comparatively poor thermal stability of several insecticides make it difficult to assess how much is actually retained in the end product and thus how much protection is given. In addition, the possibility of interaction with other functional ingredients or with the polymer itself needs to be studied. Also, health hazards to the operators concerned with mixing and processing in the factory must be considered.

Insect repellents are substances that are offensive in some way or other to insects, thus discouraging them from approaching the protected article. Most of these substances are used for the protection of wood, but some could be incorporated in rubber compounds. The problems mentioned above with incorporation of insecticides in the compound also apply to repellents. In the case of cellular rubber most of these repellents could easily be sprayed into the pores, as dust or emulsion according to their nature. Some solid elastomeric articles could possibly be redesigned with orifices or pockets capable of carrying repellents of this kind (3).

The difficulty in using insect repellents is due to their action being dependent on uniform evolution of an obnoxious vapor, which can result only from a slowly controlled volatilization rate. However, the extent of volatilization and, accordingly, the efficiency and duration of protection are considerably affected by ambient conditions such as temperature and humidity.

Other solutions are limited to few items, such as cables. A sure but expensive method involves adding a **barrier** such as a thin brass or steel tape. Aluminum or lead tapes are of doubtful value because of their softness. Other factors that may provide solutions on a much wider scale include the surface hardness and thickness of the elastomeric item. In general, the resistance to penetration increases as the surface hardness and cross section increase.

5.13 Damage from Rodents

Elastomeric items such as cables, hoses, seals and tires are also susceptible to rodent attack. The motives for attack have little connection with the search for food; in fact, rodents nibble these materials even in the presence of food. The true motives remain obscure, but it has been suggested that animals' curiosity may be a factor.

5.13.1 Prevention of Damage from Rodents

Three approaches have been made to prevent or minimize rodent attacks:
1) using rodenticides to kill the animal;
2) using rodent repellents to prevent attack; and
3) adding barriers such as steel tape or increasing the surface hardness and thickness of the elastomeric item.

Much of what has been said above, regarding prevention of attack by insects, also applies to rodents.

5.14 Guidelines for Storage of Vulcanized Rubbers

Many elastomers are liable to changes in physical properties during storage and may become unserviceable because of excessive hardening, softening, cracking, crazing or other surface degradation. These changes may be the result of one particular factor or a combination of factors, namely, the action of oxygen, ozone, light, heat and humidity. However, the deleterious effects of these factors can be minimized if the elastomeric parts are properly packaged and stored. The storage conditions are given in ISO 2230. The most important of these are the following:

1) **Temperature:** the storage temperature should be below 25 °C, preferably 15 °C.
2) **Humidity:** moist conditions should be avoided.
3) **Light:** a dark room is preferred. If this is not possible, the elastomeric parts should be protected from direct sunlight and strong artificial light with a high ultraviolet content.
4) **Oxygen and ozone:** vulcanized rubbers should be protected from circulating air by wrapping, storing in air-tight containers or other suitable means. This applies particularly to articles with large surface-area-to-volume ratios (e.g., cellular rubbers). Furthermore, the storage rooms should not contain any equipment that is capable of generating ozone, such as electric motors, fluorescent or mercury vapor lamps and high-voltage electrical equipment.
5) **Deformation:** vulcanized rubbers should be stored in a relaxed condition free from tension, compression or other deformation. If it is not possible to avoid deformation, it should at least be kept to a minimum.
6) **Contact with metals:** elastomeric parts should not be stored in direct contact with copper or manganese, which are known to have deleterious effects on many vulcanized rubbers. They should be protected by wrapping or by separation with a layer of a suitable material such as paper or polyethylene. Plasticized films such as plasticized PVC should not be used.
7) **Contact between different elastomers:** contact between rubber compounds of different compositions should be avoided.
8) **Contact with liquids or with their vapors:** vulcanized rubbers should not come in contact with vapors, liquids or semisolid materials (e.g., solvents, oils and greases) at any time during storage.
9) **Radiation:** exposure to all sources of radiation must be avoided.
10) **Cleaning:** washing with soap and water is the least harmful. Abrasives, sharp objects and solvents such as trichloroethylene and hydrocarbons must not be used. Articles that have been cleaned should be dried at room temperature.

Most elastomers will remain in serviceable condition for many years under proper storage conditions. Saturated elastomers may last 10 to 20 years; unsaturated, 2 to 5 years or more.

References

1. K. Nagdi, unpublished work.
2. W. M. Heap, "Microbiological Deterioration of Rubbers and Plastics," RAPRA Information Circular 476, September 1965.
3. J. Pacitti, "Attack by Insects and Rodents on Rubbers and Plastics," RAPRA Information Circular 475, July 1965.

CHAPTER 6

Effects of Selected Contiguous Materials on Elastomers

6.1 Introduction

Many elastomeric products, particularly seals and hoses, come in contact with a wide range of materials, such as:
– lubricants, working fluids and greases based on petroleum, natural or synthetic oils;
– gasolines, gasohols and diesel and jet fuels;
– refrigerants such as chlorofluorohydrocarbons;
– solvents such as aliphatic and aromatic hydrocarbons, chlorinated hydrocarbons, alcohols, ethers, ketones and so forth;
– water, water solutions and steam;
– aggressive chemicals such as organic and inorganic acids, alkalis and organic bases;
– aggressive gases such as chlorine, hydrogen chloride and nitrogen oxides;
– deep sour gas and oil-field fluids including corrosion inhibitors; and
– solid materials such as metals, plastics and glass.

The first thing to be considered when selecting an elastomeric material is its resistance to all media that it will contact at the maximum anticipated service temperature. This may include, for example, oils, any grease, outside air or an occasional cleaning agent. A lack of knowledge in elastomer/medium compatibility can result in premature system failure.

By proper selection of rubber compounds, elastomeric components can be designed for satisfactory use with a wide range of contacting media. However, choosing the right rubber compound for a given duty is a complex problem involving, in many cases, compromise in which one property is, in part, sacrificed to achieve another. For the successful solution of this problem, cooperation between the user and rubber manufacturer is essential.

6.2 Physical and Chemical Effects of Fluids on Elastomers

Elastomers that are in contact with fluids are subject to chemical and physical effects

6.2.1 Chemical Effects

Some base fluids and additives react chemically with elastomers, particularly at elevated temperatures, resulting in additional cross-linking or scission of the polymer chains. In addition, the action of a liquid on elastomers can be markedly affected by the presence of atmospheric oxygen. For some elastomers the effect of aeration is considerable and for others, insignificant (1, 2).

A chemical reaction between fluid and elastomer can lead to serious changes in the physical properties of the elastomer. When the attack is severe, the elastomer loses its elasticity and becomes hard and brittle or soft and tacky.

6.2.2 Physical Effects

Changes in the physical properties of elastomers that are in contact with fluids may result from two simultaneous actions:
1) absorption of the liquid by the elastomer; and
2) extraction of soluble constituents such as plasticizers and antioxidants from the elastomer.

The result is a change in volume (i.e. swelling if **1** is greater than **2** or shrinkage if **2** is greater than **1**. Swell increases from time of immersion up to a point where no more fluid will be absorbed and the volumetric expansion remains constant. The time taken to reach this state of equilibrium is largely dependent on the temperature, shape and thickness of the part.

The change in volume can alter such physical properties of the elastomer as hardness, modulus, tensile strength and elongation. A swell has the same effect as adding plasticizer to the elastomer by making it more flexible with a decrease in hardness, modulus and tensile strength. Such changes are more or less proportional to the percentage of volume increase. A shrinkage normally causes a reduction in flexibility and an increase in hardness, modulus and tensile strength.

Where dimensional accuracy is functionally necessary, as in the case of dynamic seals, excessive swelling or shrinkage would disqualify an elastomer regardless of its retention of other physical properties. The maximum volume increase that can be tolerated will vary with the application. In general, a volume increase of as much as 25% may be acceptable for static seals and up to 10% for dynamic seals. Beyond this, the dimensional change coupled with the marked increase in friction will shorten the seal life to an unacceptable level. Shrinkage is usually unacceptable and should be avoided because it can result in a loose seal and leakage, particularly at low temperatures.

If the contiguous fluid is nonvolatile (e.g., mineral oils), the swell will remain permanent. If the fluid is volatile (e.g., gasolines, gasohols and solvents), shrinkage can occur if the elastomer is allowed to dry out. Drying out does not occur as long as the elastomeric part is continously in contact with the fluid or its vapor.

6.3 Prediction of the Fluid Resistance of Elastomers

The most reliable method for selecting suitable elastomeric materials for use with particular fluids is to carry out individual immersion tests (section 10.17) under controlled conditions. Changes in volume, hardness, tensile strength and ultimate elongation of standard test pieces after immersion are used as measures of the fluid resistance. The test results will indicate whether the property changes are within acceptable limits. However, there are simple methods that may provide enough information to eliminate totally unsuitable elastomer/fluid combinations without carrying out extensive tests. These simple methods are based on the following:

- the rule of thumb "like dissolves like";
- the solubility parameter;
- the aniline point; and
- the elastomer compatibility index (ECI) using the standard elastomers specified in ISO 6072.

6.3.1 Like Dissolves Like

A general rule of thumb states that like dissolves like. For example, benzene dissolves mineral oil because both are hydrocarbons, whereas water does not dissolve mineral oil because they are chemically not alike.

This rule of thumb applies also to linear polymers (e.g., plastics, thermoplastic elastomers and nonvulcanized rubber compounds) when exposed to chemically related solvents. Consequently, polar polymers dissolve in polar solvents and nonpolar polymers in nonpolar solvents.

Elastomers, having a network structure, do not dissolve, but swell excessively in chemically related fluids. For example, EPDM elastomers, which are hydrocarbon polymers, swell excessively in hydrocarbon fluids such as mineral oils and hydrocarbon fuels. Similarly, silicone elastomers swell in silicone oils, and fluoro- and perfluoroelastomers swell in fluorinated hydrocarbon fluids such as polychlorotrifluoroethylene. **Table 6.1** shows the results of a laboratory test that illustrates this. **Table 6.2** gives examples of the swelling behavior of selected rubber compounds in chemically different fluids. Aside from the chemical action of

Table 6.1: Swelling Behavior of Selected Elastomers in Chemically Related Fluids

Elastomer Base	Medium	Test Temp. (°C)	Test Duration (h)	Original Hardness (Shore A)	Change in Shore A Hardness (points)	Volume Change (%)
EPDM (hydrocarbon rubber)	ASTM-oil No. 3 (hydrocarbon fluid)	100	168	50	−30	+185
VMQ (silicone rubber)	Silicone oil	200	168	70	−47	+ 80
FPM (Viton GF®)	PCTFE*	200	168	80	−48	+ 90
FFKM (Kalrez®)	PCTFE*	200	168	75	−24	+ 54
TFE/P** (Aflas®)	PCTFE*	150	168	70	−34	+182

* polychlorotrifluoroethylene   ** tetrafluoreethylene/propylene rubber

Table 6.2: Swelling Behavior of Selected Elastomers in Chemically Different Fluids

Elastomer Base	Medium	Test Temp. (°C)	Test Dura-tion (h)	Original Hardness (Shore A)	Change in Shore A Hardness (points)	Volume Change (%)
NBR (plasticizer-free)	ASTM-oil No. 3	100	168	85	− 2	+ 2
NBR (plasticized)	ASTM-oil No. 3	100	168	70	+ 3	− 5
EPDM (plasticizer-free)	Silicone oil	100	168	75	± 0	± 0
EPDM (plasticized)	Silicone oil	100	168	75	+17	−29
NBR (plasticizer-free)	Silicone oil	100	168	80	± 0	± 0
NBR (plasticized)	Silicone oil	100	168	70	+ 5	− 5
NBR (plasticized)	PCTFE*	100	672	80	+10	− 2
HNBR (plasticizer-free)	PCTFE*	150	672	85	+11 (brittle)	+ 2

* polychlorotrifluoroethylene

polychlorotrifluoroethylene on NBR and HNBR compounds (hardening and brittleness), it is evident that dissimilar fluids cause low swelling in the plasticizer-free elastomers and shrinkage in the plasticized ones because of plasticizer extraction.

Therefore, it is of great importance to know the chemical nature of both elastomer and fluid. This helps in recognizing totally unsuitable elastomer/fluid combinations without the need for carrying out lengthy immersion tests on each combination.

6.3.2 Solubility Parameter

The solubility parameter (δ) is a basic property of all materials. It is defined as the square root of the cohesive energy density C.E.D.:

$$\delta = (C.E.D.)^{1/2} = \left[\frac{\Delta H - RT}{Vm} \right]^{1/2}$$

In the above equation ΔH is the enthalpy of evaporation, **Vm** is the molar volume, **R** is the gas constant and **T** is the absolute temperature. The solubility parameters of common solvents and many polymers, including elastomers, have been reported in the literature. The behavior of a polymer in a fluid can be related to the solubility parameters of both polymer and fluid such that a polymer will dissolve in a liquid having the same solubility parameter.

An elastomer (being cross-linked) will swell to its maximum extent in a fluid having the same solubility parameter. However, the complexity of rubber compounds and the difficulty of determining their solubility parameters have rendered this simple approach of limited practical use. In addition, most of the industrial fluids are products of ill-defined chemical composition with additive packages to improve particular properties.

6.3.3 Aniline Point

Aniline, an aromatic amine (C_6H_5-NH_2), is a poisonous liquid, boiling at 184 °C and having a faint odor, which is common to many amino compounds. The aniline point of a liquid is the lowest temperature in degrees centigrade at which the liquid sample is miscible with an equal volume of aniline. The methods for determining the aniline point of petroleum oils and hydrocarbon solvents are specified in ISO 2977. In principle, specified volumes of aniline and the liquid sample are placed in a tube and mixed mechanically. The mixture is heated at a controlled rate until the two phases become miscible. The mixture is then cooled at a controlled rate and the temperature at which the two phases separate is recorded as the aniline point.

The aniline point is a measure of the solubility of a liquid in aniline. Aromatic hydrocarbons are readily soluble in aniline and therefore show the lowest aniline points. In contrast, paraffinic hydrocarbons are less soluble in aniline and accordingly have the highest values. Consequently, the aniline point can be used to estimate the aromatic content in mineral oils that correlates with the swelling effect of the oil on elastomers. As the aniline point of the oil decreases (indicating a high aromatic content) the swelling effect on elastomers becomes more pronounced. Oils with the same aniline points usually have similar effects on elastomers. The ASTM reference oils (section 6.4) cover a range of aniline points found in lubricating oils. Oil No. 1 has a high aniline point (124 °C) and causes slight swelling or shrinkage; oil No. 2 has a medium aniline point (93 °C) and causes intermediate swelling; and oil No. 3 has a low aniline point (70 °C) and causes high or extreme swelling of elastomeric materials. Any other commercial oil with the same or similar aniline point can be expected to have a similar effect on a particular rubber compound as the corresponding ASTM oil.

This method has been used for many years as a means of predicting the effect of mineral oils on elastomers. However, the method can be reliable only for straight oils known to be free from additives, but not for those oils containing additive packages. It has been found that different service oils with similar aniline points can differ significantly in their swelling power because they contain different sorts and amounts of additives.

6.3.4 Elastomer Compatibility Index (ECI) Using Standard Test Elastomers

The elastomer compatibility index, ECI (which will be discussed in more detail later), provides enough information about the physical and chemical effects of petroleum-based and fire resistant fluids upon specified **standard elastomers** that are representative of various commercial elastomeric materials for actual service.

Standard elastomers, or **test elastomers**, are rubber vulcanizates with known composition that are intended to simulate different types of commercial elastomers. They are used for predicting the effects of service fluids upon commercial rubber compounds of similar composition. They are also used by producers of additives and fluids for the development of products that do not severely attack elastomers. Furthermore, test elastomers are recommended for quality control of commercial fluids because they are sensitive to fluid variations and have high swelling characteristics.

In order to minimize error, test elastomers contain a minimum number of ingredients, each of which is obtained from one source. Plasticizers and processing aids, for example, are not added in order to avoid shrinkage. A stable vulcanization system is used to give adequate storage life of several years under suitable storage conditions.

Standard elastomers should not be confused with **commercial elastomers** for actual service, whose compositions are not given by their manufacturers. In general, commercial elastomers contain many more ingedients than the standard test elastomers in order to fulfill processing and service requirements. It is advisable not to use commercial elastomers for quality control of service fluids as they are generally subject to more quality tolerances than the standard test elastomers.

There are many test elastomers in existence. However, several of these are not included in international or national standards. The most common standard elastomers are described in ISO 6072 titled "Hydraulic fluid power – Compatibility between elastomeric materials and fluids." This international standard provides formulations, mixing and vulcanization procedures for three standard elastomers:
1) **NBR 1**, based on acrylonitrile rubber;
2) **FPM 1**, based on fluorocarbon rubber; and
3) **EPDM 1**, based on ethylene-propylene-diene rubber.

The changes in volume, hardness, tensile strength and elongation at break (which standard test specimens of the suitable standard elastomer undergo when immersed in a certain fluid under specified test conditions) establish an ECI, for this fluid, which can be expressed as a simple one-line symbolic designation including the following details:
a) the test elastomer used
b) the percentage change in volume
c) the change in hardness expressed in IRHD (microtest)
d) the percentage change in tensile strength
e) the percentage change in elongation at break

Example:
ECI of a fluid **x**: NBR 1, +10, −3, −10, −25
  a   b   c   d   e

The ECI (which should be quoted by fluid suppliers) allows selection of suitable combinations of fluids and elastomeric materials. In the case of petroleum-based oils, it is possible to predict the percentage volume change of commercial elastomers by using a simple method described in Annex A, which forms an integral part of the international standard. The method involves the use of standard elastomer NBR 1 and is based on the principle that there is an approximate linear relationship between the equilibrium percentage volume changes of an NBR compound in a number of mineral-oil-based fluids and those of another NBR compound in the same oils. Therefore, if the equilibrium percentage volume changes of different commercial NBR compounds in different mineral oils are plotted against those of standard NBR 1 in the same oils, a linear relationship would be obtained (as shown in **Fig. 6.1**). With the exception of VMQ, this relationship applies not only to NBR but also to many other oil-resistant elastomer types, such as HNBR, ACM, ECO, CO and FPM.

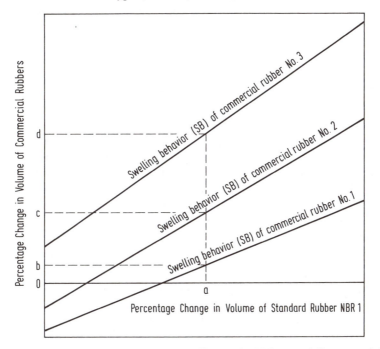

Fig. 6.1: Relationship between Percentage Change in Volume of Commercial Rubbers in Mineral Oils and of Standard Rubber NBR 1

If rubber manufacturers quote the **swelling behavior (SB)** of their rubber compounds graphically **(Fig. 6.1)** and, at the same time, the oil suppliers quote percentage volume changes of standard elastomer NBR 1 in their oils, interested parties would be able to predict volume changes of those commercial rubber compounds in those oils. By SB of a commercial rubber compound is meant, in this connection, the correlation of its percentage volume changes in a range of mineral oils with those of the standard elastomer NBR 1 in the same oils.

Example: If the percentage volume change of standard elastomer NBR 1 after immersion in a mineral oil **x** is equal to **a** (Fig. 6.1), it would be possible to predict percentage volume changes equal to **b**, **c** and **d** for commercial rubber compounds

Nos. **1**, **2** and **3**, respectively, without having to carry out individual immersion tests in this oil. This method is becoming quite popular because it allows one to predict the percentage volume change of commercial elastomers more accurately than is possible using the aniline point method.

It should be pointed out that this method is applicable only to mineral-oil-based fluids. It is also important to keep in mind that an elastomer may not be swelled, but could be degraded by the oil. Therefore, the changes in hardness, tensile strength and elongation at break of NBR 1 should also be considered. If the changes are not tolerable, commercial NBR compounds should not be used with the oil in question. In this case, other elastomer types, such as HNBR, ACM or FPM, should be considered.

A simple and rapid method for measuring percentage volume changes of standard elastomer NBR 1 in mineral oils is specified in Annex B, which forms an integral part of the international standard. This method can be used for purposes where rapidity and ease of measurement are more important than accuracy (i.e., for quality control). It is particularly suitable for users with limited laboratory facilities to safeguard themselves against faulty batches of oils.

The Annex B method involves measuring the percentage linear swell of a standard test ring (made of standard elastomer NBR 1) after a 22-hour immersion test using a specified tapered rod gauge. The percentage linear swell is then converted into the percentage volume change using a conversion table given in the standard. The results are expressed in terms of **volume change index (VCI)**, which is defined as the percentage volumetric change expressed to the nearest whole number. The Annex B method is applicable only to mineral-oil-based fluids and is considered more reliable than the aniline point method described earlier.

Annex C, which does not form an integral part of the international standard, gives an information report on types of hydraulic fluids and elastomers.

6.4 Review of Standard Test Liquids

For test purposes, it is usually desirable to use the liquid with which the elastomer will come in contact in service. However, it has long been common practice to use standard liquids with known composition that are representative of various types of service fluids.

The standard test liquids consist of well-defined chemical compounds or mixtures of compounds. They are used not only for evaluating the fluid resistance of vulcanized rubbers, but also for their quality control. It is not advisable to use commercial fluids for quality control or comparative tests because such fluids, particularly those of petroleum origin, are often not well defined and are liable to vary appreciably in chemical composition. Consequently, misleading results may be obtained.

If standard liquids are not available and nonstandard liquids of unknown or doubtful composition are employed for comparative tests, samples of liquids from the same drum or shipment must be used. The variations in commercial fluids can be detected by using a standard test elastomer (section 6.3.4).

The principal standard test liquids defined in ISO 1817 and in national standards are the same test oils and fuels described in ASTM D 471. There are three types of **standard oils** specified in ISO 1817:
1) Oil No. 1 (ASTM oil No. 1): a "low volume increase" oil
2) Oil No. 2 (ASTM oil No. 2): a "medium volume increase" oil
3) Oil No. 3 (ASTM oil No. 3): a "high volume increase" oil

Table 6.3: Alcohol-Free Test Fuels in Accordance with ISO 1817

Liquid	Constituents	Content % (V/V)
A	2,2,4-trimethylpentane	100
B	2,2,4-trimethylpentane	70
	toluene	30
C	2,2,4-trimethylpentane	50
	toluene	50
D	2,2,4-trimethylpentane	60
	toluene	40
E	toluene	100
F	straight-chain paraffin (C_{12} to C_{18})	80
	1-methylnaphthalene	20

Table 6.4: Alcohol-Containing Test Fuels in Accordance with ISO 1817

Liquid	Constituents	Content % (V/V)	
1	2,2,4-trimethylpentane	30	
	toluene	50	
	di-isobutylene	15	
	ethanol	5	
2	2,2,4-trimethylpentane	25.35	equivalent to
	toluene	42.25	84.5% (V/V)
	di-isobutylene	12.68	of liquid 1
	ethanol	4.22	above
	methanol	15.00	
	water	0.50	
3	2,2,4-trimethylpentane	45	
	toluene	45	
	ethanol	7	
	methanol	3	
4	2,2,4-trimethylpentane	42.5	
	toluene	42.5	
	methanol	15	

Oil No. 1 and oil No. 3 are the most commonly used test oils. In addition, ASTM D 471 now includes a fourth oil, ASTM oil No. 5, but its purpose is not explained. This oil is not included in ISO 1817. It has generally been accepted that the ASTM oils, although defined in the standards, are satisfactory only if obtained from a single source.

The **standard fuels** listed in **Table 6.3** are representative of petroleum-derived fuels, and those shown in **Table 6.4** are intended to simulate motor gasolines containing alcohol. The liquids A, B, C and D in Table 6.3 are identical to ASTM reference fuels A, B, C and D, respectively. Liquid F (not included in ASTM D 471) is intended to simulate diesel fuel, domestic heating oils and similar light furnace oils.

Furthermore, the international standard specifies three simulated liquids: 101, 102 and 103. The liquids 101 and 102 are identical to ASTM service fluids No. 101 and No. 102, respectively. Liquid 103 is not included in ASTM D 471. **Liquid 101** is a blend composed of 99.5% (m/m) of di-2 ethylhexyl sebacate with 0.5% (m/m) of phenothiazine and is intended to simulate synthetic diester-type lubricating oils. **Liquid 102** is a blend composed of 95% (m/m) of standard oil No. 1 with 5% of a hydrocarbon oil additive containing 29.5% to 33% of sulphur, 1.5% to 2% of phosphorus and 0.7% of nitrogen. It is intended to simulate certain high-pressure hydraulic oils. **Liquid 103** is tri-n-butyl phosphate intended to simulate phosphate ester hydraulic fluids used in aircrafts.

6.4.1 NACE Test Inhibitors

The National Association of Corrosion Engineering (NACE) has defined two different amine solutions as **NACE Fluid A** and **NACE Fluid B**. They represent the types of corrosion inhibitors that are used in oil-field operations. Fluid A, which is described in **Table 6.5**, is a water soluble amine inhibitor; Fluid B, which is described in **Table 6.6**, is an oil-soluble amine inhibitor.

Table 6.5: NACE Test Inhibitor A (26)

0.2 g	equivalent of acetic acid
0.1 g	equivalent of N-coco 1,3-propylene-diamine
20 g	isopropyl alcohol
30 g	fresh water

Table 6.6: NACE Test Inhibitor B (26)

0.1 g	equivalent of a vegetable residue acid described as a dimer trimer residue with an acid number approximately 150
0.1 g	equivalent of N-tallow 1,3 propylene diamine
0.01	theoretical mol of nonylphenol condensed with 9.5−10 mol of ethylene oxide
100 g	solvent described as heavy aromatic solvent, 90% of which will distill below 260 °C at atmospheric pressure

6.5 Review of Lubricants and Working Fluids

Nearly every lubricant and working fluid consists of two components: the base fluid and the ingredients added to improve certain properties of the base fluid.

Lubricants and working fluids are designated according to the chemical composition of the base fluids. However, these terms are generic; that is, a variety of different compositions exists under one name (e.g., mineral oil, organic ester, phosphate ester, polyalkylene glycol, etc.). All of the compositions may have certain general properties, but specific properties can differ according to the formulation.

6.5.1 Base Fluids

Base fluids may be classified into groups according to, for example:
- origin;
- fire resistance; and
- biodegradability.

6.5.1.1 Origin

According to **origin**, base fluids may be classified into three groups:
1) vegetable oils;
2) mineral oils; and
3) synthetic oils.

Vegetable oils, such as olive, palm and rapeseed oil (which are obtained by pressing the fruits or seeds of certain plants), are **esters** of a mixture of fatty acids (e.g., oleic, palmitic and stearic acids) derived from the trihydric alcohol **glycerol**. These esters are collectively termed **glycerides**, which (like other esters) are decomposed (hydrolyzed) by water at moderately high temperatures and are converted into glycerol and a mixture of fatty acids.

The main advantages of vegetable oils over mineral oils are their non-toxicity and biodegradability in short periods of time. However, vegetable oils have some severe disadvantages when compared with mineral oils. These include poor low-temperature fluidity, rapid oxidation at elevated temperatures and susceptibility to hydrolysis, giving a mixture of fatty acids and glycerol.

Mineral or **petroleum oils** are undoubtedly the most widely used base oils for service fluids. Their most serious disadvantages are their high toxicity and extreme flammability. Furthermore, they are minimally biodegradable. Petroleum oils are not well-defined chemical products, consisting mainly of a complex mixture of paraffinic, naphthenic (cycloparaffinic) and aromatic hydrocarbons. They vary appreciably in aromatic content. In practice, mineral oils are divided into two main categories:
- paraffinic oils, being composed chiefly of paraffins; and
- naphthenic oils, consisting mainly of naphthenes (cycloparaffins) and aromatic hydrocarbons.

Synthetic oils are based on different classes of organic fluids. They are produced by chemically reacting low-molecular weight substances to give fluids of higher molecular weight with planned and predictable properties. The types of synthetic base oils commonly used in the production of commercial synthetic lubricants and working fluids are listed in **Table 6.7**. Synthetic fluids have a number of advantages over mineral oils. The main advantages are:
– improved thermal and oxidation stability;
– wider temperature range of application; and
– lower volatility and reduced oil consumption.
      The major drawbacks of synthetic fluids when compared with mineral oils are:
– the high price;
– the different additive response;
– the different elastomer compatibility; and
– the poor miscibility of certain types with mineral oils.

Table 6.7: Types of Base Fluids Used in the Production of Commercial Lubricants and Working Fluids

Composition	Examples
Synthetic hydrocarbons	Polyalphaolefins Dialkylbenzene
Polyalkylene glycols	Water-free Polyethylene/propylene Glycols HFC-Hydraulic fluids
Organic esters	Dicarboxylic esters Polyol esters
Phosphate esters	Trialkyl phosphate esters Triaryl phosphate esters Trialkylaryl phosphate esters
Silicon-containing oils	Silicone oils (Polysiloxanes) Silicate esters
Fluorine-containing oils	Polyperfluoroalkyl ethers Polychlorotrifluoroethylene
Aromatic ethers	Polyphenyl ethers
Fully synthetic water solutions	HFAS Hydraulic fluids
Chlorinated Aromatics	Polychlorobiphenyls

6.5.1.2 Fire Resistance

According to **fire resistance**, base fluids can be divided into three groups:
1) flammable fluids;
2) fire-resistant fluids;
3) nonflammable fluids.

Flammable fluids ignite readily and continue to burn. They include vegetable oils, mineral oils and certain types of synthetic fluids such as nonaqueous polyalkylene glycols and synthetic hydrocarbons.

Fire-resistant fluids are difficult to ignite and show little tendency to propagate flame. They have been designed for safety reasons to replace conventional mineral oils in all applications where fire and explosion risks have to be reduced to a minimum.

Fire-resistant fluids obtain their fire resistance either from the presence of water or from their chemical composition. They are classified in accordance with the international standard 6743-4 into four categories:

1) **HFA**: This category is divided into two subcategories:
    – **HFAE:** oil-in-water emulsions, normally containing up to a maximum of 10% mineral oil dispersed in water.
    – **HFAS:** water solutions of synthetic fluids of nonuniform compositions.
2) **HFB**: water-in-oil emulsions (invert emulsions) normally containing about 40% water dispersed in a continuous phase of mineral oil.
3) **HFC**: water solutions of high viscosity polyalkylene glycols containing approximately 45% water.
4) **HFD**: synthetic fluids containing no water. This category is divided into four subcategories.
    – **HFDR:** fluids consisting of phosphate esters.
    – **HFDS:** fluids consisting of chlorinated hydrocarbons.
    – **HFDT:** fluids consisting of mixtures of phosphate ester and chlorinated hydrocarbons.
    – **HFDU:** synthetic fluids of other compositions.

The **nonflammable** fluids are highly fluoronated liquids that do not ignite. At the present time, there are two commercially available types:
– polyperfluoroalkyl ethers; and
– polychlortrifluoroethylene.

6.5.1.3 Biodegradability

According to **biodegradability**, lubricants and working fluids can be divided in two groups:
1) environmentally acceptable (EA) fluids; and
2) polluting fluids, mainly mineral oils and chlorinated hydrocarbons.

The **environmentally acceptable (EA)** fluids are readily biodegradable and non-toxic, while providing satisfactory service performance (3, 4, 5). They are classified into three different categories according to their base:
1) vegetable oils, typically rapeseed oil;
2) polyalkylene glycols such as polyethylene glycol; and
3) synthetic organic esters.

The EA fluids are used in environmentally sensitive industries such as fishing, construction, forestry and mining. In cases where involuntary or accidental spills do occur, fluids that are readily biodegradable and nontoxic will minimize the damage of forests or the high risk of groundwater contamination.

If the cost factor is considered, all the EA fluids are more expensive than mineral oils; this is the main limitation to their acceptance. However, protection laws recently issued by many governments, specifications and individual consciences will all contribute toward the acceptance of EA products even if they are more expensive than conventional fluids.

6.5.2 Additives

Certain chemicals are added to modify a wide range of physical properties of the base fluid used. Whatever their role, the majority of these additives are chemically active substances compared with the base fluids. **Table 6.8** gives examples of commonly used types of additives.

Table 6.8: Commonly Used Types of Lubricant Additives

Additive Type	Function	Examples of Chemical Composition
Antioxidants	Prevent or slow oxidation of base fluid at high temperatures	Amines, phenol derivates, sulphur compounds, sulphur-phosphorus compounds
Corrosion Inhibitors	Limit corrosion of metals	– Basic nitrogen compounds (e.g., tertiary amines and their salts with benzoic, salycylic or naphthenic acids) – Esters of fatty acids, naphthenic or dicarboxylic acids with triethnol amine – Fatty acidamides – Derivates of phosphoric acid – Sulphur compounds
Detergents / Dispersants	Prevent formation of solid deposits	Metal sulphonates, phenolates, Polymers with basic side groups
Viscosity Index Improvers and Pour Point Depressants	Improve VI of lubricants; prevent formation of large wax crystals	Polymers (e.g., polymethacrylate, polyisobutylene)
Foam Inhibitors	Destabilize foam in oil	Silicone oils
EP (Extreme Pressure)	Form protective film on rubbed metal	– Chloroparaffins – Phosphor and phosphor-sulphur compounds (e.g., zinc-dialkyldithiophosphates)

6.6 Effects of Vegetable-Oil-Based Fluids on Elastomers

Oxidation stability and low-temperature fluidity are two well-known performance concerns when working with vegetable-oil-based fluids. Compared with mineral oils, they have a much narrower temperature range of application, typically between -20 and $+80\,°C$.

Normally, vegetable oils do not cause high swell to polar or oil resistant elastomers. NBR is the preferred elastomer to use with these oils. Shrinkage may be expected if highly plasticized compounds are used because vegetable oils usually have a low swelling effect on NBR elastomers.

There is no reason for using high-temperature elastomers such as HNBR, ACM, AEM or FPM, simply because the oil temperature should not exceed $80\,°C$. VMQ elastomers are used not because of their high-temperature performance but because of their chemical inertness, which is an important requirement in the food industry.

The use of AU, EU and YBPO with vegetable-oil-based fluids is restricted even though these materials exhibit low volume change. Low swell does not always mean good fluid resistance; it may actually mask a large deterioration of the physical properties due to chemical attack, for example, by condensed water, acidic or basic additives or decomposition products of the oil. Therefore, it is essential, before deciding to use these elastomers, to carry out immersion tests (at least 1,000 h at the maximum anticipated service temperature) measuring not only the volume change but also the changes in hardness, tensile strength and elongation at break. As mentioned in section 6.5.1.1, vegetable oils are hydrolyzed by water (and this could be condensed water) to give glycerol and a mixture of fatty acids. These products will cause rapid deterioration of AU, EU and YBPO elastomers. In addition, glycerol is hygroscopic (i.e., it will absorb water from humid atmosphere, and the hydrolysis of the oil and the deterioration of these elastomers will continue). Therefore, in all applications where the formation of condensed water in the system is likely to occur (and this is usually the case), the long-term immersion tests, mentioned above, must be carried out in "wet" oils (e.g., by adding 1% water). It is important to note that only specially formulated AU, EU and YBPO with improved hydrolysis resistance may be used for an acceptable life period in "wet" vegetable oils.

Of the hydrocarbon elastomers, EPDM and IIR show the highest resistance to vegetable oils. Although the volume swell is fairly high (typically 30−40%), they do retain their physical properties sufficiently well enough, that they should not be rejected as unusable with vegetable oils. They can be used, for example, in static applications not requiring dimensional accuracy.

NR, IR and SBR elastomers are not recommended for use with vegetable oils because of the high volume swell and the degrading of the physical properties by the fluid.

6.7 Effects of Mineral-Oil-Based Fluids on Elastomers

Almost all mineral-oil-based fluids, particularly engine and gear oils, contain quite a number of chemically active additives that can cause deterioration of many elastomers, especially at high temperatures.

As would be expected (section 6.3.1), all nonpolar hydrocarbon elastomers (e.g., NR, IR, SBR, IIR, EPM and EPDM) are badly swollen by mineral oils. Conversely, the polar elastomers (e.g., NBR, HNBR, CR, CSM, ECO, CO, AEM, ACM, FPM, VMQ, FMQ, AU, EU and YBPO) are considerably more resistant to a wide variety of mineral-oil-based fluids at different temperature ranges. Besides the effect of temperature, the swelling behavior of these elastomers is influenced by three main factors:
1) the amount of aromatic hydrocarbons in the oil;
2) the amount of extractable ingredients in the rubber compound; and
3) the concentration and chemical nature of the additives.

As mentioned above, the swelling effect of an oil on elastomers becomes more pronounced as the aromatic content increases. Elastomers that are very sensitive to aromatic hydrocarbons are CR, CSM, AEM and VMQ as well as the low-temperature grades of NBR, HNBR and ACM. Less sensitive are NBR with high acrylonitrile (ACN) content, CO, ECO, AU and YBPO elastomers. FPM and FMQ are hardly affected by increasing the aromatic content.

Some rubber ingredients, such as low-temperature plasticizers, processing aids and antioxidents, can be leached by the oil, thus resulting in low swell or shrinkage of the rubber compound. Also, certain additive packages can chemically attack the polymer chain. In severe cases the elastomer becomes hard and brittle or soft and sticky.

NBR elastomers are the most effective materials used for oil seals and other items that come in contact with mineral oils. Their resistance to mineral oils increases by increasing the ACN content of the crude rubber. The high nitriles have the highest oil resistance but poorer low-temperature properties. Conversely, low nitriles have good low-temperature properties but at some sacrifice in oil resistance. Shrinkage may be expected when plasticized compounds are used in contact with oils of low swelling power. However, NBR elastomers, having double bonds in the polymer chains, tend to embrittle or case harden when exposed to permanent temperatures above 120°C because of additional cross-linking by oxygen or sulphur-containing oil additives.

As compared with conventional NBR elastomers, the highly saturated nitriles **HNBR** exhibit markedly improved resistance to mineral-oil-based fluids, including those containing active sulphur, up to a temperature range of 140−150°C. However, long-term oil aging tests on selected HNBR compounds show that aerated oils cause significantly higher volume swell and loss in the mechanical properties than do the nonaerated oils (2). This is probably due to the high sensitivity of HNBR elastomers to the oxidation products of base oils and their additives (resulting from their reaction with atmospheric oxygen at high temperatures).

CR elastomers are not widely used with mineral oils because their oil resistance is limited to paraffinic oils. They show considerable swell and softening in naphthene-based oils.

The resistance of **CSM** elastomers to mineral oils increases with increasing the chlorine content, but, at the same time, low-temperature flexibility decreases. General-purpose compounds can be used only with paraffinic oils. They are not recommended for use in naphthenic oils because of the high volume swell and the degrading of the physical properties by the fluid.

ACM elastomers, having a saturated backbone, show excellent resistance to mineral-oil-based fluids at permanent temperatures in excess of 150 °C. The degree of oil resistance depends on the chemical structure of the acrylic ester polymers. Polymers of ethyl acrylate show the highest oil resistance, but their low temperature properties are inferior.

AEM elastomers (with trade name Vamac) offer better low-temperature flexibility than ACM elastomers but at some sacrifice in oil resistance. They usually exhibit fairly good resistance to paraffinic oils. In naphthenic oils, however, the volume swell is considerably higher.

FPM elastomers are generally serviceable almost indefinitely up to 200 °C at some sacrifice in low-temperature flexibility. They have outstanding resistance to a wide range of mineral-oil-based fluids, including those with high aromatic content. They are also resistant to a great number of oil additives, except certain amines such as those found in engine and gear oils. These amines may cause severe hardening and loss of elongation. However, the peroxide-curable highly fluorinated FPM grades (containing about 70% fluorine) exhibit improved resistance to amine-based additives, and FFKM elastomers show the highest resistance.

Krumm et al. (6) investigated the effect of used oils (i.e., oils taken from vehicle sumps after a period of service operation) and came to the conclusion that, generally, used oils affect fluoroelastomers less than do new oils, probably because of the oxidation of the harmful basic additives.

Although **VMQ** elastomers retain their flexibility down to −60 °C and can withstand continuous temperatures above 200 °C in dry air, their resistance to mineral-oil-based fluids is only moderate. They appear not to be sensitive to the majority of oil additives, but they are largely influenced by the viscosity of the base oil, considerably more than all other polar elastomers. The swelling becomes more pronounced as the viscosity of the oil decreases. Consequently, VMQ elastomers can be used with confidence in contact with high viscosity oils. They are not recommended for low-viscosity oils, because of considerable swelling, softening and high loss in the physical properties.

FMQ elastomers, which are much more expensive than VMQ elastomers, have excellent resistance to mineral-oil-based fluids, but with a more restricted temperature range than that of conventional silicone elastomers (about −60 to +175 °C).

Both **CO** and **ECO** elastomers have good resistance to mineral oils, comparable to that of high nitriles. The homopolymers (CO) can be used at a temperature range from -20 to $+130\,°C$ and the copolymers (ECO) from -40 to $+120\,°C$. However, their corrosive nature is a limiting factor in some applications. Therefore, it is recommended, before use, to carry out corrosion tests with the contacting metal surface.

AU, **EU** and **YBPO** elastomers usually exhibit low to moderate volume change with mineral-oil-based fluids. However, their use with these oils is restricted because of their susceptibility to hydrolysis (section 6.6).

6.7.1 Oil-in-Water Emulsions

Oil-in-water emulsions, or HFAE fluids (section 6.5.1.2), usually contain up to 10% mineral oil (with special emulsifiers, stabilizers and inhibitors) dispersed in water. Such emulsions are normally prepared on site by the user, according to the fluid supplier's recommendation.

In general, the oil-in-water emulsions cause considerably more swell to NBR than do water-free mineral oils. The temperature and the oil concentration are the major factors influencing the degree of swell. Furthermore, it should be recognized that the time required for equilibrium swelling is considerably longer for oil-in-water emulsions than for water-free mineral oils.

In general, specially formulated NBR elastomers can be used with HFAE fluids if a moderate or fairly high swell can be tolerated. In applications requiring low swell, properly formulated FPM compounds should be used. Such compounds contain lead oxide instead of magnesium oxide.

The use of AU, EU and YBPO in HFA fluids is restricted because of their susceptibility to hydrolysis (section 6.6). For a longer life period, the service temperature should not exceed $50\,°C$.

6.7.2 Water-in-Oil Emulsions

Water-in-oil emulsions, or HFB fluids (section 6.5.1.2), consist of approximately 40% water dispersed in a continuous phase of mineral oil with special emulsifiers, stabilizers and inhibitors. They are usually supplied ready for use.

The swelling action of HFB fluids on NBR elastomers is similar to that of HFAE. Properly formulated NBR elastomers are used where fairly high swell can be tolerated. If low swell is required, suitably formulated FPM elastomers (with lead oxide) should be used.

As would be expected, the use of AU, EU and YBPO is also restricted in these fluids because of their susceptibility to hydrolysis.

6.8 Effects of Synthetic Hydrocarbon Fluids on Elastomers

The main types of synthetic hydrocarbon fluids (SHFs) are polyalphaolefins (PAOs) and alkylated aromatics. Unlike mineral oils, which are complex mixtures of paraffinic, naphthenic and aromatic hydrocarbons, SHFs are man-made, having controlled molecular structure.

As would be expected, all nonpolar hydrocarbon-based elastomers (e.g., NR, IR, IIR, SBR and EPDM) are badly swollen by hydrocarbon fluids (section 6.3.1). Conversely, the polar elastomers (e.g., NBR, HNBR, CR, CSM, ECO, AEM, ACM, FPM, VMQ, FMQ, AU, EU and YBPO) are resistant to a wide variety of hydrocarbon fluids.

6.8.1 Polyalphaolefins (PAOs)

PAOs are synthesized by polymerization of alphaolefins (e.g., 1-decene) followed by hydrogenation of the product to remove any remaining double bonds. They are chemically related to paraffin-based mineral oils but offer a number of significant advantages, including:
– superior low-temperature properties (in contrast to paraffinic oils);
– good oxidation and thermal stability; and
– high viscosity index.

In addition, PAOs have, in general, a weak swelling effect on polar elastomers, similar to paraffinic oils. In other words, PAOs combine the good low-temperature properties of naphthenic oils with the low swelling effect of paraffinic oils. Consequently, elastomer types designed for low-temperature applications [e.g., NBR with very low ACN content (ca. 18%), CR and AEM (which normally show excessive swell in the conventional low-temperature mineral oils)] may perform very well in PAOs without swelling problems (7).

Although a PAO-based oil may contain different amounts of additives and other base fluids, it seems necessary at first to have an understanding of the swelling effect of pure PAO base fluids. As has been mentioned, these fluids have a weak swelling effect on most polar elastomers and consequently they cause shrinkage to many elastomeric materials originally designed for mineral oils. This problem can be solved by one of the two following means:
1) by incorporating an "elastomer swell component" in the service fluid (e.g., about 5% organic ester); or
2) by using plasticizer-free rubber compounds designed for PAOs.

The volume swell figures of a nonplasticized NBR compound shown in **Table 6.9** and **Table 6.10** illustrate the difference in swelling effect between PAOs and mineral oils. It is evident from Table 6.9 that PAOs, in general, have a weak swelling effect on nonplasticized low nitriles and that their swelling effect decreases further with the increase of their viscosity. Table 6.10 illustrates the strong swelling action of ASTM oils Nos. 2 and 3 (section 6.4) on the same rubber compound. Similar results would be obtained with other nonplasticized elastomer types, such as HNBR, CR, CSM and AEM.

Table 6.9: Swelling Behavior of a Nonplasticized NBR Elastomer with 18% ACN in PAO Base Fluids of Different Viscosity Grades (after 168 h at 100 °C)

Changes in:	PAO Viscosity 4 mm²/s at 100 °C	PAO Viscosity 6 mm²/s at 100 °C	PAO Viscosity 8 mm²/s at 100 °C	PAO Viscosity 100 mm²/s at 100°
Volume (%)	+ 7.7	+4.8	+3.4	±0
Shore A hardness (points)	− 3	−1	−2	+1
Tensile modulus (%)*	− 7.4	−4.6	+2.8	+1.9
Tensile strength (%)	−10.8	−8.5	−7.4	−5.7
Elongation at Break (%)	− 6.7	−6.7	−8.7	−3.3

* at 100% strain

Table 6.10: Swelling Behavior of a Nonplasticized NBR Elastomer with 18% ACN in ASTM Standard Oils Nos. 1, 2 and 3 (after 168 h 100 °C)

Changes in:	ASTM Oil No. 1	ASTM Oil No. 2	ASTM Oil No. 3
Volume (%)	+ 7.3	+29.3	+45.8
Shore A hardness (points)	− 4	−12	−14
Tensile modulus (%)*	− 7.4	–	–
Tensile strength (%)	+13.6	–	–
Elongation at break (%)	+12.7	–	–

* at 100% strain

To avoid high shrinkage, plasticized rubber compounds should not be used with PAO base fluids. Such elastomers can be used only in PAO blends containing other base fluids. Their swelling behavior will depend largely on the concentration and chemical nature of the other components in the mixture. An example is shown in **Table 6.11**.

The volume swell of **VMQ** elastomers is largely influenced by the viscosity of PAO base fluids, considerably more than all other polar elastomers. Excessive swell will result in low-viscosity PAO fluids, as shown in **Table 6.12**. Conversely, **FMQ** elastomers show excellent resistance to PAO fluids and are not sensitive to viscosity variations.

FPM elastomers do not contain extractable ingredients because they are post-cured in hot air and, accordingly, almost all ingredients or by-products will volatilize. Consequently, FPM elastomers do not shrink but remain almost unchanged in PAOs of all viscosity grades.

Table 6.11: Swelling Behavior of a Plasticized NBR Elastomer with 28% ACN in 100% PAO Base Fluid and 80% PAO Blend (after 168 h at 100 °C)

Changes in:	100% PAO	80% PAO 20% Diester + Additives
Volume (%)	− 5.6	+ 6.2
Shore A hardness (points)	+ 6	− 2
Tensile modulus (%)*	+53.3	+25.0
Tensile strength (%)	+ 1.4	± 0
Elongation at break (%)	−42.1	−33.3

* at 100% strain

Table 6.12: Swelling Behavior of a VMQ Elastomer in PAO Base Fluids with Different Viscosity Grades (after 168 h 150 °C)

Changes in:	PAO Viscosity 4 mm²/s at 100 °C	PAO Viscosity 6 mm²/s at 100 °C	PAO Viscosity 8 mm²/s at 100 °C
Volume (%)	+35.2	+15.5	+ 8.4
Shore A hardness (points)	−35	−21	−20
Tensile modulus (%)*	−42.9	−33.3	−33.3
Tensile strength (%)	+54.4	−19.0	−26.6
Elongation at break (%)	−16.9	+ 4.0	+ 4.5

* at 100% strain

AU, EU and **YBPO** show good resistance to PAO base fluids. However, their use is restricted in PAO fluids containing additives or other base fluids because of their susceptibility to hydrolysis. As mentioned before, it is necessary to carry out long-term immersion tests before deciding to use these elastomers (section 6.6).

6.8.2 Alkylated Aromatics

The swelling effect of alkylated aromatics or alkylated benzenes on elastomers is similar to that of naphthenic oils. In other words, they exhibit medium to high swelling power, depending mainly on the viscosity of the oil. Low-viscosity grades have normally a greater swelling effect than the high-viscosity grades of the same composition.

Much of what has been said about mineral oils in section 6.7 also applies to alkylated aromatics.

6.9 Effects of Polyalkylene-Glycol-Based Fluids on Elastomers

Polyalkylene glycols (PAGs) are linear polyethers with two or more terminal hydroxyl groups. They are synthesized from alkylene oxides (normally ethylene oxide and propylene oxide) and hydroxy-compounds such as water, alcohols and glycols. The final viscosity is a function of the molecular weight. As mentioned before (section 6.5.1.3) some PAG based fluids, particularly polyethylene glycols, belong to the environmentally acceptable fluids.

The swelling effect of PAGs on elastomers as well as the extent of their miscibility with water or mineral oils depend on whether the PAG is a homopolymer of ethylene oxide (i.e., polyethylene glycol) or propylene oxide (i.e., polypropylene glycol), or whether it is a copolymer of both (i.e., polyethylene/ propylene glycol). The viscosity of the fluid also has a significant effect on most elastomers. The low-viscosity PAGs have a greater swelling power than the high-viscosity grades of the same composition. However, it should be noted that PAG-based fluids of the same viscosity class, but from different suppliers, may have completely different swelling effects on many elastomers because of differences in the chemical composition (8). An example is shown in **Table 6.13**.

Table 6.13: Swelling Behavior of Selected NBR Compounds in PAGs from Two Different Suppliers   (4 weeks at 100°C)

Compound	Hardness in Shore A	Low Temp. Property TR 10* (°C)	Supplier of PAG	Hardness Change (points)	Volume Change (%)
NBR with low ACN (plasticized)	80	−28	A	−14	+20.6
			B	− 1	+ 4.6
NBR with medium ACN (plasticized)	90	−22	A	−11	+10.6
			B	− 5	+ 6.9
NBR with medium ACN (plasticizer-free)	90	−12	A	−15	+14.4
			B	− 8	+10.6

Note: The PAGs are of the same viscosity class (32) but have different composition.

* TR 10 = Temperature Retraction 10% in accordance with ISO 2921.

Most low-temperature plasticizers incorporated in elastomers will be extracted by PAGs. This can either compensate for high swell or result in shrinkage of the elastomeric material if the fluid has a small swelling effect.

Generally speaking, properly formulated **NBR** and **HNBR** compounds may be used with a wide range of PAG-based fluids. Their volume swell is determined by the **ACN** content of the basic rubber. The high nitriles have the lowest swell but poorer low-temperature properties. Conversely, low nitriles show good low-temperature flexibility but higher swell.

Properly compounded **CR** elastomers exhibit a fairly good resistance to PAGs and at the same time good low-temperature properties. However, they are not widely used in PAGs because their resistance to mineral oils is moderate. Consequently, swelling problems may arise if the PAG is contaminated with mineral oil.

EPDM elastomers exhibit excellent resistance to almost all types of PAGs up to 150°C. It should be noted, however, that they are not resistant to mineral oils.

FPM elastomers are not recommended for use with PAG-based fluids because certain additive packages (which contain strong organic bases) have a deleterious effect on the physical properties of FPM compounds.

As would be expected, the use of **AU**, **EU** and **YBPO** with PAGs is not recommended because of their great tendency to hydrolyze in the presence of strong basic additives.

6.9.1 HFC Fluids

The water-soluble polyalkylene glycols are used as water-based fire-resistant hydraulic fluids, which are designated as HFC fluids (section 6.5.1.2). They are used in the temperature range of −20 to +60°C.

In general, properly formulated **NBR** elastomers perform adequately in HFC fluids. Although **EPDM** compounds exhibit excellent resistance to these fluids, it is not advisable to use them because any contact with mineral oils can cause excessive swell.

FPM elastomers should not be used with HFC fluids, as they tend to degrade slowly because of their susceptibility to basic additives.

AU, **EU** and **YBPO** elastomers are not recommended for use with HFC fluids because of their great tendency to hydrolyze in the presence of basic additives.

6.10 Effects of Synthetic Organic Esters on Elastomers

Synthetic organic esters are subdivided into diesters and polyol ester types. **Diesters** are esters derived from dicarboxylic acids and monohydric alcohols. **Polyol esters** are those derived from monocarboxylic acids and polyhydric alcohols.

Some of these synthetic organic esters belong to the environmentally acceptable fluids (section 6.5.1.3). In comparison with the natural esters (vegetable oils or glycerides) the synthetic esters offer a number of significant advantages, including:
– wider temperature range of application;
– better thermal and oxidation stability;
– long-term hydrolytic stability; and
– improved fire resistance (not equivalent to the fire-resistant phosphate esters).

Generally speaking, both diesters and polyol esters tend to cause more swell to NBR and HNBR than do mineral oils of the same viscosity. The molecular size and chain length appear to be the major factors influencing the swell of elastomers. Consequently, immersion tests are indispensable for selecting elastomeric materials. In general, properly formulated **NBR**, **HNBR** and **FPM** elastomers are used with these fluids. The use of **AU**, **EU** and **YBPO** is restricted because of their susceptibility to hydrolysis. As mentioned before (section 6.6) long term immersion tests are necessary before deciding to use these elastomers.

6.11 Effects of Phosphate Esters on Elastomers

Phosphate esters are subdivided into three categories:
1) trialkyl phosphates;
2) triaryl phosphates; and
3) alkyl-aryl phosphates.

They are used as lubricants and working fluids primarily because of their good fire resistance. Their swelling effect on elastomers depends on the viscosity of the fluid and the chemical nature of the organic part of the molecule (i.e., whether it is trialkyl, triaryl or alkyl-aryl phosphate ester).

In general, properly formulated **FPM** compounds show good resistance to phosphate esters except the trialkyl and alkyl-aryl types. **VMQ** elastomers are also resistant to many phosphate esters, but their use is limited because of their poor mechanical properties. **EPDM** and **IIR** elastomers can be used with phosphate esters, including the trialkyl and alkyl-aryl grades, provided that they do not contain mineral oils. The presence of small amounts of mineral oil can cause high swell (8), as shown in **Table 6.14.**

Table 6.14: Action of Traces of Mineral Oils in Phosphate Esters on a Selected EPDM Compound
(168 h at 100 °C)

Medium	Hardness Change (Shore A points)	Volume Change (%)
Pure phosphate ester	− 4	+ 6.0
Phosphate ester +2% ASTM Oil No. 1	− 8	+13.8
Phosphate ester +3% ASTM Oil No. 1	− 9	+18.7
Phosphate ester +5% ASTM Oil No. 1	−11	+25.8

6.12 Effects of Silicon-Containing Fluids on Elastomers

Silicon-containing fluids are subdivided into two categories:
1) silicone oils; and
2) silicate esters.

6.12.1 Silicone Oils

Silicone oils have a very wide temperature range of application and excellent oxidation and thermal stability.

As would be expected, silicone elastomers tend to swell and soften excessively in silicone oils, particularly at high temperatures (section 6.3.1). All other elastomer types such as NR, SBR, EPDM, NBR, HNBR and FPM, perform adequately as long as they are plasticizer-free. In general, silicone oils cause hardly any swell, but they extract soluble components (particularly plasticizers) from the elastomers, causing them to shrink. The effect is most severe with low-viscosity silicone oils at high temperatures. Consequently, to avoid excessive shrinkage, plasticized elastomers should not be used with silicone oils.

6.12.2 Silicate Esters

Silicate esters have good low-temperature properties but very poor hydrolytic stability. They break down to form gels (SiO_2) when they merely come in contact with atmospheric moisture (9). This property limits their use in closed systems.

The action of silicate esters on elastomers depends mainly on the molecular size and the chemical nature of the organic groups. Therefore, the best way to find out the most suitable rubber compound for a silicate ester is to carry out immersion tests. In general, suitably formulated **NBR**, **CR**, **FPM** and **FMQ** compounds may be used with silicate esters. **EPDM** and **VMQ** elastomers usually exhibit poor resistance to these fluids.

6.13 Effects of Fluorine-Containing Fluids on Elastomers

As stated earlier (section 6.5.1.2), polyperfluoroalkyl ethers and polychlorotrifluoroethylene are synthetic fluids characterized by nonflammability, extreme chemical inertness and wide temperature range of application (9).

6.13.1 Polyperfluoroalkyl Ethers

Laboratory immersion tests (8) have suggested that EPDM compounds would probably perform adequately in polyperfluoralkyl ethers up to 100°C and FPM elastomers up to 200°C.

6.13.2 Polychlorotrifluoroethylene

Laboratory immersion tests indicate that all known elastomer types do not perform adequately in these fluids. The majority of them show a high swell and loss in tensile strength. Volume swell figures in the neighborhood of 20 to 30% are the best available for this fluid (10). **NBR** and **HNBR** elastomers show low volume swell or even shrink but become hard and brittle (8), as shown in **Table 6.2**.

6.14 Effects of Polyphenylethers on Elastomers

Polyphenylethers are the most radiation resistant fluids available, combined with unusually high thermal and oxidation stability (9). Laboratory immersion tests indicate that suitably formulated EPDM compounds may be used with these fluids up to 100 °C and FPM elastomers up to 200 °C (8). However, it should be noted that the radiation resistance of FPM compounds is not outstanding (section 5.10).

6.15 Effects of HFAS Fluids on Elastomers

HFAS fluids form a relatively new group of water-based fire-resistant fluids consisting of water solutions of synthetic fluids of nonuniform compositions (section 6.5.1.2). Therefore, it is not possible to recommend certain elastomer types for these fluids. The only way to find out the most suitable rubber compound is to carry out individual tests under the working conditions.

6.16 Effects of Chlorinated Hydrocarbons on Elastomers

Chlorinated hydrocarbons belong to the nonwater-containing fire-resistant fluids and are designated as HFDS fluids (section 6.5.1.2). They are usually based on polychlorinated biphenyls (PCBs). Their use has been banned in most countries because of their pollutive nature. In general, FPM and VMQ elastomers show good resistance to PCBs and other chlorinated hydrocarbons. Other elastomer types (such as NBR, HNBR, CR, ACM and ECO) cannot be used because they are badly swollen by these fluids.

6.17 Effects of Brake Fluids on Elastomers

Before discussing the effects of brake fluids on elastomeric materials, it would be useful to review briefly the different types of commercial brake fluids. At the present time, brake fluids are subdivided into three categories:
1) glycol-based brake fluids (DOT 3 and DOT 4) (DOT = Department of Transportation);
2) silicone-based brake fluids (DOT 5); and
3) mineral-oil-based brake fluids.

The **glycol-based** brake fluids absorb water when exposed to humid atmosphere. The water absorbed causes dramatic decrease of the boiling point of the brake fluid. If a wet fluid becomes sufficiently hot enough to vaporize, then the condition known as "vapor lock" is produced. As vapor is compressible, the brake pedal can be fully depressed without pressure being transmitted to the wheel brake.

The **silicone-based** brake fluids (SBBFs) are not miscible with water and thus maintain indefinitely a constant very high boiling point and very low viscosity at $-40\,°C$. However, if contamination with water occurs, it remains as a separate phase, which will boil at $100\,°C$ and become solid at $0\,°C$. This can lead to brake failure due to vapor lock under high-temperature operation conditions.

SBBFs are also immiscible with conventional brake fluids. Therefore, complete conversion of a brake system already filled with DOT 3 or DOT 4 to SBBFs is a complex operation.

Mineral oils are ideal hydraulic fluids and can be expected to perform well in brake systems. In addition, synthetic hydrocarbons that have excellent low-temperature properties (e.g., polyalphaolefins) (section 6.8.1), are now available, although at a considerably higher price as mineral oils. It is therefore possible to produce synthetic hydrocarbon-based brake fluids with improved properties.

Mineral oils and synthetic hydrocarbons are not miscible with water and thus will maintain a high boiling point and low viscosity indefinitely. However, there is the same concern that small amounts of water could enter the brake system. It is possible to neutralize the effects of minor water contamination by including "water scavenging" additives in the brake fluid formulation. These additives react with water and convert it to substances having much less effect on brake system performance (11).

6.17.1 Glycol-Based Brake Fluids

The oil-resistant elastomers such as NBR, HNBR, ACM and FPM swell excessively in glycol-based brake fluids. Conversely, the nonoil-resistant elastomers such as NR, SBR and EPDM perform well in these fluids, depending on the temperature range of application. Properly formulated EPDM compounds can be used with DOT 3 and DOT 4 at a temperature range of -40 to $+150\,°C$. On the other hand, NR and SBR elastomers, being unsaturated polymers, should not be used at temperatures exceeding $100\,°C$, but they would perform better than EPDM elastomers at temperatures below $-40\,°C$.

6.17.2 Silicone-Based Brake Fluids

The silicone-based brake fluid DOT 5 is relatively new. Laboratory immersion tests (12) suggest that EPDM elastomers would probably not perform adequately in DOT 5 at $150\,°C$ because of excessive softening and loss in the physical properties. For a longer life period the temperature should not exceed $125\,°C$.

6.17.3 Mineral-Oil-Based Brake Fluids

The effects of mineral oils and synthetic hydrocarbon fluids have been discussed in sections 6.7 and 6.8, respectively. At the present time, specially formulated NBR compounds are the preferred materials for these fluids.

6.18 Effects of Greases on Elastomers

Greases generally consist of a base fluid, a thickener and additives, as required. Depending on the application, the base fluid can be, for example, a vegetable oil, a mineral oil, a synthetic hydrocarbon, an organic ester, a polyalkylene glycol, a phosphate ester, a silicone oil, a silicate ester, a polyphenylether or a polyperfluoroalkyl ether (13). Thickeners include soaps (such as lithium soap), fumed silica, organo-modified clay (Bentone), carbon black and PTFE. Chemical additives are usually incorporated to modify or enhance performance.

The base fluid of the grease and the additives are the major factors influencing the effect of greases on elastomers. The best way to ensure the suitability of a rubber compound is to carry out immersion tests under the working conditions.

6.19 Elastomer Selection for Synthetic Fluids

Table 6.15 is a general guide for selecting elastomeric materials for use with typical synthetic lubricants and working fluids at different temperature ranges. However,

Table 6.15: Guideline for Selection of Elastomeric Materials for Typical Synthetic Fluids

Lubricant Base Fluid	Elastomer Types to be Considered for Use At:			
	100 °C	120 °C	150 °C	200 °C
PAOs	CR* low NBR*	CSM* ECO*	AEM* HNBR*	FPM
Alkylated aromatics	NBR	ECO	HNBR ACM	FPM
PAGs	NBR CR	EPDM HNBR	EPDM HNBR	–
Organic esters	NBR	HNBR FPM	FPM	–
Phosphate esters	EPDM	EPDM FPM	FPM	–
Silicone oils	NR*, SBR* CR*, NBR*	CSM* ECO*	EPDM* HNBR* AEM*	FPM
Polyperfluoro-alkyl ethers	EPDM FPM	FPM	FPM	FPM
Polyphenyl-ethers	EPDM FPM	FPM	FPM	FPM
Chlorinated hydrocarbons	FPM	FPM	FPM	–

* plasticizer-free compounds to avoid shrinkage

the final choice should be made after carrying out individual tests under the working conditions.

6.20 Review of Hydrocarbon and Alternative Fuels

Hydrocarbon fuels may be subdivided into two main groups:
1) automotive fuels; and
2) jet fuels.

The most common **automotive fuels** are diesel, leaded and unleaded gasolines. The leaded gasolines are now of limited interest in many countries, but their use will continue in some parts of the world for a long time.

The use of fuels alternative to gasolines and diesel is already practiced to some extent, as, for example, the use of ethanol in Brazil or the use of propane and butane in some countries. There are also indications that other alternative fuels could become important in the future. In particular straight methanol could become an important fuel of the future because of its "clean-burning" characteristics (14). At the present time it is added to gasolines in different proportions to obtain gasoline/alcohol blends, or **gasohols**.

6.20.1 Gasolines

Gasolines differ in composition in various countries. They consist mainly of a mixture of a great number of low-molecular-weight hydrocarbons with varying amounts of paraffins, cycloparaffins, olefins, cycloolefins and aromatics. They have a very broad boiling range, from about 25 °C to 210 °C. The density may range from 0.72 to 0.76.

The gasoline distilled in oil refineries has a very low **octane number**. If the octane number is low, the engine will knock. This means that combustion of the air/fuel mixture is uncontrolled, which can lead to engine damage. The octane number is, therefore, a measure of the antiknock performance of a gasoline. The higher the octane number, the greater the fuel resistance to knock.

There are two types of octane numbers that are based on different engine operating conditions. These are:
1) the Research Octane Number (**RON**); and
2) the Motor Octane Number (**MON**).

Both are determined under standard conditions in standard engines where the fuel is compared with a mixture of iso-octane (octane number = 100) and normal heptane (octane number = 0). If the gasoline has the same knocking behavior as, for example, a mixture of 90% by volume of iso-octane and 10% by volume of normal heptane, it is said to have an octane number of 90.

The most common additives that considerably raise the octane number of fuels are certain organic lead compounds, mainly **tetraethyl lead**. Gasoline grades that contain organic lead compounds are called **leaded** gasolines. The elimination of lead compounds (to obtain **nonleaded** gasolines) results in lowering of the octane number, which must be compansated for. This can be achieved by adding aromatic fractions or oxygenated components such as methanol, ethanol, tertiary butanol and methyl tertiary butyl ether (MTBE). Both aromatics and oxygenated compounds have a high octane number and are used as alternative antiknock agents.

The global warming, acid rain and health hazards resulting partly from the burning products of automotive fuels have created concern and led to a call for alternative-fuel vehicles (15). There are two possible alternative-fuel vehicles:

1) **flexible-fuel** vehicles capable of using methanol/gasoline in all ratios; and
2) **methanol-fuel** vehicles powered by M 85, an 85:15 blend of methanol and gasoline.

Flexible-fuel vehicles may be introduced first, since M 85 would most likely be available only in certain areas and current methanol production capacity might not meet the demand. In the long run, however, vehicles powered by M 85 may prevail (15).

When fuel-injected engines are used with gasolines, **peroxidized** fuel or "sour gasoline" may be produced. The formation and breakdown of hydroperoxides is catalyzed by traces of metal ions in the fuel system. The formation of sour gasoline has not been reported in Europe, because of differences in composition of gasolines. The North American gasolines have a higher content of unsaturated hydrocarbons (olefins) than do the European gasolines (16). It is known that unsaturated compounds are easily oxidized and can, therefore, form hydroperoxides in fuel-injected engines.

6.20.2 Gasoline Additives

Lead alkyls and other antiknock compounds have already been discussed. In addition, gasolines contain other additives at low dose rates [in the range of parts per million (ppm)], for purposes other than enhancing antiknock properties. These include, for example, antioxidants, corrosion inhibitors, metal deactivators (to prevent oxidation reactions catalyzed by metal ions), dyes (to distinguish one product from another), biocides (to prevent microbial growth in the bottom of tanks), antistatic additives (where there is a danger of explosion due to a charge of static electricity building up during pumping at high rate) and demulsifiers and dehazers (if the fuel becomes hazy because of the presence of finely dispersed droplets of water) (14).

6.20.3 Pure Methanol

Pure methanol (methyl alcohol or wood spirit), $CH_3\text{-}OH$, is a mobile liquid having a density of 0.7869 at 25°C. It boils at 64.5°C and mixes with water in all proportions. It can be prepared from the products of destructive distillation of wood or synthetically from carbon monoxide and hydrogen.

Infrared studies of the molecular structure of pure methanol indicate that the methanol molecules are bound together by hydrogen bonds. Evidence has been found for the existence of monomeric, dimeric, trimeric, tetrameric and higher polymeric species (17, 18). **Fig. 6.2** shows plausible structures of dimeric methanol.

The concentration of hydrogen-bonded structures is increased as the temperature is lowered. In other words, the hydrogen-bonding capability of methanol is reduced with increasing temperature.

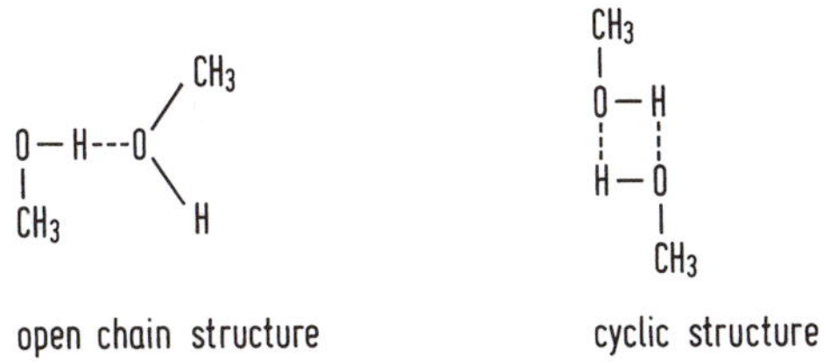

open chain structure   cyclic structure

Fig. 6.2: Plausible Structures of Dimeric Methanol (17)

6.20.4 Pure Ethanol

Ethanol (ethyl alcohol, alcohol or spirit of wine), CH_3-CH_2-OH, is contained in all fermented liquors. In pure form, it is a mobile liquid having a boiling point of 78.32°C and a density of 0.79367 at 15°C. It is very hygroscopic, and the anhydrous product is called **absolute** alcohol.

Ethanol mixes with water in all proportions with development of heat and diminution of volume; 52 vols. of ethanol and 48 vols. of water give a mixture occupying only 96.3 vols. A mixture of 95.57 wt % of ethanol and 4.43 wt % of water is an **azeotropic** mixture (i.e., it has a constant boiling point of 78.2°C). Consequently, the water portion cannot be separated simply by fractionation.

In Brazil, ethanol containing about 5% water has been used in vehicles specially designed for this fuel. The ethanol has been produced by fermentation of sugar cane.

6.20.5 Diesel Fuels

Diesel fuels consist mainly of complex mixtures of high-boiling hydrocarbons with varying amounts of paraffins, cycloparaffins, olefins, cycloolefins and aromatics. The boiling range is typically between 200 and 360°C. The density ranges from about 0.83 to 0.88.

The ease with which a diesel fuel is subjected to combustion is determined by the **cetane number**. Testing is carried out in a standard engine where the fuel is compared with mixtures of cetane (cetane number = 100) and alphamethylnaphthalene (cetane number = 0).

In northern European countries, diesel fuels will normally be mixed during the winter with up to 30% gasoline in order to lower the freezing point. As with gasolines, diesel fuels also contain small amounts of additives, which are expressed in ppm. These include, for example, antioxidants, metal deactivators, cetane improvers, combustion improvers, detergents, antistatic additives, anti-icers, biocides, antifoamants, odor masks or odorants, dyes and demulsifiers and dehazers (14).

In the search for environmentally acceptable diesel fuels, chemically modified rapeseed oils have been tested. Favorable results have been obtained with the methyl ester of rapeseed fatty acids, indicating that biodegradable natural products may be used in the future as diesel fuels (19).

6.20.6 Jet Fuels

Gasoline and diesel cannot be used as a jet fuel because, in the high atmosphere, gasoline will evaporate because of the low atmospheric pressure and diesel fuel will freeze because the outside temperature is usually below −55°C. Therefore, jet fuels consist mainly of kerosene with anti-icing additives.

Kerosene is a mixture of hydrocarbons with an intermediate boiling range (between that of gasolines and diesel fuels). The boiling range is typically 180−250°C. The density can range from 0.75 to 0.84 and the aromatic content from 20 to 25%.

The octane number is of no importance for jet fuels, but a high heating value (high energy output) is essential.

6.21 Effects of Hydrocarbon and Alternative Fuels on Elastomers

Generally speaking, the majority of hydrocarbon fuels cause considerably higher swell to elastomers than do mineral oils. Most elastomers with good swelling resistance have rather poor low-temperature flexibility in air, but in the fuels that swell them the low-temperature properties will improve. The best rubber compound to use depends not only on the nature of the fuel but also on the temperature range in service and the type of application (i.e., whether static or dynamic).

6.21.1 Gasolines and Gasohols

The elastomeric components for automotive fuel systems must withstand the physical and chemical effects of gasolines and gasohols at the temperature range anticipated. The emphasis on heat resistance is very marked in western Europe, where high temperatures under the hood can be reached in cars with more efficient engines when driven at high speeds (15). In cold countries such as Scandinavia and Canada, temperatures as low as −40°C or even lower can be expected.

The elastomers that meet a wide range of fuel demands include properly formulated compounds based on NBR, CO/ECO, FPM and FMQ. The use of **HNBR** elastomers is restricted because they swell markedly more than NBR compounds of the same nitrile level. Other elastomer types, such as **CR** and **EPDM**, swell to a large extent in gasolines and gasohols and hence cannot be used in the fuel systems. However, they may be used under the hood and can come in contact with the fuel by an accidental spill.

The most critical gasolines are the unleaded types that gain their high octane number from aromatics and oxygenates. Both cause more marked swelling of elastomers. In general, methanol blends cause more swelling to elastomers than ethanol blends at equivalent alcohol concentrations (20).

The resistance of **NBR** elastomers to swelling in gasolines and gasohols depends primarily upon the acrylonitrile level of the basic rubber. Specially formulated high nitrile compounds (whose equilibrium volume swell is less than 30%) appear to be best suited for static applications. If dryout conditions are present (section 6.2.2), then compounds with low extractables (nonplasticized) should be used.

The resistance of **CO/ECO** compounds to alcohol-free gasolines is comparable to that of high nitriles. In gasoline/alcohol blends, both NBR and CO/ECO elastomers show considerably higher swell than in alcohol-free gasolines. Here again, ethanol blends cause comparatively less swell than their methanol counterparts.

The resistance of **FPM** compounds to swelling in gasolines and gasohols depends primarily upon their combined fluorine level, which varies between approximately 65 and 70%. The highly fluorinated types (about 70% fluorine) provide the best resistance to swelling in gasolines and gasohols. In addition, they have the lowest permeation to automotive fuels. Therefore, they are prime candidates for elastomeric components in modern fuel systems. However, the material choice becomes more difficult if both low swell and good low-temperature flexibility are required. There are elastomer types available that meet these demands, but they are very expensive. These include low-temperature (LT) FPM grades (with perfluoromethylvinyl ether instead of hexafluoropropylene) and FMQ grades with high tensile strength.

It is not recommended to use **AU**, **EU** or **YBPO** elastomers in gasohols because of their susceptibility to hydrolysis and **alcoholysis** (a chemical reaction similar to hydrolysis).

6.21.2 Sour Gasoline

Both NBR and ECO elastomers will be attacked by sour gasoline (section 6.20.1). **NBR** compounds become hard and brittle, and **ECO** elastomers show excessive softening. Either type of attack can cause premature failure of elastomeric fuel system components. **HNBR** elastomers show better resistance to sour fuels but their use seems restricted because they tend to swell markedly more than NBR compounds with the same nitrile level. **FPM** elastomers are chemically unaffected by exposure to sour fuel (20).

6.21.3 Pure Methanol

Elastomers in contact with fluids normally swell more as the temperature increases. However, immersion tests show that conventional FPM elastomers swell less in pure methanol as the temperature increases **(Table 6.16)**. This unusual behavior is believed to be due to the reduction of the hydrogen-bonding capability of methanol with increasing temperature (section 6.20.3).

It is most likely that the methylene hydrogens of the vinylidene fluoride ($-CH_2-CF_2-$) segments of the FPM polymer chains are capable of forming hydrogen bonds with methanol (21). Consequently, the volume swell of an FPM compound in pure methanol will increase (with decreasing temperature) as the polymer hydrogen content increases.

The volume change figures in **Table 6.16** show that this effect is more pronounced on FPM copolymers containing about 1.9% hydrogen and 66% fluorine. The effect becomes markedly less on the terpolymer with 1.4% hydrogen and 68% fluorine. The terpolymer compound with 1.1% hydrogen and 69.5% fluorine shows the lowest volume swell. In contrast to the other two compounds, it behaves normally in methanol (i.e., it swells more as the temperature increases).

Table 6.16: Volume Swell of Selected FPM Elastomers after 168 h Immersion in Pure Methanol at Different Temperatures

Polymer Type	Hydrogen Content (%) (approx.)	Fluorine Content (%) (approx.)	Volume Change (%) at:		
			−30°C	+23°C	+65°C
Copolymer	1.9	66	+118.1	+74.6	+47.8
Terpolymer	1.4	68	+ 71.7	+25.6	+14.7
Terpolymer	1.1	69.5	− 0.3	+ 1.4	+ 6.1

The effect of pure methanol on FPM elastomers is considerably reduced by adding small amounts of water to the alcohol, as shown in **Table 6.17**.

Table 6.17: Volume Swell at Room Temperature of a Selected FPM Copolymer Compound after 168 h Immersion in Methanol Containing Different Amounts of Water

Methanol (%)	Water (%)	Volume Change (%)
100.0	0.0	+113.1
99.5	0.5	+ 89.3
95.0	5.0	+ 5.5
90.0	10.0	+ 2.1

Other elastomer types, such as **EPDM**, **NBR** and **FMQ**, behave normally in methanol; that is, volume swell increases as the temperature increases **(Table 6.18)**, indicating that these elastomers are not capable of forming hydrogen bonds with methanol.

The volume change figures in **Table 6.18** show that **EPDM** elastomers have the best resistance to swelling in methanol over a wide temperature range. As would be expected (section 6.3.1), other hydrocarbon elastomers such as **NR**, **IR**, **IIR** and **SBR** also show excellent resistance to methanol. However, it should be remem-

Table 6.18: Volume Swell of Selected EPDM, NBR and FMQ Elastomers after 168 h Immersion in Pure Methanol at Different Temperatures

Elastomer	Volume Change (%) at:		
	−30°C	room temperature	+65°C
Standard elastomer EPDM 1 (ISO 6072)	±0	± 0	+ 0.3
Standard elastomer NBR 1 (ISO 6072)	+3.8	+13.0	+18.6
Commercial FMQ compound	+4.2	+ 5.7	+ 5.7

bered that these elastomers are not resistant to mineral oils and hydrocarbon fuels. Therefore, they cannot be used with gasoline/alcohol blends.

CO/ECO elastomers usually show moderate to fairly high swelling in methanol. **AU**, **EU** and **YBPO** should not be used in methanol because of their susceptibility to hydrolysis and alcoholysis.

6.21.4 Pure Ethanol

FPM elastomers swell considerably less in ethanol than in methanol. **NBR** elastomers swell nearly to the same extent as in methanol **(Table 6.18)**. However, the highly plasticized compounds may shrink because of extraction of plasticizers. **CO/ECO** compounds tend to swell more than NBR elastomers with low extractables.   Hydrocarbon elastomers such as **NR, IR, IIR, SBR** and **EPDM** show excellent resistance to ethanol. As has been mentioned, they are not resistant to mineral oils and hydrocarbon fuels.

AU, **EU** and **YBPO** elastomers should not be used in ethanol because of their susceptibility to hydrolysis and alcoholysis.

6.21.5 Fuel Permeation

Besides the required resistance to swelling in hydrocarbon and alternative fuels, the elastomers need to meet the **SHED** (Sealed Housing Evaporation Determination) test requirements (especially in the United States), which have become progressively more restrictive.

Fuel emission by permeation depends in part upon thickness and in part on the elastomer selected. As has been mentioned, the highly fluorinated **FPM** elastomers have the lowest permeation to fuels (22).

6.21.6 Diesel Fuels

Diesel fuels are markedly less aggressive to elastomers than are gasolines and gasohols. Therefore, there are fewer problems with volume swell and higher permeation. Only the required temperature range will determine the basis of the elastomer. Usually, elastomer types used with gasolines or gasohols (high nitriles, FPM and FMQ) will perform very well in diesel fuels. **HNBR** elastomers can also be considered because they tend to swell considerably less in diesel fuels than in gasolines or gasohols.

The newly developed "bio-diesel fuels" (section 6.20.5) cause high swelling to conventional NBR compounds. Only properly formulated high nitriles or FPM compounds may be used with these diesel fuel types.

6.21.7 Jet Fuels

The swelling effect of jet fuels on elastomers is between that of gasolines and diesel fuels. Usually, rubber compounds with good swelling resistance to gasolines or gasohols can be used with jet fuels.

6.22 Review of Organic Refrigerants

A **refrigerant** is defined as the medium of heat transfer in a refrigerating system that absorbs heat on evaporating at a low temperature and a low pressure, and gives up heat on condensing at a higher temperature and pressure.

The most common organic refrigerants are **halohydrocarbons**, that is, halogenated hydrocarbons containing one or more halogens (fluorine, chlorine, bromine and iodine). They are identified by number designations in accordance with ISO standard 817 (23) instead of using chemical names, formulas or trade names. However, there is no intention of precluding the use of a chemical name or formula.

The identifying number is preceded by the letter **R** or the word "Refrigerant". It may also be used in combination with the trade name (e.g., R 12, Refrigerant 12 or (trade name) R 12.

The rules of the fixed number designations are as follows:
1) The first digit on the right is the number of fluorine (F) atoms in the molecule.
2) The second digit from the right is one more than the number of hydrogen (H) atoms in the molecule.
3) The third digit from the right is one less than the number of carbon atoms in the molecule. When this digit is zero, it is omitted from the number.
4) The number of chlorine (Cl) atoms in the molecule is calculated by subtracting the sum of the F and H atoms from the total number of atoms that can be connected to the C atoms.

   In the case of **saturated** hydrocarbons, the total number of attached atoms is calculated as follows:

   For **n** C atoms, the total number of attached atoms is **2n + 2** (e.g., for **2** C atoms, the total number of attached atoms is **6**).

   In the case of **mono-unsaturated** and **cyclic saturated** hydrocarbons the total number of attached atoms is calculated as follows:

   For **n** C atoms the total number of attached atoms is **2n** (e.g., for **2** C atoms, the total number of attached atoms is **4**).

   Examples:
   R 12 = 2 **F** atoms, 0 **H** atoms, 1 **C** atom and 2 **Cl** atoms (CCl_2F_2)
   R 22 = 2 **F** atoms, 1 **H** atom, 1 **C** atom, 1 **Cl** atom ($CHClF_2$)
   R 113 = 3 **F** atoms, 0 **H** atoms, 2 **C** atoms, 3 **Cl** atoms ($C_2Cl_3F_3$ or $FCl_2C\text{-}CClF_2$)
   R 218 = 8 **F** atoms, 0 **H** atoms, 3 **C** atoms, 0 **Cl** atoms (C_3F_8 or $F_3C\text{-}CF_2\text{-}CF_3$)
5) For **cyclic** compounds the letter **C** is used before the identifying refrigerant number.

   Examples:
   C 316 = cyclic compound with 6 **F** atoms, 0 **H** atoms, 4 **C** atoms, 2 **Cl** atoms ($C_4Cl_2F_6$)
   C 318 = cyclic compound with 8 **F** atoms, 0 **H** atoms, 4 **C** atoms, 0 **Cl** atoms (C_4F_8).

6) In those cases where bromine (Br) is present in place of part or all of the chlorine, the same rules apply except that the letter **B** is added after the designation of the parent chloro-fluorohydrocarbon. A number following the letter **B** shows the number of bromine atoms present.

Examples:
R 13 = the parent chloro-fluorohydrocarbon ($CClF_3$)
R 13 B 1 = 1 **Br** atom is in place of 1 **Cl** atom ($CBrF_3$)
R 114 = the parent chloro-fluorohydrocarbon ($C_2Cl_2F_4$)
R 114 B 2 = 2 **Br** atoms are in place of 2 **Cl** atoms ($C_2Br_2F_4$)

7) In the case of **isomers** of the ethane series, the most symmetrical one is identified by the refrigerant number without any letter following it. As the isomers become more and more unsymmetrical, the letters **a**, **b**, **c** and so on are appended. Symmetry is determined by adding the atomic weights of the elements attached to **each** carbon atom and subtracting one sum from the other. The smaller the difference, the more symmetrical the compound.

Example:
R 114 = $C_2Cl_2F_4$ or $F_2ClC\text{-}CClF_2$
high degree of symmetry
R 114a = $C_2Cl_2F_4$ or $FCl_2C\text{-}CF_3$
low degree of symmetry
R 114**a** is an isomer of R 114 (i.e., it has the same empirical or molecular formula but the arrangement of the atoms is different).

8) In the case of the **ethylene** series (i.e., unsaturated compounds) the above rules apply, except that the number **1** is used as the fourth digit from the right.

Examples:
R 1113 = chlorotrifluoroethylene ($FClC = CF_2$)
R 1114 = tetrafluoroethylene ($F_2C = CF_2$)

9) Mixtures are designated by their respective refrigerant numbers and mass proportion. Refrigerants are named in order of increasing boiling points. For example, a 90%/10% mixture of refrigerants 22 and 12 will be designated by R 22/12 (90/10).

10) Arbitrary identifying numbers of 500 series are assigned to **azeotropes** (i.e., mixtures of refrigerants whose vapor and liquid phases have identical composition at a given temperature).
The refrigerants should be named in increasing order of boiling points.

Examples:
R 500 = R 12/152 a, 73.8/26.2 by weight
R 501 = R 22/12, 75/25 by weight
R 502 = R 22/115, 48.8/51.2 by weight

6.22.1 Effects of Halocarbons on the Ozone Layer

The chlorine in chlorofluorocarbons such as R 12 (which is used in automotive air-conditioning systems) can react photolytically with ozone in the upper atmosphere and deplete the ozone layer.

The refrigerant generally regarded as the replacement for R 12 is **R 134a** (CF_3-CH_2F). Since this product contains no chlorine, it is believed to be harmless to the ozone layer.

6.23 Effects of Organic Refrigerants on Elastomers

Many of the halohydrocarbon refrigerants have a high swelling effect on elastomers. The extent of linear swelling is a valuable guide in determining whether an elastomer is suitable for use in contact with a particular halohydrocarbon. In pressure systems, it is more practical to measure linear swell rather than volumetric swell (24). Other important effects, such as extraction of plasticizers and changes in the physical properties of the elastomer, should also be considered. Highly plasticized elastomers may shrink. In some cases, appreciable swelling may be masked by extraction. However, shrinkage can occur if the elastomer is allowed to dry.

The swelling effect of a halohydrocarbon refrigerant depends on its molecular structure. The swell tests show certain regularities (24):

1) Halohydrocarbons containing more fluorine atoms in their molecules have less swelling effect on elastomers than those containing a higher proportion of chlorine atoms.

   Examples:
   a) swell is considerable in **R 11** (CCl_3F) but becomes much less in **R 12** (CCl_2F_2) and still less in R 13 ($CClF_3$)
   b) **R 115** ($CClF_2$-CF_3) and **R 218** (CF_3-CF_2-CF_3) have very weak swelling effect on elastomers

2) Halogenated one-carbon compounds containing one hydrogen atom cause more swelling than completely halogenated compounds.

   Examples:
   a) **$CHCl_3$** causes more swelling than **CCl_4**
   b) **R 21** ($CHCl_2F$) causes more swelling than **R 11** (CCl_3F)
   c) **R 22** ($CHClF_2$) causes more swelling than **R 12** (CCl_2F_2)

3) Substitution of a second hydrogen atom for chlorine (to give two hydrogen atoms in the molecule) leads to a decrease in swelling.

   Examples:
   a) **CH_2Cl_2** causes less swelling than **$CHCl_3$**
   b) **R 31** (CH_2ClF) causes less swelling than **R 21** ($CHCl_2F$)
   c) **R 32** (CH_2F_2) causes less swelling than **R 22** ($CHClF_2$)

The elastomer types that may be considered for use in refrigeration systems include CR, CSM, NBR, HNBR, EPDM, FPM and T. The resistance ratings of different elastomer types in halohydrocarbon refrigerants given in chapter 15 (**Table 15.1;** under refrigerants) are only a general guide. It should be noted that differences in rubber compounding may cause significant differences in swelling. Therefore, it is always best to conduct tests that are specific to the application involved.

In a refrigeration or air-conditioning system where a lubricating fluid is mixed with the refrigerant, the elastomeric component must withstand the effects of both the refrigerant and the lubricant. Their combined effects may be greater than a simple addition of the individual effects. This can be found out only by conducting tests under the working conditions.

As has been mentioned, **R 12** will be replaced by the new refrigerant **R 134a** in the coming years (section 6.22.1). Since the mineral oils used as lubricant in R 12 systems are not compatible with R 134a, certain types of polyalkylene glycols will most likely be used by the automotive industry. For other industrial applications, certain polyolesters may be used. The elastomeric materials that may be considered for R 134a systems include specially formulated **CR** and **NBR** in applications where the temperature is limited to 100°C. At higher temperatures (up to 140–150°C) **HNBR** elastomers are recommended. Peroxide-cured **EPDM** compounds may also be used where the presence of any mineral oil is excluded.

6.24 Effects of Organic Solvents on Elastomers

Organic solvents are normally low-molecular-weight liquids. The most common solvents include:
– aliphatic hydrocarbons (e.g., pentane, hexane and petrol ether);
– aromatic hydrocarbons (e.g., benzene, toluene and xylene);
– chlorinated hydrocarbons (e.g., chloroform, trichloroethylene and carbon tetrachloride);
– alcohols (e.g., methanol, ethanol, propanol and butanol);
– ethers (e.g., diethyl ether, dibutyl ether and dioxan);
– ketones (e.g., acetone and methylethyl ketone); and
– esters (e.g., ethyl acetate and butyl acetate).

Generally speaking, polar elastomers such as NBR, HNBR, ECO and FPM swell excessively in polar solvents, particularly in ketones and esters, because of similarity in the chemical structure (section 6.3.1). Conversely, the nonpolar (hydrocarbon) elastomers such as IIR and EPDM show markedly better resistance to swelling in these solvents because of dissimilarity in the chemical composition.

However, this rule of thumb should not be applied literally, because the swelling effect of a liquid depends not only on the presence or absence of polar groups but also on the molecular size of the hydrocarbon part of the molecule. In the case of low-molecular-weight liquids such as acetone and ethyl acetate, the swelling effect of the polar group is the predominating factor because the hydrocarbon part of the molecule is small. In high-molecular-weight liquids, such as ester oils, the swelling effect of the polar group will be masked by the swelling effect of the large hydrocarbon part of the molecule. The following example should illustrate this:

FPM elastomers swell enormously in the low-molecular-weight ethyl acetate, but show excellent resistance to swelling in high-molecular-weight ester oils. Conversely, **EPDM** elastomers show high resistance to swelling in ethyl acetate, but swell excessively in ester oils. Both liquids are esters, but with different molecular weight. In ethyl acetate, the swelling effect of the polar (ester) group is predominating; in ester oils, the large hydrocarbon part of the molecule is the controlling factor for swelling.

Table 6.19 is a general guide for selecting elastomeric materials for use in different types of organic solvents. However, the final choice should be made after conducting immersion tests. If dryout conditions are present (section 6.2.2), then compounds with low extractables (plasticizer-free) should be used. Problems usually arise when mixtures of different types of solvents are used (e.g., the nitro lacquers solvents). These are usually mixtures containing different amounts of esters, ketones, alcohols and aromatics. The combined effects of the different components on elastomers are usually greater than a simple addition of the individual effects. In some cases, the very expensive **FFKM** elastomers are the only choice for use with these mixtures.

Table 6.19: Guideline for Selection of Elastomeric Materials for Different Types of Solvents

Solvent Type	Elastomer Types to be Considered for Use
Aliphatic hydrocarbons	NBR, HNBR, CO, ECO, ACM, FPM, FMQ, T, AU, EU, CR, CSM
Aromatic hydrocarbons	FPM, FMQ
Chlorohydrocarbons	FPM
Alcohols	EPDM, IIR, SBR, NR, CR, CSM, T
Ethers	FFKM, partly EPDM, AU, FPM, T
Ketones	EPDM, IIR, T
Esters	EPDM, IIR, T
Blends of different types	FFKM, Partly T

6.25 Effects of Water and Steam on Elastomers

Many elastomer users think that water is a harmless liquid, but they will be surprised to learn that elastomeric components exposed to water for extended periods or at high temperatures may absorb very large amounts of water and swell enormously if the proper compound has not been used. The penetration of water into elastomers is very slow compared with most organic liquids; therefore, a very long time is required to reach equilibrium.

Fillers, metal oxides and other compounding ingredients have a significant effect on the water resistance because many of these ingredients are hydrophilic (i.e., they absorb water). In addition, soluble impurities largely contribute to water absorption. Therefore, maximum purity of all compounding ingredients is essential.

The compounds should not contain water-soluble ingredients, as this may result in shrinkage and considerable changes in the physical properties. In addition, undesirable tastes or odors may be imparted by water-extractable materials.

Almost all elastomers (with suitable compounding ingredients) may be used in cold water. However, it is advisable, whenever possible, not to use AU, EU, YBPO and ACM because of the danger of hydrolysis after long periods of time.

For those applications requiring high resistance to hot water, careful attention must be given when selecting the elastomeric materials. When CR, CSM and FPM elastomers are used, the preferred curing system contains lead oxide. Other curing systems (e.g., with magnesium oxide) cause higher swelling and greater deterioration.

Suitably formulated **NBR** compounds can be used in hot water up to 100°C. Peroxide-cured **HNBR** elastomers show good resistance in hot water and steam up to 150°C. Under these conditions, conventionally cured **FPM** elastomers will deteriorate. Only some of the peroxide-cured grades have improved resistance to water and steam at temperatures not exceeding 150°C.

Peroxide-cured **EPDM** compounds provide the highest resistance to hot water and steam, up to 200°C in the absence of air (oxygen). If one side of the elastomeric part is exposed to air, then the temperature should not exceed 150°C, otherwise it will be attacked by oxygen. It is important to remember that EPDM compounds (and other hydrocarbon elastomers) will deteriorate when exposed to petroleum-based lubricants. When lubrication is required, silicone oil, glycerine or ethylene glycol are suggested.

VMQ elastomers show good resistance to hot water up to 100°C. They can also be used in steam for short periods up to 130°C (in such applications as sterilization and pressure cooking).

ACM, **AU**, **EU** and **YBPO** elastomers should not be used in hot water because of their susceptibility to hydrolysis (section 5.9). **CO/ECO** elastomers are also not recommended because of high swelling and deterioration of the physical properties.

After dryout, shrinkage will not occur if the compound does not contain water-soluble or hydrolyzable ingredients, particularly ester plasticizers. These can be decomposed by hot water into fatty acids and alcohols. If these products, or some of them, are soluble in hot water, shrinkage and hardening of the elastomer can occur.

6.26 Effects of Acids on Elastomers

According to the ionic theory, acids are those substances that in water solution yield hydrogen ions. They can be divided into two groups:
1) inorganic acids; and
2) organic acids.

Inorganic acids include, for example, nitric acid (HNO_3), sulphuric acid (H_2SO_4), hydrochloric acid (HCl) and phosphoric acid (H_3PO_4).

Organic acids form a very important class of acidic substances, including a huge number of compounds. The acidity is mostly due to the presence of carboxyl groups **(−COOH)** and, in some cases, sulphonic groups **(−SO$_3$H)** and hydroxyl groups **(OH)**.

Some organic acids are liquids at room temperature. These include, for example, formic acid (H-COOH), acetic acid (CH_3-COOH), propionic acid (CH_3-CH_2-COOH) and butyric acid (CH_3-CH_2-CH_2-COOH). However, the majority of organic acids are solids at room temperature; for example, oxalic acid (HOOC-COOH), succinic acid (HOOC-CH_2-COOH), benzoic acid (C_6H_5-COOH), benzenesulphonic acid (C_6H_5-SO$_3$H) and carbolic acid or phenol (C_6H_5OH).

6.26.1 Inorganic Acids

Inorganic acids, when concentrated, are very aggressive and can chemically attack conventional elastomers. In severe cases the elastomeric materials can be completely deteriorated. In strong solutions, **FPM** compounds usually show good resistance at room temperature. Maximum resistance to concentrated acids is obtained by using suitably formulated compounds containing lead oxides rather than magnesium oxide. For those applications requiring greatly increased acid resistance, properly formulated **FFKM** compounds should be used.

In dilute acids and at room temperature, **EPDM** compounds are preferred because, as mentioned before, they have excellent resistance to water.

6.26.2 Organic Acids

The action of organic acids on elastomers depends not only on the acidic group but also on the molecular size and chemical structure of the hydrocarbon part of the molecule. Therefore, immersion tests are indispensable for selecting elastomeric materials.

It should be noted that **FPM** elastomers (which usually show high resistance to most inorganic acids) will be severely attacked by low-molecular-weight carboxylic acids, particularly formic and acetic acids. However, they are usually resistant to high-molecular-weight carboxylic acids (e.g., stearic acid) because the effect of the carboxylic group will be masked by the large hydrocarbon part of the molecule. On the other hand, **EPDM** and **IIR** elastomers show good or moderate resistance to many low-molecular-weight acids because the hydrocarbon part of the molecule is small. Their resistance becomes less as the size of the hydrocarbon part of the acid molecule increases. For example, they swell to a large extent in melted stearic acid (melting point = 69−71 °C).

6.27 Effects of Bases on Elastomers

Bases are alkaline substances defined broadly as those that will combine with acids (i.e., hydrogen ions) to form salts. Bases are subdivided in two groups:
1) inorganic bases; and
2) organic bases.

Inorganic bases, in terms of the ionic theory, are substances that yield hydroxyl ions (OH^-) when dissolved in water. Examples are sodium hydroxide (NaOH), potassium hydroxide (KOH) and ammonium hydroxide (NH_4OH).

Organic bases are derivatives of hydrocarbons that contain nitrogen (N) [sometimes phosphorus (P) or arsenic (As)] in addition to carbon (C) and hydrogen (H). **Amines** are the most important category of organic bases and include a huge number of compounds.

6.27.1 Inorganic Bases

Although **FPM** elastomers are resistant to most inorganic compounds, they will be chemically attacked by anhydrous ammonia and aqueous solutions of alkali metal hydroxides when exposed for long periods of time or at elevated temperatures. Conversely, peroxide-cured **EPDM** compounds show excellent resistance to inorganic bases even in concentrated solutions and at elevated temperatures. Other elastomers that have also good resistance to inorganic bases include suitably formulated **IIR**, **CR** and **CSM**.

6.27.2 Organic Bases

The effect of an organic base on elastomers depends not only on its basicity but also on the molecular size and structure of the hydrocarbon part of the molecule. Therefore, the best way to find out the most suitable rubber compound for an application is to run immersion tests.

Generally speaking, **FPM** elastomers are not recommended for use with organic bases, particularly amines. **EPDM, IIR,CR** and **CSM** elastomers show moderate resistance to some organic bases. In many cases, the very expensive **FFKM** elastomers are the only choice for use with those aggressive bases that attack all other elastomer types.

6.28 Effects of Gases on Elastomers

Gases may be divided into three groups:
1) elements such as nitrogen, oxygen, hydrogen, chlorine, argon, helium and neon;
2) chemical compounds such as carbon dioxide, methane, acetylene or vapors of water, ethanol and benzene; and
3) mixtures such as air, lighting gas and fuel vapors.

The effects of gases on elastomers can be physical or chemical. The physical action is indicated by swell or permeation through the elastomer or both (section 4.9).

Gases that act **physically** include, for example, nitrogen, argon, helium, neon, methane, ethane, propane and vapors of benzene and fuels.

As mentioned in section 4.10, elastomeric parts may be damaged because of explosive decompression if the gas pressure is reduced too rapidly. Generally, carbon dioxide causes more swelling and damage than nitrogen does. Suggested solutions to explosive decompression are as follows:
– Increase depressurization time to allow the trapped gas to escape harmlessly.
– Choose hard materials with high strength and good resistance to explosive decompression.
– Whenever possible, use elastomeric parts with small cross sections.

Chemically reactive gases such as oxygen, ozone, chlorine, fumes of hydrochloric or nitric acids are very aggressive and can cause total destruction of the elastomeric part if the proper compound has not been used. The best rubber compound to use depends not only on the nature of the gas but also on the temperature and concentration. As a general rule, unsaturated elastomers should not be used with chemically reactive gases. Elastomer types that meet a wide range of demands include suitably formulated **FPM**, **FFKM** and, to some extent, **EPDM**, **CSM** and **IIR**.

6.29 Effects of Oil-field Environments on Elastomers

Elastomeric components intended for use in oil-field operations are required to function in a wide range of fluids, temperatures and pressures. In long-term use under these conditions, elastomeric materials suffer chemical and physical deterioration from the combined influences of stress, well fluids and high temperatures.

Elastomeric seals performing under differential pressure conditions will often fail because of extrusion through the clearances between members being sealed. The resistance to high-pressure extrusion is a composite effect of hardness, modulus, high-temperature stiffness and compression set. The use of antiextrusion rings and minimum extrusion gaps can reduce this problem to a minimum. However, it is sometimes not feasible to use either of these methods.

In gaseous environments, elastomeric seals can suffer extensive damage caused by explosive decompression (section 4.10). Resistance to rapid pressure drops in service is often an important parameter with which seals must comply. In general, rubber compounds designed to be "decompression resistant" should have high mechanical strength at the decompression temperature. Plastics like PTFE and polyamides are usually rigid enough to be resistant to this effect.

The hostile environments that elastomeric components must resist in service include **sour gas** [hydrogen sulphide (H_2S) in combination with methane (CH_4), carbon dioxide (CO_2) and water], **sour crude oil** and **saline** at elevated pressures (above 1,000 bar) and temperatures (above 200°C). In addition, several chemicals are added to alleviate a particular drilling or production problem. These include, for example, hydrochloric acid, sulphuric acid, formic acid, hydrofluoric acid, certain inhibitors with amines, ketones and peroxides (25). It is becoming increasingly apparent that these chemicals, particularly amine-based corrosion inhibitors, can attack elastomeric components, resulting in degradation and premature failure (26).

The elastomeric materials that may be considered for use in oil-field environments include properly formulated compounds based on NBR, HNBR, XNBR, ACM, FPM, TFE/P (tetrafluoroethylene propylene rubber with the trade name Aflas), FFKM, EPDM, FMQ, FZ and ECO.

NBR elastomers perform well in mineral oils at around 100 °C. However, they undergo cross-linking and become hard and brittle when exposed to oil-field environments containing H_2S gas. The amine-based corrosion inhibitors accelerate this cross-linking and cause increased swell.

The effect of H_2S gas on NBR elastomers does not appear to be strongly influenced by either the polymer type or the cure system (sulphur or peroxide) (27).

Nowadays, it is generally agreed that NBR elastomers are not acceptable in most hot sour environments. In these cases, **HNBR** elastomers are preferred because they show a better resistance to H_2S and corrosion inhibitors (28, 29). Furthermore, they offer a higher application temperature limit (around 150 °C, compared with 100 °C for NBR elastomers).

XNBR elastomers have excellent abrasion resistance and high tensile strength, but the overall heat and oil resistance are not better than conventional NBR compounds.

ACM elastomers have excellent oil resistance at temperatures exceeding 150 °C, but they will be badly affected by hydrolysis in watery environments. **AEM** elastomers offer markedly better resistance to hydrolysis at some sacrifice in oil resistance.

FPM elastomers are resistant to a wide range of well fluids and chemicals, except amine-based corrosion inhibitors. These amines may cause dehydrofluorination of conventional FPM elastomers, which leads to severe hardening and embrittlement. However, the peroxide-cured highly fluorinated FPM compounds are less affected by amines (30).

TFE/P elastomers have good heat and oil resistance. In addition, they show good resistance to amine-based corrosion inhibitors. For this reason they are finding use in oil-field operations (31). Wider use, at the present time, is not expected because of relatively poor low-temperature properties and poorer compression set compared with FPM elastomers.

FFKM elastomers (e.g., Kalrez), which are more expensive than any other elastomer, offer complete resistance to well fluids at temperatures exceeding those of FPM elastomers. However, they have poor resistance to extrusion and therefore must be backed up by harder materials such as PTFE.

Specially formulated **EPDM** compounds can be used in steam injection wells, as they have excellent resistance to steam at temperatures exceeding 200 °C. However, they deteriorate from intimate contact with the oil at elevated temperatures.

The choice of material becomes more difficult for applications requiring elastomeric components to operate under arctic conditions. This is because elastomers with good oil resistance usually have poor low-temperature properties. Although **FMQ** elastomers have excellent low-temperature properties and good oil resistance, their use in oil-field environments is restricted because of their low mechanical strength. **FZ** elastomers (section 8.27) are similar to FMQ elastomers in many respects, but they show, in addition, better mechanical properties and lower gas permeability. These property advantages suggest that they can be used in oil and gas exploration.

ECO elastomers have good low-temperature properties (down to $-40\,°C$) and good oil resistance. However, their corrosive effect on metals must be considered.

Finally, it can be concluded that there is no universal elastomer that resists all physical and chemical effects of oil-field environments. Therefore, it is always best to conduct simulated tests that are specific to the application involved. It is also important to consider the resistance to high-pressure extrusion and explosive decompression.

6.30 Effects of Contiguous Surfaces of Rigid Materials on Elastomers

Contiguous surfaces of rigid materials, such as metals, plastics and glass, can have adverse effects on the performance of elastomeric parts. The following examples will illustrate this:

1) A rough metal surface can cause excessive wear of dynamic seals, which may result in premature leakage.
2) NR compounds may deteriorate after prolonged contact with certain heavy metals (such as copper, manganese, nickel, iron and cobalt) resulting from metal-catalyzed oxidation (section 5.8).
3) NBR compounds tend to stick to surfaces of plasticized PVC after prolonged contact as a result of **plasticizer migration** into the elastomer. In severe cases, the NBR compound becomes soft and loses a great deal of its mechanical properties.
4) Silicone elastomers tend to adhere to glass surfaces after prolonged contact because of similarity in the chemical structure of the two materials. The Si-O-Si linkage in silicone elastomers is similar to the linkage in glass.

References

1. "Effects of Air Bubbling on Elastomer/Fluid Compatibility," *The TSF Journal*, Vol. 8 (1988), pp. 103–106.
2. J. G. Bauerle and D. W. Bruhnke, "The Effects of Aeration of Test Fluids on the Retention of Physical Properties of Fluoroelastomer Vulcanizates," SAE Technical Paper 890362.
3. S. D. Scott, "Biodegradable Fluids for Axial Piston Pumps and Motors, Application Considerations," SAE Technical Paper 910963.
4. H. F. Eichenberger, "Biodegradable Hydraulic Lubricant, an Overview of Current Developments in Central Europe," SAE Technical Paper 910962.
5. V. M. Cheng, A. A. Wessol, P. Bandouin, M. T. Ben Kinney and N. J. Novic, "Biodegradable and Nontoxic Hydraulic Oil," SAE Technical Paper 910964.
6. H. Krumm, H. D. Müller and A. Marx, "Observations and Findings of the Compatibility of Elastomer Materials with Modern Engine Oils," *Mineraloeltechnik*, February 1982.
7. K. Nagdi, "Polyalphaolefins (PAO) – The Seal Friendly Fluids," *Tribologie + Schmiertechnik*, May 1990, pp. 281–288.

8. K. Nagdi, "Seal Materials for Synthetic Lubricants and Working Fluids," *Kautschuk + Gummi. Kunststoffe*, Vol. 43 (1990) No. 3, pp. 227–234.

9. J. W. Miller, "Synthetic Lubricants and their Industrial Applications," Paper presented at the 4th International Colloquium on Synthetic Lubricants and Operational Fluids, January 10–12, 1984, Technische Akademie Esslingen, Germany.

10. G. W. Lawless, A. K. Behme, R. P. Mortimer, H. W. Polley and T. H. Wical, "Volume Swell and Elastomeric Seal Hydraulic Fluid Compatibility," *Elastomerics*, November 1984, pp. 22–25.

11. C. J. Harrington, "Brake Fluids – An Opportunity for Change," Paper presented at the 4th International Colloquium on Synthetic Lubricants and Operational Fluids, January 10–12, 1984, Technische Akademie Esslingen, Germany.

12. K. Nagdi, unpublished work.

13. P. S. Coffin, "Characteristics of Synthetic Lubricating Greases," Paper presented at the 4th International Colloquium on Synthetic Lubricants and Operational Fluids, January 10–12, 1984, Technische Akademie Esslingen, Germany.

14. K. Owen and T. Coley, *Automotive Fuels Handbook*, SAE, 1990.

15. J. R. Dunn, "Specialty Elastomers Meet Emerging Needs for Underhood Applications," *Elastomerics*, January 1991, pp. 15–20.

16. F. Leibbrandt, "The Status of HNBR in West European Automotive Industry," SAE Technical Paper 890360.

17. M. van Thiel, E. D. Becker and G. C. Pimentel, "Infrared Studies of Hydrogen Bonding of Methanol by the Matrix Isolation Technique," *Journal of Chemical Physics*, Vol. 27, No. 1, July 1957, pp. 95–99.

18. R. G. Inskeep, J. M. Kelliher, P. E. Mc Mahon and B. G. Somers, "Molecular Association of Methanol Vapour," *The Journal of Chemical Physics*, Vol. 28, No. 6, June 1958, pp. 1033–1036.

19. H. Menrad, K. Weidmann, W. Bernhard, G. Heilmann and U. Behn, "Rapeseed Oil an Engine Fuel," *Mineralöltechnik*, 5–6, May 1989.

20. A. Nersasian, "Compatibility of Fuel-Handling Rubbers with Gasoline/Alcohol Blends," *Elastomerics*, October 1980, pp. 26–27.

21. A. Nersasian, "The Volume Increase of Fuel-Handling Rubbers in Gasoline/Alcohol Blends," SAE Technical Paper 800789.

22. B. Spoo, "High Performance Fuel Line for Emerging Automotive Needs," SAE Technical Paper 800787.

23. International Standard ISO 817–1974 E, Organic Refrigerants-Number Designation.

24. R. O. Menard, "Effect of Freon Fluorocarbons and other Halohydrocarbons on Elastomers," Report from the Elastomer Chemicals Department, Du Pont.

25. W. M. Taylor, "Operating Conditions for Elastomers Used in Oil Field Surface Equipment," *Elastomerics*, July 1982, pp. 14–16.

26. M. J. Watkins and G. C. Derringer, "Effects of Oilfield Corrosion Inhibitors on Nitrile Elastomers," *Kautschuk + Gummi. Kunststoffe*, Vol. 38 (1985), No. 10, pp. 901–903.

27. "Guidelines for Selection of Materials for H_2S Services, Phase II," *Polymeric Materials*, Vol. 5, Summary Report, Battele Petroleum Technology Center, Houston, Tex.

28. L. A. Peters and D. E. Cain, "Saturated Nitrile (HSN) vs Nitrile (NBR) in Temperature and Compatibility Tests," *Elastomerics*, June 1986, pp. 28–31.

29. J. Thoermer, J. Mirza and Shoen, "Therban Hydrogenated NBR in Oilfield Applications," *Elastomerics*, September 1986, pp. 28–32.

30. G. C. Sweet, "A Review of Elastomers Used for Oilfield Environments," Proceedings of Offshore Engineering with Elastomers Conference, June 1985, Aberdeen, Scotland, Plastics and Rubber Institute (PRI).

31. D. Hull, "Copolymer of Tetrafluoroethylene and Propylene Finds Oil Field Applications," *Elastomerics*, July 1982, pp. 27–30.

CHAPTER 7

Effects of Elastomers on Selected Contiguous Materials

In chapter 6 the effects of contiguous materials on elastomers have been discussed in detail. We will now consider the adverse effects of elastomers on various contiguous materials.

7.1 Effects of Elastomers on Metals

Some rubber compounds can cause corrosion of metal surfaces with which they are in direct contact or to which they are adjacent. Quite frequently the elastomer tends to stick to the metal surface. Corrosion and adhesion may be caused by certain compounding ingredients or through the formation of some reaction products under service conditions.

Examples:
1) Rubber compounds containing uncombined or free sulphur (section 2.5) will promote the corrosion of copper, brass, silver and lead. After prolonged contact, the elastomer may tend to adhere to the surface of these metals because of the formation of metal sulphide. In these cases sulphur-free compounds should be used.
2) Chlorine-containing elastomers such as CO, ECO and CR may cause corrosion and pitting of metal surfaces because of the formation of hydrochloric acid under the service conditions. This may be avoided by using chlorine-free compounds.

Furthermore, **galvanic** corrosion may also occur even if the elastomer does not contain corrosive substances. This type of corrosion is found particularly at seal regions, probably because of the accumulation of moisture and contaminants (thus producing an electrolyte) at or adjacent to the elastomer/metal contact area. Factors that support galvanic corrosion include nonhomogeneity of the alloy, rough metal surface, high humidity and elevated temperatures.

7.2 Effects of Elastomers on Plastics

Plasticized elastomers may seriously change the properties of the contiguous plastic as a result of **plasticizer migration**, and the rate of degradation may increase as the temperature increases. For example, if a plasticized NBR compound is in direct contact with a plastic material for a long time, the plasticizer will transfer to the plastic, causing serious changes of the physical properties of both materials. In addition, the two surfaces tend to stick together.

Table 7.1 shows the results of a laboratory test in which a plasticized NBR compound was placed on a thermoplastic polyurethane under load and subsequently aged for eight weeks at 70°C in circulating air. It can be seen that the

Table 7.1: Property Changes of a Thermoplastic Polyurethane and a Plasticized NBR Compound after Eight Weeks of Direct Contact at 70 °C in Circulating Air

Property Changes	Thermoplastic Polyurethane	Plasticized NBR Compound
Change in hardness (points)	− 3	+10
Change in 100% modulus (%)	−15.0	+38.9
Change in 300% modulus (%)	−35.2	+42.1
Change in tensile strength (%)	−59.4	+ 0.7
Change in elongation at break (%)	− 2.3	−18.7

physical properties of both materials changed to a large extent. The same test was carried out under the same conditions with a nonplasticized NBR compound. The test results given in **Table 7.2** show that the property changes of both materials after aging are considerably less significant than those obtained by using the plasticized compound.

Table 7.2: Property Changes of a Thermoplastic Polyurethane and a Nonplasticized NBR Compound after Eight Weeks of Direct Contact at 70 °C in Circulating Air

Property Changes	Thermoplastic Polyurethane	Nonplasticized NBR Compound
Change in hardness (points)	± 0	+ 3
Change in 100% modulus (%)	− 1.5	+16.3
Change in 300% modulus (%)	−14.1	+21.7
Change in tensile strength (%)	−13.6	+ 9.3
Change in elongation at break (%)	−14.3	−20.2

In some cases, fine cracks may be formed on the plastic surface. This sort of "crazing" has been noticed most frequently with polycarbonate plastics, but it has also been found in other plastic materials. This problem can be avoided by using plasticizer-free rubber compounds.

In addition to the influence of elastomers on plastics, it is necessary also to consider the adverse effects of plasticized plastics on rubber compounds (section 6.30).

7.3 Effects of Elastomers on Paints

Paints and other organic materials can become stained by some rubber compounds with which they come in contact. There are four types of stain:

1) **contact stain**, which occurs on the area in direct contact with the elastomer;

2) **migration stain**, which occurs on the surface surrounding the contact area;
3) **extraction stain**, which is caused by contact with water containing leached-out constituents of the rubber compound; and
4) **penetration** or **diffusion stain**, which occurs on the external surface of an organic material bonded to the surface of an elastomer.

The staining is caused by staining ingredients of the rubber compound, particularly antioxidants. Heat and light may intensify the degree of staining. This problem can be solved by using compounds containing nonstaining ingredients.

7.4 Effects of Elastomers on Refrigerants and Insulating Oils

Extractable ingredients of elastomers, particularly plasticizers, may considerably change the properties of contiguous media such as refrigerants and insulating oils. The effect will be more pronounced in small equipment. In these applications the use of specially formulated rubber compounds with low extractables is necessary.

7.5 Effects of Elastomers on Food and Drinks

Applications involving contact with food and drinks require the use of specially formulated elastomers. In these formulations attention is drawn to the requirements and recommendations of agencies such as the U.S. Food and Drug Administration (FDA) and the German Bundesgesundheitsamt (BGA).

The FDA has established a list of rubber compounding ingredients that are neither toxic nor carcinogenic (cancer producing). Rubber compounds produced entirely from these ingredients and which pass the FDA extraction tests are said to meet the FDA requirements. Normally, the FDA does not approve rubber compounds. It is the responsibility of the manufacturer to compound food-grade materials from the FDA list of ingredients and establish whether they pass the extraction requirements.

The BGA has also established a list of compounding ingredients and extraction tests. Rubber compounds produced entirely from these ingredients and which pass the standardized extraction tests require an approval from the BGA. Moreover, the manufacturer must submit the compound formula.

7.6 Effects of Elastomers on Explosives

Rubber compounds used in contact with explosives should contain only ingredients that do not sensitize them. In addition, it is necessary to consider the effect of the explosive on the elastomer in question. For example, many elastomers are severely attacked by nitrogen oxides and nitroglycerine.

7.7 Effects of Elastomers on Vacuum Conditions

Many rubber compounds contain plasticizers and other ingredients that evaporate or sublimate under high vacuum conditions and deposit as a thin film on the surrounding surface. Therefore, it is particularly important in vacuum applications to choose rubber compounds with the least weight loss under high vacuum conditions. **IIR** compounds have long been the preferred material for vacuum applications because of their low permeability rates for gases and their low weight loss. However, if resistance to high temperatures and aggressive chemicals is required, it is necessary to use **FPM** or even **FFKM**, depending on the working conditions.

7.8 Effects of Elastomers on Meters

Rubber compounds used in meters or other devices that must be read through glass, a liquid or plastic must be free from volatile ingredients that can discolor these materials and hinder vision. For these applications properly post-cured **VMQ** and **FPM** are recommended.

CHAPTER 8

Types of Crude Rubbers – Chemistry, Compounding, Vulcanizate Properties and Applications

8.1 Introduction

The nomenclature and classification of elastomers according to different aspects have been briefly reviewed in chapter 3. Furthermore, factors of their environmental aging and resistance to various contiguous materials have been described in chapters 5 and 6, respectively.

The purpose of this chapter is to give a brief, up-to-date summary of the principal types of crude (base) rubbers, starting with general-purpose (nonoil-resistant) types and ending with special-purpose (oil-resistant) grades. The topics that are considered for each rubber type include its chemistry and compounding as well as the important properties and applications of its vulcanizates. (Thermoplastic elastomers will be treated separately in chapter 9.)

The figures and tables at the end of this chapter give a summary of the important physical and chemical properties of the most common elastomer types. They should be regarded as guidelines for selecting elastomeric materials for different applications. More details on chemical resistance to particular liquids are given in chapter 15. However, the final choice should be made after carrying out individual tests.

The typical trade names given below are examples only; the references are not intended as a complete list of trade names.

8.2 Natural Rubbers (NR)

8.2.1 Chemistry

The chemical name for NR is polyisoprene, which is a homopolymer of isoprene. It has the **cis-1,4** configuration **(Fig. 8.1)**, which means that carbon atoms **1** and **4** are both on the same side of the double bond. (In the **trans-1,4** configuration, these two carbon atoms are on opposite sides of the double bond.) In addition, the polymer contains small amounts of nonrubber substances, notably fatty acids, proteins and resinous materials that function as mild accelerators and activators for vulcanization.

NR is available in a variety of types and grades, including smoked sheets, air-dried sheets and pale crepes.

8.2.2 Compounding

NR compounds usually contain peptizers, carbon black or nonblack fillers or both, zinc oxide, fatty acids, processing aids, plasticizers, antioxidants, antiozonants,

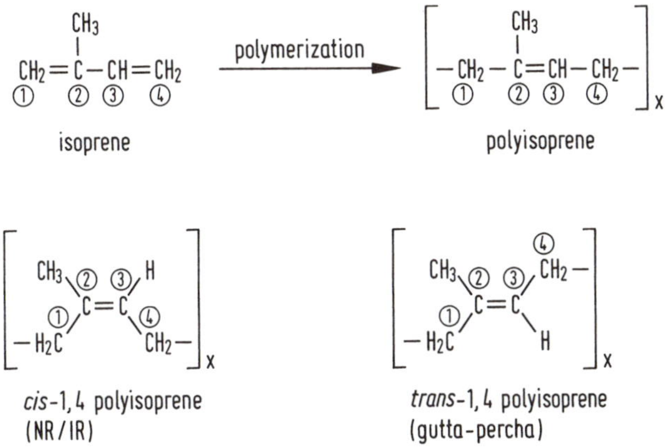

Fig. 8.1: Possible Configurations of 1,4 Polyisoprene

protective waxes and vulcanizing ingredients (usually sulphur, low sulphur or nonelemental sulphur vulcanizing systems; less frequently peroxides).

NR can be blended with other diene rubbers such as IR, SBR and BR.

8.2.3 Vulcanizate Properties

NR vulcanizates have high tensile strength over a wide hardness range. The high strength is due to crystallization of the polymer chains at high strains (section 1.7), enabling NR to be used in unfilled compounds. Furthermore, NR vulcanizates have the highest resilience of all elastomers (except BR), which is responsible for very low heat buildup (section 4.8). Further advantages include low compression set and stress relaxation, good electrical insulation and good resistance to abrasion, tear and fatigue.

NR can be compounded for continuous use at 90°C and for intermittent periods up to 100°C. The vulcanizates remain flexible at temperatures down to −55°C without adding plasticizers. However, they tend to crystallize readily when stored for long periods at low temperatures (section 4.15).

Like other unsaturated elastomers, NR vulcanizates are susceptible to attack by atmospheric ozone. However, the ozone and weather resistance can be improved by blending with a saturated rubber such as EPDM or by incorporating antiozonants and protective waxes in the compound.

NR vulcanizates are not resistant to petroleum-based oils and fuels but they can be used with a wide range of organic and inorganic chemicals, such as nonpetroleum-based automotive brake fluids, silicone oils and greases; glycols; alcohols; water; and nonoxidizing aqueous solutions of acids, alkalis and salts.

8.2.4 Applications

NR elastomers remain the best choice for many applications that require low heat buildup, such as large tires, carcasses of passenger-car tires, vibration mounts, springs and bearings. Other products include hoses, conveyor belts, gaskets, seals, rolls, rubberized fabrics, elastic bands and pharmaceutical goods.

8.3 Synthetic Polyisoprene Rubbers (IR)

Trade Names

Natsyn (Goodyear Tire and Rubber Co.)
Shell Isoprene Rubber (Shell International Chemical Co.)

8.3.1 Chemistry

IR is synthetic natural rubber; that is, **cis-1,4** polyisoprene **(Fig. 8.1)**. However, it does not contain the nonrubber substances that are present in NR.

One can differentiate between two basic types of synthetic polyisoprene. These depend upon the polymerization catalyst system used and are commonly referred to as "high" cis and "low" cis types.

The **high** cis grades contain approximately 96−97% cis-1,4 polyisoprene. Because of the high degree of stereoregularity, they are able to crystallize on stretching, like NR. Consequently, they can be compounded without fillers, giving tensile strength nearly as high as that of unfilled NR vulcanizates.

The **low** cis grades contain about 92−93% cis-1,4 polyisoprene. They have limited use because the physical properties of their vulcanizates are inferior to those of high cis types.

8.3.2 Compounding

In general, synthetic IR can be compounded using the same ingredients used for NR. However, the addition of high levels of fatty acids, activators and accelerators to synthetic IR is necessary to achieve the same vulcanization rates of NR.

Synthetic IR can be blended with other diene rubbers such as NR, SBR and BR.

8.3.3 Vulcanizate Properties

The vulcanizates of synthetic IR have less tendency to crystallize than do NR vulcanizates, which is advantageous for low-temperature applications. The aging properties and resistance to chemicals are similar to those of NR vulcanizates. However, the physical properties are not as good as those of NR elastomers.

8.3.4 Applications

In general, synthetic IR can be used alone or in blends with NR in the manufacture of most products where NR is the traditional choice.

8.4 Styrene-Butadiene Rubbers (SBR)

Former Designations

Buna S
GRS (Government Rubber Styrene)

Trade Names

Buna Hüls (Chemische Werke Hüls AG)
Plioflex, Pliolite (Goodyear Tire and Rubber Co.)
Cariflex S (Shell International Chemical Co.)

8.4.1 Chemistry

SBRs are copolymers of butadiene and styrene **(Fig. 8.2)**. The regular grades contain 23% styrene. Increasing styrene content leads to a loss in resilience and a rise in the freezing point of the vulcanizates.

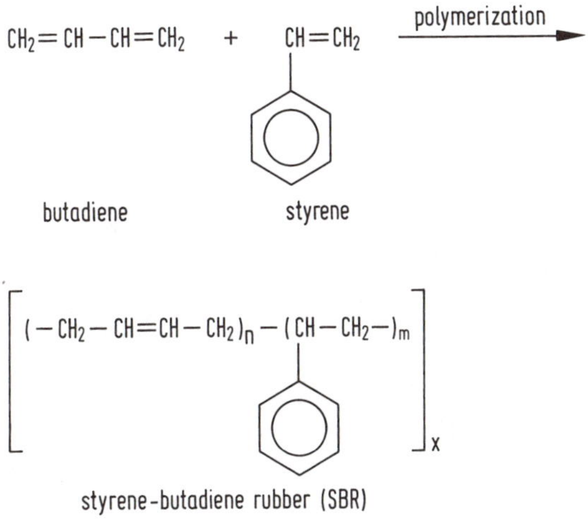

$$CH_2=CH-CH=CH_2 \quad + \quad CH=CH_2 \xrightarrow{\text{polymerization}}$$

butadiene   styrene

$$\left[(-CH_2-CH=CH-CH_2)_n - (CH-CH_2-)_m \right]_x$$

styrene-butadiene rubber (SBR)

Fig. 8.2: Synthesis of SBR

The oil-extended grades (with and without carbon black) contain naphthenic or highly aromatic oils in the range of 25–50 parts by weight per 100 parts by weight of polymer.

8.4.2 Compounding

In general, SBR can be compounded using the same ingredients for NR. However, SBR cures more slowly than NR and hence either more accelerator or a more active accelerator system is required than for NR.

SBR can be blended with other diene rubbers such as NR, IR and BR. Polymers containing a high proportion of styrene are widely used in blends with diene rubbers to give improved wear resistance and high hardness in conjunction with low specific gravity.

8.4.3 Vulcanizate Properties

In contrast to NR, the tensile strength of SBR gum vulcanizates (i.e., unfilled compounds) is very poor (about 10–15% of that of NR elastomers). This is because of the absence of crystallization on stretching the gum vulcanizate (section 1.7). Consequently, these rubbers do not develop high tensile strengths without the aid of reinforcing fillers. The resilience and low-temperature behavior of SBR vulcanizates are inferior to those of NR, but heat aging characteristics are better. The vulcanizates have an operational temperature range of −50 to +100°C and they show no tendency to crystallize at low temperatures.

Like other highly unsaturated elastomers, SBR vulcanizates show poor ozone resistance, which can be improved by blending with EPDM or by incorporating antiozonants and protective waxes.

SBR vulcanizates are not resistant to petroleum-based oils and greases or hydrocarbon fuels, but they are resistant to nonpetroleum-based automotive brake fluids, silicone oils and greases; glycols; alcohols; water; and nonoxidizing aqueous solutions of acids, alkalis and salts.

8.4.4 Applications

SBR was produced during the Second World War as a substitute for NR. Generally speaking, SBR can be used in many applications as a replacement for NR, except in severe dynamic applications requiring low heat buildup on flexing (e.g., high-performance tires for trucks).

8.5 Polybutadiene Rubbers (BR)

Trade Names

Budene (Goodyear Tire and Rubber Co.)
Buna CB (Bayer AG)

8.5.1 Chemistry

BR is a homopolymer of butadiene. The high cis grades contain approximately 97–98% cis-1,4 butadiene units **(Fig. 8.3)**. Oil-extended grades (with and without carbon black) are also available.

8.5.2 Compounding

Polybutadiene rubbers are more difficult to process than NR or SBR. Therefore, they are normally used in blends with other rubbers such as NR, IR, SBR or NBR

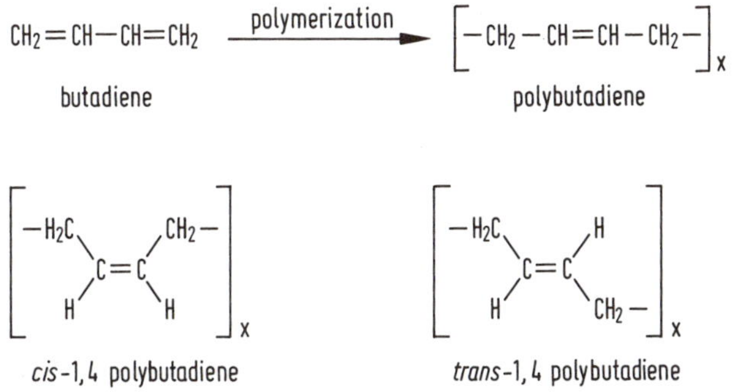

$$CH_2=CH-CH=CH_2 \xrightarrow{\text{polymerization}} \left[-CH_2-CH=CH-CH_2-\right]_x$$

butadiene   polybutadiene

cis-1,4 polybutadiene   trans-1,4 polybutadiene

Fig. 8.3: Possible Configurations of 1,4 Polybutadiene

to improve the abrasion resistance, resilience and low-temperature flexibility. The blends usually contain less than 50% of BR and often only 10−25%.

8.5.3 Vulcanizate Properties

The vulcanizates of 100% BR have high abrasion resistance, the highest resilience of all known elastomers and, with the exception of silicone vulcanizates, the lowest glass transition temperature (T_g). However, the skid resistance on wet roads is poor.

The characteristics of environmental aging and chemical resistance to fluids are similar to those of SBR vulcanizates.

8.5.4 Applications

Polybutadiene rubbers are used mainly in blends with SBR in the production of tire treads and with NR for truck tires. They are also used in blends with other rubbers such as NBR in manufacturing a great number of mechanical goods to increase their resilience, to improve their low-temperature flexibility or to reduce their heat buildup on flexing.

8.6 Polynorbornene Rubber

Trade Name

Norsorex (at the present time, CDF Chimie is the sole producer of polynorbornene)

8.6.1 Chemistry

Norsorex is a homopolymer based on norbornene monomer. The polymerization occurs through ring opening rather than through the reaction of a double bond or

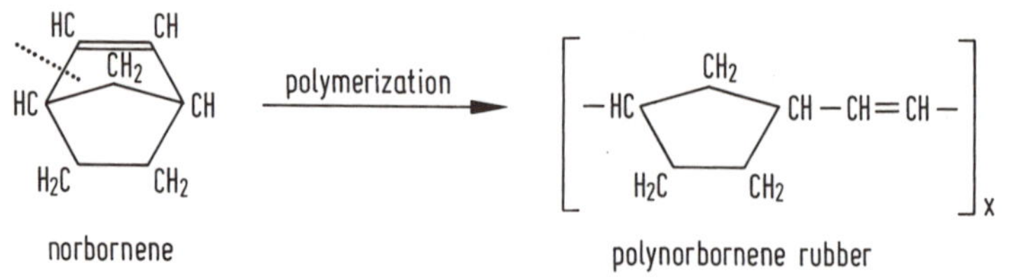

Fig. 8.4: Synthesis of Polynorbornene Rubber

by condensation. The polymerization reaction is illustrated in **Fig. 8.4**. This type of polymerization produces very high molecular weights. The molecular weight of norsorex exceeds 2,000,000.

Since the unsaturation of the monomer is retained in the polymer, polynorbornene belongs to the group of highly unsaturated hydrocarbon rubbers. Polynorbornene rubber is not yet identified by a standard designation.

The basic polymer is a thermoplastic powder with a glass transition temperature (Tg) of about 35°C. By adding a wide variety of mineral oils or ester plasticizers, the Tg can be lowered to about −60°C and the polymer acquires rubbery properties. In this respect, it resembles polyvinyl chloride (PVC).

8.6.2 Compounding

Polynorbornene formulations usually contain plasticizers, fillers (carbon black or mineral fillers or both), antioxidants, antiozonants, protective waxes, zinc oxide, processing aids and a curing system.

Plasticizers are necessary since they will depress the Tg below room temperature and thus determine the ultimate low-temperature flexibility of the vulcanizate. Aromatic oils are most compatible with polynorbornene, followed by naphthenic, paraffinic and, finally, ester plasticizers. Polynorbornene is capable of accepting very high levels of both oil and filler. In many formulations 200 phr of a naphthenic oil plus 200 phr filler are used.

Vulcanization is achieved with sulphur and conventional accelerators. Polynorbornene can be blended with EPDM to improve resistance to ozone and weather.

8.6.3 Vulcanizate Properties

Polynorbornene can be compounded to give very soft vulcanizates having a hardness as low as 20 Shore A with tensile strengths in excess of 10 N/mm².

Resistance to ozone and aging is poor. However, this resistance can be improved by adding antioxidants, antiozonants and protective waxes or by blending with EPDM. The normal operating temperature range is −30 to +70°C.

Resistance to liquids depends not only on the nature of the liquid but also on the type and level of plasticizer in the vulcanizates. Generally speaking, polynorbornene vulcanizates swell in liquids considerably less than do the other hydrocarbon elastomers. This is because of plasticizer extraction, which results in either a reduced swelling or a shrinkage. The extent of swelling or shrinkage depends on the plasticizer level in the vulcanizate.

The resistance to mineral oils is comparable to that of some oil-resistant elastomers. **Table 8.1** shows the volume changes of a selected norbornene compound (containing 200 phr naphthenic oil plus 200 phr carbon black) in ASTM oil Nos. 1, 2 and 3 at 70°C. High shrinkage usually occurs in oils with low swelling effect, such as ASTM oil No. 1. On the other hand, liquids with high swelling power (such as 100% aromatic and chlorinated hydrocarbons) cause rather high swelling to polynorbornene vulcanizates. However, the volume increase is still considerably lower than that of other hydrocarbon elastomers in the same liquid.

Table 8.1: Resistance of a Typical Polynorbornene Vulcanizate (Containing 200 phr Naphthenic Oil and 200 phr Carbon Black) to ASTM Oils after 70 h at 70°C

Medium	Approximate Volume Change (%)
ASTM oil No. 1	−15
ASTM oil No. 2	+ 3
ASTM oil No. 3	+60

Table 8.2: Resistance of a Typical Polynorbornene Vulcanizate (Containing 200 phr Naphthenic Oil and 200 phr Carbon Black) to Organic Liquids after 70 h at Room Temperature

Medium	Approximate Volume Change (%)
Acetone	− 25
Methylethyl ketone	− 30
Ethyl acetate	− 25
Ethanol	− 10
ASTM fuel A	− 15
ASTM fuel B	+ 30
ASTM fuel C	+ 80
ASTM fuel D	+130
Carbon tetrachloride	+170
Trichloroethylene	+175

Table 8.2 shows the volume changes of the same norbornene compound as mentioned above but in different types of liquids at room temperature.

8.6.4 Applications

In general, polynorbornene vulcanizates can be advantageously used as a substitute for cellular elastomers in many applications. They can be the first choice for sealing at low pressures between components with surface irregularity. Other applications include printing roll coverings, vibration and shock absorbers and electrical insulators.

8.7 Butyl Rubbers (IIR)

Trade Names

Exxon Butyl (Exxon Chemical Co.)

8.7.1 Chemistry

Isobutene-isoprene rubbers (IIR), or butyl rubbers, are copolymers containing mostly isobutene (isobutylene) units with just a small percentage of isoprene units (**Fig. 8.5**). Unlike NR, IR, SBR, BR and NBR, butyl rubbers are highly saturated hydrocarbons containing only a small amount of double bonds. This small extent of unsaturation is introduced to furnish the necessary sites for vulcanization.

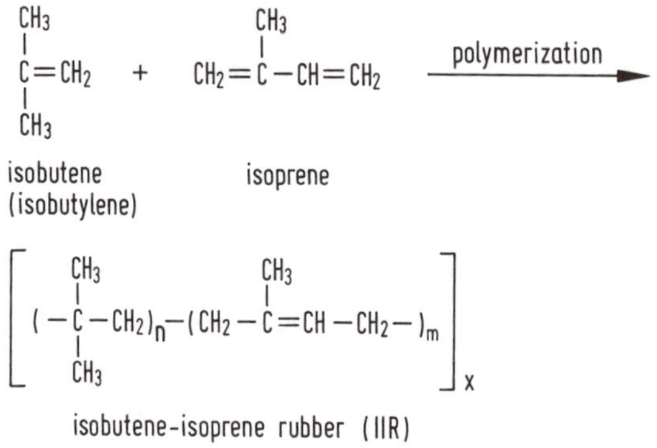

$$\underset{\substack{\text{isobutene}\\\text{(isobutylene)}}}{\overset{\displaystyle \underset{\text{CH}_3}{\overset{\text{CH}_3}{\underset{|}{\overset{|}{C}}}}=\text{CH}_2}{}} \quad + \quad \underset{\text{isoprene}}{\overset{\displaystyle \text{CH}_2=\underset{|}{\overset{\overset{\text{CH}_3}{|}}{C}}-\text{CH}=\text{CH}_2}{}} \quad \xrightarrow{\text{polymerization}}$$

$$\left[\left(-\underset{\underset{\text{CH}_3}{|}}{\overset{\overset{\text{CH}_3}{|}}{C}}-\text{CH}_2 \right)_n - \left(\text{CH}_2 - \underset{}{\overset{\overset{\text{CH}_3}{|}}{C}}=\text{CH}-\text{CH}_2 - \right)_m \right]_x$$

isobutene-isoprene rubber (IIR)

Fig. 8.5: Synthesis of IIR

The various grades of IIR differ in their levels of unsaturation (determined by the ratio of isoprene to isobutene). The grades with highest unsaturation have the fastest cure rate and somewhat lower ozone resistance than the more saturated grades. For maximum ozone resistance, the butyl grades with low levels of unsaturation should be used.

8.7.2 Compounding

IIR compounds usually contain carbon black or mineral fillers or both, plasticizers (mineral oils or esters), processing aids (e.g., zinc stearate, waxes, coumarone-indene resins), antioxidants, antiozonants and vulcanizing ingredients.

There are three types of cure systems:
1) sulphur and sulphur donor systems in conjunction with zinc oxide;
2) p-quinone dioxime activated by lead oxide (PbO_2); and
3) phenolic resins activated by tin chloride ($SnCl_2$) or halogen-containing rubbers such as CR.

Butyl rubbers cannot be cross-linked with organic peroxides since the peroxides degrade the polymer.

Sulphur cures are widely used in general-purpose compounds. The **p-quinone dioxime** cure is largely used in electrical insulation formulations to provide a maximum of ozone and aging resistance to the vulcanizates. The **resin** cure provides outstanding resistance to both wet and dry heat and is utilized in formulations of tire-curing bladders.

Because of their low unsaturation, butyl rubbers are not compatible with highly unsaturated rubbers such as NR, IR, SBR, BR and NBR. Even very small amounts of these rubbers will react preferentially with the curatives, resulting in undercured butyl rubber. Consequently, equipment that has been used for mixing or processing highly unsaturated rubbers must be thoroughly cleaned before it is used for butyl rubbers. Conversely, small amounts of IIR contamination in highly unsaturated rubbers must also be avoided because delamination of the vulcanizates will occur when the contaminant is present in the matrix.

8.7.3 Vulcanizate Properties

The distinctive properties of IIR vulcanizates are:
- very low gas and moisture permeability;
- high damping (ability to absorb mechanical energy);
- excellent electrical insulation properties;
- good ozone and weathering resistance, which increases with decrease in unsaturation of the polymer chain;
- good resistance to dry heat and steam; and
- good resistance to a great number of organic and inorganic products such as phosphate ester hydraulic fluids (section 6.11), silicone oils and greases, glycols, alcohols, ketones (e.g., acetone, MEK), low-molecular-weight esters (e.g., ethyl acetate), aqueous solutions of inorganic acids, alkalis and salts.

IIR vulcanizates are not resistant to:
- mineral-oil-based fluids and greases;
- synthetic hydrocarbon lubricants (e.g., polyalphaolefins);
- organic-ester-based lubricants; and
- hydrocarbon fuels.

Their resistance to animal and vegetable oils and fats is moderate; these substances can be tolerated in many static applications.

The mechanical properties of IIR vulcanizates are generally poorer than those of NR and SBR. The resilience is low at room temperature. However, low resilience can be of use in applications requiring high damping characteristics. The compression set is usually high but, when suitably compounded, low values can be achieved.

The operational temperature range of IIR elastomers is about -40 to $+120\,°C$. At $-40\,°C$ the vulcanizates are not brittle, but they do not exhibit elastic properties.

Butyl elastomers degrade by chain scission, becoming soft and tacky.

8.7.4 Applications

The main use for IIR elastomers is in gas retention applications such as tire inner tubes, ball bladders, vacuum seals and membranes. Other applications include tire curing bladders, steam hoses, shock absorbers, gaskets, wire and cable insulations, printing rolls and pharmaceutical closures.

8.7.5 Cross-linked Butyl Rubbers

Cross-linked butyl rubbers are obtained by polymerizing isobutene and isoprene with divinylbenzene to form cross-linked terpolymers. The extent of cross-linking is controlled by the level of divinylbenzene. The terpolymer is used mostly in an uncured state as a sealant, but it can also by cured with any of the systems used to cure unmodified butyl rubbers.

8.8 Halobutyl Rubbers (BIIR and CIIR)

8.8.1 Chemistry

Halobutyl rubbers include brombutyl rubbers (BIIR) and chlorobutyl rubbers (CIIR) and are produced by reacting elemental bromine or chlorine, respectively, with IIR dissolved in a light aliphatic hydrocarbon such as hexane.

The halogenation is carried out under carefully controlled conditions to ensure that the original double bonds are largely retained. After halogenation, the unsaturation remains but the double bonds move from the backbone to adjacent pendant positions (**Fig. 8.6**).

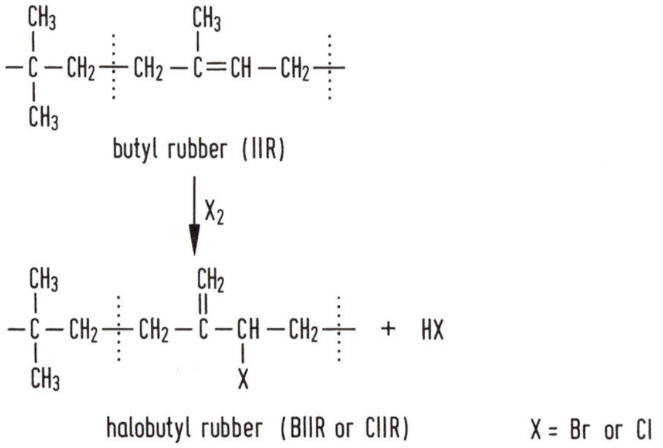

Fig. 8.6: Synthesis of Halobutyl Rubbers

Commercial bromobutyls contain typically 1.9−2.1 wt % bromine and chlorobutyls 1.1−1.3 wt % chlorine.

The halogenated IIRs do not belong to polar rubbers because the halogen contents are very low. They retain most of the distinctive and desirable properties of unmodified IIR.

8.8.2 Compounding

The same compounding ingredients and cure systems of regular IIR can be used with the halogenated grades. In addition, several other vulcanizing systems can be used because of the presence of both double bonds and reactive halogen atoms. The chlorobutyls are appreciably more cure-reactive than unmodified butyls (i.e., they cure much faster and reach a higher state of cure), but they are less reactive than bromobutyls.

The phenolic resin cure does not require the addition of halides to activate the resin, because halogen is already present in the rubber.

Unlike regular butyls and chlorobutyls, bromobutyls can be vulcanized with peroxides. Furthermore, they are capable of vulcanizing without zinc oxide or any other zinc salt using diamines as curatives. This is of particular importance for special applications requiring zinc-free compounds (e.g., in some special pharmaceutical closures).

Unlike regular IIR, the halobutyls can be blended and covulcanized with highly unsaturated rubbers such as NR, IR, SBR, BR and NBR. Consequently, there is no need for the stringent contamination precautions associated with the mixing and processing of regular butyl rubbers (section 8.7.2).

8.8.3 Vulcanizate Properties

BIIR and CIIR vulcanizates retain the characteristic properties of regular IIR elastomers such as low gas permeability, high hysteresis and high resistance to ozone, weather and chemicals.

Halobutyl vulcanizates usually contain small quantities of vulcanization by-products, mainly water-soluble salts. Consequently, they are less moisture resistant than IIR vulcanizates and are less suitable for use in electrical insulation.

8.8.4 Applications

The major applications of halobutyl rubbers include chemical-resistant O-rings and gaskets, vacuum seals and membranes, steam hoses, pharmaceutical closures, white tire sidewalls and tire inner tubes.

8.9 Ethylene-Propylene Rubbers (EPM and EPDM)

Trade Names

Nordel (Du Pont)
Vistalon (Exxon Chemicals Co.)
Keltan (DSM)
Buna AP (Chemische Werke Hüls AG)

8.9.1 Chemistry

The ethylene-propylene rubbers are of two types:
1) **EPM**: fully saturated copolymers of ethylene and propylene **(Fig. 8.7)**; and

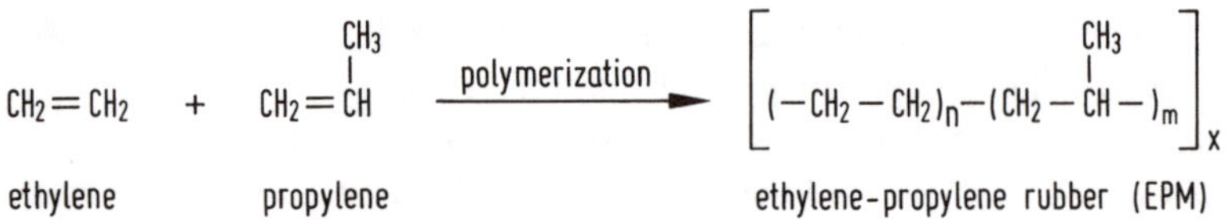

$$CH_2=CH_2 \quad + \quad CH_2=\underset{\underset{CH_3}{|}}{CH} \quad \xrightarrow{\text{polymerization}} \quad \left[(-CH_2-CH_2)_n-(CH_2-\underset{\underset{CH_3}{|}}{CH}-)_m \right]_x$$

$$\text{ethylene} \qquad\qquad \text{propylene} \qquad\qquad\qquad \text{ethylene-propylene rubber (EPM)}$$

Fig. 8.7: Synthesis of EPM

2) **EPDM**: terpolymers of ethylene, propylene and a small percentage of a noncon-
    jugated diene, which provides unsaturation in side chains pendent from the fully
    saturated backbone.
      There are three basic dienes **(Fig. 8.8)** used as the third monomer:
1) 1,4 hexadiene (1,4 **HD**);
2) dicyclopentadiene (**DCPD**); and
3) 5-ethylidene norbornene (**ENB**).

$$CH_2=CH-CH_2-CH=CH-CH_3$$

1,4 hexadiene (1,4 HD)

dicyclopentadiene (DCPD)   5-ethylidene norbornene (ENB)

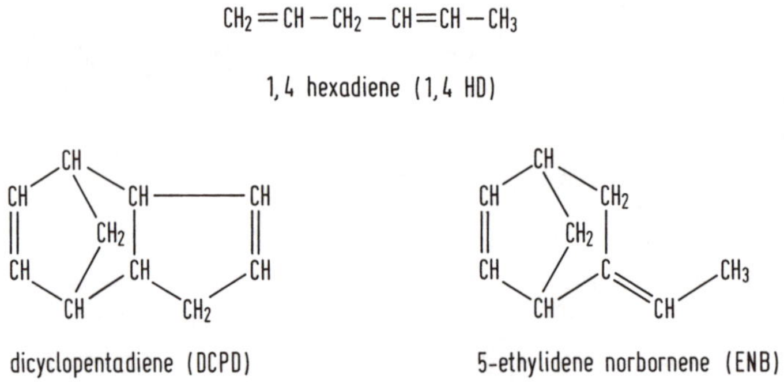

Fig. 8.8: Basic Dienes Used for the Synthesis of EPDM

The EPM rubbers, being completely saturated, require organic peroxides or
radiation for vulcanization. The EPDM terpolymers can be vulcanized with perox-

ides, radiation or sulphur. EPDM grades containing ENB as a diene component **(Fig. 8.9)** have greater reactivity toward sulphur vulcanization, and the reactivity increases with increasing the ENB level.

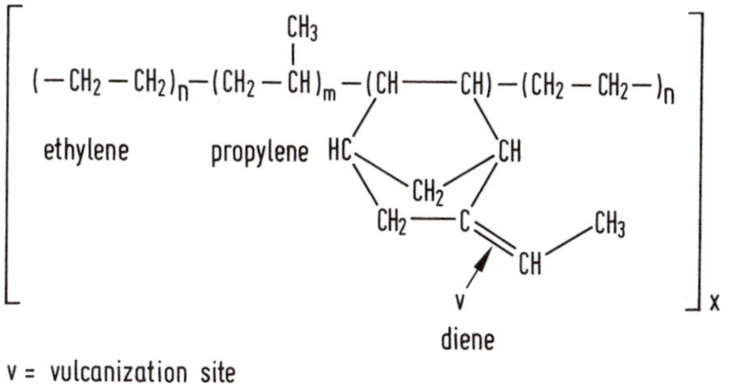

v = vulcanization site

Fig. 8.9: Structural Formula of an EPDM with ENB

EPM and EPDM rubbers have varying ethylene/propylene ratios. The ethylene content in the polymer can vary from about 75 to 45%. Rubber grades of very high molecular weight are extended with large amounts of mineral oil, typically 25 to 50 phr.

8.9.2 Compounding

EPM and EPDM compounds usually contain carbon black or light fillers or both, zinc oxide, antioxidants, processing aids, petroleum-based plasticizers and curing ingredients.

Rubber grades with a higher ethylene content can be more easily processed and more highly loaded with fillers and oils, but the vulcanizates will exhibit inferior low-temperature properties and high compression set.

As has been mentioned, EPM rubbers can be cured only with peroxides and EPDMs with peroxides or conventional sulphur cure systems. Peroxides are used for applications requiring good high-temperature performance and low compression set.

It should be noted that many fillers, antioxidants, plasticizers and processing aids inhibit vulcanization by peroxides. Consequently, the compounding ingredients should be selected with care.

EPDM grades containing a high level of ENB have the greatest tendency to be blended with highly unsaturated rubbers such as NR, IR, SBR, BR and NBR.

8.9.3 Vulcanizate Properties

The properties of vulcanizates produced from EPM and EPDM rubbers are basically the same. Both have fair tensile strength over a wide hardness range and excellent resistance to ozone, weathering and chemical attack. Furthermore, they exhibit very good electrical insulation properties.

Other properties, particularly compression set, high-temperature performance and low-temperature flexibility, are highly dependent on the formulation and polymer composition. Peroxide-cured compounds exhibit excellent heat aging properties and resistance to compression set up to 150°C. As the ethylene content of the polymer increases, compression set resistance and low-temperature flexibility will deteriorate.

Sulphur-cured EPDM compounds have high compression set and are less resistant to high temperatures. Peroxide-cured EPM and EPDM grades with low ethylene content have a service temperature range from −40 to +150°C and short exposures to even higher temperatures.

In contrast to IIR, the double bonds in EPDM are located in the side groups. Consequently, the EPDM vulcanizates (when peroxide cured) retain the excellent properties that the EPM elastomers possess.

EPM and EPDM vulcanizates are resistant to:
- nonpetroleum-based automotive brake fluids;
- aryl and alkyl-aryl phosphate esters (section 6.11);
- hot water and steam, up to 200°C with peroxide-cured vulcanizates (in the absence of air);
- aqueous solutions of inorganic acids, alkalis and salts;
- polyalkylene-glycol-based fluids;
- alcohols, glycols, ketones (e.g., acetone, MEK) and low-molecular-weight esters (e.g., ethyl acetate); and
- silicone oils and greases.

Their resistance to animal and vegetable oils and fats is moderate; these substances can be tolerated in many static applications.

EPM and EPDM vulcanizates are not resistant to:
- mineral-oil-based fluids and greases;
- synthetic hydrocarbon lubricants (e.g., polyalphaolefins);
- organic-ester-based lubricants; and
- hydrocarbon fuels.

8.9.4 Applications

Ethylene-propylene rubbers are used for a wide range of products, including O-rings, gaskets, window and door seals, wire and cable insulations, roller covers, conveyor belts, hoses and water-proofing sheets.

8.10 Chemically Cross-linked Polyethylene (PE)

8.10.1 Chemistry

Polyethylene (PE) is a thermoplastic homopolymer (plastomer) produced by polymerizing ethylene gas (see Fig. 1.1). Like rubbers, PE can be converted to an elastomeric material by cross-linking the polymer chain using a cross-linking agent, usually organic peroxides or electron beams (radiation cure).

Chemical cross-linking provides flow resistance above the melting point of the polymer. This allows applications of cross-linked PE at temperatures above 125°C.

8.10.2 Compounding

Chemically cross-linked PE is used extensively without any fillers being compounded, only with antioxidants and cross-linking agents. However, incorporation of fillers can impart advantageous properties such as resistance to deformation, flame and corona.

Both peroxide and radiation cures require proper selection of the compounding ingredients, such as co-agents, antioxidants and fillers.

8.10.3 Vulcanizate Properties

Generally speaking, the environmental aging, electrical properties and fluid resistance are similar to those of EPM vulcanizates (section 8.9.3).

8.10.4 Applications

Chemically cross-linked PE compounds are most extensively used in the wire and cable industry.

8.11 Acrylonitrile-Butadiene Rubbers (NBR)

Former Designation

Buna N

Trade Names

Chemigum (Goodyear Tire and Rubber Co.)
Perbunan (Bayer AG)

8.11.1 Chemistry

Acrylonitrile-butadiene rubbers (NBR), or, simply, nitrile rubbers, are copolymers of butadiene and acrylonitrile **(Fig. 8.10)**. They are available in five grades based on the acrylonitrile (**ACN**) content:
1) very low nitriles: typically 18−20% ACN;
2) low nitriles: typically 28−29% ACN;
3) medium nitriles: typically 33−34% ACN;
4) high nitriles: typically 38−39% ACN;
5) very high nitriles: typically 45−48% ACN.

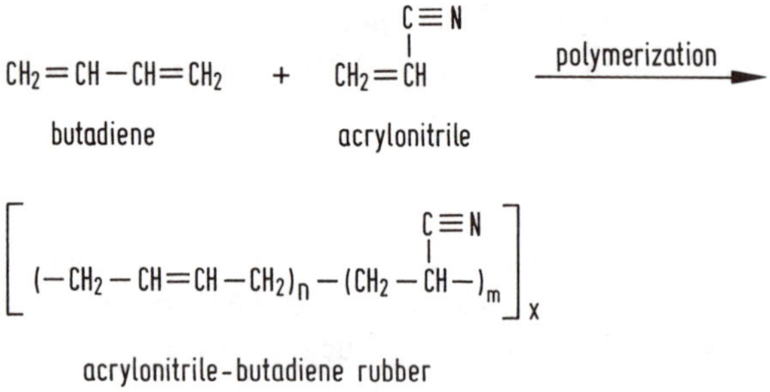

$$CH_2=CH-CH=CH_2 \quad + \quad CH_2=\overset{\overset{\displaystyle C\equiv N}{|}}{CH} \qquad \xrightarrow{\text{polymerization}}$$

butadiene   acrylonitrile

$$\left[(-CH_2-CH=CH-CH_2)_n -(CH_2-\overset{\overset{\displaystyle C\equiv N}{|}}{CH}-)_m \right]_x$$

acrylonitrile - butadiene rubber

Fig. 8.10: Synthesis of NBR

Many of the vulcanizate properties are directly related to the proportion of acrylonitrile in the rubber. As the ACN content is increased, the following changes in the vulcanizate properties occur:
– resistance to petroleum-based fluids and hydrocarbon fuels increases;
– low-temperature flexibility decreases;
– rebound resilience decreases;
– compression set deteriorates;
– gas permeability decreases;
– heat resistance improves;
– ozone resistance improves;
– abrasion resistance improves;
– tensile strength increases;
– hardness increases; and
– density increases.

In general, the high and very high nitriles are used in applications requiring good resistance to hydrocarbons of high aromatic contents (e.g., aromatic oils, gasolines).

The medium grades are used in cases where the oil is of lower aromatic content or where higher swelling of the elastomer is tolerable. The low and very low nitriles are used with liquids of low swelling effect [e.g., paraffinic oils and polyalphaolefins (section 6.8.1)] or in cases where low-temperature flexibility is of greater importance than is oil resistance.

8.11.2 Compounding

As with SBR, nitrile rubbers require reinforcing fillers to obtain high strength, because the unfilled vulcanizates do not crystallize on stretching.

The polymer selection is an important factor in obtaining the best balance of oil resistance and low temperature flexibility.

Basically, nitrile rubber compounds contain nearly the same compounding ingredients used in NR and SBR. Ester-based plasticizers are generally used in NBR compounds to improve low-temperature properties. Sulphur donor and peroxide-curing systems are normally used for applications requiring good high-temperature performance and low compression set. NBR has poor compatibility with natural rubber, but it can be blended with SBR in all proportions. This reduces the overall oil resistance of the vulcanizate, but it is sometimes used also as a technique to counteract shrinkage caused by oils with low swelling power such as polyalphaolefins.

8.11.3 Vulcanizate Properties

As has been mentioned, many of the vulcanizate properties will vary depending upon the ACN content. However, it can be said that NBR vulcanizates have, in general, good physical properties over a wide hardness range. They are (like other highly unsaturated elastomers) not inherently ozone resistant. However, this property can be improved through compounding or through the use of NBR/PVC blends.

The electrical insulation properties are poor, although adequate for sheathing when oil resistance is required. Instead, conductive compounds can be obtained by using high nitriles with suitable compounding ingredients (section 4.17).

Gas permeability is generally low. Vulcanizates of high nitriles exhibit greater resistance to permeation approaching that of IIR elastomers. The low-temperature flexibility of NBR vulcanizates can be improved by adding ester-based plasticizers at some sacrifice in mechanical properties and heat resistance.

Suitably formulated NBR compounds have low compression set, and continuous operational temperature range from −40 to +100°C and for intermittent periods (in the absence of air) up to 120°C.

NBR vulcanizates are resistant to a wide range of petroleum-based greases and fluids, hydrocarbon fuels, vegetable and animal oils, silicone greases and oils, organic-ester-based fluids, polyalkylene glycols, water and aqueous solutions of nonoxidizing chemicals. However, they are not resistant to phosphate ester hydraulic fluids, nonpetroleum-based automotive brake fluids, aromatic hydrocarbons (e.g. benzene, toluene, xylene), halogenated hydrocarbons (e.g., trichloroethylene, carbon tetrachloride), ketones (e.g., acetone, MEK), low-molecular-weight esters (e.g., ethyl acetate), strong acids and oxidizing chemicals.

8.11.4 Applications

NBR elastomers are the most widely used materials for oil- and fuel-resistant components such as seals, gaskets, diaphragms, hoses and cable jacketing.

8.11.5 Carboxylated Nitrile Rubbers (XNBR)

Carboxylated nitrile rubbers (XNBR) are terpolymers of butadiene, acrylonitrile and an acidic monomer with a carboxylic group such as methacrylic or acrylic acid. The acrylonitrile and acidic monomers are distributed randomly through the polymer chain.

Carboxylated nitriles are available in grades that differ in ACN and acid content. The latter varies between about 2 and 10%. The carboxylic groups provide additional cure sites for zinc oxide or zinc peroxide.

XNBR vulcanizates retain the distinctive properties of regular NBR elastomers, but they show in addition much higher modulus, tensile strength and abrasion and tear resistance. Therefore, they are used in applications that require oil resistance, toughness and high abrasion resistance.

8.11.6 NBR/PVC Blends

Medium and high nitriles give a homogeneous polymer phase with PVC. Some of these blends are commercially available. They usually contain 30% PVC.

NBR/PVC vulcanizates have improved resistance to ozone, fire and swelling in mineral oils and hydrocarbon solvents. However, their use is restricted because of deficiencies in low-temperature flexibility and compression set resistance. Their main areas of application include hose covers, hose tubes and wire and cable covers.

It must also be pointed out that there are blends in which PVC predominates. In such blends, the rubber acts as a polymeric plasticizer for the PVC, which does not migrate and which improves properties such as cold flow and low-temperature flexibility.

8.12 Hydrogenated Acrylonitrile-Butadiene Rubbers (HNBR)

Former Designation

HSN (Highly Saturated Nitriles)

Trade Names

Therban (Bayer AG)
Zetpol (Nippon Zeon Co.)

8.12.1 Chemistry

Hydrogenated acrylonitrile-butadiene rubbers (HNBR) are currently produced by selective and controlled hydrogenation of NBR (section 8.11). The degree of hydrogenation can be varied by changing catalyst levels and reaction conditions. The hydrogenated product consists essentially of polymethylene chains containing known amounts of unsaturation (double bonds) and carrying nitrile ($-C\equiv N$) side groups **(Fig. 8.11)**. The highly saturated polymethylene chains provide excellent heat and ozone resistance whereas the nitrile groups give oil and fuel resistance. Increasing the degree of hydrogenation results in improved heat and ozone resistance.

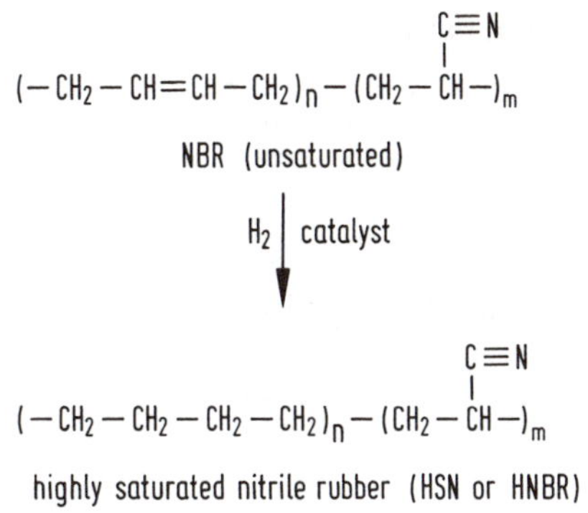

$$(-CH_2-CH=CH-CH_2)_n-(CH_2-\underset{\underset{C\equiv N}{|}}{CH}-)_m$$

NBR (unsaturated)

H_2 | catalyst

$$(-CH_2-CH_2-CH_2-CH_2)_n-(CH_2-\underset{\underset{C\equiv N}{|}}{CH}-)_m$$

highly saturated nitrile rubber (HSN or HNBR)

Fig. 8.11: Synthesis of HNBR

Depending on the degree of hydrogenation, there are two types of commercially available products. The first (almost saturated) contains just 1% or less of the original double bonds and can be cross-linked only with peroxides. The other type retains a larger percentage of the original double bonds (about 5−10%) and can be vulcanized with either peroxide or sulphur. However, peroxide cure is generally recommended for better compression set and heat resistance. Best results are obtained with the almost completely hyrogenated polymers. They combine the oil resistance of NBR with nearly the same amount of heat and ozone resistance of EPDM. As would be expected, increasing the nitrile content in HNBR results in reduced swelling in mineral oils, but with a surprisingly small amount of loss in low-temperature flexibility, compared with the regular NBR. This suggests that HNBR grades derived from a high acrylonitrile NBR should be used for the best balance of fluid resistance and low-temperature flexibility.

HNBR is considerably more expensive than regular NBR because a low-cost, specific hydrogenation catalyst has not yet been found.

8.12.2 Compounding

In general, the compounding principles applied to NBR are applicable to HNBR. As has been mentioned, peroxides are used for the highly saturated grades and sulphur cure systems or peroxides are used for the less saturated types.

A postcure in an oven with circulating hot air (typically three hours at 160°C) improves the physical properties, particularly compression set (section 2.10).

8.12.3 Vulcanizate Properties

HNBR vulcanizates have very good mechanical properties and show good resistance to:
- ozone and weather;
- aging in hot air and hot industrial lubricants (including those containing sulphur);
- hot water and steam up to 150°C;

– amine-based corrosion inhibitors and sour gas; and
– high-energy radiation.

The swelling behavior of HNBR vulcanizates in mineral oils and hydrocarbon fuels depends on the nitrile content. It is important to note that hydrogenation of NBR results in an increase of the volume changes of the vulcanizates in oils and fuels. In other words, HNBR vulcanizates swell more than the vulcanizates of the parent NBR. A vulcanizate of a hydrogenated NBR with 38% ACN, for example, will have nearly the same swelling behavior as regular NBR containing 34% ACN. The operational temperature range of peroxide-cured HNBR is −25 to +150°C and for short periods up to +170°C.

8.12.4 Applications

HNBR elastomers fill a gap between NBR and FPM in many areas of application. In general, they are replacing NBR elastomers in cases where resistance to excessive heat or especially aggressive environments is critical. In contrast to conventional FPM compounds, HNBR elastomers can withstand basic additives such as amine-based corrosion inhibitors. For this reason, HNBR components are finding wide applications, particularly in oil-field operations, where extreme hard conditions exist (section 6.29). They seem to maintain their performance under these conditions, whereas NBR and most conventional FPM elastomers show a degradation.

8.13 Chloroprene Rubbers (CR)

Trade Names

Neoprene (Du Pont)
Baypren (Bayer AG)

8.13.1 Chemistry

Chloroprene rubbers (CR) are essentially homopolymers of chloroprene (chlorobutadiene). The polymer chains have an almost entirely trans-1,4 configuration **(Fig. 8.12)**. Because of this high degree of stereoregularity they are able to crystallize on stretching (section 1.7). Consequently, the gum vulcanizates have high tensile strength. In this respect they resemble NR gum vulcanizates (section 8.2.3).

The chlorine atoms in the polymer chains reduce the reactivity of the double bonds toward many oxidizing agents, particularly oxygen and ozone (section 3.5.1). They also impart oil and flame resistance to the vulcanizates.

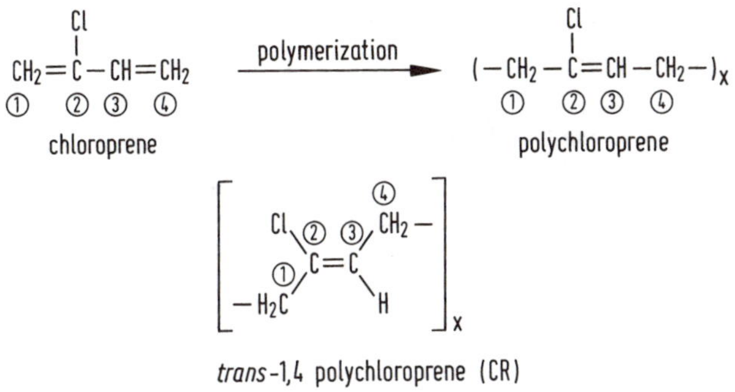

$$CH_2{=}\overset{\underset{\displaystyle |}{Cl}}{C}{-}CH{=}CH_2 \quad \xrightarrow{\text{polymerization}} \quad ({-}CH_2{-}\overset{\underset{\displaystyle |}{Cl}}{C}{=}CH{-}CH_2{-})_x$$

chloroprene ① ② ③ ④   polychloroprene ① ② ③ ④

trans-1,4 polychloroprene (CR)

Fig. 8.12: Synthesis of CR

8.13.2 Compounding

Typical CR compounds usually contain carbon black or mineral fillers or both, processing aids (e.g., petroleum oils, stearic acid, waxes and low-molecular-weight polyethylene), ester-based plasticizers, antioxidants, antiozonants and a vulcanizing agent.

In contrast to other highly unsaturated rubbers (e.g., NR, IR, SBR and NBR), sulphur is not an effective vulcanizing agent for CR. Instead, metal oxides in combination with an organic accelerator are used. The metal oxides serve also as acid acceptors for trace amounts of hydrogen chloride (HCl) that may be released from the polymer during processing, curing and vulcanizate aging. Usually a combination of zinc oxide (ZnO) and magnesium oxide (MgO) is used for general-purpose applications. For improved resistance to water, lead oxide (Pb_3O_4) is recommended in place of the MgO/ZnO combination.

8.13.3 Vulcanizate Properties

The distinctive properties of CR vulcanizates include:
- good resistance to ozone cracking, heat aging and chemical attack;
- low flammability (they burn when exposed to open flame and self-extinguish within a short time after removal from the flame); this property can be enhanced by special compounding;
- good resistance to silicate ester lubricants, silicone oils and greases;
- moderate to good resistance to a wide range of refrigerants, aliphatic hydrocarbons, mineral oils and greases (**Table 8.3** shows the average volume changes of typical CR vulcanizates in ASTM oil Nos. 1, 2 and 3 at different temperatures); and
- tendency to crystallize at low temperatures (section 4.15). This tendency can be reduced by the correct choice of polymer type and by compounding. However, crystallization is useful in the case of rubber-based adhesives because crystallization develops high bond strength to the contiguous materials (metals, rubbers, plastics, etc.).

Table 8.3: Resistance of Typical CR Vulcanizates to ASTM Oils after 70 h at Different Temperatures

Medium	Temperature (°C)	Average Volume Increase (%)
ASTM oil No. 1	70	0− 5
	100	5−10
	120	5−10
ASTM oil No. 2	70	20−25
	100	25−30
	120	25−30
ASTM oil No. 3	70	45−50
	100	50−60
	120	60−70

Properly formulated compounds permit service temperature between −40 and +100°C. Low compression set can be obtained by effecting a very tight cure.

The electrical properties are poor, although adequate for sheathing. The gas permeability is fairly low.

CR vulcanizates are not resistant to hydrocarbon fuels, phosphate esters and aromatic and chlorinated hydrocarbons.

8.13.4 Applications

Some of the most important applications of CR elastomers include adhesives, hoses, V belts, coated fabrics, wire and cable jackets, tire sidewalls and a variety of components (e.g. seals and gaskets) in contact with refrigerants, mild chemicals and atmospheric ozone.

8.14 Chlorinated Polyethylene Rubbers (CM)

Trade Names

CPE Elastomers (Dow Chemical)
Kelrinal (Hoechst AG)

8.14.1 Chemistry

The chlorinated polyethylene rubbers (CM) are unusual among synthetic rubbers in that they are produced by chemical modification of an existing polymer and not by polymerizing monomers.

As the name implies, chlorinated polyethylene rubbers are produced by reacting polyethylene with chlorine **(Fig. 8.13)**. They are supplied in a wide variety of grades with chlorine contents ranging from about 25 to 42% by weight. As the

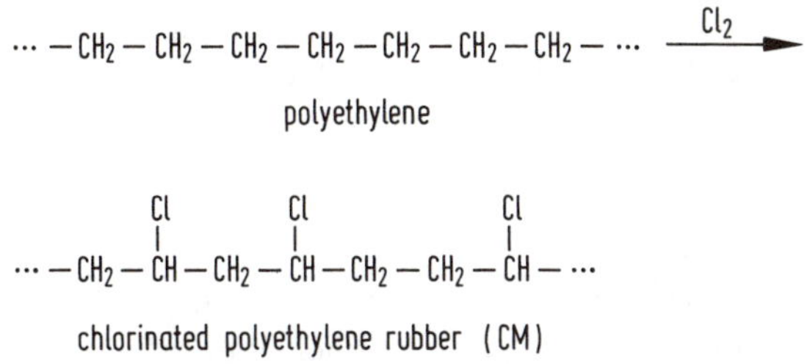

$$\cdots -CH_2-CH_2-CH_2-CH_2-CH_2-CH_2-CH_2- \cdots \xrightarrow{Cl_2}$$

polyethylene

$$\cdots -CH_2-\underset{\underset{Cl}{|}}{CH}-CH_2-\underset{\underset{Cl}{|}}{CH}-CH_2-CH_2-\underset{\underset{Cl}{|}}{CH}- \cdots$$

chlorinated polyethylene rubber (CM)

Fig. 8.13: Synthesis of CM

chlorine content increases, the oil and flame resistance are improved, but the low-temperature flexibility and heat resistance are impaired.

8.14.2 Compounding

The formulations of CM compounds normally include fillers, heat stabilizers, ester-based plasticizers, processing aids, antioxidants and a cure system. Organic peroxides are usually the preferred cross-linking agents for CM rubbers. Co-agents are often added to improve the rate and state of cure and to permit a lower peroxide dosage. As with peroxide cures in general, the compounding ingredients should be selected with care since acidic and unsaturated materials can seriously impair cross-linking efficiency. There are also other disadvantages in using peroxides, which have led to the development of "peroxide-less" vulcanization systems (based on N,N dialkylthiourea or a thiadiazole derivative). They provide much greater flexibility to the compounder, but the vulcanizates show less satisfactory heat aging and compression set resistance.

Like all chlorinated polymers, CM rubbers require heat stabilizers (or acid acceptors) to prevent the release of hydrochloric acid (HCl) at high processing or service temperatures. Magnesium oxide is most commonly used for this purpose. Where low water absorption is required, lead compounds (e.g., lead silicate) are used. Zinc oxide and other zinc compounds must be avoided because they catalytically decompose the polymer.

CM rubbers can be blended with peroxide vulcanizable rubbers such as EPDM.

8.14.3 Vulcanizate Properties

The major characteristics of CM vulcanizates are:
- high resistance to ozone, weather and a great number of corrosive and oxidizing chemicals;
- very good color stability;
- good resistance to dry heat (continuously up to about 125°C and for limited periods at temperatures as high as 150°C);
- fair resistance to mineral oils and aliphatic solvents (resistance to swelling increases as the chlorine content increases);
- low flammability, which can be enhanced by adding flame retardants;

– low compression set at high temperatures (when peroxide cured); and
– poor low-temperature flexibility (addition of ester plasticizers is frequently needed for low-temperature applications).

8.14.4 Applications

CM elastomers find wide application in wire and cable sheathing where resistance to oils, chemicals, ozone and flame is required. Other applications include hoses and automotive parts.

8.15 Chlorosulphonated Polyethylene Rubbers (CSM)

Trade Names

Hypalon (Du Pont)
Noralon (Denki Kagaku Chemical Co.)

8.15.1 Chemistry

Like CM (section 8.14), the chlorosulphonated polyethylene rubbers (CSM) are also produced by modification of an existing polymer. As the name implies, CSM rubbers are produced by reacting polyethylene with a mixture of chlorine (Cl) and sulphur dioxide (SO_2) gas in appropriate ratio. The resulting polymer has the chemical structure shown in **Fig. 8.14**. The chlorosulphonation changes the rather rigid polyethylene into a rubber with reactive cure sites which can be processed and vulcanized like any other rubber.

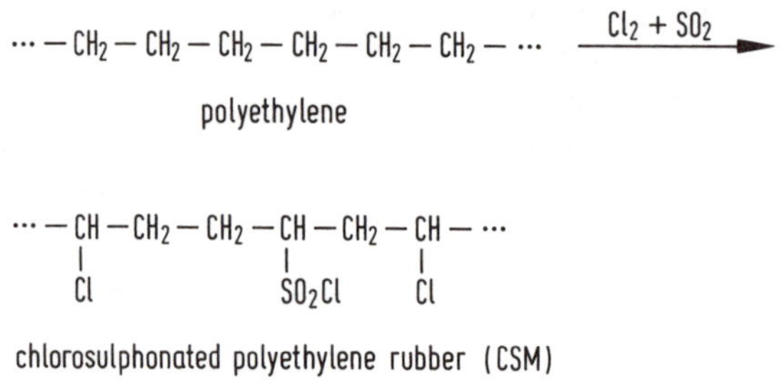

$$\cdots - CH_2 - CH_2 - CH_2 - CH_2 - CH_2 - CH_2 - \cdots \xrightarrow{\quad Cl_2 + SO_2 \quad}$$

polyethylene

$$\cdots - \underset{\underset{Cl}{|}}{CH} - CH_2 - CH_2 - \underset{\underset{SO_2Cl}{|}}{CH} - CH_2 - \underset{\underset{Cl}{|}}{CH} - \cdots$$

chlorosulphonated polyethylene rubber (CSM)

Fig. 8.14: Synthesis of CSM

The chlorine content of commercially available CSM grades ranges from about 24 to 43% by weight. The range of sulphur contents is about 1.0–1.5% by weight, the majority having a sulphur content of about 1.0%.

8.15.2 Compounding

Typical CSM compounds usually contain carbon black or mineral fillers or both, plasticizers, processing aids, antioxidants and vulcanizing ingredients.

The high reactivity of the sulphonyl chloride offers a wide choice of curing systems. However, the vulcanization is normally accomplished by metal oxides in the presence of conventional sulphur donors and accelerators. Magnesium oxide is usually used unless a vulcanizate of high water resistance is required. In this case lead oxide (litharge) is recommended. The cross-linking reaction probably involves interaction between the metal oxide and sulphonyl chloride groups of the polymer chains to form metal sulphonate bridges.

The metal oxides have another function in the compound. They act as acid acceptors; that is, they absorb acid by-products of the curing reaction and maintain sufficient alkalinity to allow effective curing. Zinc oxide and other zinc compounds are excluded because they cause polymer degradation on heat aging or natural weathering.

CSM rubbers can also be cured with peroxides, provided that care is excercised in the selection of fillers and other ingredients. Usually a co-agent is added to improve the effectiveness of the peroxide. An acid acceptor must also be added. The significant advantages of peroxide cure systems are the improvements in heat aging and compression set resistance.

8.15.3 Vulcanizate Properties

The distinctive properties of CSM vulcanizates include:
- excellent resistance to ozone, weather and discoloration by sunlight and ultraviolet light;
- excellent resistance to a great number of corrosive or oxidizing chemicals;
- good resistance to dry heat (continuously up to about 125°C and for limited periods at temperatures as high as 150°C);
- low flammability (the best flame resistance is obtained with the high-chlorine grades);
- moderate to good resistance to mineral oils, depending on the chlorine content of the base rubber (**Table 8.4** shows the average volume changes of general-purpose CSM vulcanizates in ASTM oil Nos. 1, 2 and 3 at 120°C); lower swell values are obtained with CSM grades having high chlorine contents at some sacrifice in low-temperature flexibility;
- good resistance to silicone oils and greases;
- good hot water resistance (when cured with lead oxide); and
- low gas permeability.

Table 8.4: Resistance of Typical CSM Vulcanizates to ASTM Oils after 70h at 120°C

Medium	Average Volume Increase (%)
ASTM oil No. 1	8–12
ASTM oil No. 2	30–45
ASTM oil No. 3	70–90

The low-temperature resistance is generally limited depending on the chlorine content of the CSM grade used. It can be improved by adding plasticizers. In general, the compression set resistance is not satisfactory.

8.15.4 Applications

CSM elastomers are widely used in electrical applications as protective jacketing where resistance to heat, flame, ozone, weather, corrosive chemicals and oils are important properties.

Other applications include coating, weather-resistant membranes, hoses, roll covers, colored extrudates and acid-resistant tank linings.

8.15.5 Alkylated Chlorosulphonated Polyethylene Rubbers (ACSM)

Trade Name

Ascium (Du Pont)

Alkylated CSM (ACSM) is a chemically modified version of Du Pont's CSM (Hypalon) that has extra alkyl groups in the polymer chains, as shown in **Fig. 8.15**. According to Du Pont, belts made from ACSM have better aging resistance at 140 °C than those based on HNBR.

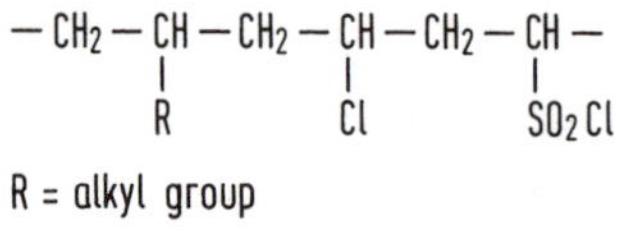

$$- CH_2 - CH - CH_2 - CH - CH_2 - CH -$$
$$\qquad\quad | \qquad\qquad | \qquad\qquad |$$
$$\qquad\quad R \qquad\qquad Cl \qquad\quad SO_2Cl$$

R = alkyl group

Fig. 8.15: Structural Formula of Alkylated CSM (ACSM)

8.16 Polyacrylate Rubbers (ACM)

Trade Names

Cyanacryl (Enichem Elastomeri)
Europrene AR (Enichem Elastomeri)

8.16.1 Chemistry

Polyacrylate rubbers (ACM) of today are saturated copolymers of monomeric acrylic esters and reactive cure site monomers. The first commercial products were based predominantly upon ethyl acrylate or butyl acrylate and, in some grades, together with acrylic monomers of the alkoxyalkyl type such as methoxyethyl acrylate and ethoxyethyl acrylate **(Fig. 8.16)**.

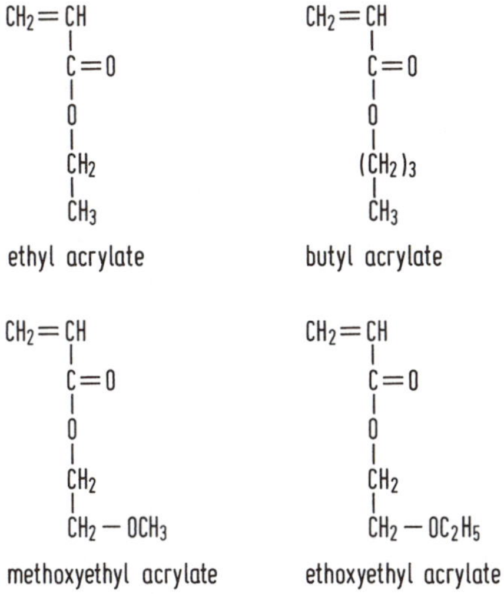

$$
\begin{array}{ll}
\text{CH}_2\!=\!\text{CH} & \text{CH}_2\!=\!\text{CH} \\
\quad\ |\ & \quad\ |\ \\
\quad \text{C}\!=\!\text{O} & \quad \text{C}\!=\!\text{O} \\
\quad\ |\ & \quad\ |\ \\
\quad \text{O} & \quad \text{O} \\
\quad\ |\ & \quad\ |\ \\
\quad \text{CH}_2 & \quad (\text{CH}_2)_3 \\
\quad\ |\ & \quad\ |\ \\
\quad \text{CH}_3 & \quad \text{CH}_3 \\
\text{ethyl acrylate} & \text{butyl acrylate}
\end{array}
$$

$$
\begin{array}{ll}
\text{CH}_2\!=\!\text{CH} & \text{CH}_2\!=\!\text{CH} \\
\quad\ |\ & \quad\ |\ \\
\quad \text{C}\!=\!\text{O} & \quad \text{C}\!=\!\text{O} \\
\quad\ |\ & \quad\ |\ \\
\quad \text{O} & \quad \text{O} \\
\quad\ |\ & \quad\ |\ \\
\quad \text{CH}_2 & \quad \text{CH}_2 \\
\quad\ |\ & \quad\ |\ \\
\quad \text{CH}_2-\text{OCH}_3 & \quad \text{CH}_2-\text{OC}_2\text{H}_5 \\
\text{methoxyethyl acrylate} & \text{ethoxyethyl acrylate}
\end{array}
$$

Fig. 8.16: Typical Basic Monomers Used for the Synthesis of ACM

The more modern types of ACM rubbers contain minor amounts (less than 5% by weight) of cure site monomers with functional groups whose presence increases the cure rate and improves the vulcanizate properties. The cure site monomers can

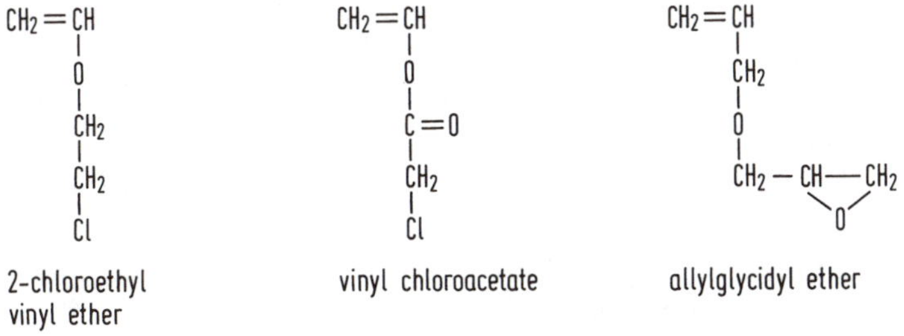

$$
\begin{array}{lll}
\text{CH}_2\!=\!\text{CH} & \text{CH}_2\!=\!\text{CH} & \text{CH}_2\!=\!\text{CH} \\
\quad\ |\ & \quad\ |\ & \quad\ |\ \\
\quad \text{O} & \quad \text{O} & \quad \text{CH}_2 \\
\quad\ |\ & \quad\ |\ & \quad\ |\ \\
\quad \text{CH}_2 & \quad \text{C}\!=\!\text{O} & \quad \text{O} \\
\quad\ |\ & \quad\ |\ & \quad\ |\ \\
\quad \text{CH}_2 & \quad \text{CH}_2 & \quad \text{CH}_2-\text{CH}\!-\!\!-\!\text{CH}_2 \\
\quad\ |\ & \quad\ |\ & \quad\qquad\ \backslash\text{O}\diagup \\
\quad \text{Cl} & \quad \text{Cl} & \\
\text{2-chloroethyl} & \text{vinyl chloroacetate} & \text{allylglycidyl ether} \\
\text{vinyl ether} & &
\end{array}
$$

Fig. 8.17: Typical Cure Site Monomers Used for the Synthesis of ACM

be divided into two groups: one containing labile chlorine atoms and the other chlorine-free. The names and chemical structures of the most widely used cure site monomers are given in **Fig. 8.17**. The polymer chain of an ACM rubber with a chlorine-containing site monomer is shown in **Fig. 8.18**.

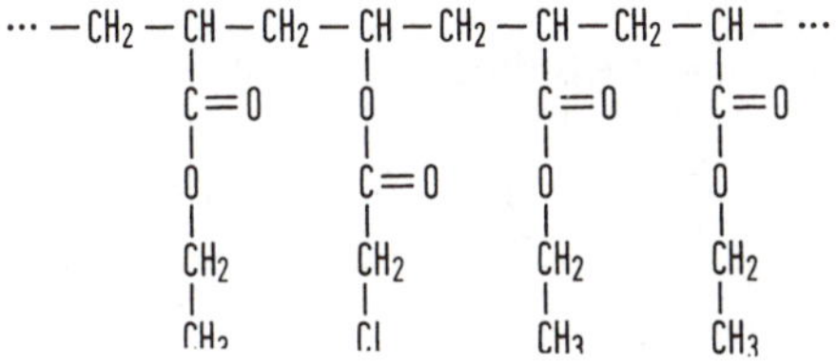

$$
\cdots-\text{CH}_2-\text{CH}-\text{CH}_2-\text{CH}-\text{CH}_2-\text{CH}-\text{CH}_2-\text{CH}-\cdots
$$

$$
\begin{array}{llll}
\quad \text{C}\!=\!\text{O} & \quad \text{O} & \quad \text{C}\!=\!\text{O} & \quad \text{C}\!=\!\text{O} \\
\quad\ |\ & \quad\ |\ & \quad\ |\ & \quad\ |\ \\
\quad \text{O} & \quad \text{C}\!=\!\text{O} & \quad \text{O} & \quad \text{O} \\
\quad\ |\ & \quad\ |\ & \quad\ |\ & \quad\ |\ \\
\quad \text{CH}_2 & \quad \text{CH}_2 & \quad \text{CH}_2 & \quad \text{CH}_2 \\
\quad\ |\ & \quad\ |\ & \quad\ |\ & \quad\ |\ \\
\quad \text{CH}_2 & \quad \text{Cl} & \quad \text{CH}_3 & \quad \text{CH}_3
\end{array}
$$

Fig. 8.18: Structural Formula of a Chlorine-Containing ACM

The fully saturated backbone provides the excellent heat and ozone resistance of the vulcanizates, and the polar side groups give the oil resistance. The latter depends on the nature of the basic monomers **(Fig. 8.16)**. ACM grades based on ethyl acrylates have excellent oil resistance but poor low-temperature properties, whereas those based on butyl acrylate show improved low-temperature flexibility but inferior oil resistance. For this reason, some ACM grades are based on compromise blends of these monomers together with alkoxyalkyl acrylates to achieve the best balance of fluid resistance and low-temperature flexibility.

8.16.2 Compounding

A typical ACM compound contains a limited number of ingredients: reinforcing fillers, processing aids and a cure system. Antioxidants are usually not necessary because the vulcanizates have excellent heat aging properties. The addition of plasticizers to improve the low-temperature properties is impractical because they volatilize during postcure or when the finished parts are exposed to high service temperatures. If plasticizers are required, they must have low volatility, but they usually do not improve low-temperature flexibility.

Acidic fillers must be avoided, as they can seriously impair the cross-linking. Processing aids are essential to prevent or reduce mill and mold sticking.

ACM rubbers cannot be cured with sulphur, because the backbone is fully saturated. Many curing systems have been proposed over the years, such as polyamines, ammonium benzoate and ammonium adipate. The most commonly used vulcanizing system for more modern types is the "sulphur-soap" cure system consisting of a combination of sodium stearate, potassium stearate and small amounts of sulphur (about 0.3 phr). In this case, sulphur functions as an accelerator. This system offers improved processibility but results in vulcanizates with relatively high compression set at 150 °C.

ACM vulcanizates require postcure in an oven with circulating air (typically 6 h at 175 °C) to complete the cross-linking process and to develop optimum physical properties, especially compression set.

8.16.3 Vulcanizate Properties

The useful properties that ACM elastomers offer can be summarized as follows:
- excellent heat resistance (they can be used continuously at temperatures up to 150 °C and can withstand limited exposure to temperatures as high as 175 °C);
- high resistance to ozone and oxygen; and
- good resistance to hot industrial oils, including those containing sulphur, sulphur-bearing chemicals and other additives. The extent of swelling depends on the aromatic content of the oil and the composition of the base polymer. **Table 8.5** shows the average volume changes of ACM vulcanizates with different polymer bases in ASTM oil Nos. 1, 2 and 3 at 150 °C.

Resistance to water is usually poor. Other properties, such as compression set and low-temperature flexibility, depend on compounding and polymer choice.

Table 8.5: Resistance of Various ACM Vulcanizates to ASTM Oils after 70 h at 150 °C

Medium	Polymer Base	Average Volume Increase (%)
ASTM oil No. 1	Ethyl acrylate	0– 2
	Butyl acrylate	5–10
	Acrylate blends	2– 5
ASTM oil No. 2	Ethyl acrylate	3– 6
	Butyl acrylate	15–25
	Acrylate blends	7–12
ASTM oil No. 3	Ethyl acrylate	12–15
	Butyl acrylate	40–55
	Acrylate blends	20–30

8.16.4 Applications

ACM elastomers are used primarily in applications requiring combined resistance to heat, oils and oil additives (e.g., O-rings, lip seals and gaskets).

8.17 Ethylene-Acrylic Rubbers (AEM)

Trade Name

Vamac (at the present time Du Pont is the sole producer of ethylene-acrylic rubbers)

8.17.1 Chemistry

Vamac is a terpolymer of ethylene and methyl acrylate with a cure site monomer that contains a carboxylic acid group **(Fig. 8.19)**. The presence of carboxylic acid

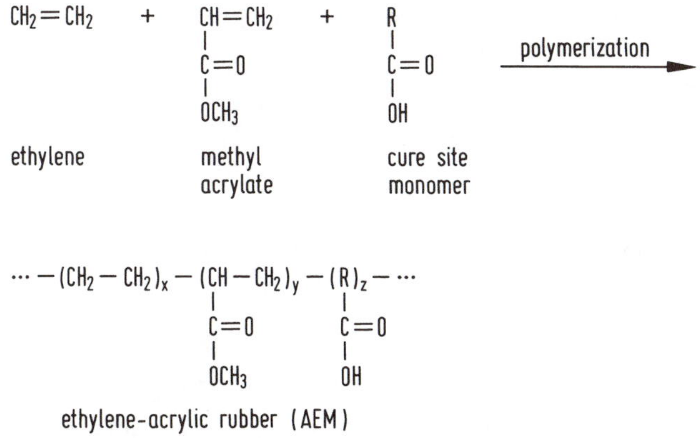

Fig. 8.19: Synthesis of AEM

groups in the polymer chain permits cross-linking by reaction with certain bifunctional reagents such as diamines. The fully saturated backbone provides excellent heat and ozone resistance, whereas methyl acrylate groups provide oil resistance. The polymer does not contain halogens.

8.17.2 Compounding

Vamac is compounded in the same way as ACM rubbers. The most common curing system is a combination of a guanidine and a blocked primary diamine (Diak No. 1). Peroxide systems may be used, particularly for cable applications.

AEM vulcanizates require postcure (usually 6 h at 175 °C) to complete the vulcanization process and to produce optimum properties, particularly compression set.

8.17.3 Vulcanizate Properties

AEM vulcanizates offer an interesting combination of properties:
- high heat resistance intermediate between that of CSM and that of VMQ elastomers (they can be used continuously at temperatures up to 150 °C and for short periods up to 175 °C);
- excellent ozone and weather resistance;
- moderate resistance to mineral oils;
- good low-temperature flexibility (down to −30 °C);
- good resistance to hot water (in contrast to ACM); and
- high tensile strength.

8.17.4 Applications

The applications of ACM and AEM elastomers are similar. Vamac is specified when low-temperature flexibility is required. The main applications include seals, gaskets, boots, hoses, ignition-wire jackets and cable jackets.

8.18 Ethylene-Vinyl Acetate Rubbers (EAM)

Former Designation

EVA

Trade Names
Levapren (Bayer AG)
Elvax (Du Pont)

8.18.1 Chemistry

Ethylene-vinyl acetate rubbers (EAM) are copolymers of ethylene and vinyl acetate with fully saturated backbones **(Fig. 8.20)**. The commercially available EAM rubbers have vinyl acetate contents ranging usually from 40 to 70% by weight. The fully saturated backbone provides excellent heat and ozone resistance, whereas the vinyl acetate groups provide oil resistance. As the vinyl acetate content increases, the oil resistance improves, but the electrical insulation properties are impaired.

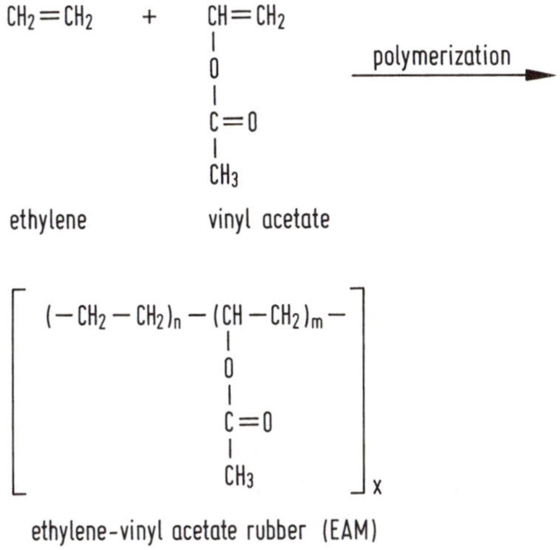

$$CH_2{=}CH_2 \quad + \quad \begin{array}{c} CH{=}CH_2 \\ | \\ O \\ | \\ C{=}O \\ | \\ CH_3 \end{array} \qquad \xrightarrow{\text{polymerization}}$$

ethylene   vinyl acetate

$$\left[\begin{array}{c} (-CH_2-CH_2)_n - (CH-CH_2)_m - \\ | \\ O \\ | \\ C{=}O \\ | \\ CH_3 \end{array} \right]_x$$

ethylene-vinyl acetate rubber (EAM)

Fig. 8.20: Synthesis of EAM

8.18.2 Compounding

EAM rubbers cannot be vulcanized with sulphur because they have a saturated backbone. Vulcanization is achieved either by exposure to high-energy radiation or by reacting with peroxides, usually in conjunction with a co-agent for increased state of cure. Carbon black is the preferred filler. Mineral fillers, plasticizers and processing aids should be selected carefully because acidic fillers and unsaturated compounds can seriously impair the peroxide cure.

The addition of antioxidants is usually not necessary. However, they may be added for optimum heat resistance. If a plasticizer is required, low-volatile paraffinic oils or esters may be used.

8.18.3 Vulcanizate Properties

The main characteristic properties of EAM vulcanizates include:
- high resistance to ozone and weather;
- good dry-heat resistance (continuously up to about 125°C and for limited periods at temperatures as high as 150°C);
- low compression set at high temperatures;
- fair oil resistance, depending on the vinyl acetate content;
- moderate electrical insulation properties with low vinyl acetate grades; and
- poor low-temperature flexibility.

8.18.4 Applications

EAM elastomers find wide application in wire and cable sheathing where resistance to ozone, weather, dry heat and oils are important properties.

8.19 Fluorocarbon Rubbers (FPM)

Trade Names

Viton (Du Pont)
Fluorel (3M)
Dai-el (Daikin Industries)
Tecnoflon (Montefluos)

8.19.1 Chemistry

Fluorocarbon rubbers are highly fluorinated hydrocarbon polymers. In general, all highly fluorinated polymers are very stable and possess exceptional resistance to oxidation, weather, flame, chemical attack and swelling in a wide range of liquids. This stability is mainly due to the high strength of the C-F bond as compared with the C-H bond. The names and chemical structures of the monomers that are used for the production of these rubbers are given in **Fig. 8.21**.

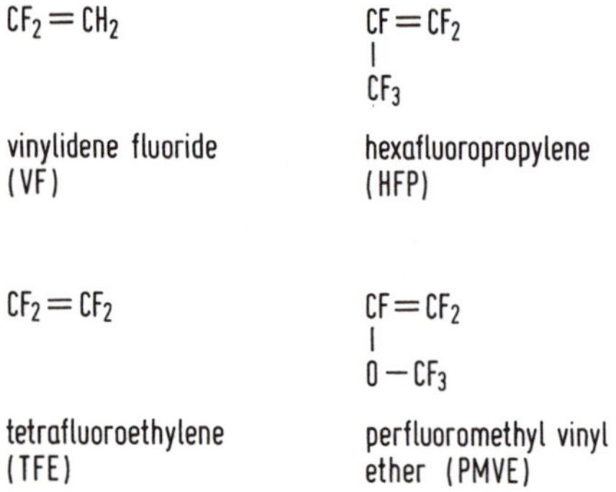

$$CF_2 = CH_2 \qquad\qquad CF = CF_2$$
$$\qquad\qquad\qquad\qquad\qquad |$$
$$\qquad\qquad\qquad\qquad\qquad CF_3$$

vinylidene fluoride   hexafluoropropylene
(VF)   (HFP)

$$CF_2 = CF_2 \qquad\qquad CF = CF_2$$
$$\qquad\qquad\qquad\qquad\qquad |$$
$$\qquad\qquad\qquad\qquad\qquad 0 - CF_3$$

tetrafluoroethylene   perfluoromethyl vinyl
(TFE)   ether (PMVE)

Fig. 8.21: Basic Monomers Used for the Synthesis of FPM

Table 8.6: Fluorine and Hydrogen Contents of Different FPM Rubbers

Polymer Type	Monomers Used	Fluorine Content (%) (approx.)	Hydrogen Content (%) (approx.)
Copolymer	VF-HFP	65	1.9
Terpolymer	VF-HFP-TFE	68	1.4
Tetrapolymer	VF-HFP-TFE-CS	70	1.1
LT tetrapolymer	VF-PMVE-TFE-CS	67	1.1

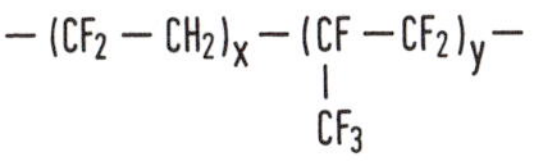

$$-(CF_2-CH_2)_x-(CF-CF_2)_y-$$
$$\hspace{3.5cm}|$$
$$\hspace{3.5cm}CF_3$$

copolymers

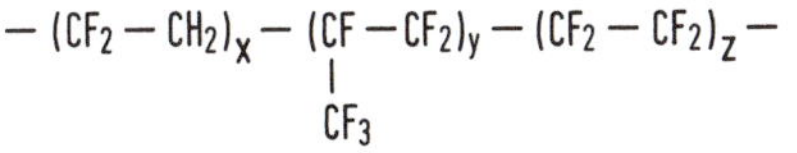

$$-(CF_2-CH_2)_x-(CF-CF_2)_y-(CF_2-CF_2)_z-$$
$$\hspace{3.5cm}|$$
$$\hspace{3.5cm}CF_3$$

terpolymers

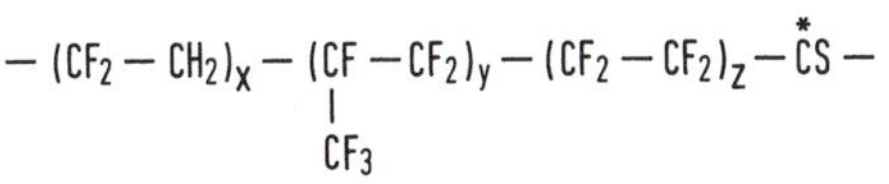

$$-(CF_2-CH_2)_x-(CF-CF_2)_y-(CF_2-CF_2)_z-\overset{*}{C}S-$$
$$\hspace{3.5cm}|$$
$$\hspace{3.5cm}CF_3$$

peroxide-curable tetrapolymers

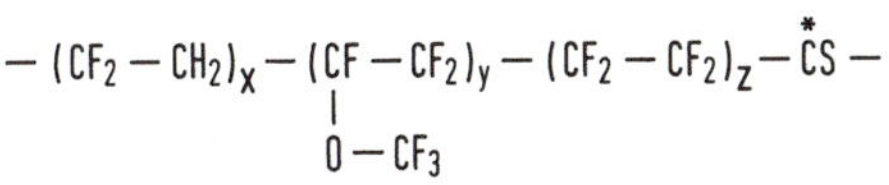

$$-(CF_2-CH_2)_x-(CF-CF_2)_y-(CF_2-CF_2)_z-\overset{*}{C}S-$$
$$\hspace{3.5cm}|$$
$$\hspace{3.5cm}O-CF_3$$

peroxide-curable tetrapolymers [low-temperature (LT) types]

* CS = cure site monomer [e.g., trifluoro-monobromo-ethylene $(-CF_2-CFBr-)$]

Fig. 8.22: Types of FPM Polymers

FPM rubbers are available in various grades, which differ mainly in the polymer composition and fluorine content. The different polymer types and their chemical structures are shown in **Fig. 8.22**. The fluorine and hydrogen contents of the different FPM rubbers are listed in **Table 8.6**.

The terpolymer vulcanizates exhibit, in general, better fluid and chemical resistance than do copolymers. The resistance to swelling improves with increasing the fluorine content of the polymer, but at a sacrifice in low-temperature properties. FPM grades with perfluoromethyl vinyl ether (PMVE) instead of hexafluoropropylene (HFP) offer improved low-temperature performance over conventional FPM elastomers, with no associated sacrifice in the fundamental properties (section 6.21.1). However, these low-temperature grades are much more expensive than the conventional types.

8.19.2 Compounding

FPM compounds contain rather few ingredients as compared with other rubber compounds. In addition to the curing system, a typical FPM compound usually contains a filler (carbon black or mineral filler or both), a metal oxide and a small amount of a processing aid (typically carnauba wax or low-molecular-weight polyethylene).

FPM rubbers accept limited amounts of fillers (typically 30−50 phr). The addition of plasticizers such as mineral oils or organic esters is impractical because of their limited compatibility with the rubber and volatilization during the postcure at 230−260°C. If a plasticizer is required, a low-molecular-weight FPM liquid rubber may be used.

The addition of metal oxides (or acid acceptors) is essential since they serve to neutralize hydrogen fluoride generated during the cure or when the vulcanizates are exposed to high service temperatures. Magnesium oxide is probably the most widely used oxide. However, it is not recommended when optimum water, steam or acid resistance is required. In such cases, lead oxides such as litharge should be used.

There are three types of cure systems:
1) diamines;
2) bisphenols; and
3) organic peroxides.

The preferred **amines** are blocked diamines such as hexamethylene diamine carbamate (Diak No. 1).

The **bisphenol** cure systems are supplied either already mixed in the base polymer or separately as master batches. The preferred accelerator is a phosphonium salt. In addition, calcium hydroxide is added to act as a vulcanization promotor. The bisphenol cure systems provide vulcanizates with outstanding resistance to compression set.

The **peroxide** cure systems are applicable only to FPM grades containing cure site monomers. A co-agent such as triallyl isocyanurate is usually added. These cure systems provide vulcanizates with improved resistance to steam and amine-based lubricant additives.

FPM vulcanizates usually require an oven postcure up to 24 h at temperatures in the range of 230−260°C to develop optimum physical properties, particularly compression set. During the postcure, dissolved or trapped air as well as volatile vulcanization by-products, mainly water, will be expanded and driven from the press-cured article. In order to avoid fissuring or cracking of thick parts, postcure is done gradually, starting at 100°C and increasing in increments of 25°C until the desired oven cure temperature is reached. This gradual postcure permits the slow diffusion of gases.

For applications where extreme temperatures will not be encountered, such as in coated fabrics or hose linings, elimination or reduction of the postcure may be allowed.

8.19.3 Vulcanizate Properties

Certain vulcanizate properties (e.g., resistance to compression set, methanol, amine-based additives, hot water and steam) depend upon the base polymer composition, curing system and metal oxide used. However, it can be said that FPM vulcanizates, in general, have outstanding resistance to heat, oxygen, ozone, weather, flame and oxidative chemicals. They maintain, for example, their elas-

tomeric properties in hot air almost indefinitely up to 200°C and can be used at temperatures as high as 300°C for short-term applications. Coupled with this excellent heat aging resistance, FPM elastomers exhibit excellent resistance to swelling in a wide variety of oils, fuels, solvents and chemicals. For example, they are recommended for:
- petroleum oils and hydrocarbon fuels;
- organic-ester-based lubricants;
- silicate-ester-based lubricants;
- silicone fluids and greases;
- aryl phosphate ester fluids (e.g., selected Pydraul types);
- aromatic hydrocarbons (e.g., benzene, toluene, xylene); and
- halognated hydrocarbons (e.g., trichloroethylene, carbon tetrachloride).

Table 8.7 shows the average volume changes of typical FPM vulcanizates in ASTM test fluids.

Table 8.7: Resistance of Typical FPM Vulcanizates to ASTM Test Fluids after 70 h Immersion Test

Medium	Temperature (°C)	Average Volume Increase (%)
ASTM oil No. 1	150	0— 1
ASTM oil No. 2	150	1— 2
ASTM oil No. 3	150	3— 5
ASTM fuel A	RT	0— 1
ASTM fuel B	RT	2— 4
ASTM fuel C	RT	3— 8
ASTM fuel D	RT	8—12

Despite this excellent resistance to a wide variety of fluids, there are certain chemicals that severely attack FPM vulcanizates. For example, they are not recommended for:
- polar solvents such as ketones (e.g., acetone, MEK) and esters (e.g., ethyl acetate);
- low-molecular-weight organic acids such as formic acid and acetic acid;
- hot water and steam, unless compounded with lead oxide;
- methanol, unless based on highly fluorinated polymers [with low hydrogen content (section 6.21.3)];
- alkyl-aryl phosphate ester hydraulic fluids (Skydrol fluids) [however, they are resistant to aryl phosphate esters (section 6.11)];
- glycol-based-automotive brake fluids;
- anhydrous ammonia and amines [the highly fluorinated peroxide-curable FPM grades result in vulcanizates with improved resistance to amine-based additives such as those found in engine and gear oils (section 6.7)];

– hot hydrofluoric or chlorosulphonic acids; and
– high-energy radiation above 10^6 rads.

The compression set resistance is strongly affected by the cure system. Bisphenol cure systems offer the best high-temperature compression set resistance. The peroxide cure systems do not provide the same resistance to compression set, although they are better than diamine systems.

The low-temperature properties of conventional FPM elastomers are, in general, less than satisfactory. They are usually serviceable down to −20°C in dynamic applications. In many static applications, effective sealing at about −40°C has been achieved with O-rings based upon conventional bisphenol-cured FPM copolymers. This indicates that where static seals are involved, conventional laboratory low-temperature tests may be poor indicators for service performance.

As has been mentioned, the FPM base polymers containing PMVE provide enhanced low-temperature flexibility, but their major disadvantage is their very high price.

The gas permeability of FPM elastomers is generally very low, approaching that of IIR elastomers. The highly fluorinated FPM elastomers have the lowest permeation to fuels (section 6.21.5).

The electrical insulation properties are not outstanding but are adequate for sheathing where exceptionally high resistance to elevated temperatures, ozone, chemicals and flame is required.

8.19.4 Applications

FPM elastomers are widely used in critical applications requiring high resistance to oils, fuels, flame and chemicals at elevated temperatures. The main uses are as O-rings, shaft seals, gaskets, fuel hoses, diaphragms and cable sheathing for extreme conditions.

8.20 Perfluorocarbon Rubbers (FFKM)

Trade Names

Kalrez (Du Pont)
Dai-el Perfluor (Daikin Industries)

8.20.1 Kalrez Perfluoroelastomer Parts

Kalrez parts are made from a perfluorocarbon rubber (FFKM) that is chemically a terpolymer of tetrafluoroethylene (TFE) and perfluoromethyl vinyl ether (PMVE) with a small amount of a perfluorinated cure site monomer **(Fig. 8.23)**. The resultant cured polymer does not contain hydrogen atoms in the molecule. The absence of hydrogen dramatically increases the heat and chemical resistance as compared with FPM elastomers.

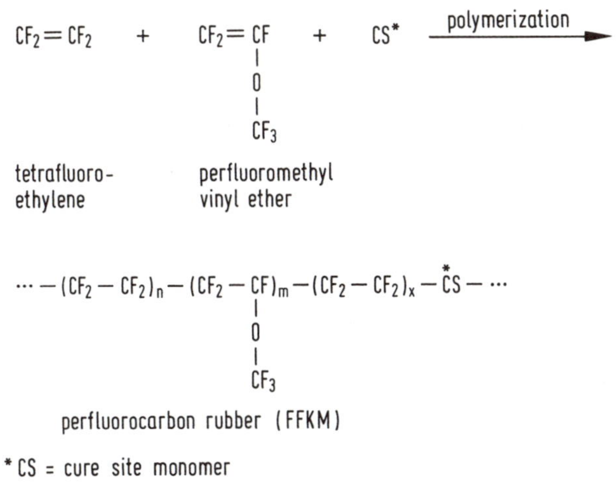

$$CF_2\!=\!CF_2 \quad + \quad CF_2\!=\!CF \quad + \quad CS^* \xrightarrow{\quad \text{polymerization} \quad}$$

$$\begin{array}{c} | \\ O \\ | \\ CF_3 \end{array}$$

tetrafluoro-   perfluoromethyl
ethylene   vinyl ether

$$\cdots - (CF_2 - CF_2)_n - (CF_2 - CF)_m - (CF_2 - CF_2)_x - \overset{*}{C}S - \cdots$$

$$\begin{array}{c} | \\ O \\ | \\ CF_3 \end{array}$$

perfluorocarbon rubber (FFKM)

*CS = cure site monomer

Fig. 8.23: Synthesis of FFKM

Owing to complex manufacturing techniques, Kalrez perfluoroelastomer parts are available only from Du Pont. These include O-rings, tubing, rods, sheeting and custom-designed parts that are offered in different hardnesses, ranging between about 70 and 95 Shore A.

Generally speaking, these products combine the resilience and sealing force of an elastomer with the thermal stability and chemical resistance of polytetra-fluoroethylene (PTFE) resin. They retain their elastic properties in long-term service at temperatures as high as 260 °C and can be used at temperatures up to 315 °C for short-term applications. Furthermore, they resist the majority of chemicals that attack other elastomers, including FPM (e.g., amines, oil-field sour gas, hot sodium hydroxide, fuming nitric acid, ketones, tetrahydrofuran, acrylonitrile, styrene, vinyl chloride and low-molecular-weight esters and ethers). However, they are not recommended for use with perfluorinated hydrocarbons (section 6.3.1) and molten alkali metals.

Table 8.8 compares the resistance of Kalrez and FPM elastomers to selected fluids.

Kalrez elastomers have poor resistance to extrusion and therefore must be backed up by harder materials when subjected to relatively high pressure. The low-temperature flexibility is very poor.

8.20.2 Dai-el Perfluor

In contrast to Kalrez, Dai-el Perfluor is offered in the form of uncured stocks that can be manufactured and marketed directly by the producers of elastomeric parts.

As compared with Kalrez, the vulcanizates of Dai-el Perfluor have a similar chemical resistance profile, better compression set and low-temperature flexibility, but at a considerable sacrifice in the heat resistance.

Table 8.8: Fluid Resistance of Typical Kalrez FFKM Vulcanizates versus FPM Vulcanizates after 168 h at Room Temperature

Medium	Average Volume Increase (%)	
	FFKM Vulcanizates	FPM Vulcanizates
Hexane	<1	1
Cyclohexane	<1	3
Benzene	3	15
Toluene	<1	8
Acetone	<2	>200
Methylethyl ketone	<1	>200
Ethyl acetate	3	>200
Perchloroethylene	2	2
Tetrahydrofuran	<1	>200
Ethanol	0	6
Chlorobenzene	<1	8
Nitrobenzene	<1	25

8.20.3 Applications

FFKM elastomeric parts, although extremely expensive, are used in chemical plants, oil refineries, oil-field operations and analytical instruments.

8.21 Tetrafluoroethylene-Propylene Rubbers (TFE/P)

Trade Name

The base rubber is produced solely by Asahi Glass Company and sold under the trade name Aflas. Since 1987, 3M Company has become the western European and North American supplier of the Japanese-made Aflas.

8.21.1 Chemistry

Throughout this book, Aflas tetrafluoroethylene-propylene rubbers will be referred to as TFE/P. Chemically, TFE/P is a copolymer of tetrafluoroethylene ($CF_2=CF_2$) and propylene ($CH_2=CH-CH_3$) with a fluorine content of only 53.5% (compared with 65% in FPM copolymers). The tetrafluoroethylene and propylene are arranged alternately in an orderly manner, as shown in **Fig. 8.24**.

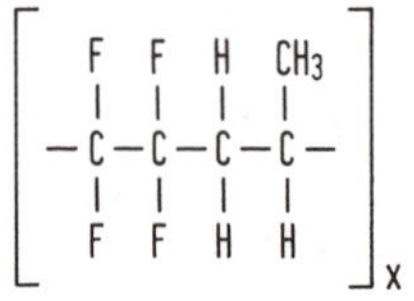

$$\begin{bmatrix} \begin{array}{cccc} F & F & H & CH_3 \\ | & | & | & | \\ -C & -C & -C & -C - \\ | & | & | & | \\ F & F & H & H \end{array} \end{bmatrix}_x$$

Fig. 8.24: Structural Formula of Tetrafluoroethylene-Propylene Rubber (TFE/P)

TFE/P can be considered as an improved ethylene-propylene rubber **(Fig. 8.7)**, in which the hydrogen atoms of ethylene are replaced by fluorine. The $C-F$ bond and the saturated polymer chain provide the excellent chemical and heat resistance of the vulcanizates.

8.21.2 Compounding

Like FPM, TFE/P compounds contain few ingredients, namely a filler, small amounts of a processing aid and a cure system. Carbon blacks are the most common fillers used. The addition of small amounts of a processing aid (typically carnauba wax or low-molecular-weight polyethylene) is essential to reduce mold sticking. The vulcanization is effected by organic peroxides in conjunction with a co-agent, usually triallylisocyanurate (TAIC).

Postcure is necessary to develop optimum properties, particularly compression set resistance. A typical postcure is 16 h at 200 °C, but thick parts require gradual postcure to avoid fissuring or cracking (similar to FPM compounds).

8.21.3 Vulcanizate Properties

As compared with FPM elastomers, TFE/P vulcanizates have about the same thermal stability but better electrical insulation properties and a different chemical resistance profile. They resist a wide variety of chemicals, including:
– amines, amine corrosion inhibitors and additive packages;
– steam and hot water;
– sour oil and gas (H_2S);
– all types of hydraulic fluids (including alkyl-aryl phosphate esters);
– all types of brake fluids (glycol base, mineral oil, silicone oil);
– petroleum oils and greases (better than NBR, ACM, ECO and AU, but not as good as FPM elastomers);
– alcohols and various industrial solvents;
– acids, alkalis and oxidizing chemicals;
– ozone and weather; and
– high-energy radiation.
   TFE/P vulcanizates are not resistant to:
– aromatic hydrocarbons (e.g., benzene, toluene, xylene);
– chlorinated hydrocarbon (e.g., trichloroethylene and carbon tetrachloride);
– ketones (e.g., MEK, acetone);
– ethers (e.g., diethyl ether);
– acetic acid and organic acetates; and
– most organic refrigerants (section 6.22).
   Table 8.9 shows the resistance of a typical TFE/P compound to selected fluids.

The compression set resistance is not as good as that of FPM elastomers. The low temperature flexibility is poor. However, it has been found that TFE/P seals frequently perform at lower temperatures than laboratory tests would indicate. This is because some fluids plasticize the elastomer to some extent, making it more flexible at low temperatures when they are in contact with these fluids. Therefore, it is recommended to carry out functional tests under the working conditions.

Table 8.9: Fluid Resistance of a Typical TFE/P Vulcanizate with 70 IRHD

Medium	Temperature (°C)	Time (h)	Volume Increase (%)
ASTM oil No. 3	100	168	8
Brake fluid (glycol base)	100	168	4
HFDR (section 6.5)	100	168	5
HFC (section 6.5)	60	672	1
HFA (section 6.5)	60	672	6
Water	100	672	9
ASTM fuel C	50	70	76
Trichloroethylene	50	168	94
Carbon tetrachloride	50	168	83
Acetone	RT	70	68

8.21.4 Applications

TFE/P elastomers are finding wide application mainly in oil-field operations and chemical processing as O-rings and different types of seals. Other applications include roll covering, hose liners, wire and cable insulation and jacketing. None of these applications should call for low-temperature requirements.

8.22 Silicone Rubbers (Q)

Trade Names

Silastic (Dow Corning Corporation)
Silopren (Bayer AG)

8.22.1 Chemistry

Silicone rubbers are unusual among synthetic rubbers in that they are partly inorganic and partly organic in nature. They have a backbone that consists of alternating silicon and oxygen atoms ($-Si-O-Si-$) in place of the more usual carbon-carbon ($-C-C-$) linkage. The silicon-oxygen linkage in silicone rubbers is similar to the linkage in quartz and glass.

Chemically, silicone rubbers are substituted polysiloxanes **(Fig. 8.25)**. They are denoted generically by the letter **Q**. The letters **MQ** denote the basic silicone rubbers that have only methyl substituents in the polysiloxane chain. By replacing small amounts of these methyl groups with other groups, significant variations in properties can be achieved. The presence of vinyl groups in **VMQ** improves vul-

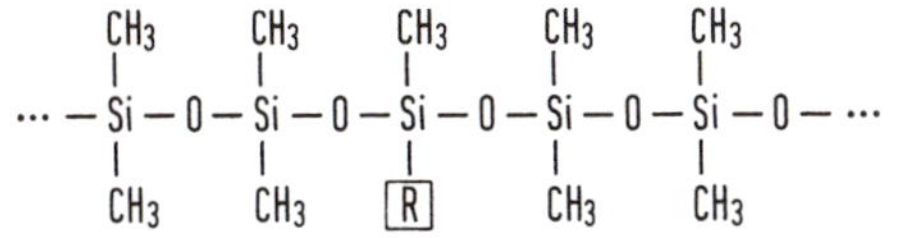

$$\cdots - \underset{\underset{CH_3}{|}}{\overset{\overset{CH_3}{|}}{Si}} - O - \underset{\underset{CH_3}{|}}{\overset{\overset{CH_3}{|}}{Si}} - O - \underset{\underset{\boxed{R}}{|}}{\overset{\overset{CH_3}{|}}{Si}} - O - \underset{\underset{CH_3}{|}}{\overset{\overset{CH_3}{|}}{Si}} - O - \underset{\underset{CH_3}{|}}{\overset{\overset{CH_3}{|}}{Si}} - O - \cdots$$

R group is : methyl (CH$_3$) in MQ
vinyl (CH=CH$_2$) in VMQ
phenyl (C$_6$H$_5$) in PMQ
trifluoropropyl (CH$_2$—CH$_2$—CF$_3$) in FMQ

PVMQ rubbers have phenyl, vinyl and methyl groups.
FVMQ rubbers have trifluoropropyl, vinyl and methyl groups.

Fig. 8.25: Types of Silicone Rubbers

canization rate and compression set resistance. The phenyl groups in **PMQ** and **PVMQ** improve low-temperature flexibility and resistance to high-energy radiation. The addition of trifluoropropyl groups to the polymer chain results in a special type of silicone rubbers commonly known as fluorosilicone rubbers (**FMQ** and **FVMQ**). The vulcanizates of these rubbers exhibit excellent resistance to oils, fuels and many solvents while retaining the basic properties of silicone elastomers. (Fluorosilicone rubbers are described in section 8.22.5.)

Silicone rubbers can be divided into three groups:
1) heat-vulcanizable solid rubbers;
2) heat-vulcanizable liquid rubbers (**LSR**) designed for the automated production of molded parts; and
3) room-temperature vulcanizing rubbers (**RTV**), usually flowable liquids supplied in a "ready to use" form for such applications as building sealants, encapsulation, coating and flexible molds.

8.22.2 Compounding

Heat-vulcanizable solid silicone rubbers are usually supplied already reinforced in a base form requiring only addition of pigments, curing agent or other ingredients on a two-roll mill. Some of these ingredients are available as pastes or master batches. However, many manufacturers prefer to purchase silicone compounds in a "ready to use" form rather than mixing their own formulations.

The compounding ingredients are usually few in number. Typical silicone compounds contain reinforcing or extending fillers or both, pigments and organic peroxides as curing agent. Special additives may be added to achieve specific processing or performance properties. There is no necessity for antioxidants.

Very fine fumed silica is the main reinforcing filler used to develop high tensile and tear strength. Extending fillers include ground quartz, calcium carbonate, diatomaceous earth and calcined china clay. These fillers impart only fair strength, but they offer other advantages, such as improved processing and performance characteristics or cost reductions. Acetylene carbon blacks and metals, such as silver, are used to develop electrically conductive or antistatic compounds.

Inorganic pigments are used to color silicone compounds. They are usually added in the form of master batches in silicone oil or gum. Red iron oxide is suitable as both a pigment and a heat aging improver.

Most silicone vulcanizates need a postcure in an air-circulating oven. A period of several hours (up to 24 h) at 250 °C is typical. Thick parts should be gradually cured (starting at 100 °C) to avoid fissuring or cracking. During this postcure, the decomposition products and volatiles are driven off, resulting in improvements in compression set, electrical properties, heat aging and chemical resistance.

Heat-vulcanizable liquid silicone rubbers (**LSR**) are "ready to use" products in the form of two components: A and B mixed in a 1:1 ratio before use. Pigments or any additive can be added during the mixing stage. They are used for manufacturing small parts by injection molding at about 180–220 °C. The vulcanization is effected by an addition cure mechanism and the process is completed within a few seconds. Postcuring is usually not necessary, as no by-products are formed during vulcanization. However, postcuring is required where low compression set at elevated temperatures is needed or to modify hardness and modulus.

The room-temperature-vulcanizing (**RTV**) liquid silicone compounds are supplied in both one and two-component systems. In the one-component systems, the cross-linking agent is incorporated in the base compound at the time of manufacture. The vulcanization takes place upon exposure to atmospheric moisture. It will start first at the surface and then progress inward with the diffusion of moisture into the rubber compound. In the two-component systems, the cross-linking agent is added to the base compound just before use.

8.22.3 Vulcanizate Properties

The distinctive properties of silicone elastomers can be listed as follows:
- outstanding resistance to ozone and corona, outdoor weather and sunlight;
- excellent high-temperature stability (if dry heat is the only criterion, special compounds will offer acceptable service life up to 300 °C; however, in the absence of air, silicone elastomers can revert to a paste, even at lower temperatures, probably because of hydrolysis promoted by trapped moisture; only slight ventilation is required to prevent reversion; the usual high-temperature limit recommended for continuous service in **dry** air is about 200 °C);
- excellent low-temperature flexibility (MQ and MVQ vulcanizates maintain flexibility at temperatures as low as −60 °C; PMQ and PVMQ rubbers can yield compounds flexible at −90 to −100 °C);
- excellent electrical insulation properties, which are maintained fairly constant at the service temperature range (electrically conductive compounds are also available);
- low level of combustible components, (even when exposed to flame, the elastomer will burn to a nonconducting silica ash);
- excellent compression set over the entire service temperature range;
- high physiological inertness (when properly postcured, the vulcanizates are odorless, tasteless and completely nontoxic);

- excellent resistance to bacteria, fungus and soil;
- good resistance to hot water, vegetable and animal oils, paraffinic oils (e.g., ASTM oil No. 1) and glycol-based brake fluids (however, they are not resistant to naphthenic and aromatic oils, hydrocarbon fuels, silicone oils and greases, ketones and many low-viscosity fluids; the swelling is reversible if the swelling medium is volatile, because the vulcanizates are not susceptible to solvent extraction; for good resistance to swelling by solvents and fuels fluorosilicone elastomers should be used);
- excellent surface release properties, preventing adhesion of sticky materials (however, it should be noted that silicone elastomers tend to adhere to glass surfaces after prolonged contact because of similarity in the chemical structure of the two materials);
- good resistance to high-energy radiation up to 10^7 rad (compounds based on PMQ and PVMQ show improved radiation resistance);
- very high permeability to gases, the highest of all other elastomers;
- poor to fair physical properties (in contrast to many organic elastomers, the physical properties of silicone elastomers are maintained fairly constant at the operational temperature range); and
- poor resistance to chemical degradation caused by acids, alkalis and steam above 120°C.

8.22.4 Applications

The major applications of silicone elastomers include electrical insulators, ignition cables, gaskets, O-rings, static seals (dynamic seals are not recommended), oxygen masks, food and medical grade tubing and roll coverings.

8.22.5 Fluorosilicone Rubbers (FMQ and FVMQ)

Fluorosilicone rubbers are fluorine-modified silicone rubbers containing trifluoro-propyl side groups (**Fig. 8.25**). They are designated according to ISO 1629 as FMQ and FVMQ. Throughout this book, all fluorosilicone rubbers (including the vinyl-containing types) are denoted by the letters FMQ.

In general, FMQ rubbers are compounded and processed in the same fashion as conventional silicone rubbers. Their vulcanizates have the most useful properties of regular silicone elastomers plus improved fluid resistance, but they have a more restricted high temperature limit. The long-term heat resistance of FMQ elastomers is not as good as that of conventional silicones or FPM vulcanizates. Consequently, the recommended high-temperature limit for continuous service is about 175°C.

FMQ elastomers, which are considerably more expensive than regular silicones, are used where best low-temperature flexibility and low swell in fluids are required. With few exceptions, such as ketones and some esters, the fluid resistance of FMQ elastomers is generally good. **Tables 8.10** and **8.11** show the fluid resistance of typical FMQ elastomers compared with that of VMQ and PMQ vulcanizates.

Table 8.10: Resistance of Typical FMQ, VMQ and PMQ Vulcanizates to ASTM Oils after 168 h at 125°C

Elastomer Base	Average Volume Increase (%) in		
	ASTM Oil No. 1	ASTM Oil No. 2	ASTM Oil No. 3
FMQ	<1	<2	<5
VMQ	3– 6	6–12	25–40
PMQ	6–12	15–25	40–60

Table 8.11: Resistance of Typical FMQ and VMQ Vulcanizates to ASTM Fuels after 168 h at Room Temperature

Elastomer Base	Average Volume Increase (%) in			
	ASTM Fuel A	ASTM Fuel B	ASTM Fuel C	ASTM Fuel D
FMQ	< 15	< 25	< 25	< 25
VMQ	>100	>100	>100	>100

Typical applications of FMQ elastomers include O-rings, seals, diaphragms and tank linings.

8.23 Polyurethane Rubbers (AU/EU)

Trade Names

Vulkollan, Urepan, Desmopan (Bayer AG)
Pellethane (Dow Chemical)
Adiprene (Uniroyal)

8.23.1 Chemistry

The chemical basis of polyurethanes is the isocyanate group ($-N=C=O$) and its ability to react with hydroxyl ($-OH$) groups to form the urethane linkage ($-NH-CO-O-$). **Fig. 8.26** shows the reaction of a monoisocyanate with a monohydroxy compound such as ethanol.

The formation of polyurethanes requires difunctional reactants to enable the building of large chains, as shown in **Fig. 8.27**. The basic components used to prepare polyurethanes are:
– a diisocyanate ($O=C=N-R-N=C=O$);
– a long-chain macroglycol or polyol ($HO-R-OH$);
– a short-chain glycol ($HO-R'-OH$) or amine ($H_2N-R'-NH_2$) as chain extender and cross-linker.

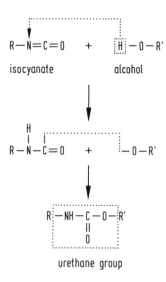

Fig. 8.26: Formation of Urethane Groups

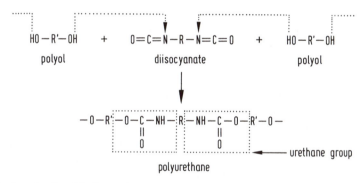

Fig. 8.27: Synthesis of Polyurethanes

The diisocyanates have relatively small molecules. Examples of the diisocyanates most commonly used for the production of polyurethanes are shown in **Fig. 8.28**.

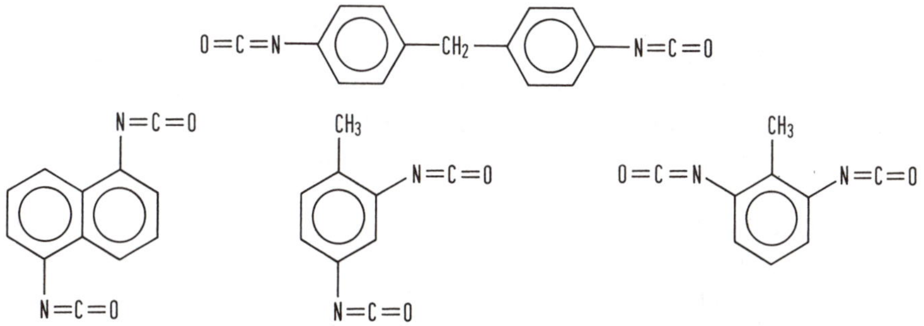

$O=C=N-\bigcirc-CH_2-\bigcirc-N=C=O$

Fig. 8.28: Most Common Diisocyanates Used for the Synthesis of Polyurethanes

The macroglycols or polyols have a large influence on the properties of the final product. Both polyester and polyether macroglycols are used. The polymers derived from these two classes are known as polyester urethanes (**AU**) and polyether urethanes (**EU**), respectively.

The chain extenders have relatively small molecules, about the same size as the diisocyanates. One of the most frequently used chain extender for the production of polyurethanes is 1,4 butane-diol ($HO-(CH_2)_4-OH$).

Unsaturation (double bonds) can be introduced into both AU and EU by using an unsaturated diol such as glycerol monoallyl ether to enable sulphur cure.

The great variety of starting materials results in a wide range of polyurethane grades that differ in processing, curing systems and also in properties of the final products.

8.23.2 Compounding

Polyurethane rubbers can be classified according to the way in which they are processed in three main groups:
1) millable rubbers that are processed and subsequently cured using the conventional mixing and processing methods of the rubber industry;
2) liquid reactants that are processed by casting and reaction injection molding (**RIM**) techniques; and
3) thermoplastic elastomers that are processed by techniques used for thermoplastics.

The polyurethane millable rubbers are available in various grades that differ mainly in the polymer composition. The compounding principles of these rubbers are similar to those applied to other rubbers. Reinforcing fillers are usually required to develop optimum physical properties. Small amounts of lubricants are normally added to improve mold release. Ester-based plasticizers are sometimes added to improve the processibility and lower the hardness of the vulcanizates without seriously affecting other properties unless used in excessive amounts. Antioxidants are usually not required, but the addition of a hydrolysis protective agent (polycarbodiimide) is important for the hydrolysis-prone AU types. On the other hand, the EU types require the addition of an ultraviolet protective agent.

The main vulcanizing agents used are organic peroxides and diisocyanates. Grades that have double bonds in the rubber molecule can be cross-linked with sulphur and accelerators. Each vulcanizing system offers a distinct set of vulcanizate properties. For example, compounds cured with peroxides have the best heat stability and compression set resistance. Isocyanate-cured compounds may be useful where low heat buildup is required. The sulphur-cured compounds may be used in general-purpose applications.

Liquid reactants offer energy-saving processing methods such as casting and reaction injection molding (RIM). Most of the components are room-temperature liquids or low-melting solids. Chain extension and cross-linking are part of the polymerization process in the liquid systems. If high fluidity is required, solid additive levels must be restricted to a few parts of inert materials.

The procedure of casting is relatively simple: the preheated reaction mixture is briefly degased under reduced pressure with stirring and then promptly poured into preheated lubricated molds. The parts are demolded as soon as their green strength allows and subsequently postcured in an oven at about 110 °C for 24 h.

RIM is a process of growing importance in the polyurethane elastomer production. It differs from casting in that the reaction components are rapidly impingement-mixed under pressure and instantly injected into a lubricated mold, all in very short cycles. After demolding, the parts are postcured to develop optimum properties.

Thermoplastic polyurethane elastomers are block copolymers that do not require vulcanization (section 9.5). They are usually supplied in dice form or granulate, which can be directly processed on conventional plastics equipment. Additives, if required, are normally restricted to a few parts of pigments, light stabilizers, hydrolysis protective agents, and so on.

8.23.3 Vulcanizate Properties

In view of the several types and compositions of polyurethane elastomers, it is preferable to discuss the polymer properties in very general terms.

The distinctive properties of polyurethane elastomers can be summarized as follows:
- outstanding tensile strength, tear and abrasion resistance, better than all other elastomers;
- excellent resistance to degradation by oxygen and ozone because of chemical saturation of the polymer chains (in practice, however, polyurethanes do deteriorate outdoors, particularly in hot and tropical climates; the main reasons for outdoor deterioration are susceptibility to hydrolytic and microbiological attack in the case of **AU** elastomer types and susceptibility to attack by ultraviolet light in the case of **EU** elastomer types);
- upper temperature limit for continuous use in dry conditions is about 80–100 °C;
- fair to good low-temperature flexibility, typically between −25 and −35 °C (the **EU** elastomer types have better low temperature properties than the **AU** types);
- excellent resistance to high-energy radiation (usually little deterioration is experienced after exposure to 10^7 rad);
- low gas permeability, comparable to that of IIR elastomers;
- poor compression set resistance above 70 °C, unless based on peroxide-curable millable rubbers;
- good resistance to mineral oils and greases [the EU types are less resistant and show higher swelling; as mentioned earlier (section 6.7), many industrial oils and greases contain additives that can cause deterioration of AU and EU elastomers];
- fair to good resistance to swelling in aliphatic hydrocarbon solvents (section 6.24); and
- good resistance to cold water (about 20–25 °C) (however, hydrolytic deterioration is catalyzed by any acidic or alkaline environment; concentrated solutions of acids or alkalis will corrode polyurethanes rapidly, even at room temperature).

As a general rule, the rate of hydrolysis increases rapidly with increasing temperature. In applications involving contact with neutral water, the service temperature should not exceed 60°C if long-term service is required.

In the case of AU elastomers, hydrolysis will occur at the ester linkage and the urethane linkage. EU elastomers are more resistant to hydrolysis because ether linkages are more hydrolytically stable than ester linkages and hydrolysis can occur only at the urethane linkage. However, specially formulated AU elastomers (stabilized with polycarbodiimide) will also provide adequate hydrolysis resistance. The carbodiimide group reacts with the carboxylic groups generated by the hydrolysis of ester groups that otherwise would catalyze further hydrolysis.

Polyurethane elastomers, as a group, are not recommended for use in:
- glycol-based brake fluids;
- phosphate ester hydraulic fluids;
- polyalkylene-glycol-based fluids;
- aromatic hydrocarbons such as benzene, toluene and xylene;
- chlorinated hydrocarbons such as trichloroethylene and carbon tetrachloride; and
- ketones such as acetone, MEK and cyclohexanone.

8.23.4 Applications

Polyurethane elastomers are used mainly in applications requiring high abrasion resistance or oil and solvent resistance or both. Typical applications include hydraulic seals, gaskets, diaphragms, hoses, cable sheathing, conveyor belts, wheels for roller skates and skateboards, soling for high-quality shoes, and coated fabrics. In all applications, the danger of hydrolysis and the limited heat resistance should be considered.

8.24 Epichlorohydrin Rubbers (CO, ECO and GECO)

Trade Names

Hydrin (Nippon Zeon Co.)
Epichlomer (Osaka Soda Co.)

8.24.1 Chemistry

Epichlorohydrin rubbers are saturated polymers of aliphatic polyethers with chloromethyl side chains. Three types of epichlorohydrin rubbers are currently available:
1) homopolymers of epichlorohydrin **(Fig. 8.29)** designated as **CO**;
2) copolymers of epichlorohydrin and ethylene oxide **(Fig. 8.30)** designated as **ECO**; and

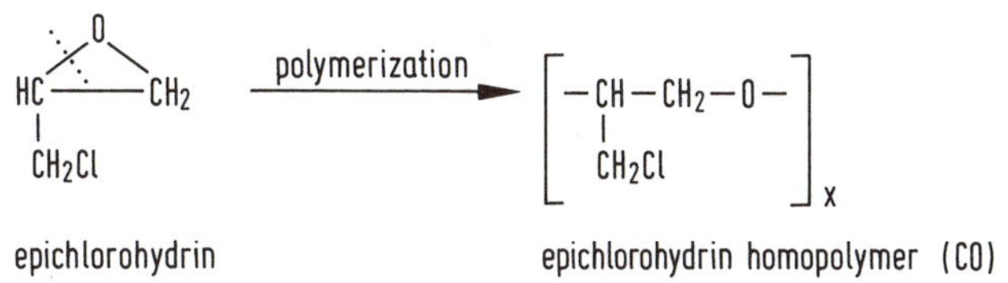

epichlorohydrin   epichlorohydrin homopolymer (CO)

Fig. 8.29: Synthesis of CO

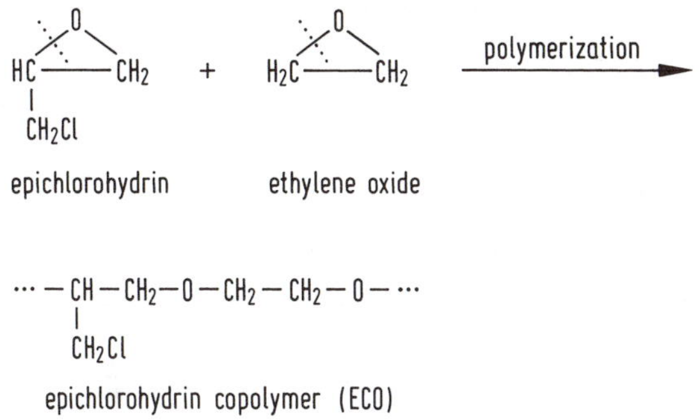

epichlorohydrin   ethylene oxide

··· — CH — CH$_2$—O—CH$_2$ — CH$_2$ — O — ···
     |
   CH$_2$Cl

epichlorohydrin copolymer (ECO)

Fig. 8.30: Synthesis of ECO

3) terpolymers of epichlorohydrin, ethylene oxide and an unsaturated monomer (allyl glycidyl ether) **(Fig. 8.31)** designated according to ASTM D 1418 as **GECO** (the unsaturated monomer provides double bonds in side chains pendant from the fully saturated backbone to enable sulphur cure).

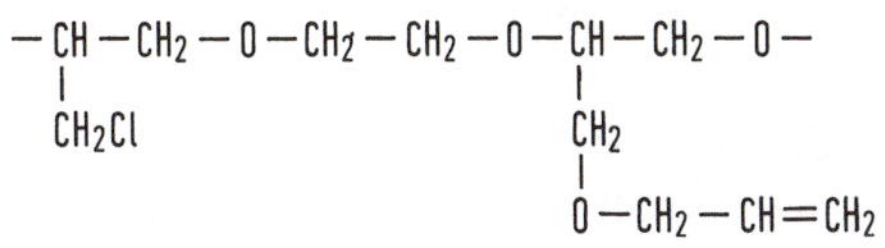

— CH — CH$_2$ — O — CH$_2$ — CH$_2$ — O — CH — CH$_2$ — O —
   | |
 CH$_2$Cl   CH$_2$
                                  O—CH$_2$ — CH=CH$_2$

Fig. 8.31: Structural Formula of GECO Terpolymer

The saturation of the backbone imparts high resistance to oxygen and ozone, while the oxygen and chlorine atoms provide polarity to the polymer chains and hence resistance to nonpolar or hydrocarbon fluids.

8.24.2 Compounding

Epichlorohydrin compounds usually contain carbon black or mineral fillers or both, processing aids, ester-type plasticizers, antioxidants, acid acceptors and a cure system. Satisfactory acid acceptors include red lead oxide, dibasic lead phosphite, basic lead silicate and magnesium oxide. Their presence is essential to stabilize the vulcanizate by reacting with the small amounts of hydrogen chloride, which may be released when the elastomer is exposed to high temperatures.

CO and ECO rubbers, being fully saturated, cannot be cured with sulphur. They can be cured with diamines or ethylene thiourea, which react with the chloromethyl groups. The terpolymer (GECO) can be cured with conventional sulphur, peroxide systems or ethylene thiourea.

Blends of CO, ECO and GECO offer vulcanizates with intermediate properties that are dependent on the amount of each polymer. The terpolymer GECO can be blended with conventional rubbers such as SBR and NBR using sulphur or peroxide as a common curing agent.

Most ECO vulcanizates need a postcure in an oven with circulating air to develop optimum physical properties, particularly compression set. A period of 6 h at 175 °C is typical.

8.24.3 Vulcanizate Properties

Many of the vulcanizate properties will vary depending on the polymer type. However, it can generally be said that the vulcanizates of the three epichlorohydrin types are resistant to high temperatures, oils, ozone and flame.

The vulcanizates of the homopolymer (CO) are outstanding in their low air permeability, being less than half that of IIR elastomers. In addition, their flame, ozone and heat resistance are superior to those of the copolymer (ECO). On the other hand, the copolymer vulcanizates are much more resilient and flexible at low temperatures, but the air permeability is higher, being comparable to that of medium/high NBR elastomers.

The vulcanizates of both CO and ECO show good resistance to swelling in mineral oils and aliphatic hydrocarbons. Their electrical insulation properties and radiation resistance are generally poor. The temperature range for continuous use is about $-15\,°C$ to $+130\,°C$ with CO and $-40\,°C$ to $+120\,°C$ with ECO elastomers.

The properties of the terpolymer (GECO) vulcanizates are comparable to those of the copolymer. However, the heat resistance and compression set are poorer when sulphur-cured. These disadvantages will be eliminated when peroxide cure is used.

Epichlorohydrin elastomers, as a group, are not recommended for use in:
- aromatic and chlorinated hydrocarbons;
- alcohols;
- ketones and esters;
- glycol-based brake fluids;
- phosphate ester hydraulic fluids;
- gasohols and sour gasolines (section 6.21); and
- hot water and steam.

Tables 8.12 and 8.13 show the resistance of typical ECO compounds to different liquid classes.

The widespread use of epichlorohydrin elastomers has been inhibited because of other drawbacks, mainly their corrosive effects on metals and their tendency to revert (soften) after long-term exposure to high temperatures. However, these drawbacks can be overcome to some extent by compounding.

Table 8.12: Resistance of Typical ECO Vulcanizates to ASTM Oils after 168 h at 125 °C

Medium	Average Volume Increase (%)
ASTM oil No. 1	0 – 2
ASTM oil No. 2	2 – 4
ASTM oil No. 3	8 – 12

Table 8.13: Resistance of Typical ECO Vulcanizates to Various Liquids after 168 h at Room Temperature

Medium	Average Volume Increase (%)
ASTM fuel A	1 – 2
ASTM fuel B	15 – 20
ASTM fuel C	40 – 45
ASTM fuel D	>100
Water	5 – 10
Ethanol	20 – 25
Methanol	20 – 25
Trichloroethylene	>100
Acetone	>100
Ethyl acetate	>100

8.24.4 Applications

Typical applications of epichlorohydrin elastomers include seals, gaskets, diaphragms, hoses, belting, wire and cable jackets, coated fabrics and printing rolls. In all these applications the corrosion resistance of contiguous metals must be considered.

8.25 Propylene Oxide Rubbers (GPO)

Trade Name

Parel (Nippon Zeon Co.)

8.25.1 Chemistry

Propylene oxide rubbers (**GPO**) are copolymers of propylene oxide and allyl glycidyl ether, which provides double bonds in side chains pendant from the fully saturated backbone (**Fig. 8.32**).

The double bonds in the side chains enable vulcanization with sulphur and conventional accelerators. The saturated backbone imparts resistance to oxygen, ozone and elevated temperatures.

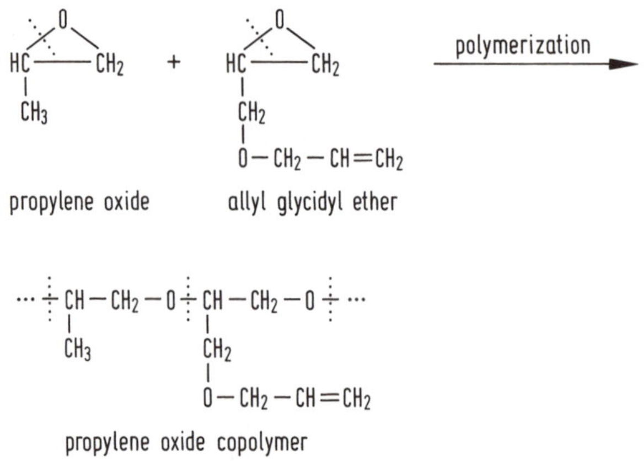

Fig. 8.32: Synthesis of GPO

8.25.2 Compounding

A typical GPO compound usually contains carbon black, zinc oxide, an antioxidant, a processing aid and a vulcanizing agent consisting of sulphur and conventional accelerators.

8.25.3 Vulcanizate Properties

GPO elastomers show high resilience, excellent flex-crack resistance and excellent low-temperature flexibility. In several respects they are similar to NR elastomers, but have in addition the following advantages:
– good resistance to heat aging and ozone; and
– moderate resistance to mineral oils and aliphatic hydrocarbons.

The normal service temperature range is about $-50\,°C$ to $+120\,°C$.

However, GPO elastomers are not recommended for use in aromatic and chlorinated hydrocarbons, alcohols, ketones and esters. **Table 8.14** shows the fluid resistance of typical GPO vulcanizates.

8.25.4 Applications

GPO elastomers can be expected to perform similarly to NR vulcanizates in dynamic applications. They may be used where high temperature and weather resistance are required in addition to good dynamic properties.

Table 8.14: Fluid Resistance of Typical GPO Vulcanizates after 168 h Immersion Test

Medium	Temperature (°C)	Average Volume Increase (%)
ASTM oil No. 1	100	10−15
ASTM oil No. 2	100	40−45
ASTM oil No. 3	100	95−105
Brake fluid (glycol base)	100	>100
ASTM fuel A	Room	50−60
ASTM fuel B	Room	>150
ASTM fuel C	Room	>200
ASTM fuel D	Room	>250
Water	Room	3− 6
Water	100	10−20
Ethanol	Room	>150
Methanol	Room	>100
Trichloroethylene	Room	>300
Acetone	Room	>150
Ethyl acetate	Room	>200

8.26 Polysulphide Rubbers (T)

Trade Names

FA and ST Polysulphide Rubbers
LP Liquid Polysulphide Polymers (Marton Thiokol is the major manufacturer of polysulphide rubbers worldwide. Other manufacturers include Toray Thiokol, a Marton joint venture in Japan. It is also believed that both the former Soviet Union and China produce polysulphide rubbers.)

8.26.1 Chemistry

Polysulphide rubbers (T) are produced by reacting a suitable aliphatic dichloride with aqueous solution of sodium polysulphide, as shown in **Fig. 8.33**. They are available in two forms: solids and liquids.

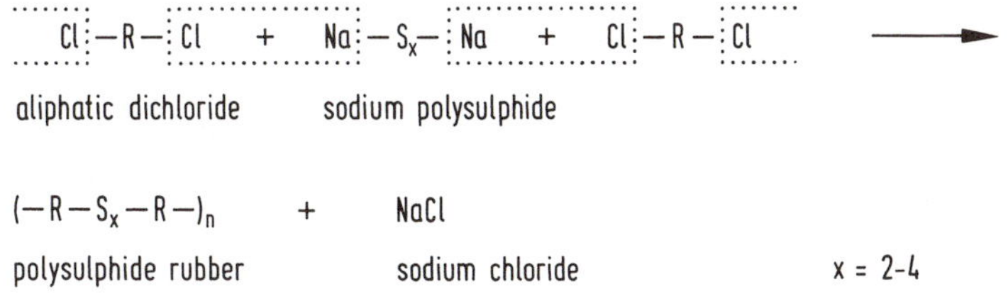

$$Cl-R-Cl \quad + \quad Na-S_x-Na \quad + \quad Cl-R-Cl \quad \longrightarrow$$

aliphatic dichloride   sodium polysulphide

$$(-R-S_x-R-)_n \quad + \quad NaCl$$

polysulphide rubber   sodium chloride $x = 2-4$

Fig. 8.33: General Method for Synthesis of Polysulphide Rubbers

The solid rubbers can be processed on conventional rubber equipment and subsequently cured at high temperatures. The liquid polymers are obtained by controlled chain-scission of high-molecular-weight polymers and can be cured in place at room temperature to solid polymers without shrinkage. They are discussed separately below because they are different materials from the processing point of view.

8.26.2 Solid Polysulphide Rubbers

The solid rubbers to be considered are the polysulphide types: A, FA and ST of Marton Thiokol. The raw materials for production of these rubbers, the total sulphur content, the terminal groups of the polymer chains and the specific gravity of the rubbers are given in **Table 8.15.**

Table 8.15: Polysulphide Rubbers and Raw Materials for Production

Polysulphide Type	Base Monomer	Sulphur Rank* (x)	Sulphur Content (%)	Terminals	Specific Gravity
A	Ethylene dichloride	4	84	−OH	1.60
FA	Dichloroethyl formal + Ethylene dichloride	2	47	−OH	1.34
ST	Dichloroethyl formal + 2% 1,2,3 trichloropropane (to provide branching and cross-linking)	2.2	37	−SH	1.25

* Sulphur rank is the amount of sulphur in the specific sodium sulphide used (N_2S_x). It represents an average value.

Thiokol A was the first commercial polysulphide rubber. It was made from ethylene dichloride and sodium tetrasulphide, as shown in **Fig. 8.34**. After vulcanization, it showed the highest solvent resistance, which is due to its high sulphur content, about 84%. The main disadvantage of this type was the difficult processibility. It had an unpleasant odor and gave off irritating fumes during processing. In addition, the compression set, heat resistance and low-temperature flexibility of its vulcanizates were very poor.

Subsequently, the improved type, **FA**, was developed to replace type A. It is a linear polysulphide polymer, synthesized by reacting a mixture of ethylene dichloride and dichloroethyl formal ($Cl-CH_2-CH_2-O-CH_2-O-CH_2-CH_2-Cl$) with sodium polysulphide. The terminals of the polymer chains are presumably hydroxyl groups (−OH) formed by hydrolysis of the organic chlorides during the polymerization process.

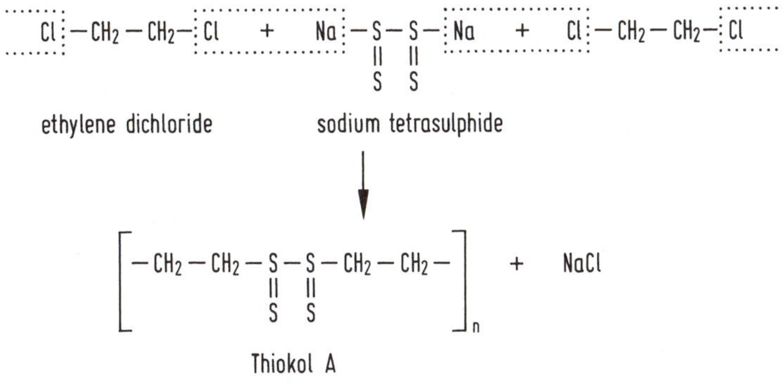

Fig. 8.34: Synthesis of Thiokol A

Type FA has eliminated many of the disadvantages of type A. Its vulcanizates have less odor, better physical properties and a wider service temperature range. However, the solvent resistance is not as good as that of type A vulcanizates. The compression set is also poor.

ST polysulphide rubber was developed later. The chlorides used for its synthesis are dichloroethyl formal and about 2% 1,2,3 trichloropropane ($CH_2Cl-CHCl-CH_2Cl$). The latter is included to introduce some branches in the polymer chains.

After polymerization, the water dispersion of the obtained high-molecular-weight polymer is given an additional treatment prior to coagulation and drying. This process is carried out to cleave some of the disulphide links in the polymer and thus lower its molecular weight. The terminals of the polymer chains and the branches are mercaptan or thiol ($-SH$) groups, being generated in the "splitting operation."

The vulcanization of polysulphide rubbers proceeds via the terminal groups. With type FA, the process is a chain extension rather than cross-linking. The rubber, even when vulcanized, has no compression set because it is a linear polymer without cross-linking.

In the case of type ST (being a branched polymer), chain extension could proceed in three directions to give few chemical cross-links. After prolonged press cure followed by oven postcuring, the elastomer exhibits fair compression set up to 70°C. Other advantages include the absence of much odor and the excellent low-temperature flexibility, compared with former types. However, these improved properties are obtained at some sacrifice in the solvent resistance, because of its low sulphur content of 37%.

FA polysulphide rubber is normally cured with zinc oxide. The actual mechanism is not clear. Presumably, zinc oxide reacts with the hydroxyl terminal groups in the following manner:

$$R-OH + ZnO + HO-R \rightarrow R-O-R + Zn(OH)_2$$

Since type FA has a very high viscosity, the rubber must be plasticized chemically by adding a peptizer (section 2.6) prior to further compounding. After plasticizing, reinforcement fillers, normally various grades of carbon black, are added. Stearic acid is usually included as a mill and mold release agent.

ST polysulphide rubber is vulcanized via oxidation of the mercaptan end groups to sulphide bonds. The most frequently used oxidizing agent is zinc peroxide. The vulcanization mechanism may be illustrated as follows:

$$R-SH + ZnO_2 + HS-R \rightarrow R-S-S-R + ZnO + H_2O$$

Peptization is not necessary because, as has been mentioned, the molecular weight (i.e., viscosisty) of the ST type can be adjusted to the desired range during manufacture. As with type FA, reinforcement is obtained by incorporating carbon black. Stearic acid is also included as a mill and mold release agent.

Both FA and ST polysulphide rubbers can be blended with other rubbers, primarily NBR and CR, to overcome some of the drawbacks in processing and physical properties. At the same time, advantage is taken of polysulphide's high resistance to solvents, ozone and weather.

8.26.3 Liquid Polysulphide Polymers

Liquid polysulphide (LP) polymers are available in various viscosities. The chlorides used for their synthesis are dichloroethyl formal and small amounts of 1,2,3 trichloropropane to introduce some branching. They are manufactured using a procedure similar to that described for the solid type ST, except that the molecular weight of the polymer is reduced to a considerably greater degree. They have a certain proportion of branched chains and can be cured without shrinkage at room temperature to solid rubbers with very little cross-linking. The cured compounds exhibit more or less the general properies of solid ST vulcanizates, but the physical properties are poorer.

LP polysulphides can be compounded with a variety of fillers to give the required viscosity and to improve the vulcanizate properties. Curing is accomplished by oxidizing the mercaptan terminals to sulphide bonds, as with the solid type ST (see above).

The most commonly used curing agents are lead dioxide, certain grades of manganese dioxide, calcium peroxide, zinc peroxide and p-quinone dioxime. The rate of curing may be accelerated or retarded by using small amounts of specific additives.

Adhesion of LP compounds to various substrates is achieved by adding adhesion promoters. It can be improved by treating the substrate with suitable primers such as epoxy resins.

LP compounds are commonly formulated as one- or two-component systems. The one-component mix contains all ingredients (including the curing agent) in a dry condition. It is package-stable and will cure when exposed to atmospheric moisture. The two-component systems include a base component (containing the LP polymer with all ingredients except curing agent) and a curing agent component in paste form. The two components are blended on site just before use.

LP compounds are applied by pouring or by pressure gun, spatula or brush, depending upon the viscosity.

8.26.4 Vulcanizate Properties

The properties of polysulphide elastomers are determined by the type of chain structure (linear or branched) and the sulphur content of the base rubber. As the sulphur content is increased, the solvent resistance is improved. High sulphur content also reduces the permeability to vapors and gases. However, the basic characteristics of polysulphide elastomers, as a group, can be summarized as follows:
- excellent resistance to mineral oils and greases (however, they tend to shrink excessively at temperatures above 70°C, as shown in **Table 8.16**;

Table 8.16: Resistance of Typical FA and ST Polysulphide Vulcanizates to ASTM Oils at 70 and 100°C after 168 h

Medium	Temperature (°C)	Average Volume Change (%)	
		FA Vulcanizates	ST Vulcanizates
ASTM oil No. 1	70	− 2	−2
	100	−11	−7
ASTM oil No. 2	70	− 1	+1
	100	−10	−3
ASTM oil No. 3	70	+ 2	+3
	100	− 9	+4

- good resistance to swelling in various solvents, depending upon the sulphur content of the base polymer (**Table 8.17** shows the solvent resistance of typical FA vulcanizates versus ST vulcanizates; the solvent resistance of cured LP polymers is comparable to that of ST elastomers);

Table 8.17: Fluid Resistance of Typical FA Polysulphide Vulcanizates versus ST Vulcanizates after 168 h at Room Temperature

Medium	Average Volume Increase (%)	
	FA Vulcanizates	ST Vulcanizates
Benzene	95	115
Toluene	55	75
Xylene	30	40
Carbon tetrachloride	35	45
Acetone	20	35
Methylethyl ketone	30	50
Ethyl acetate	20	35
Water	1	1

- excellent resistance to oxidation, ozone, sunlight and weather in general;
- low permeability to gases and vapors, depending upon the sulphur content of the base polymer; and

– temperature range for continuous use of about −35°C to +80°C with type FA and −45°C to +80°C with type ST.

The drawbacks of polysulphide elastomers include:
– unpleasant odor;
– relatively low heat resistance;
– poor physical properties, especially those of cured liquid polymers; and
– poor compression set, unless based on type ST.

8.26.5 Applications

Typical applications of polysulphide elastomers include gasoline and aromatic fuel hoses, coating and printing rolls, gas meter diaphragms, O-rings, putties, sealants, paint spray, coated paper gaskets and binders for cork.

The use of polysulphide elastomers could have been greater if they did not have the above-mentioned drawbacks. They are usually used when no suitable alternative can be found for the fluid resistance offered.

8.27 Polyphosphazene Rubbers (FZ and PZ)

Trade Name

Eypel F, Eypel A (Ethyl Corporation)

Former Name

PNF Elastomer (Firestone; Firestone sold its polyphosphazene tecnology to Ethyl Corporation)

8.27.1 Chemistry

The polyphosphazenes FZ and PZ are similar to silicone rubbers in that they are semi-inorganic materials (i.e., partly organic and partly inorganic in nature). They are characterized by a polymer backbone consisting of alternate phosphorus and nitrogen atoms with pendant organic groups attached to the phosphorus atoms.

Polyphosphazene rubbers are made from an inorganic polymer, poly-dichlorophosphazene, by replacing the chlorine atoms with organic groups. If the inorganic polymer is reacted with the sodium salts of mixed fluoroalcohols, a poly-fluoroalkoxyphosphazene rubber (FZ) is obtained. Replacement of the chlorines with phenoxy and substituted phenoxy groups yields a nonhalogenated polyaryl-oxyphosphazene rubber (PZ). The synthesis of FZ and PZ rubbers are shown in **Fig. 8.35**.

Ethyl Corporation is currently commercializing two polyphosphazenes: Eypel F (FZ) and Eypel A (PZ).

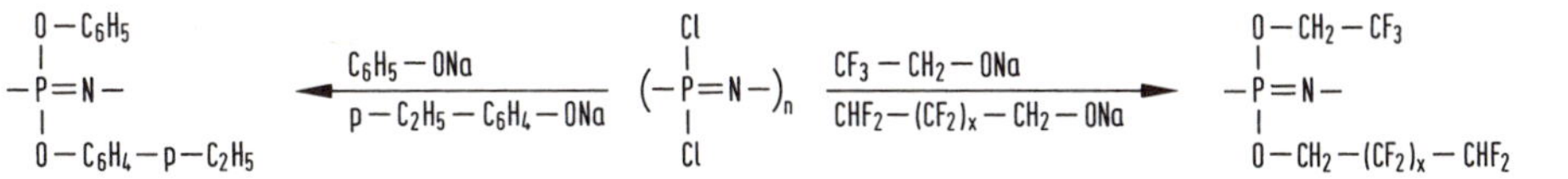

$$\begin{array}{ccccc}
\begin{matrix} O-C_6H_5 \\ | \\ -P=N- \\ | \\ O-C_6H_4-p-C_2H_5 \end{matrix}
& \xleftarrow[p-C_2H_5-C_6H_4-ONa]{C_6H_5-ONa}
& \begin{matrix} Cl \\ | \\ (-P=N-)_n \\ | \\ Cl \end{matrix}
& \xrightarrow[CHF_2-(CF_2)_x-CH_2-ONa]{CF_3-CH_2-ONa}
& \begin{matrix} O-CH_2-CF_3 \\ | \\ -P=N- \\ | \\ O-CH_2-(CF_2)_x-CHF_2 \end{matrix}
\end{array}$$

polyaryloxyphosphazene rubber (PZ)　　　　polydichlorophosphazene　　　　polyfluoroalkoxyphosphazene rubber (FZ)

Fig. 8.35: Synthesis of FZ and PZ

8.27.2 Polyfluoroalkoxyphosphazene Rubber (FZ)

FZ can be compounded in much the same manner as conventional rubbers. Typical FZ compounds contain reinforcing fillers, pigments and organic peroxides as curing agents. Special additives may also be included to achieve specific properties.

FZ compounds are commercially available in "ready to use" form, with or without the peroxide curative added. Most compounds have a distinctive dark green color to provide easy identification of the FZ parts.

The vulcanizates usually require an oven postcure to develop optimum physical properties, particularly compression set. A period of 4 h at 175 °C is typical.

The distinctive properties of FZ vulcanizates can be listed as follows:
– wide service temperature range (about −60 °C to +175 °C);
– excellent resistance to oxygen, ozone and flame;
– good compression set resistance;
– good flex fatigue resistance and damping properties;
– improved tear and abrasion resistance, better than that of fluorosilicone elastomers;
– gas permeability about half that of fluorosilicones; and
– good to excellent resistance to a broad range of fluids, including petroleum oils, hydrocarbon fuels, silicone fluids and greases, silicate esters, diester synthetic lubricants and aryl phosphate esters (e.g., selected Pydraul types).

However, there are certain fluids that cause excessive swelling to FZ elastomers, such as:
– oxygenated solvents, including ketones, ethers and low-molecular-weight esters;
– alkyl-aryl phosphate esters (skydrol types); and
– methanol-containing fuels.

Furthermore, FZ elastomers are not recommended for permanent service at temperatures exceeding 175 °C.

The above-mentioned properties of FZ elastomers suggest that they can be used as O-rings, shaft seals, gaskets, hoses and shock mounts in aerospace, military, oil-field and petrochemical applications. In spite of the very high price, it is expected that interest in these materials will increase. They may replace other materials currently used as "the best available compromise" for some applications.

8.27.3 Polyaryloxyphosphazene Rubber (PZ)

PZ is also cured by peroxides. The vulcanizates offer excellent fire resistance without the presence of halogens. In case of fire they produce low levels of smoke.

These properties suggest that they are suited for electrical insulation applications where low flammability and low toxicity are required.

8.28 Selection of the Basic Rubber

Tables 8.18−8.20 and **Figures 8.36−8.55** give a summary of the basic properties of most common rubber vulcanizates currently available commercially. They are intended only as a guide to help designers and users in selecting the basic rubber for the appropriate compound.

After defining the operating requirements, designing the optimum shape and size of the component and selecting the candidate compound, functional tests are carried out. If necessary, final adjustments are made to the component design or the compound or both. As previously mentioned, properties can be modified considerably by compounding.

Table 8.18: Scheme for Selecting Elastomeric Materials

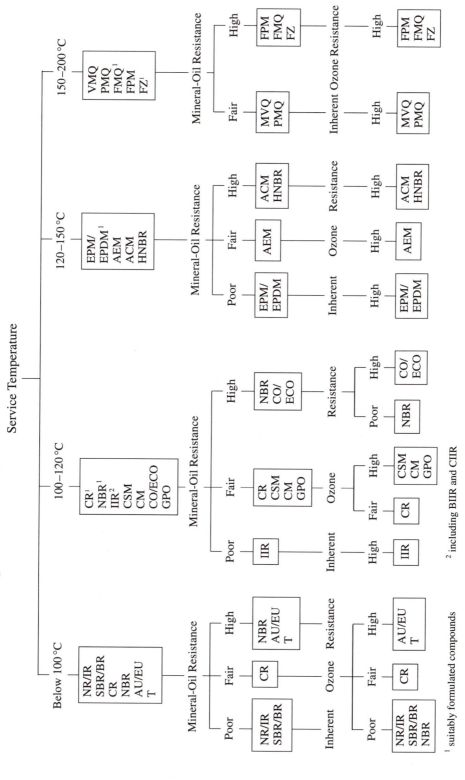

Table 8.19: Temperature Range of Most Common Elastomer Types

Elastomer Base	Temperature Range (°C)	
	−	+
CR	40	100
IIR	40	120
IR	55	90
NBR	40	100
HNBR*	25	150
NR	55	90
SBR	50	100
ACM	20	150
AEM	30	150
CSM	20	120
EPDM*	50	150
FPM	20	200
FFKM	0	250
VMQ	60	200
FMQ	60	175
ECO	40	120
AU/EU	25	100
YBPO	50	100

* peroxide cure

Table 8.20: Price Index of Unvulcanized Rubber Compouds

Rubber Base	Price Index (SBR = 1)
CR	2.5
IIR	1.5
IR	1.3
NBR	1.8
HNBR	11.2
NR	1.1
SBR	1.0
ACM	3.5
AEM	4.3
CSM	2.7
EPDM	1.5
FPM	30.0
FFKM	5,600.0
VMQ	8.5
FMQ	75.0
ECO	4.5
AU/EU	4.5
YBPO	5.0

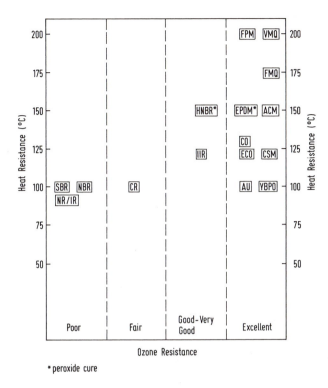

Fig. 8.36: Heat and Ozone Resistance of Different Elastomer Types

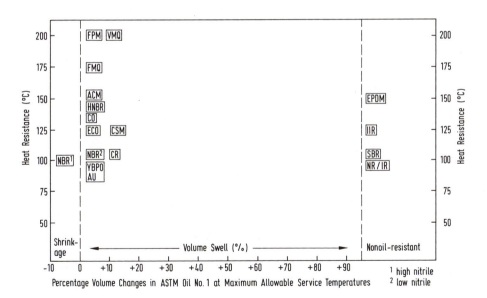

Fig. 8.37: Heat and Swell Resistance of Different Elastomer Types in ASTM Oil
No. 1

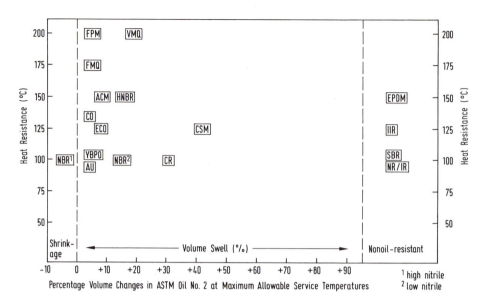

Fig. 8.38: Heat and Swell Resistance of Different Elastomer Types in ASTM Oil No. 2

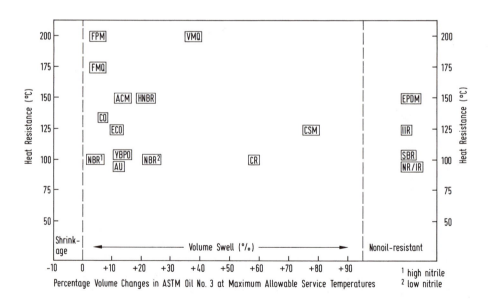

Fig. 8.39: Heat and Swell Resistance of Different Elastomer Types in ASTM Oil No. 3

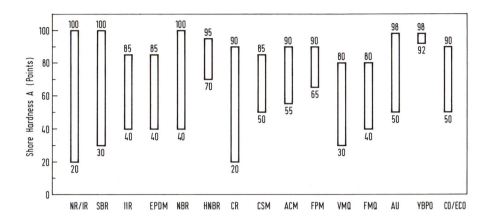

Fig. 8.40: Common Ranges of Shore Hardness A of Different Elastomer Types at Room Temperature

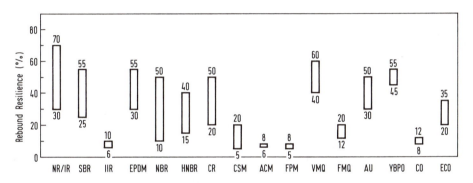

Fig. 8.41: Common Ranges of Rebound Resilience of Different Elastomer Types at Room Temperature

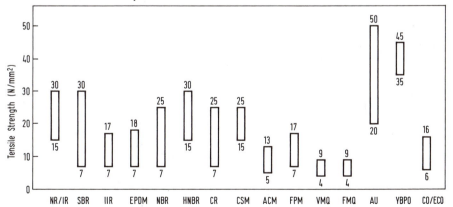

Fig. 8.42: Common Ranges of Tensile Strength of Different Elastomer Types at Room Temperature

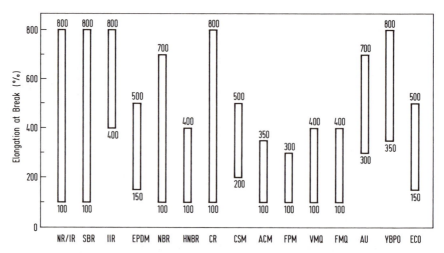

Fig. 8.43: Common Ranges of Elongation at Break of Different Elastomer Types at Room Temperature

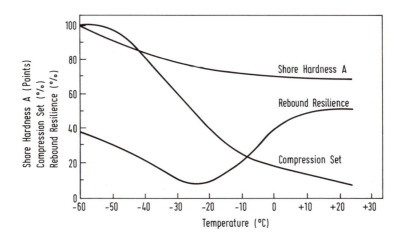

Fig. 8.44: Changes in Hardness, Compression Set and Rebound Resilience of a Conventional EPDM Compound with Decreasing Temperatures

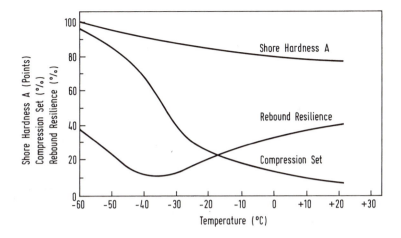

Fig. 8.45: Changes in Hardness, Compression Set and Rebound Resilience of a Low-Temperature EPDM Compound with Decreasing Temperatures

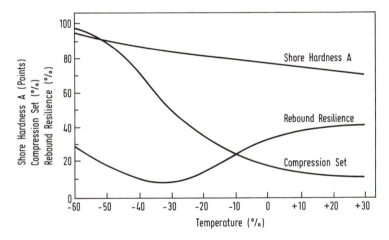

Fig. 8.46: Changes in Hardness, Compression Set and Rebound Resilience of an SBR Compound with Decreasing Temperatures

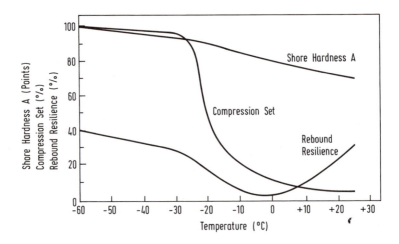

Fig. 8.47: Changes in Hardness, Compression Set and Rebound Resilience of a Conventional NBR Compound with Decreasing Temperatures

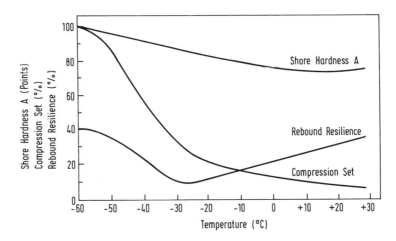

Fig. 8.48: Changes in Hardness, Compression Set and Rebound Resilience of a Low-Temperature NBR Compound with Decreasing Temperatures

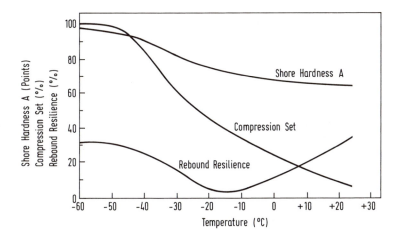

Fig. 8.49: Changes in Hardness, Compression Set and Rebound Resilience of a Conventional CR Compound with Decreasing Temperatures

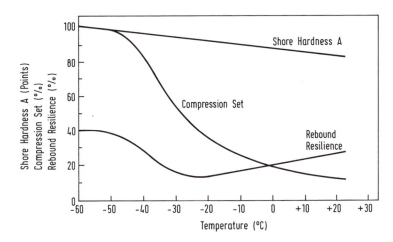

Fig. 8.50: Changes in Hardness, Compression Set and Rebound Resilience of a Conventional ECO Compound with Decreasing Temperatures

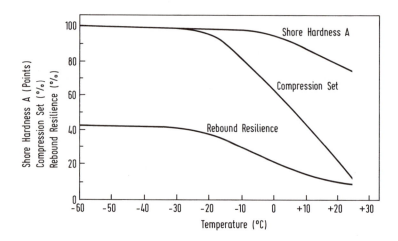

Fig. 8.51: Changes in Hardness, Compression Set and Rebound Resilience of a Conventional ACM Compound with Decreasing Temperatures

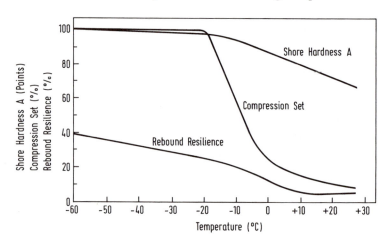

Fig. 8.52: Changes in Hardness, Compression Set and Rebound Resilience of a Conventional FPM Compound with Decreasing Temperatures

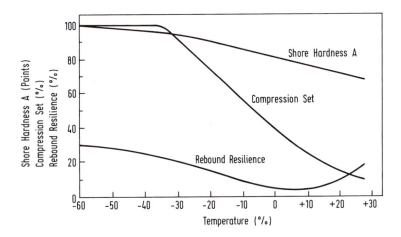

Fig. 8.53: Changes in Hardness, Compression Set and Rebound Resilience of a Low-Temperature FPM compound (Viton GLT) with Decreasing Temperatures

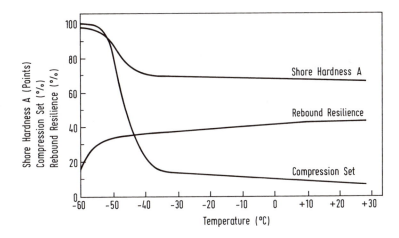

Fig. 8.54: Changes in Hardness, Compression Set and Rebound Resilience of a Selected VMQ Compound with Decreasing Temperatures

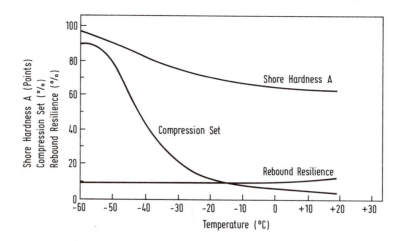

Fig. 8.55: Changes in Hardness, Compression Set and Rebound Resilience of a Selected FMQ Compound with Decreasing Temperatures

CHAPTER 9

Thermoplastic Elastomers (TPEs)

9.1 Introduction

As has been mentioned in section 1.6, thermoplastic elastomers **(TPEs)**, also called elastoplastics, are polymers that combine the processibility of plastomers (e.g., polyethylene, PVC) and the functional performance of conventional elastomers (i.e., the chemically cross-linked rubbers).

Unlike conventional rubbers, TPEs need no vulcanization and yet they show elastomeric properties within a certain temperature range. They can be processed on conventional plastic equipment such as injection molders, blow molders, extruders and so on. The transition from a processible melt to a solid elastomeric material is rapid and reversible. The elastomeric properties are developed immediately on cooling. The scrap generated during processing can be granulated and reused in blends with virgin material without any significant loss in physical properties. The advantages in processing simplicity, coupled with many useful properties of the end product, have resulted in rapid growth of TPEs. They are steadily replacing vulcanized rubbers in a large number of applications.

9.2 Advantages and Disadvantages of TPEs

The practical advantages of TPEs versus comparable vulcanized rubbers include the following:
– Little or no compounding is required. Most TPEs are "ready to use" materials, thus eliminating the batch-to-batch variations of conventional rubber compounds as well as the high energy consumption during mixing and vulcanization.
– Injection molding cycles are very fast, leading to lower finished part costs.
– The scrap can be easily recycled, whereas the scrap of vulcanized rubbers is usually discarded because it is difficult to recycle.
– Most TPEs have lower density.
– Product consistency is better than Comparable vulcanized rubbers.
– There is tighter dimensional tolerance of the parts.
– TPEs are very easy to color with many types of pigments or dyes.
– Less skilled labor is needed.
– Hazardous fumes (e.g., nitrosamines) are normally not generated during processing.
    The disadvantages of TPEs include the following:
– They have higher compression set and less thermal stability.
– They melt at elevated temperatures with the result that they are not suitable for applications requiring brief exposures beyond the upper service temperature. Comparable vulcanized rubbers would be suitable for such a brief exposure because they do not melt at high temperatures.

– There is a limited number of low hardness compounds.
– They may require drying before processing. This step is not common with conventional rubbers.

The high compression set and low thermal stability of TPEs don't allow these materials to be used in areas where the compression set is important and the working conditions are critical, for example, at temperatures above normal and at high strain.

9.3 Types of TPEs

As has been mentioned in chapter 3 (section 3.2), thermoplastic elastomers are identified by inserting the letter Y in front of the rubber designation. There are two major groups of commercially available TPEs:
1) Block copolymers consisting of chain molecules, each of which contains sequences of "soft" and "hard" segments (section 9.4). This group includes the following types:
    – thermoplastic polyurethanes (YAU, YEU);
    – ether-ester block copolymers (YBPO);
    – ether-amide block copolymers;
    – styrene-diene block copolymers (YSBR and YSIR); and
    – styrene-(ethylene-butylene) block copolymers (SEBS).
2) Olefin based elastomeric alloys consisting of cured rubber particles dispersed in a continuous thermoplastic matrix such as polypropylene (PP) and chlorinated polyolefins. More details are given in section 9.10.

It is expected that more types of TPEs may become available over the next few years.

9.4 Morphology of Block Copolymers

Block copolymers (section 1.5) consist of chain molecules, each of which contains sequences of "soft" and "hard" segments **(Fig. 9.1)** These are dissimilar and incompatible with each other so that they act as individual phases. The dominant soft

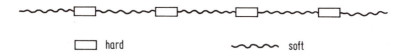

☐ hard   ∿∿∿ soft

Fig. 9.1: A Chain Molecule of a Block Copolymer

segments are flexible, amorphous and have low glass transition temperatures. Conversely, the hard segments have a high melting point and tend to aggregate at ordinary temperatures into rigid domains to form physically effective "pseudo" cross-links, as illustrated in **Fig. 9.2**.

When the block copolymer is heated to the processing temperature, the forces that bind the hard segments together will be destroyed. It is then possible to

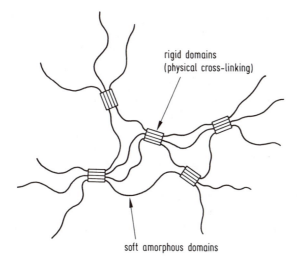

Fig. 9.2: Morphology of Thermoplastic Elastomers

process the polymer as a conventional thermoplastic, because the macromolecules are not any longer bound together. On cooling, the hard segments reassociate into rigid domains and the material shows elastomeric properties once again.

Suitable solvents are also able to destroy the pseudo cross-links. When the solvent is evaporated, the hard segments reassociate into rigid domains.

The properties of the block copolymers can be adjusted by varying the ratio of the monomers and the lengths of hard and soft segments. The polymers become harder and stiffer as the ratio of the hard to soft phase is increased. The upper service temperature of the block copolymer will depend on the softening point of the hard phase. On the other hand, the low-temperature properties and fluid resistance are controlled largely by the soft segments.

The molecular weight usually controls the processibility of the polymer. Low-molecular-weight polymers are easier to process but have poorer service properties than high-molecular-weight analogues.

9.5 Thermoplastic Polyurethane Elastomers (YAU and YEU)

Trade Names

Desmopan (Bayer AG)
Pellethane (Dow Chemical)

9.5.1 Chemistry

The millable and castable polyurethane types have been discussed separately in chapter 8 (section 8.23). The thermoplastic polyurethane elastomers (YAU and YEU) are block copolymers consisting of soft amorphous segments and hard crystalline segments. The soft segments are the long flexible polyester or polyether chains. The hard segments are formed through the reaction between the diisocyanate and the low-molecular-weight chain extender (section 8.23).

At room temperature, the soft segments are incompatible with the hard segments, which leads to phase separation. Because of the phase separation, the hard segments of different molecules agglomerate to produce semi-ordered regions that act as physical cross-links and reinforcing filler. The forces of association are believed to be hydrogen bonding. The soft segments form an amorphous matrix, which accounts for the elastomeric properties. At elevated temperatures the rigid domains soften, allowing the polymer to be processed by the usual methods for thermoplastic materials.

After processing, the parts achieve their optimum properties by postcuring at about 110°C for 24 h. Parts that are not postcured should be left for 30 days to develop optimum properties, although they will not show minimum compression set.

9.5.2 Properties of End Products

The heat stability and compression set resistance of thermoplastic polyurethanes are inferior to those of cross-linked types, but the other basic properties given in section 8.23 are similar.

9.5.3 Applications

(See section 8.23.)

9.6 Ether-Ester Block Copolymers (YBPO)

Trade Names

Hytrel (Du Pont)
Arnitel (Akzo)

9.6.1 Chemistry

Ether-ester block copolymers, designated YBPO according to ASTM D 1418, are block copolymers of hard crystalline segments and soft amorphous segments. The hard segment is an aromatic polyester, typically polybutylene terphthalate. The soft segment is an aliphatic polyether. The copolymers have the generalized structure shown in **Fig. 9.3**.

As with the thermoplastic polyurethane elastomers, the crystallizable hard segments associate to produce rigid regions that act as physical cross-links and reinforcing fillers. These physical cross-links will be destroyed at the processing temperature and the rigid domains soften, allowing the polymer to be processed on conventional plastic equipment.

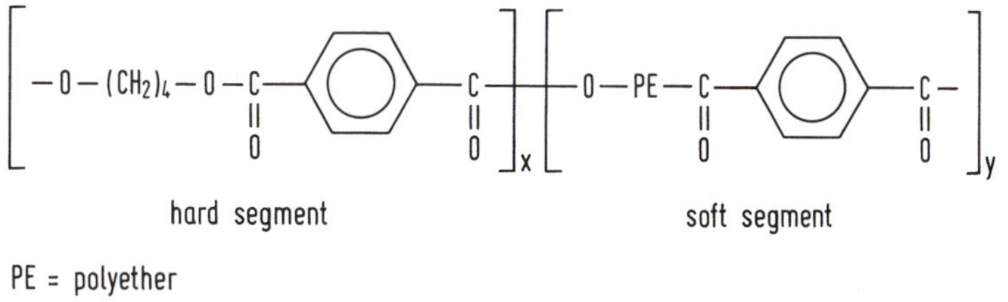

hard segment   soft segment

PE = polyether

Fig. 9.3: General Formula of YBPO

By varying the ratio of hard to soft segments, polymers can be obtained with a wide range of hardness grades.

9.6.2 Compounding

Ether-ester block copolymers are intended to be used as supplied. Additives, if required, are normally restricted to small amounts of pigments, light stabilizers, hydrolysis protective agents, flame retardants, blowing agents and other such materials.

After processing, the parts are postcured at about 110°C for 24h to achieve optimum properties, particularly compression set.

9.6.3 Properties of End Products

The distinctive properties of YBPO elastomeric products can be listed as follows:
- high hardness, typically between about 85 Shore A (35 D) and 72 Shore D;
- excellent mechanical properties;
- good resistance to flex fatigue;
- high resistance to degradation by oxygen and ozone due to chemical saturation of the polymer chains (however, YBPO elastomers are susceptible to oxidative degradation when exposed to ultraviolet light; for outdoor applications, the addition of light stabilizers is necessary);
- service temperature range of about −50 to +100°C;
- poor compression set above 70°C;
- good resistance to mineral oils and aliphatic hydrocarbons (in general, the fluid resistance increases considerably with increasing hardness of the polymer, as illustrated in **Table 9.1** and **Table 9.2**); and
- susceptibility to degradation by hydrolysis at elevated temperatures, even though the rate is much less than that of polyester urethanes (AU) [the hydrolysis resistance can be enhanced by adding a hydrolysis protective agent (Polycarbodiimide)].

YBPO elastomers are not recommended for permanent use with:
- phosphate ester hydraulic fluids;
- polyalkylene-glycol-based fluids;
- glycol-based brake fluids;

– aromatic hydrocarbons such as benzene and toluene;
– chlorinated hydrocarbons such as trichloroethylene and carbon tetrachloride;
– low-molecular-weight solvents such as ketones and esters; and
– acids and bases.

Table 9.1: Resistance of Various YBPO Elastomers (with Different Hardness) to ASTM Oils after 168 h at 100°C

Medium	Average Volume Increase (%) of YBPO with:		
	40 Shore D	55 Shore D	63 Shore D
ASTM oil No. 1	3	<1	0
ASTM oil No. 2	16	6	3
ASTM oil No. 3	25	10	6

Table 9.2: Resistance of Various YBPO Elastomers (with Different Hardness) to Organic Liquids after 168 h at Room Temperature

Medium	Average Volume Increase (%) of YBPO with:		
	40 Shore D	55 Shore D	63 Shore D
ASTM fuel A	10	6	2
ASTM fuel B	35	17	11
ASTM fuel C	53	21	17
ASTM fuel D	102	36	25
Trichloroethylene	195	60	40
Acetone	40	17	14
Ethyl acetate	56	20	16
Methanol	10	7	5

9.6.4 Applications

Typical applications of YBPO thermoplastic elastomers include hoses, tubing, seals, gaskets, various molded parts, wire and cable jacketing, thin-walled hollow articles and sports-shoe soles.

9.7 Ether-Amide Block Copolymers

Trade Names

Pebax (Atochem)

9.7.1 Chemistry

Ether-amide block copolymers are obtained by reacting a polyether diol with a dicarboxylic polyamide. The general formula of these block copolymers is shown in **Fig. 9.4**. They consist of linear and regular chains of rigid polyamide segments and flexible polyether segments.

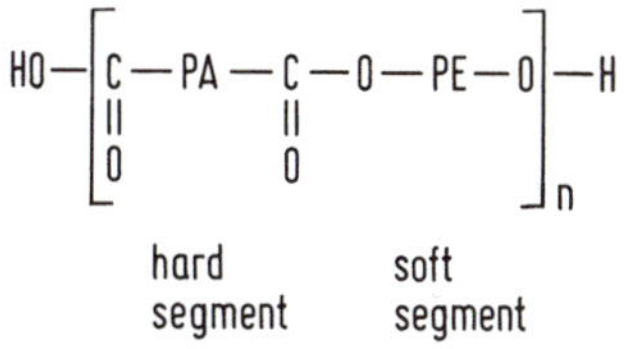

PA = polyamide block
PE = polyether block

Fig. 9.4: General Formula of Ether-Amide Block Copolymers

The polyamide and polyether segments are incompatible, resulting in the formation of a two-phase structure. As with other block copolymers, the hard polyamide segments associate at normal temperatures to produce rigid regions that act as physical cross-links and reinforcing fillers. At the processing temperature, the rigid domains soften, thus allowing the polymer to be processed on conventional plastic equipment.

9.7.2 Compounding

These block copolymers require stabilizers to achieve good resistance to ultraviolet light and high temperatures. Special grades can be filled with calcium carbonate, carbon black or glass fibers.

9.7.3 Properties of End Products

The properties of ether-amide block copolymers are controlled by the nature and length of polyether and polyamide segments. Because of the wide variety of available polyethers and polyamides, it is possible to obtain a great number of grades of ether-amide block copolymers with different properties. However, the main properties that characterize this entire family of polymers include:
– high mechanical properties;
– high resilience,

– high resistance to flex fatigue; and
– good resistance to mineral oils and greases as well as to many chemicals and
solvents (the fluid resistance is dependent on the polyamide content; rigid grades
with high polyamide content have good solvent and chemical resistance; the soft
grades with high polyether content are less resistant and show higher swelling).

9.7.4 Applications

The ether-amide block copolymers are relatively new. The main application areas
foreseen for these thermoplastic elastomers are hoses, tubing, wire and cable jacketing and molded components.

Because of their relatively high price, they are likely to be used only in special
cases.

9.8 Styrene-Diene Block Copolymers (YSBR and YSIR)

Trade Names

Kraton D in the United States and Cariflex TR in Europe (Shell Chemical Company)
Solprene (Phillips Chemical Company)

9.8.1 Chemistry

Thermoplastic styrene-diene block copolymers are block copolymers of styrene
and either butadiene or isoprene. The types are respectively designated SBS (or
YSBR) and SIS (or YSIR), where **S** indicates polystyrene, **B** indicates polybutadiene and **I** indicates polyisoprene. The simplest types are linear polymers
having molecules that consist of diene blocks in the middle and two terminal
styrene blocks, as illustrated in **Fig. 9.5 (a)**. Accordingly, they are called triblock
copolymers.

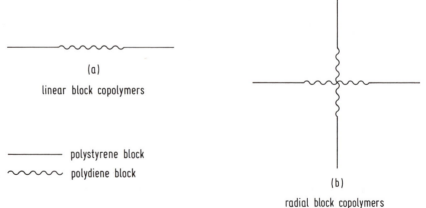

(a)
linear block copolymers

——————— polystyrene block
∿∿∿∿∿ polydiene block

(b)
radial block copolymers

Fig. 9.5: Structure of Linear and Radial Styrene-Diene Block Copolymers

Rather more complex are the radial types illustrated in **Fig. 9.5 (b)**. These consist of three or more arms of polydiene chains radiating from a central point. The outer end of each of these chains is attached to a polystyrene endblock.

The main differences between the linear and radial types are found in the solution and melt viscosity. The radial types have lower viscosity at equal molecular weight.

The hard polystyrene endblocks and the soft polydiene midblocks are incompatible, resulting in the formation of a two-phase structure at ordinary temperatures. The hard polystyrene segments associate to form rigid domains within a rubbery matrix of flexible polydiene segments. These hard segments act as physical cross-links and reinforcing filler. When the polymer is heated above the softening point of polystyrene, the material can be processed as conventional thermoplastics.

9.8.2 Compounding

SBS and SIS block copolymers are supplied both as compounds and as pure polymers for further compounding. Fillers, extenders, resins and other compounding ingredients can be incorporated to obtain properties required for different applications.

9.8.3 Properties of End Products

The distinctive properties of SBS and SIS block copolymers include:
– hardness ranges of about 40 Shore A to 50 Shore D;
– service temperature range of about $-50\,°C$ to $+65\,°C$;
– poor compression set above room temperature; and
– environmental aging and fluid resistance similar to those of SBR vulcanizates (section 8.4.3).

9.8.4 Applications

Typical applications of SBS and SIS block copolymers include shoe soles, hoses, tubing, insulation and jacketing for wires and cables, solvent-based and hot-melt adhesives, sealants, modifiers for bitumen, sporting goods and toys.

9.9 Styrene-Ethylene-Butylene Block Copolymers (SEBS)

Trade Names

Kraton G, Elexar (Shell Chemical Company)

9.9.1 Chemistry

A major disadvantage of SBS and SIS block copolymers (section 9.8) is their poor ozone and weathering resistance, due to the presence of unsaturation in the mid-block. This has led to the development of a new material with a saturated midblock consisting of poly (ethylene-butylene), as shown in **Fig. 9.6**. They are designated SEBS, where **S** is polystyrene and **EB** is poly (ethylene-butylene).

$$S \underset{}{\overline{}} \left[(CH_2 - CH_2)_x - (CH_2 - \underset{\underset{C_2H_5}{|}}{CH})_y \right]_n \underset{}{\overline{}} S$$

poly (ethylene-butylene) midblock

S = polystyrene block

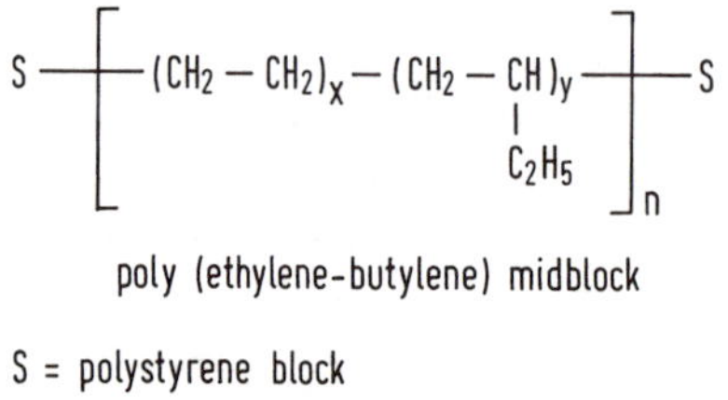

Fig. 9.6: General Formula of SEBS

As with SBS and SIS block copolymers, the hard polystyrene and the soft poly (ethylene-butylene) segments are incompatible. This leads to phase separation at normal temperature. The hard polystyrene segments associate to form rigid domains within an amorphous matrix of soft poly (ethylene-butylene) segments. When the material is heated, it can be processed in the same way that conventional thermoplastics are processed.

9.9.2 Compounding

SEBS block copolymers are available as pure polymers, as oil-extended polymers and as compounds. The pure polymers and oil extended polymers can be further compounded by incorporating fillers, resins, other polymers and extenders.

9.9.3 Properties of End Products

SEBS block copolymers show high resistance to attack by oxygen and ozone. In addition they show improved retention of strength at elevated temperatures.

9.9.4 Applications

The improved properties of SEBS block copolymers give them a wider area of application than the SBS and SIS block copolymers. They are specifically designed for outdoor applications.

9.10 Olefin-Based Elastomeric Alloys

Elastomeric alloys are blends of a rubber and a plastic in which the rubber component has been "dynamically" vulcanized. Dynamic vulcanization means in-situ cross-linking of the rubber during mixing with the thermoplastic. This in-situ vulcanization generates cured rubber particles dispersed in a continuous thermoplastic matrix, as shown in **Fig. 9.7**.

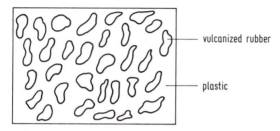

Fig. 9.7: Morphology of Elastomeric Alloys

Although it is theoretically possible to produce a great number of elastomeric alloys, three major commercial products have gained large acceptance. These are:
– Santoprene (Monsanto);
– Geolast (Monsanto); and
– Alcryn (Du Pont).

9.10.1 Santoprene

Santoprene TPEs are blends of in-situ cross-linked EPDM and polypropylene (PP). They are supplied as precompounded materials ready for processing on conventional thermoplastic equipment.

Santoprene compounds are available in hardness grades ranging between about 65 Shore A and 50 Shore D. The compression set is good at room temperature and fair at elevated temperatures up to 100 °C. The upper service temperature is about 100 °C for permanent use and 120 °C for short periods. The environmental aging, electrical properties and fluid resistance are similar to those of EPDM vulcanizates (section 8.9.3).

Santoprene finished parts can displace EPDM vulcanizates in some applications. They would also compete with SEBS block copolymers because of their higher heat stability combined with excellent electrical properties.

9.10.2 Geolast

Geolast TPEs are blends of in-situ cross-linked NBR and PP. As with Santoprene, they are supplied as "ready to use" materials in different grades ranging in hardness from about 80 Shore A to 50 Shore D. The compression set of the finished parts is good at room temperature and fair at elevated temperature up to 100 °C. The upper service temperature is about 100 °C for permanent use and 120 °C for short periods.

The oil resistance is comparable to that of cross-linked NBR. Accordingly, it is expected that Geolast parts will displace NBR vulcanizates in many applications.

9.10.3 Alcryn

Alcryn TPEs are elastomeric alloys based on chlorinated polyolefins, whose detailed formulations are not published. Presumably, they are blends of in-situ cross-linked ethylene vinyl acetate rubber (EAM) and polyvinyledene chloride, in which fillers, plasticizers and stabilizers have been incorporated. They are supplied as "ready to use" materials in different grades ranging in hardness between about 60 to 80 Shore A. All grades can be blended with each other to adjust the properties of the finished products. They can also be blended with PVC.

Alcryn parts have good resistance to oils and weather. Their oil resistance is equal to that of NBR vulcanizates with medium acrylonitrile content. The compression set is good at room temperature and fair at elevated temperatures up to 100 °C. The upper service temperature is about 100 °C for permanent use and 120 °C for short periods.

The desirable combination of resistance to heat, oils and weather make Alcryn blends suitable for use in many applications, including hoses, tubing, wire and cable jacketing, automotive parts, seals and gaskets, coated fabrics and sheeting.

CHAPTER 10

Standard Tests and Their Significance

10.1 Introduction

Elastomers are complex materials that differ very considerably from other engineering materials. This unusual class of materials requires its own carefully worked-out testing procedures. Tests used for other solid materials are seldom directly applicable to elastomers.

The physical properties of elastomers are very dependent on temperature, rate of deformation and shape and thickness of the test piece. For example, the tensile strength of a rubber compound at 100°C may be as little as 10 to 20% of the value measured at room temperature. Repeated deformation of the test piece may also result in substantial changes in the measured property values.

It should also be noted that the measured physical data of rubber compounds are not accurate or constant values because in mixing and curing many variables are involved that are very difficult to control accurately. Great care is necessary to obtain precision of ±10%. It is important to remember this in considering the significance of tests on rubber compounds.

In order to obtain reproducible test results within narrow limits only standardized test methods should be adopted.

10.2 Reasons for Testing

Tests on crude rubber and its products may be classified in three groups:
1) control tests;
2) specification tests; and
3) research and development tests.

Control tests are made to determine properties of the raw materials, the in-process materials and the finished products, in order to ensure their uniformity (section 2.12).

Specification tests are applied to rubber products that are made to meet customers' specifications. First, the manufacturer runs the specified tests to ensure that the company's product meets the property limits imposed by the specification. If this is found to be the case, the product is submitted to the customer, who also tests it.

Research and development tests are designed mainly to achieve a better understanding of the physics or chemistry of rubber, such as vulcanization, aging and performance in service. They may also involve the evaluation of new crude rubbers, fillers, chemicals and so on. The results of this work will be the basis for developing new elastomeric materials.

10.3 Significance of Testing

There are probably thousands of procedures for testing elastomeric materials and products. Several of these tests are now included in national and international standards. It is essential to know that these tests are valuable only for quality control and compound development, but they are seldom reliable for predicting serviceability of the elastomeric part because service conditions are so varied.

The purpose of this chapter is to discuss the significance of most common standard test methods and to emphasize that the serviceability of elastomeric products can be predicted only by actual or high-quality simulated service tests.

10.4 Testing of Hardness

Hardness is a property of considerable importance, usually included in rubber specifications along with tensile properties. As mentioned in section 4.2, durometers (type A and D) or IRHD instruments are used for measuring hardness. The durometers (utilizing a spring to produce the indenting force) are not as precise as the standard dead load instrument for measuring IRHD. However, durometers are very widely used, mainly because of their low cost.

The standard methods for determination of hardness are given in **Table 10.1**. Although there is no international standard for elastomers covering Shore hardness, ISO 868 for plastics and ebonites can be used for elastomers. **Fig. 10.1** shows a bench hardness tester, and **Fig. 10.2** shows the different types of indentors used

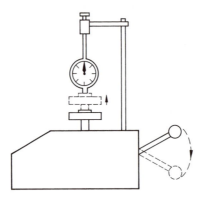

Fig. 10.1: Bench Hardness Tester

Shore A   Shore D   IRHD

Fig. 10.2: Different Types of Indentors

Table 10.1: Standard Test Methods for Hardness Measurement

ISO Standard	Title	Corresponding National Standards
868	Plastics and ebonites – Determination of indentation hardness by means of a durometer (Shore hardness)	ASTM D 2240 BS 2719 DIN 53505
48	Vulcanized rubbers – Determination of hardness (hardness between 30 and 85 IRHD)	ASTM D 1415 BS 903, Part A 26 DIN 53519
1400	Vulcanized rubbers of high hardness (85 to 100 IRHD) – Determination of hardness	ASTM D 1415 BS 903, Part A 26 DIN 53519
1818	Vulcanized rubbers of low hardness (10 to 35 IRHD) – Determination of hardness	ASTM 1415 BS 903, Part A 26 DIN 53519

for measuring the hardness. The test piece should have its upper and lower surfaces flat, smooth and parallel to one another. The hardness readings depend on the dimensions of the test piece, thickness being the most critical dimension. For the normal IRHD test, the standard test piece should be 8 to 10 mm thick. Nonstandard test pieces are either thicker or thinner. The measurement is not accurate at test pieces less than 4 mm thick. For thinner test pieces a micro IRHD instrument (a scaled-down version of the normal test) is used. The standard test piece for the microtest should be 2.0 (±0.5) mm. Only a thickness in this range will frequently give results agreeing with those of the normal test, using its standard test piece. Thicker or thinner test pieces may be used, but in no case should they be less than 1 mm thick.

If readings are taken too near the edge of a test piece, there will be an "edge effect"; consequently, minimum distances from the edge for various thicknesses are given in ISO 48, 1400 and 1818.

The hardness test should be carried out at a standard laboratory temperature [20 (±2)°C, 23 (±2)°C or 27 (±2)°C]. The test report should include (a) dimensions of the test piece, (b) temperature, (c) type of surface tested (molded, buffed or otherwise) and (d) type of apparatus used.

All measurements made on nonstandard test pieces are called **apparent hardness**. The term **standard hardness** refers to measurements made on standard test pieces [8–10 mm for normal test and 2.0 (±0.5) mm for microtest]. Elastomeric parts made from the same material may have different apparent hardnesses based on their shape and thickness. Test results obtained on curved surfaces (e.g., O-rings) are arbitrary values applicable only to the particular part and may differ from the standard hardness by as much as 10 IRHD or even more.

10.4.1 Significance of Hardness Tests

Hardness is not a reliable measure of stiffness. Hardness measurements derive from small deformations at the surface, whereas stiffness measurements, such as measurement of tensile modulus (section 10.5), derive from large deformations of the entire mass.

Unlike with metals, there is no correlation between hardness and tensile strength of elastomers. As the hardness increases, the tensile strength of an elastomer may increase to a maximum, then decrease, or it may decrease from the beginning, depending on the formulation of the compound.

10.5 Testing of Tensile Properties

As mentioned in section 4.3, tensile stress-strain properties include tensile strength, elongation at break and tensile modulus. Standard methods for determining these properties are given in ISO 37, ASTM D 412, BS 903: Part A 2 and DIN 53504.

The tensile test involves stretching standard test pieces to breakage at constant speed using a tension testing machine. The test pieces are cut from molded sheets. Two types of test pieces are used: rings and dumbbells **(Fig. 10.3)**.

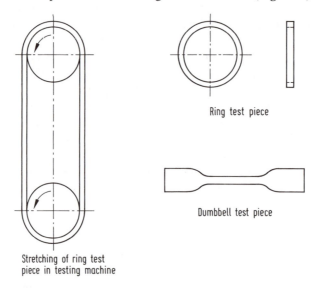

Ring test piece

Dumbbell test piece

Stretching of ring test piece in testing machine

Fig. 10.3: Different Types of Tensile Test Pieces

The standards permit a variety of test piece dimensions, although it is known that the various types and sizes can give different results. The measured tensile strength usually decreases with increasing cross sectional area of the test piece. Furthermore, ring test pieces give lower tensile strength values than do dumbbells. This is mainly because in stretched rings, the tensile stress and strain are not uniform over the cross section but vary from a maximum at the inside circumference to a minimum at the outside circumference. Therefore, it is important to make comparisons only between test pieces of nominally the same size and type.

The temperature at which the test is made has a pronounced effect on the results (section 4.14) and therefore it must be controlled and included in the test report. The standard laboratory temperature specified in ISO 37 is 20 ($\pm$2)°C, 23 ($\pm$2)°C or 27 ($\pm$2)°C.

Variations in the rate of elongation have a great effect on the modulus and the ultimate elongation: As the elongation speed is increased, the modulus increases, the ultimate elongation decreases and the tensile strength may either increase or decrease. An example to illustrate this is given in **Table 10.2**.

Table 10.2: Effects of Elongation Speed on Tensile Stress-Strain Properties of an NBR Compound Using Standard Ring Test Piece

Property	Elongation Speed	
	200 mm/min	500 mm/min
100% modules (N/mm$_2$)	3.0	4.5
200% modules (N/mm$_2$)	9.0	11.0
Tensile strength (N/mm$_2$)	13.7	14.6
Elongation at break (%)	320	270

It is also important to note that tensile properties may be influenced by the grain effect caused by the action of the mixing mill, leading to regular orientation of the chain molecules in one direction. For example, high values of tensile strength may be obtained when the tension tests are made along the grain (i.e., parallel to the direction of passage through the mill).

Finally, it should be emphasized that tension tests are conducted on test specimens that have not been stretched previously. The stress-strain curve of a rubber compound is unique and cannot be obtained again on subsequent stretching because of material changes. **Fig. 10.4** shows an original stress-strain curve (I) and a

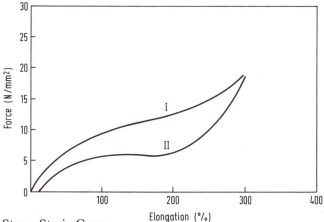

Fig. 10.4: Stress-Strain Curve

second curve (II) of a duplicate specimen that was prestretched once to 300% elongation. Up to 300% elongation, the second curve shows lower stress, but beyond that elongation, it almost coincides with the first curve. This behavior is called **stress softening**.

10.5.1 Significance of Tension Tests

Tension tests are useful for production control. The tensile strength in particular is very sensitive to any change in rubber compounds resulting from manufacturing mishaps (section 2.12).

The tensile tests are also useful for determining the resistance of elastomers to deterioration by heat, liquids, gases, chemicals, ozone, weather and the like. For this purpose, the tensile strength, tensile modulus and ultimate elongation are measured before and after an exposure test. If minor changes in these properties result, long service life may be expected; if appreciable changes occur, service life may be short.

It is important to recognize that the tensile properties are of limited use to the design engineer. They cannot be used in design calculations, and they bear little relation to performance in practice.

Unlike steel, stress and strain in tension are not proportional when applied to elastomers, particularly at high strains.

It is often argued that tensile strength is a general index of quality, of wear resistance in particular. This may be true to some extent at the extremes of tensile strength range. For example, polyurethane elastomers with their superior tensile strength show in general good abrasion resistance when subjected to rough surfaces and poor lubrication. On the other hand, compounds with poor tensile strength, such as silicone elastomers, show excessive wear after a short time. However, in the middle range (about $10-20$ N/mm$_2$), where the great majority of rubber compounds fall, tensile strength has little, if any, direct bearing on serviceability. This is understandable when we consider that rubber products are seldom stretched in service. In practice, it has been found that rubber compounds with lower tensile strength may perform in service as well as materials having higher tensile strength, and sometimes even better.

10.6 Testing of Tear Resistance

Methods for measurement of tear resistance (section 4.4) are given in ISO 34, ISO 816, ASTM D 624, BS 903: Part A 3, DIN 53507 and DIN 53515. The standards permit several types of nicked and right-angled test specimens **(Fig. 10.5)**. The test involves measuring the force (in N/mm of thickness) required to completely tear the specified test piece. The tearing force is applied by means of a tensile testing machine at a specified rate. The test results are strongly dependent on the type of specimen used, the speed of stretching and the temperature. Sometimes the tear progresses in a straight line and at other times changes direction. The latter behavior is called "**knotty tear**" and is considered advantageous.

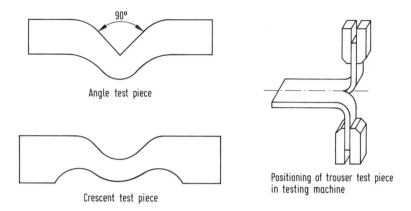

Fig. 10.5: Different Types of Tear Test Pieces

10.6.1 Significance of Tear Resistance Tests

The standard test methods are useful for laboratory comparisons but not for service evaluations. When an estimate of service behavior is required, service tests on the actual part should be carried out.

10.7 Testing of Friction and Abrasion

As mentioned in section 4.5, friction and abrasion are two properties of major importance, particularly for dynamic seals. Although friction tests are rarely standardized and are carried out in few laboratories, many testing machines for measuring abrasion resistance have been standardized, and most rubber laboratories have at least one type of these abrasion machines.

Abrasion resistance is defined as the resistance of a rubber compound to wearing away by contact with a moving abrasive surface. The test methods are described in ISO 4649, ASTM D 2228 and D1630, BS 903: Part A 9 and DIN 53516. In all these methods a test piece of the rubber compound is held against an abrasive surface under specified load and speed. The volume loss of the rubber specimen is determined and the result is expressed as a percentage in comparison with a standard elastomer.

The test results vary widely with the kind of the basic rubber and compounding ingredients. Some elastomers, such as polyurethanes, show outstanding resistance to abrasion; others, such as silicone elastomers, have poor resistance. In some cases, the tests may produce misleading results. For example, an undercured compound (soft and sticky) or one with wax bloom will appear to have excellent abrasion resistance mainly because the abrasive surface has been clogged or smeared by ingredients removed from the surface of the rubber specimen.

10.7.1 Significance of Abrasion Tests

It should be recognized that no correlation exists between abrasion test results and service performance. Silicone elastomers, for instance, can perform very well as dynamic seals under favorable working conditions that eliminate friction. Also, when comparing different rubber compounds the ranking from the laboratory test results may not follow the ranking in service.

10.8 Testing of Stress Relaxation

Stress relaxation (section 4.6) can be measured in compression, shear or tension. However, measurements in compression are used to estimate sealing efficiency.

The methods for measurement of stress relaxation in compression are described in ISO 3384, BS 903: Part A 42 and DIN 53537. The ASTM test method (D 1390−76) was discontinued in July 1989.

Two sizes of disc test pieces are allowed: large or small. The test method involves basically compressing the standard test piece to a constant strain; the force exerted by the test piece is measured at intervals under specified conditions. The compression stress relaxation is expressed as a percentage of the initial counterforce.

10.8.1 Significance of Stress Relaxation Tests

As has been mentioned, stress relaxation behavior is an important property for seals and gaskets. However, the widespread use of stress relaxation tests has been inhibited because these tests are time-consuming and require expensive equipment.

10.9 Testing of Compression Set

The standard methods for the measurement of compression set (section 4.6) at low, ambient and elevated temperatures are given in **Table 10.3**. Two sizes of disc test pieces are allowed, large or small, the same as used for stress-relaxation measurements. The test specimen is compressed to 25% of its original thickness. The

Table 10.3: Standard Test Methods for Compression Set Measurement

ISO Standard	Title	Corresponding National Standards
815	Vulcanized rubbers – Determination of compression set under constant deflection at normal and high temperatures	ASTM D 395 BS 903, Part A6 DIN 53517
1653	Vulcanized rubbers – Determination of compression set under constant deflection at low temperatures	ASTM D 1229 BS 903, Part A 39 DIN 53517

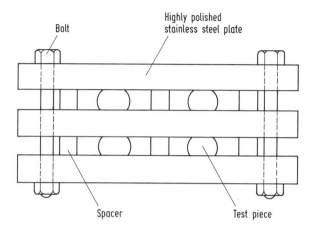

Fig. 10.6: Compression Apparatus

compression apparatus is then set for the specified time at the selected test temperature, after which the thickness of the recovered test piece is measured. The compression set is the difference between the original thickness and the thickness after recovery, expressed as a percentage of the deflection employed.

In contrast to stress relaxation, compression set is very easy to measure and requires a simple and inexpensive apparatus **(Fig. 10.6)**.

10.9.1 Significance of Compression Set Tests

Compression set is a measure of the degree of recovery of an elastomeric part, but not a measure of the force it exerts, which actually matters for sealing. However, it has been found that there is a reasonably good general correlation between compression set and stress relaxation as predicted theoretically (1).

The compression set measurements do not necessarily correlate with service performance, because there are other factors that can favor or impair the service performance. For instance, swelling caused by contact with the service fluid may compensate for compression set. On the other hand, a combination of high compression set and shrinkage may lead to leakage.

There is a widespread tendency to overemphasize compression set values. However, a good balance of all properties is usually necessary for optimum performance.

Finally, it is worth mentioning that compression set is an effective quality-control test for evaluating the state of cure.

10.10 Testing of Rebound Resilience

The measurement of rebound resilience (section 4.7) is standardized in ISO 4662, ASTM D 1054, BS 903: Part A 8 and DIN 53512. The test method involves impacting a standard test piece with a falling pendulum hammer that is free to

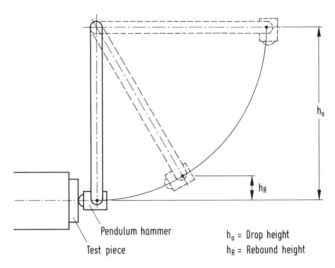

Pendulum hammer

Test piece

h_o = Drop height
h_R = Rebound height

Fig. 10.7: Rebound Resilience Apparatus

rebound after impact **(Fig. 10.7)**. The ratio of the rebound height to the drop height, expressed as a percentage, is equal to the rebound resilience of the compound tested. The obtained value is a measure of the ability of the material to recover quickly to its original shape after a temporary deformation.

10.10.1 Significance of Rebound Resilience Tests

Good resilience is vital for dynamic seals as well as components with large cross section (to reduce heat buildup).

10.11 Testing of Permeability to Gases and Vapors

The standard procedures for measuring gas permeability of elastomers (section 4.9) are described in ISO 1399 (constant volume method), ISO 2782 (constant pressure method), BS 903: Parts A 17 and A 30, as well as DIN 53536. In principle, the test procedures involve setting up a pressure differential across the test piece and measuring (by noting change in pressure or volume) the amount of gas passing to the low-pressure side. It is essential to ensure that the diffusion of the gas through the test piece has reached the steady state. This may require minutes, hours, days or even weeks, depending on the gas and elastomer combination and the thickness of the specimen.

10.11.1 Significance of Gas Permeability Tests

Most laboratory data are obtained under much lower pressures than those commonly encountered in service. Consequently, the permeability rate of elastomers at high pressures cannot be predicted accurately from such low-pressure data. For accurate results, the test should be carried out under the service conditions. However, the laboratory test methods may be useful when comparing the permeabilities of different elastomers against a control compound of known service performance.

10.11.2 Vapor Transmission of Volatile Liquids

Test methods for determining the rate of vapor transmission of volatile liquids through elastomers are described in ISO 6179, ASTM D 814 and BS 903: Part A 46. The result is expressed as a vapor transmission rate since the liquid diffuses through the elastomer and escapes into free atmosphere in vapor form. The test methods are essentially simple but require great care to achieve good reproducibility. Furthermore, they are not generally sensitive enough to measure very low transmission rates.

10.12 Testing of Explosive Decompression Resistance

Tests for evaluating the resistance to explosive decompression (section 4.10) are rarely standardized (2) and are carried out in relatively few laboratories. In principle, the procedures involve exposing test specimens to the gas or gas mixture in an autoclave under certain pressure and at a definite temperature for a specified soak period. In order to simulate explosive decompression, the gas pressure is rapidly released within a specified time, which usually varies between a few seconds and a few minutes. After removal of the test specimens from the autoclave, a combination of visual, dimensional and mechanical tests are carried out and completed as quickly as possible.

10.12.1 Significance of Explosive Decompression Tests

It should be noted that the explosive decompression characteristics of sheet molded materials can be different from those of components made from the same materials (3). Consequently, it is advisable, to carry out tests on the elastomeric part under service conditions whenever possible.

10.13 Testing of Accelerated Aging or Heat Resistance

Elastomers are usually more resistant to heat in the absence of oxygen. In order to separate the effect of heat from that of oxygen, it is necessary to carry out the tests in vacuum or in an inert gas such as nitrogen. However, in actual practice, the effects of heat and oxygen can hardly be separated. For this reason, the tests designed to determine heat resistance are normally carried out in air or oxygen. Consequently, the property changes are caused by a combination of heat and oxygen.

The test methods for determining heat resistance or accelerated aging are described in ISO 188, BS 903: Part A 19, DIN 53508 and ASTM D 572, D 573 and D 865. They allow the use of two procedures: air oven and oxygen bomb. A compromise between the two procedures is the air bomb method given in ASTM D 454.

In the **air oven method**, the test pieces are exposed to air at atmospheric pressure at a specified elevated temperature for known periods of time, after which their physical properties are determined. These are compared with the properties measured on the unaged specimens and the changes noted. The heat aging can be carried out either in the usual single-chamber type of oven or in a multicell oven. If a single chamber oven is used, only very similar compounds can be heated together, to avoid migration of plasticizers, antioxidants, sulphur or other compounding ingredients. The multicell ovens have the advantage of one compound being placed in each cell. There must be a steady flow of air through either type of oven. It is also important that the test pieces are exposed to air from all sides.

In the **oxygen bomb** method, the test pieces are exposed to the deteriorating influence of oxygen at a specified elevated temperature and pressure for known periods of time.

In the **air bomb** method given in ASTM D 454, the test specimens are exposed to high-pressure air at 125 °C for suitable periods of exposure. The periods are spaced at intervals such that the deterioration will not be so great as to prevent determination of the final physical properties. Intervals frequently used are 3, 5, 8, 12, 20 and 30 h.

10.13.1 Significance of Heat Aging Tests

Heat aging tests are carried out for three distinct purposes:
1) to measure changes in the rubber vulcanizate at the elevated service temperature;
2) as an accelerated test to estimate natural aging at normal ambient temperature; and
3) in specifications as a quality-control test.

Even when heat aging tests are used to simulate high temperature application, correlation may not be good unless the whole part is used rather than the standard thin test pieces. These have a relatively large surface-area-to-volume ratio, resulting in rapid diffusion of oxygen through the elastomer to give more uniform aging. It would be misleading to correlate results from thin test pieces to parts of markedly different size and shape.

It is also important to keep in mind that no correlation exists between accelerated aging and normal aging, which usually occurs in combination with light, humidity, ozone and other factors.

10.14 Testing of Low-Temperature Properties

There are various test methods for measuring the low-temperature properties of elastomers (section 4.15). They cover different aspects of low-temperature behavior and hence give different rankings of the rubber compounds being tested.

The low-temperature limit of an elastomer is commonly determined by using the **TR** (temperature retraction) test, which is standardized in ISO 2921, ASTM D 1329 and BS 903: Part A 29. The test involves stretching a standard test piece (normally 50%), immersing it in the stretched condition in a cold bath at $-70°$ until it becomes rigid, releasing the clamp from one end and allowing the frozen specimen to retract freely while raising the temperature at $1°C/min$. The temperature at which the test piece has retracted 10% of the original stretch is known as **TR 10**.

Other test methods used for evaluating the cold resistance of elastomers include measurements at low temperatures of stress relaxation (section 10.8), compression set (section 10.9) and rebound resilience (section 10.10).

The hardness measurement (section 10.4) is the simplest way to determine the elastic modulus of an elastomer under slight strain. Consequently, the increase in hardness as the temperature decreases is the most obvious and simple measure of stiffness of a rubber compound. A more accurate method for measuring the degree of stiffness as the temperature is lowered is the **Gehman Torsional test,** using a torsional apparatus specified in ISO1432. The Gehman test is also standardized in BS 903: Part A 13, DIN 53548 and ASTM D 1053. The British and German standards are technically identical to those in the international method, but the ASTM method differs in a few details.

The method of measuring the **brittleness point** is standardized in ISO R 812, ASTM D 2137, BS 903: Part A 25 and DIN 53546. It is defined as the lowest temperature at which all the specimens tested do not exhibit brittle failure when impacted under specified conditions.

The brittleness point only tells at which temperature the elastomeric component is most likely to be completely useless in service. However, it can be important when elastomeric parts are transported in very cold regions. Great care should be taken if the surrounding temperature is below the brittleness point of the elastomeric parts.

In principle, any of the low-temperature tests mentioned above can be used to study the **crystallization** effects (section 1.7 and 4.15) by conditioning the test pieces at low temperatures for a much longer time than is usual (for example, 168 h or longer). For such long tests, a gaseous medium should be used, to exclude the swelling effect of cooling liquids.

ISO 3387 specifies a test based on hardness measurements for determining the progressive stiffening of elastomers with time caused by crystallization. The test results may be expressed as the hardness increase after a specified storage time or as the time required for a specified increase in hardness to occur.

10.14.1 Significance of Low-Temperature Tests

Although the low-temperature tests provide useful information needed for selecting elastomeric materials, it is not possible to accurately predict whether the elastomeric component will function in a given application, because of the varying nature of the working conditions (4). The service performance of an elastomeric part at low temperature depends not only on the flexibility and rate of recovery of the material, but also on design, amount of squeeze, nature of contacting medium, pressure applied and other working conditions. Such factors can favor or impair the low-temperature performance. Following are few examples:

1) An NBR seal that would break at $-30\,°C$ before use becomes flexible at that temperature when exposed to fuel or fuel vapor due to swell. The absorbed fluid will have an effect on the compound similar to that produced with the addition of a plasticizer.

2) A plasticized NBR seal having TR 10 value of $-45\,°C$ before use may have only $-35\,°C$ after exposure to a mineral oil. This is because part of the plasticizer in the rubber compound has been extracted and replaced by the oil, which is a relatively poor plasticizer, leading to the change in TR 10 value. That means that low-temperature serviceability of plasticized elastomers depends on whether the plasticizer remains in the elastomer.

3) In some instances, fluids may extract plasticizers, causing the elastomer to shrink. Shrinkage is usually accompanied by increase in hardness and loss of some low-temperature flexibility. In the case of seals, a shrinkage usually results in premature leakage.

4) A lip of a shaft seal can warm up very quickly and become flexible because of friction.

5) Elastomers have an expansion coefficient that is approximately ten times that of steel (section 4.12). This can be critical for a seal at low temperatures if the squeeze is marginal. In this case, leakage can occur because of thermal shrinkage, even when the seal is flexible.

6) The fluid to be sealed may become so viscous at low-temperatures that it cannot possibly leak out.

The above examples show that there is no direct correlation between low-temperature tests and service performance. Consequently, it is essential to carry out functional tests with candidate materials having potential for low-temperature applications.

10.15 Testing of Resistance to Ozone Cracking

The test methods used to evaluate the resistance to ozone cracking (section 5.2) are described in ISO 1431/1 (static strain test) and 1431/2 (dynamic strain test). Corresponding national standards include BS 903: Part A 23, DIN 53509 and ASTM D 518, D 1149, D 1171 and D 3395. Briefly, the test procedures involve exposing strained test pieces to air containing ozone at specified conditions and observing the cracks. The ozone concentration can be varied and is usually much higher than that existing naturally in most parts of the world. Conditions that influence the accelerated tests include ozone concentration, amount of stretch, temperature and degree of bloom.

10.15.1 Significance of Ozone Resistance Tests

The indoor ozone tests are useful for compound development and for comparing the ozone resistance of different compounds. However, the test results do not usually correlate with the outdoor performance of the rubber compound tested, because the ozone concentration and temperature vary widely seasonally and geographically. In addition, there are other factors that influence the resistance to outdoor weather, namely the intensity of sunshine and the frequency of rainfall. Sunlight exposure causes another kind of crack (crazing), which occurs whether or not the specimen is stretched (section 5.7).

10.16 Testing of Fatigue Resistance

The test methods used to evaluate fatigue resistance (section 5.5) are given in ISO 132 and 133. The former standard is for crack initiation and the latter for cut growth. Both standards use the same test piece and the same flexing apparatus (De Mattia). The test piece is a strip with a molded groove. The essential difference between the two standards is that in ISO 133 a cut is made through the bottom of the groove in the test piece before flexing is started. Corresponding national standards include DIN 53522, BS 903: Parts A 10 and A 11 and ASTM D 430, D 813 and D 4482.

10.16.1 Significance of Fatigue Resistance Tests

The results of the standard fatigue resistance tests do not usually correlate with the service performance because the manner of flex cracking depends on the geometry of the part, the type of stressing and the environmental conditions. However, the laboratory test may be useful when comparison is made in a simultaneous test with a reference compound of known service performance.

10.17 Testing of Resistance to Fluids

The standard test methods of evaluating the resistance of elastomers to the action of fluids (chapter 6) are described in ISO 1817, ASTM D 471 and D 1460, BS 903: Part 16 and DIN 53521. Briefly, the test procedures involve exposing test specimens to the influence of liquids under definite conditions of temperature and time. Although the equilibrium or final volume change is a good general indication of the fluid resistance, it is also important to measure the changes in mechanical properties such as hardness, tensile strength and ultimate elongation. A low swell does not always mean good fluid resistance, as it may be hiding a large deterioration of the physical properties.

As mentioned before, the contiguous fluid may influence compression set and low-temperature limits, which are usually determined without reference to the contacting medium. Therefore, it is recommended to determine the effect of fluids on these properties if they are important for the application.

It is also worth mentioning that, in some cases, chemical changes in the fluid can occur during service so that an elastomer that is resistant to the new fluid may deteriorate in the same fluid after it has been used for some time. For this reason, tests are sometimes run in used fluids.

10.17.1 Significance of Fluid Resistance Tests

Although the simple free-swelling tests can provide valuable information on the suitability of a rubber compound for use with a given fluid, it should be noted that operating conditions may differ appreciably from controlled test conditions. For example, the fluid contact with the elastomeric part may be only partial or not continuous. Also, the thickness of the elastomeric part must be taken into account. Different parts made from the same batch of compound under identical conditions will give varying results when tested in exactly the same way because of their difference in shape, thickness and surface-to-volume relationship. The bulk of very thick elastomeric parts may remain almost unaffected during the projected service life.

Furthermore, elastomer parts under strain (e.g., seals) swell less than in the free state, which is the case in glassware tests.

10.18 Testing of Resistance to Microbiological Degradation

Methods for testing the resistance of elastomers to microbiological attack (section 5.11) are not standardized, although there is an international standard, ISO 846, covering evaluation of the resistance of plastics to fungi and bacteria.

Visual observations and physical testing may be used for determining the extent of deterioration caused by microorganisms. The physical testing may include tensile strength, elongation at break, insulation resistance and loss of weight due to consumption of compounding ingredients.

It is generally accepted that microbiological deterioration testing is a subject best entrusted to laboratories specializing in that field.

10.19 Testing of Effects of Elastomers on Contiguous Materials

A variety of test methods are used to evaluate the effects of elastomers on contiguous materials (chapter 7). Several of these procedures are now included in international and national standards.

Most test methods for determination of adhesion to and corrosion of metals (section 7.1) consist simply in placing the elastomer in contact with the metal in question under load, aging for a certain period under specified conditions and assessing adhesion or corrosion by visual inspection. Standard methods are described in ISO 6505 and BS 903: Part A 37, but it is rather difficult to obtain good reproducibility.

Test methods for estimating the degree of staining of organic materials caused by contacting elastomers (section 7.3) are given in ISO 3865, ASTM D 925, BS 903: Part A 33 and DIN 53540. Staining can be accelerated by heat and artificial light exposure. The degree of staining is usually estimated by visual inspection, but for more accurate results a spectrophotometer is used to measure color change.

10.20 Miscellaneous ISO Standards

Table 10.4 lists further ISO standards that may serve the needs of different applications.

Table 10.4: Miscellaneous ISO Standards

ISO Standard	Title
816	Rubber, vulcanized – Determination of tear strength of small test pieces (Delft test pieces)
2285	Rubber, vulcanized – Determination of tension set at normal and high temperatures
6056	Rubber, vulcanized – Determination of compression stress relaxation (rings)
1827	Rubber, vulcanized – Determination of modulus in shear – Quadruple shear method
4665/1	Rubber, vulcanized – Resistance to weather Part 1: Assessment of changes in properties after exposure to natural weather or artificial light
4665/2	Rubber, vulcanized – Resistance to weather Part 2: Methods of exposure to natural weather
4664	Rubber – Determination of dynamic properties of vulcanizates for classification purposes (by forced sinusoidal shear strain)
4663	Rubber – Determination of dynamic behavior of vulcanizates at low frequencies. Torsion pendulum method
2856	Elastomers – General requirements for dynamic testing
2781	Rubber, vulcanized – Determination of density
845	Cellular rubbers and plastics – Determination of apparent density
1853	Conducting and antistatic rubbers – Measurement of resistivity
2878	Rubber, vulcanized – Antistatic and conductive products – Determination of electrical resistance
2882	Rubber, vulcanized – Antistatic and conductive products for hospital use – Electrical resistance limits
2883	Rubber, vulcanized – Antistatic and conductive products for industrial use – Electrical resistance limits
2951	Vulcanized rubber – Determination of insulation resistance
36	Rubber, vulcanized – Determination of adhesion to textile fabric
4647	Rubber, vulcanized – Determination of static adhesion to textile cord – H-Pull test
2411	Fabrics coated with rubber or plastics – Determination of coating adhesion
4637	Rubber – coated fabrics – Determination of rubber-to-fabric adhesion – Direct tension method

Table 10.4: Miscellaneous ISO Standards (Cont.)

ISO Standard	Title
813	Vulcanized rubber – Determination of adhesion to metal – One-plate method
814	Vulcanized rubber – Determination of adhesion to metal – Two-plate method
1747	Rubber, vulcanized – Determination of adhesion to rigid plates in shear – Quadruple shear method
8033	Rubber and plastic hose – Determination of adhesion between components
1746	Rubber or plastic hoses and tubing – Bending tests
1420	Rubber- or plastic-coated fabric – Determination of resistance to penetration by water
1421	Fabrics coated with rubber or plastics – Determination of breaking strength and elongation at break
3011	Rubber- or plastic-coated fabrics – Determination of resistance to ozone cracking under static conditions
3303	Rubber- or plastic-coated fabrics – Determination of bursting strength
4646	Rubber- or plastic-coated fabrics – Low-temperature impact test
4675	Fabrics coated with rubber or plastics – Low-temperature bend test
4674	Fabrics coated with rubber or plastics – Determination of tear resistance
5979	Rubber- or plastic-coated fabrics – Determination of flexibility – Flat loop method
5981	Rubber- or plastic-coated fabrics – Determination of flex abrasion
5470	Rubber- or plastic-coated fabrics – Determination of abrasion resistance
5473	Rubber- or plastic-coated fabrics – Determination of crush resistance
2472	Ebonite – Determination of tensile strength and elongation at break
2473	Ebonite – Determination of cross-breaking strength
2474	Ebonite – Determination of crushing strength
2783	Ebonite – Determination of hardness by means of a durometer
3302	Rubber – Dimensional tolerances of solid molded and extruded products

10.21 Conclusion

The selection of an elastomeric material for a particular application is often difficult because laboratory measurements do not usually predict serviceability. It is therefore essential to clearly establish the expected service environment in which the elastomeric component will operate and carry out functional tests accordingly. One functional test is worth more than a thousand physical and chemical property tests.

References

1. M. D. Ellul and F. Southern, "Comparison of Stress Relaxation with Compression Set for Seal Compounds," *Plastics and Rubber Processing and Applications* 5 (1985) pp. 61–69.
2. "Guidelines," *Classification System for Elastomeric Materials Used in Oil and Gas Sealing Applications*, Offshore Engineering Group, The Plastics and Rubber Institute (PRI), 1990.
3. V. A. Cox, "Service Failures: A User's View of Explosive Decompression in Oilfield Elastomers," Proceedings of Offshore Engineering with Elastomers Conference, June 5–6, 1985, Aberdeen, PRI.
4. K. Nagdi, "Correlation between Laboratory Tests and Service Performance of Elastomeric Seals at Low Temperature," *Kautschuk + Gummi. Kunststoffe*, Vol. 41 (1988), No. 7, pp. 717–722.

CHAPTER 11

Simple Methods for Identification of Elastomers

11.1 Introduction

The complete analysis of rubber products to determine the amount and type of the rubber polymer and nonrubber constituents is a difficult task requiring specially equipped laboratories and a staff with analytical experience. In most cases, however, it is quite sufficient to determine the elastomer type to which an unknown sample belongs (for example, whether it is based on NBR, SBR, EPDM and so on). Several analytical methods may be found in the literature and in standards such as ISO 4650, BS 4181 and ASTM D 297 and D 3677. However, many of these test methods require expensive equipment and qualified staff, whereas the majority of users have limited laboratory facilities. This has created a need for simple methods that do not require expensive instruments nor specially trained staff.

The simple methods described in this chapter are based partially on selected procedures from the literature and partially on the author's experience. They do not require a special knowledge of chemistry, but great care must be taken when handling chemicals, solvents and open flame. The necessary apparatuses and chemicals are listed in section 11.2 and 11.3, respectively.

The identification of elastomers by these methods is usually rapid and accurate when dealing with vulcanizates containing only one rubber polymer. Elastomers containing more than one polymer cannot be identified with certainty by simple methods, unless comparison is made in a simultaneous test with a reference compound of known composition.

11.2 Laboratory Aids and Apparatuses

The following list contains the laboratory aids and apparatuses that are required for identification of elastomers using the simple methods described in this chapter:
- fire extinguisher, buckets of dry sand and fireproof blankets
- first-aid box and eye bath
- safety glasses
- rubber gloves
- glass test tubes (**small:** about 10 x 75 mm; **medium:** about 15 x 150 mm; and **Large:** about 20 x 200 m,)
- combustion tubes (about 15 x 100)
- test tube rack
- test tube tongs
- cork or rubber stoppers to fit the test tubes
- cork borer
- glass stirring rods (the ends should be rounded in a Bunsen flame)

- glass cutter
- glass condensing tubes or "knee-tubes" (about 5 mm in outside diameter) that are bent at least 90 degrees and extend about 100 mm beyond the bend (a condensing tube will be attached to a combustion tube by means of a cork stopper to form a pyrolysis apparatus, as show in in **Fig. 11.3 b**)
- beakers (50, 100, 250 and 500 ml)
- conical flasks (50, 100, 250 and 500 ml)
- graduated cylinders (10, 100 and 500 ml)
- stoppered brown bottles (250, 500 and 1,000 ml)
- pipets (1 and 10 ml)
- glass funnels (approximately 40 and 70 ml in diameter)
- round filter paper for the funnels
- spatula, tweezers, scissors and knife
- thermometers for high temperatures (100, 200 °C)
- areometer, or hydrometer **(Fig. 11.1)**, for density measurements in the range of $1.0 - 2.2$ g/cm^3 (section 11.6)
- Bunsen burner for the flame test (section 11.10) and pyrolysis test (section 11.11)
- heating bath (e.g., heating mantel, water bath, sand bath) for heating solvents
- Soxhlet apparatus with porous cups made of tough filter paper **(Fig. 11.2)** for sample extraction (section 11.9)

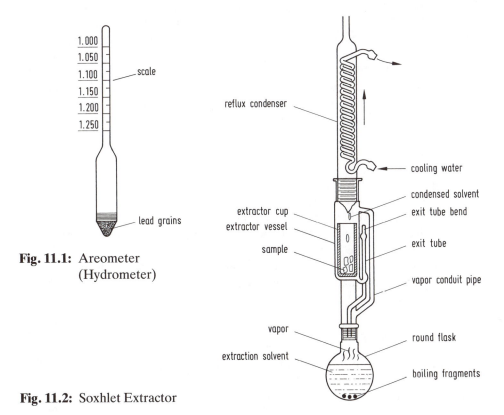

Fig. 11.1: Areometer
(Hydrometer)

Fig. 11.2: Soxhlet Extractor

- round flask to fit soxhlet apparatus
- reflux water condenser to fit soxhlet apparatus
- stand with clamps to hold the reflux condenser
- rubber tubing for water cooling of the reflux condenser
- boiling grains (e.g., unglazed porcelain fragments) to prevent a boiling liquid from superheating and "bumping"
- air oven with circulating air, for the aging test at 200 °C (section 11.8)
- a balance, accurate to 1 mg, for the swell test (section 11.12)
- stoppered weighing glasses for the swell test

11.3 Chemicals

Following is a list of the chemicals needed for carrying out the simple tests described in this chapter. Whenever possible, use only analytically pure chemicals. For the preparation of aqueous solutions, always use distilled or deionized water, never tap water.

Work with concentrated acids or bases requires that safety measures are taken, since such chemicals can cause injuries to skin and eyes. Therefore, always wear safety glasses and rubber gloves. When diluting a concentrated acid or base, always add the acid or base to the required amount of distilled or deionized water; **never add the water to the chemicals**, since the resulting heat can cause spattering.

Many organic solvents are inflammable and should, therefore, be stored in limited amounts. Whenever they are being heated, use a heating mantel, water bath or sand bath, but never an open flame or a Bunsen burner. It is also very important to add porous boiling grains in order to provide nuclei for the formation of vapor bubbles and thus to ensure steady, gentle boiling. If such grains are omitted, the liquid may become superheated and then suddenly boil with great violence.

11.3.1 Acids and Bases

- Concentrated sulphuric acid (H_2SO_4), about 95−98% (d = 1.84 g/cm^3), for the sulphuric acid test (section 11.7)
- concentrated hydrochloric acid (HCl), about 32%
- diluted hydrochloric acid (20 ml concentrated hydrochloric acid carefully dissolved in 80 ml distilled or deionized water)
- diluted sodium hydroxide (NaOH) solution (5 g NaOH carefully dissolved in 100 ml distilled or deionized water; the solution should be kept in a brown bottle with a cork)

11.3.2 Inorganic Salts

- Saturated solutions of zinc chloride or calcium chloride for density determination (section 11.6)
  To prepare a saturated solution, add zinc chloride or calcium chloride in small

portions (with shaking or stirring) to distilled or deionized water until, on further addition, the salt does not dissolve and a residue remains at the bottom. The solution process is relatively slow and the saturated solutions are rather viscous. Both solutions are hygroscopic and therefore must be kept in closed bottles. Different densities can be obtained by diluting the concentrated solution with the required amount of distilled or deionized water while stirring with an appropriate thermometer. A suitable range areometer (hydrometer) is placed in the liquid and the reading taken at 25°C **(Fig. 11.1)**.

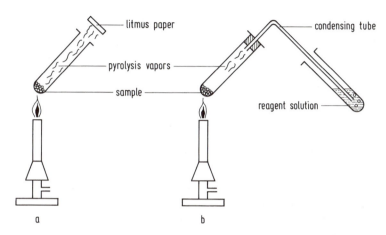

Fig. 11.3: Pyrolysis Test

– iron (II) chloride ($FeCl_2 \cdot 4H_2O$) solution (dissolve 0.2 g $FeCl_2 \cdot 4H_2O$ in 10 ml distilled or deionized water; the solution is unstable and should therefore be prepared fresh when needed).

11.3.3 Organic Solvents

– chloroform, trichloroethylene
– acetone, petrol ether, methanol (inflammable solvents)

11.3.4 Organic Reagents for Identification of Pyrolysis Vapours

– **Reagent I:** dissolve 0.1 g 4-nitrobenzo-diazonium fluoroborate (Nitrazol CF extra, Hoechst AG) in 10 ml methanol by heating them gently. The solution is unstable and should, therefore, be prepared fresh when needed.
– **Reagent II:** dissolve 1 g p-dimethyl-aminobenzaldehyde and 0.01 g hydroquinone in 100 ml methanol by heating them gently, then add to the solution 5 ml concentrated hydrochloric acid and 10 ml ethylene glycol. This reagent is stable for several months if stored in a brown bottle.

11.4 Miscellaneous

– Litmus paper (red and blue for identification of pyrolysis vapors) (section 11.11)
– copper wire for the flame test (section 11.10)

11.5 Scheme for Identification of Elastomers

The test methods for identification of elastomers described in this chapter are based on simple separation procedures. After some experience, the operator will find that it is frequently unnecessary to carry out all the tests.

Each analysis begins with preliminary tests, which often provide useful information. Such information will determine the number and kind of tests that should be conducted to identify the elastomer. Frequently, the preliminary tests permit direct conclusions so that one can then begin with confirmatory tests.

The preliminary examination of the unknown sample includes:
– examination of physical characteristics such as color, odor, bloom, elastic behavior, hardness and so on
– determination of density (section 11.6)
– treatment with concentrated sulphuric acid (section 11.7)
– accelerated heat aging at 200°C (section 11.8)

If the preliminary tests do not provide reliable information that can lead to identification of the sample, then begin a systematic analysis.

At first the sample must be extracted by suitable solvents to remove compounding ingredients such as plasticizers, processing aids and antioxidants, because these may lead to false results. For this purpose an extraction apparatus (section 11.9) is used.

After the sample has been extracted and thoroughly dried, one or more of the following tests may lead to complete identification of the sample:
– flame test (section 11.10)
– pyrolysis test (section 11.11)
– swell test (section 11.12)

If the above tests leave doubt, then it is likely that the unknown sample contains more than one rubber polymer. In this case the identification may require sophisticated methods such as infrared spectrum. For the majority of users, such tests are best entrusted to laboratories specializing in that field.

11.6 Determination of Density

Density is the weight of unit volume of the substance, usually expressed in grams per cubic centimeter (g/cm^3). It is now the preferred term to replace *specific gravity*, although they are equivalent.

The determination of density as described in ISO 2781 requires a balance, accurate to 1 mg. For many purposes, however, it is simpler to adopt the flotation procedure using salt solutions of known densities. The method involves finding the solution of known density in which the sample neither sinks to the bottom nor rises to the surface of the solution (i.e., it floats inside the liquid). It is very important to remove any air bubbles that may appear on the surface of the sample.

The density of the liquid may be determined by means of an areometer **(Fig. 11.1)**. Usually, solutions of zinc chloride or calcium chloride are used for this purpose (section 11.3.2).

The approximate density ranges listed in **Table 11.1** are typical for different elastomer types (compact solids). It is notable that FPM, FFKM and FZ elastomers have the highest densities. However, it should be kept in mind that the amount and type of fillers can lead to considerable deviations from the figures given in the table. Consequently, the density alone is seldom reliable as a means of characterization.

Table 11.1: Approximate Densities of Different Elastomer Types

Elastomer Type	Average Densities
EPM, EPDM	1.05−1.20
NBR, SBR, NR, IIR, BIIR, CIIR	1.15−1.35
ACM, AEM	1.30−1.40
CR	1.35−1.50
CO, ECO, CSM	1.45−1.60
FZ	1.75−1.90
FPM, FFKM	1.85−2.30

11.7 Sulphuric Acid Test

The sulphuric acid test is one of the most important preliminary tests for differentiation between elastomer types. The method is based on the resistance of different elastomer types to concentrated sulphuric acid at room temperature. Some elastomers deteriorate immediately or after a short time and other types remain almost unchanged.

The test procedure is very simple: place a small piece (about 0.3 g, 2 mm thick) of the unknown sample in a test tube and carefully add to it about 5 ml concentrated sulphuric acid (95−98%, density about 1.84 g/cm^3). If the sample floats on the surface, add small glass rods to keep it at the bottom. Most elastomers float on the surface of concentrated sulphuric acid because they usually have much lower density than 1.84. Normally, the FPM, FFKM and FZ vulcanizates have higher density and consequently they do not float.

Note whether the sample deteriorates immediately after adding the sulphuric acid. If this is not the case, close the test tube with a cork (sulphuric acid is hygroscopic) and allow it to stand for at least 4 h, preferably overnight, at room temperature.

At the end of the immersion period, carefully decant the sulphuric acid into a small beaker and remove the sample from the test tube after washing it several times with water. Blot lightly with filter paper and record all changes. Classify the unknown material using **Table 11.2** as a guideline.

Table 11.2: Characterization of Elastomers by Treatment with Concentrated Sulphuric Acid

Time of Exposure	Kind of Change	Rubber Polymer
Few minutes	Complete deterioration	T, GPO
4 h	Complete deterioration or dissolution	ACM, CO, ECO, AU, EU, YBPO, VMQ, PVMQ
	Softening, tacky or smeary surface	IIR, BIIR, CIIR, FMQ
	Swelling and softening, unchanged surface	AEM, FZ
	Excessive hardening, cracky or brittle	NBR, SBR, CR, NR, Polynorbornene
	No visual change	HNBR, EPM, EPDM, CM, CSM, FPM, FFKM

11.8 Accelerated Heat Aging at 200 °C

The property changes of an unknown sample after a short exposure to hot circulating air at 200 °C can provide useful information that can lead to its identification.

Place a strip of the sample (about 2 mm in thickness) in the air oven after it has been preheated to 200 °C. Note whether the specimen melts or decomposes after 30 minutes of aging. If this is not the case, continue aging for at least 4 h. Afterward, remove the specimen from the oven, cool to room temperature on a metal surface and note the changes in the material.

If the changes are minor or not clear, place the specimen again in the oven and prolong the aging test for a further 20 h. **Table 11.3** shows the property changes of different elastomer types after heat aging at 200 °C for periods of ½, 4 and 24 h.

11.9 Sample Extraction

The complete removal of extractable additives from the sample can be achieved by a mixture of 68% vol chloroform and 32% vol acetone for a period of at least 8 h, using the Soxhlet extraction apparatus shown in **Fig. 11.2**.

The mixture of solvents is heated to boiling and the resulting vapor is condensed in a reflux condenser mounted at the top of the extractor. The condensed solvent falls down into the extractor cup containing the sample and slowly fills the extractor vessel. When this condensed solvent reaches the exit tube bend, it siphons down into the round flask, taking down that portion of additives which it has extracted. The process then repeats itself indefinitely, and each time, more additives are extracted and transferred to the flask until the extraction is complete.

If a Soxhlet extractor is not available, it may be sufficient to heat the sample in the solvent for at least 8 h under reflux.

Table 11.3: Characterization of Elastomers by Heat Aging at 200°C in Circulating Air

Aging Period	Kind of Change	Rubber Polymer
½ h	Molten	Thermoplastic elastomers (e.g., YAU, YEU)
	Softening and decomposition (smell of rotten eggs)	T
4 h	Excessive hardening, cracky or brittle	NR, SBR, NBR, CR, Poly-norbornene
	Softening and tacky surface	IIR, BIIR, CIIR, GPO, AU, EU
	Slight change in hardness or minute surface cracks	High-performance NBR or CR, HNBR, EPM, EPDM, CM, CSM, CO, ECO, YBPO
	No change	ACM, AEM, FPM, FFKM, VMQ, PVMQ, FMQ, FZ
24 h	Excessive hardening, cracky or brittle	High-performance NBR or CR, HNBR, EPM, EPDM, CM, CSM, YBPO
	Excessive softening, kneadable or crumbly, smeary surface	CO, ECO, GPO
	Excessive softening, tacky or smeary surface, not kneadable or crumbly	IIR, BIIR, CIIR, AU, EU
	Hardly any change	ACM, AEM, FPM, FKKM, VMQ, PVMQ, FMQ, FZ

At the end of the extraction period, remove the specimen from the apparatus, blot lightly with filter paper and leave it to dry at room temperature, until the smell of the solvent has disappeared. For complete drying, place the specimen for about 2 h in an oven after it has been preheated to 100°C.

11.10 Flame Test

The flammability and burning behavior of rubber vulcanizates show characteristic differences, depending on the nature of the rubber polymer.

The test can be reliable only when the sample has been extracted (section 11.9) and thoroughly dried, because some additives, particularly plasticizers, can give false results.

During the course of combustion, vapors and gases evolve, which may be hazardous to the operator. Consequently, adequate precautions should be taken.

Table 11.4: Characterization of Elastomers by Burning (Flame Test)

Combustion Behavior				Rubber Polymer
Inside the Flame	Outside the Flame	Color of Residue	Beilstein Test	
Difficult to ignite	Extinguishes immediately	Black	Negative	FPM, FFKM, FZ
Combustible	Extinguishes slowly	Black	Positive	CR, CSM, CM, CO, ECO
Ignites readily	Continues burning, black smoke	Black	Positive	BIIR, CIIR, chlorine containing ACM
Ignites readily	Continues burning, black smoke	Black	Negative	NR[1], SBR, NBR, HNBR, EPM EPDM, IIR, ACM, AEM, GPO AU, EU, Polynorbornene
Combustible	Continues burning, grey smoke	White/ grey ash	Negative	VMQ, PVMQ, FMQ
Sample melts and drips, burning drops	Continues burning and dripping	Black	Negative	Thermoplastic elastomers (e.g., YAU, YEU, YBPO)
Ignites readily	Continues burning, blue flame, odor of burning sulphur	Black	Negative	T

1 NR gives a characteristic odour on burning that can be easily recognized in future testing. After extinguishing, the burnt end is smeary (rub on paper).

The flame test involves holding a small piece of the unknown sample with a pair of tweezers in a Bunsen flame and observing the burning characteristics inside and outside the flame. **Table 11.4** shows the behavior of different elastomer types in the flame. However, the flammability will be influenced by the addition of inorganic flame retardants (which cannot be extracted by solvents). Consequently, the results may deviate from those shown in the table.

11.10.1 Beilstein Test

The presence or absence of chlorine or bromine in an unknown sample can be detected by the very sensitive and rapid Beilstein test. The test is based on the formation of volatile copper halides, which cause a green coloration of the Bunsen flame. The procedure involves heating the end of a copper wire in a Bunsen flame until any initial green coloration caused by impurities on the copper has disappeared. After cooling, a small piece of the unknown sample is placed on the copper wire and heated at the edge of the colorless part of the flame. A bright green coloration, often lasting only a few seconds, indicates the presence of chlorine or bromine in the sample, most probably in the rubber polymer (e.g., CR, CSM, ECO, CIIR, BIIR, etc.). Under the same test conditions, the fluorinated elastomers do not give a green coloration, although the simple fluorinated organic compounds give positive results.

11.11 Pyrolysis Test

Pyrolysis involves thermal degradation of the material. During this process, low-molecular-weight fragments are produced that may give important information for the identification of the unknown sample.

The pyrolysis test involves heating a small quantity of the extracted and dried sample in a combustion tube with a small Bunsen flame until the sample begins to decompose. The vapors that are produced are then identified by means of different color reactions.

11.11.1 Color Reaction with Litmus Paper

Place about 0.5 g of the unknown sample in a combustion tube and heat with a small Bunsen flame. At the open end of the tube place a piece of moist litmus paper (**Fig. 11.3 a**). Depending on the reaction of the pyrolysis vapors with litmus, it is possible to distinguish three different groups:
1) acidic, when the litmus paper turns red;
2) alkaline, when the litmus paper turns blue; or
3) neutral, when the litmus paper does not change in color.

Table 11.5 shows the litmus reactions with the pyrolysis products of different elastomer types.

11.11.2 Color Reaction with Reagent I

The pyrolysis vapors of polyurethanes do not always show a clear acid reaction with litmus paper, as shown in **Table 11.5**. For their identification, pass the vapors over

Table 11.5: Litmus Reactions with Pyrolysis Vapors of Different Elastomer Types

Color Reaction	Rubber Polymer
Acidic (red color)	CR, CM, CSM, CO, ECO, FPM, FFKM, FMQ, FZ, BIIR, CIIR, IIR, ACM, AEM, AU, EU, YBPO, GPO
Alkaline (blue color)	NBR, HNBR, NR
Neutral (no color change)	SBR, EPM, EPDM, VMQ, PVMQ

a dry filter paper and then moisten it with a fresh solution of **reagent I** (section 11.3.4). Depending on the type of diisocyanate used in their synthesis, the paper will turn yellow, reddish, brown or violet.

This specific test should be made immediately after the litmus paper test in order to confirm the presence or absence of polyurethanes.

11.11.3 Color Reaction with Reagent II

Place about 0.5 g of the unknown sample in a combustion tube and attach it to a condensing tube by means of a cork stopper, as shown in **Fig. 11.3 b**. Heat with a small Bunsen flame until the pyrolysis vapors appear at the mouth of the condensing tube. Immerse the end of the tube beneath the surface of 1.5 ml of reagent II (section 11.3.4) contained in a receiver test tube. Continue the distillation and note whether a color change takes place. Remove the receiver tube and transfer the solution to a larger test tube. Add 5 ml methanol, boil for 3 minutes and note the color that develops. Record all observations and classify the material using **Table 11.6** as a guideline. If the color is red to violet, then run the specific test for NBR and HNBR, as follows.

Table 11.6: Color Reactions of Reagent II with Pyrolysis Vapors of Different Elastomers

Initial Color after the Reaction	Color after Heating with Methanol	Rubber Polymer
Red to violet Green to blue	Red to violet Green to blue	NBR, NR, GPO SBR, EPDM, IIR, Poly-norbornene
Yellow	Yellow	AU, EU

11.11.4 Specific Test for NBR and HNBR Elastomers

When nitrile-group-containing polymers such as NBR and HNBR are pyrolyzed, hydrogen cyanide (HCN) is formed. This may be identified by means of the Prussian blue reaction, as follows: pass the pyrolysis vapors in 3 ml of 5% sodium hydroxide solution. Add 1 ml of a fresh solution of iron II chloride and gently heat the mixture to boiling. Acidify with dilute hydrochloric acid. A characteristic blue color will indicate the presence of nitrile-group-containing polymers.

11.12 Swell Tests

The swelling behavior of the extracted and thoroughly dried unknown sample in different liquid classes allows further differentiation between elastomer types.

For the purpose of identification, it is sufficient to determine the percentage changes in weight of the test specimen after immersion in three different test

liquids at room temperature. These liquids are:
1) petrol ether with boiling range 100−140 °C (mixture of aliphatic hydrocarbons);
2) trichloroethylene; and
3) acetone.

Accordingly, three test specimens are required for the identification. Their shape does not matter, but their thickness should not exceed 2 mm (otherwise they should be buffed to this thickness). For the sake of accuracy, each specimen should not weigh less than 0.5 g.

weigh each test specimen to the nearest 1 mg and place it in a test tube containing at least 10 ml of the test liquid. Close each test tube with a stopper and allow to stand for at least 4 h, which is sufficient to reach equilibrium.

At the end of the immersion period, remove each test specimen from the tube and remove any excess liquid from the surface by blotting with filter paper. Place the sample immediately in a tared, stoppered weighing glass and determine its weight after immersion. Express the increase in weight as a percentage of the original weight of the test specimen. Record all changes in the three solvents and classify the material using **Table 11.7** as a guideline that is based on extensive tests.

Table 11.7: Characterization of Elastomers by Swelling in Solvents (Swell Test: 4 h at Room Temperature)

Approximate Weight Increase (%) in:			Rubber Polymer
Acetone	Petrol Ether	Trichloro-ethylene	
0− 1	0− 1	0− 1	FFKM
50−150	0− 1	0− 10	FPM
50−150	0− 10	20− 30	FMQ, FZ
50−100	0− 10	100−300	NBR, HNBR, ACM, EAM, CO, ECO, AU
15− 30	10− 20	100−300	CR, CSM
15− 30	50−100	100−400	NR, SBR, VMQ, PVMQ
0− 5	50−150	200−400	EPM, EPDM, IIR, BIIR, CIIR, Polynorbornene
>100	>50	>400	GPO

It should be noted that this method of identification is not applicable to cellular elastomers.

CHAPTER 12

Quality Control of Elastomeric Parts

12.1 Introduction

The purpose of running quality control of elastomeric parts is to ensure that they are completely cured and that the material composition is identical with that of the approved compound.

The test methods for quality control should be sensitive to the degree of cure and to any changes in the compound composition. There are already several test methods established to safeguard users against faulty materials, but the trend today is to utilize more sophisticated techniques, which require very expensive instruments and a qualified staff (see References).

This chapter gives a brief overview of the regularly used techniques for material identification, including inexpensive methods for users who cannot afford expensive instruments and qualified staff. Following is a list of the techniques to be discussed in sequence:
- infrared (IR) spectroscopy
- thermogravimetric analysis (TGA)
- differential thermal analysis (DTA)
- differential scanning calorimetry (DSC)
- density measurement
- ash content determination
- swelling behavior test
- compression set measurement
- test for apparent hardness

Furthermore, the simple methods described in chapter 11 may be used as additional tests for settling inconsistencies. It is unnecessary to run more tests if the sample has been clearly identified.

12.2 Infrared Spectroscopy

This analytical technique quickly provides a "fingerprint" that proves the identity of a rubber compound. The preparation and interpretation of IR spectra are described in ISO 4650, ASTM D 3677 and BS 4181. The basic process of IR spectroscopy involves illuminating a sample with successive wavelengths ranging from 2.5 to 15 microns (which corresponds to wavenumbers ranging from 4,000 to 667 cm^{-1}) and measuring the amount of light transmitted by the sample at each wavelength.

A modern spectrophotometer automatically computes the percentage of light transmitted at each wavelength and in a few minutes produces a curve of transmittance (%T) against wavelength or wavenumber, similar to that shown in **Fig. 12.1.**

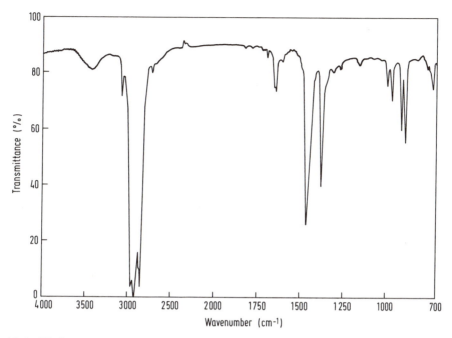

Fig. 12.1: IR Spectrum of an EPDM Compound

The obtained spectrum is then compared with that of a reference specimen (from the approved compound), which must have been prepared and scanned in an identical manner using the same infrared spectrophotometer. If other absorption bands are found in the spectrum of the sample, this will indicate that its composition differs from that of the approved compound.

(The IR spectra should be prepared and analyzed by experienced personnel and the equipment should be operated according to the manufacturer's directions for optimum performance.)

12.3 Thermogravimetric Analysis

TGA is the technique most commonly used to obtain, within a short time, a simple quantitative analysis of the sample, including the percentage of polymer, carbon black and ash.

The basic process of TGA involves recording the weight loss of a sample as a function of the temperature under controlled atmospheric conditions. This produces a curve generally similar to that shown in **Fig. 12.2**.

At first, the sample (typically 5–10 mg) is heated to 600°C at a constant rate in nitrogen atmosphere and the weight loss is recorded as a function of the temperature. The weight loss below 300°C is assumed to present moisture and volatiles such as plasticizers, processing aids and antioxidants. The weight loss between 300 and 600°C is assumed to be the polymer content. When the polymer pyrolysis is

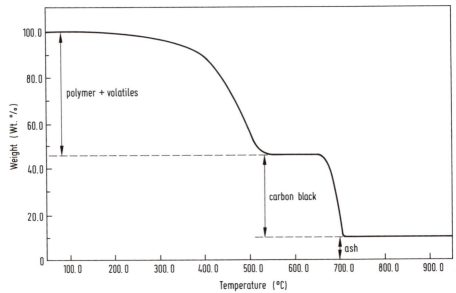

Fig. 12.2: TGA of an NBR Compound

complete, the nitrogen is replaced by oxygen and the sample is heated from 600 to 950°C. The weight loss due to oxidation gives the carbon black content and the residual weight represents noncombustibles or ash, including inorganic fillers, inorganic pigments or metal oxides.

12.4 Differential Thermal Analysis

In this technique, the sample under investigation and an inert reference substance are heated or cooled under the same conditions. The difference in temperature (ΔT) between the specimen and the reference substance is plotted against the

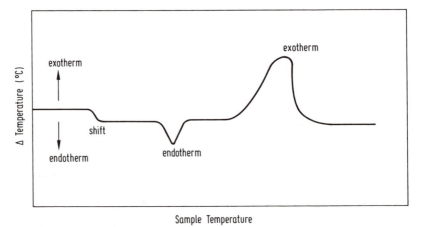

Fig. 12.3: An Idial DTA Curve

temperature (T) of the sample. The resulting curve shows the physical and chemical changes of the sample during heating and cooling. These changes appear as base line shifts, as exothermic peaks or as endothermic inverted peaks **(Fig. 12.3)**.

The DTA curves of elastomeric materials are used mainly to check the glass temperature (Tg) and the degree of cure of the incoming part.

12.5 Differential Scanning Calorimetry

DSC is a further development of DTA. In this new technique, the temperature difference, instead of being recorded, is compensated for, and the amount of energy required to maintain the sample at the same temperature as the reference material is recorded. The DSC curves are similar to those of DTA. They are also used to check the glass temperature (Tg) and the degree of cure of the sample.

12.6 Density Measurement

The density measurement is a simple, but effective, quality control test that safe-guards the users against gross errors and possible material mix-ups.

A convenient method for determining the density of incoming parts involves finding the liquid of known density in which the sample neither sinks to the bottom nor rises to the surface, as described in section 11.6.

12.7 Ash Content Determination

The ash content, which forms a part of the TGA process, can be determined by a simple method described in ASTM D 297. The method is intended for use when a muffle furnace is not available for ashing. In brief, a weighed sample is heated in a previously ignited weighed porcelain crucible with a gas burner, at first with a small flame to char it and then with a strong flame to burn off all carbonaceous matter. The residue in the crucible represents the ash content. The percentage of ash is calculated as follows:

$$\text{Ash \%} = \frac{A - B}{C} \times 100$$

where:
A = grams of crucible plus ash
B = grams of crucible
C = grams of sample

The above method is not suitable for halogen-containing elastomers because they usually contain metal oxides that can form volatile metal halides. For this reason the sample is cautiously heated with concentrated sulphuric acid to convert volatile metal halides into stable sulphates. Heating with sulphuric acid is continued until charring is complete and sulphuric acid has been driven off. Finally, the carbonaceous material is burned off and the percentage of ash is calculated as described above.

12.8 Swelling Behavior Test

The swelling behavior of an elastomeric part in a suitable test liquid under specified test conditions is a simple method to determine its identity. For control purposes, it is sufficient to determine the percentage of weight increase after a specified immersion period.

The selected test liquid should cause high swell to the sample within a few hours at room temperature, in order to detect possible variations in the material. It is suggested that the test liquid be chosen from those listed in **Table 12.1**. Commercial liquids should not be used because they are liable to vary appreciably in composition (section 6.4).

Table 12.1: Recommended Test Fluids for Quality Control of Elastomeric Parts

Rubber Polymer	Recommended Liquids
NR, SBR, IIR, BIIR, CIIR, EPM, EPDM, VMQ, PVMQ, GPO	Aliphatic hydrocarbons (e.g., hexane, iso-octane)
NBR, HNBR, CR, CSM, CO ECO, ACM, EAM, AU, EU	Aromatic hydrocarbons (e.g., toluene)
FPM, FMQ, FZ	Ketones (e.g., acetone, methyl ethyl ketone)

The test procedure is simple: weigh 0.5–1 g of the test specimen to the nearest 1 mg and place it in a test tube containing at least 10 ml of the test liquid. Close the test tube with a stopper and allow to stand for the specified time, say 4 h. At the end of the immersion period, remove the specimen from the test tube and remove any excess liquid from the surface by blotting with filter paper. Place the sample immediately in a weighed stoppered weighing glass and determine its weight. Express the increase in weight as a percentage of the original weight of the test specimen, as follows:

$$\text{Increase in weight } (\%) = \frac{(A - B) - C}{C} \times 100$$

where:
A = grams of stoppered weighing glass plus sample after immersion
B = grams of stoppered weighing glass
C = grams of sample before immersion

Again, it should be recognized that the swell values depend on the cross section of the sample. Consequently, the allowable limits for each cross section must be agreed upon between the manufacturer and the user.

12.9 Compression Set Measurement

As has been mentioned in section 10.9, compression set measurement is an effective quality control test for evaluating the state of cure.

For control purposes, the suggested test period is 22 h. Longer periods may be required for settling inconsistencies. The choice of test temperature is optional, but consideration should be given to the heat resistance of the basic rubber. It is suggested that the test temperature be chosen from those listed in **Table 12.2**. The allowable limits of compression set values must be agreed upon between the manufacturer and the user.

Table 12.2: Recommended Test Temperatures for Determination of Compression Set (After 22 h) for Different Elastomer Types

Rubber Polymer	Recommended Test Temperature (°C)
NR, IR	70 (maximum, 100)
SBR, NBR, CR, IIR, BIIR, CIIR, AU, EU	100 (maximum, 125)
CO, ECO, HNBR, EPM, EPDM	125 (maximum, 150)
ACM, AEM	150 (maximum, 175)
FMQ, FZ	175 (maximum, 200)
VMQ, FPM, FFKM	200 (maximum, 250)

It should be noted that the compression set values obtained from finished parts cannot be compared with those obtained from standard test pieces (section 10.9). Furthermore, finished parts with different cross sections made from the same material may have different compression set values when tested under the same conditions. The effect of the cross section on compression set is significant with unsaturated elastomers such as SBR and NBR, probably because the thin parts are more susceptible to heat aging than are the thick ones (sections 3.5.1 and 10.13). An example is given in **Table 12.3**, which shows compression set values of O-rings

Table 12.3: Compression Set Values (22 h at 120 °C) of O-Rings with Different Cross Sections Made from the Same Stock of an SBR Compound

Nominal Cross Section (mm)	Range of Compression Set (%)
7.0	24−27
6.0	26−29
5.0	28−32
4.0	31−36
3.5	33−38
3.0	34−40
2.5	36−42
2.0	39−44
1.5	40−46
1.3	43−50

(having 20 mm inside diameter but different cross sections) made from the same stock of an SBR compound. Similar results were obtained with NBR compounds.

With saturated elastomers, including EPDM, FPM and VMQ, the compression set values did not seem to correlate with the cross section, probably because these elastomers are much more resistant to heat aging.

12.10 Test for Apparent Hardness

As has been mentioned in section 10.4, elastomeric parts made from the same material may have different apparent hardness depending on their shape and thickness. Generally speaking, the apparent hardness increases as the test piece thickness decreases because of the effect of compression against the rigid test piece support.

The hardness test on curved surfaces (e.g., O-rings), is frequently problematic. This requires certain precautions and a holding fixture to locate the test piece, as described in a separate ASTM standard for O-rings (D 1414), which has a section on measuring hardness.

In order to avoid inconsistencies, the test procedure and the allowable limits for each cross section must be agreed upon between the producer and the user.

References

1. C.Y. Chu, "Modern Analytical Methods Used in the Rubber Industry," *Kautschuk + Gummi. Kunststoffe* 39, No. 1/88, pp. 33–39.
2. B.L. Treherne, "Thermal Analysis as quality Control Method for Elastomers," *Elastomerics*, May 1982, pp. 25–28.
3. J. Leckenby, "Made to Measure Analysis," *European Rubber Journal*, December 1986, p. 27.
4. K. Baker and J. Leckenby, "Improved quality Assurance of Elastomers with Thermal Analysis," *Kautschuk + Gummi. Kunststoffe* 40, No. 3/87, pp. 223–227.
5. R. Vaiden, "Testing Raw Materials for Quality Assurance," *Elastomerics*, February 1987, pp. 25–27.
6. D. Brück, "Analysis of Unvulcanized and Vulcanized Rubber by Physical Methods, with Particular Reference to IR Spectroscopy and Thin-Layer Chromatography," *Kautschuk + Gummi. Kunststoffe* 39, No. 12/86, pp. 1165–1174.
7. F. Merch and R. Zimmer, "Analysis of Rubber Vulcanizates by Advanced Chemical Techniques," *Kautschuk + Gummi. Kunststoffe* 39, No. 5/86, pp. 427–432.

CHAPTER 13

Health Hazards and Handling of Elastomers

13.1 Introduction

Many users think that elastomers are harmless materials, but they will be surprised to learn that some of them may emit potentially harmful volatiles. This applies not only to the production areas, but also to all places where rubber goods are found, including warehouses, storage rooms and even the atmosphere inside a car, where volatiles might evolve from a spare tire or other elastomeric parts.

The potential hazards related to raw materials, compounding, processing and general use of elastomers may result from the following:
– eye and skin contact with hazardous raw materials
– breathing dust of powdered raw materials
– breathing harmful vapors resulting from high-temperature processing or service
– prolonged breathing of minute quantities of potentially harmful monomers and other volatiles that defuse at room temperature from polymers, rubber chemicals and cured and uncured rubber compounds
– breathing toxic and corrosive combustion products in the event of fire
– handling residues of elastomeric parts that have been involved in a fire or exposed to a high service temperature

The handling precautions discussed in the next sections are offered only as guidelines. They are based, for the most part, on company reports and "material safety data sheets" for raw materials and finished parts. It should not be assumed that all necessary warnings and precautionary measures are contained in this chapter; additional measures may be required.

13.2 Potential Hazards Related to Raw Materials

As has been mentioned in previous chapters, the raw materials for manufacturing all elastomeric products may be divided into two main groups: crude rubbers and compounding ingredients.

The crude rubbers, like other polymers, may contain potentially irritating or harmful monomers (e.g., butadiene, acrylonitrile, chloroprene, epichlorohydrin, ethylene oxide, etc.), which may diffused in the atmosphere during storage and processing.

There are also potential hazards that result from certain compounding ingredients, particularly curing agents and antioxidants. Some of these are irritants, toxins or even carcinogens.

13.2.1 Protective Measures

– Adequate ventilation should be provided at all workplace, including storage areas, to ensure that hazardous quantities of dust and volatiles do not build up.
– Raw materials should be stored in a cool, dry location away from direct light to avoid product degradation and to reduce the amount of the released volatiles and residual monomers.
– Operators engaged in handling raw materials should be advised to avoid repeated or prolonged skin contact by wearing protective gloves and clothing. A dust mask is recommended to prevent routine inhalation of dust. Safety glasses should be worn if spilling or spattering of liquids is possible. Contacted skin should always be washed with soap and water after handling parts.
– Anyone who inhales dust or vapors should be taken to fresh air. If breathing is difficult, give oxygen and call a physician.
– In case of eye contact, immediately flush the eyes with plenty of water and call a physician.
– In case of spilling on skin or clothing, flush the skin with water, then wash thoroughly with soap and water. Wash contaminated clothing before reuse.

13.3 Potential Hazards Related to Nitrosamines

During the vulcanization of rubber compounds and the following cooling and storage periods, volatile organic compounds known as vulcanization fumes are released in the atmosphere. The chemical composition of these fumes depends on the type of crude rubber and the compounding ingredients. Secondary amines are known to produce nitrosamines during and after the vulcanization. They were identified many years ago as potent carcinogens, but no definite link to cancer in humans has yet been proved (1).

13.3.1 Protective Measures

– Adequate ventilation should be installed at all areas of the workplace, including storage rooms.
– Nitrosamine-free compounds should be developed.
– Operators engaged in handling vulcanized rubbers should be advised to wash their hands thoroughly after handling.

13.4 Hazards Related to High-Temperature Service

If operation at temperatures above the recommended limit is required or is possible through accident, precautions should be taken to protect personnel from breathing hazardous fumes and from contact with decomposed elastomeric components or highly corrosive condensates (which may include hydrogen fluoride if FPM parts are involved).

Before inspecting equipment that has been exposed to high temperature, it is most important not to touch any part until a substantial cooling period has been allowed. Check to see if any elastomeric parts have suffered from decomposition, which will appear as a charred or black sticky mess. The affected area should be washed well with lime water (calcium hydroxide solution) before undertaking any further work. CR or PVC gloves should be worn when handling the equipment and parts; the gloves should be discarded after use.

13.5 Hazards Related to Dust from Grinding or Abrading Rubber Vulcanizates

Fine dust resulting from grinding or abrading of rubber vulcanizates can generate toxic decomposition products if burned. Consequently, smoking should be prohibited in areas contaminated with dust, and adequate ventilation should be installed. Operators engaged in grinding or abrading should be advised to wear respirators and safety glasses and to wash their hands thoroughly before smoking anywhere.

13.6 Hazards Related to Occasional Exothermic Decomposition of FPM Compounds

Incidents of exothermic decomposition of FPM compounds have occurred during mixing, extruding and molding. The first incident, in 1958, occurred in a Du Pont laboratory when a compound of Viton containing finely divided aluminum powder underwent violent exothermic decomposition during remilling of the stock. Subsequently, warnings against the use of finely divided metals were published. It has also been found that some metal oxides at high levels in Viton can undergo an exothermic decomposition when heated to a temperature of approximately 200°C (2).

Another type of decomposition was observed during extrusion and molding of cold stocks. When this type of decomposition occurs, it is sudden and vigorous. Considerable pressure can build up inside equipment and molds, causing sudden emission of charred material from openings in the equipment. This problem may be remedied by prewarming the stock, using low-viscosity polymers or incorporating a good processing aid such as carnauba wax (which will prevent the formation of excessive frictional heat).

13.7 Hazards Related to Curing and Postcuring of FPM Elastomers

Hazardous volatiles evolve from FPM compounds during cure and postcure, particularly at temperatures above 200°C. The bulk of the volatiles evolved from diamine and bisphenol cures consists of CO_2 and H_2O along with small quantities of the toxic hydrogen fluoride, which will increase as the temperature increases. The peroxide-curable FPM rubbers liberate methyl halides, which are suspected carcinogens. Consequently, adequate ventilation is required.

Although carbon-black-filled FPM compounds are routinely postcured without incident, several O-ring producers have experienced major fires during the postcure of FPM O-rings containing iron oxide. No obvious explanations were available. However, the results of an investigation in a Du Point laboratory strongly suggest that the root cause of postcure oven fires is related to the use of austin black (which is crushed coal) as a substitute for carbon black and to the amount of air flow around the sample in the oven (3). Direct oxidation of the austin black and possible subsequent reaction with iron oxide may be the source of heat buildup when the air flow is insufficient to carry away the reaction heat. Accordingly, the problem may be remedied by providing sufficient air flow around the O-rings. In other words, stacking of elastomeric parts in the oven should be prohibited.

13.8 Precautions in the Event of Fire

Highly toxic and corrosive combustion products can be generated in fires involving elastomeric parts. The composition of the combustion products depends not only on the nature of the crude rubber and compounding ingredients but also on the amount of atmospheric oxygen. **Table 13.1** lists the main combustion products of different elastomer types.

Table 13.1: Combustion Products of Different Elastomer Types

Rubber Polymer	Main Combustion Products
FPM	HF, carbonyl fluoride, fluorocarbon fragments, CO, CO_2
NBR, HNBR	HCN, CO, CO_2
Chlorine-containing rubbers	HCl, CO, CO_2
AU, EU	Nitrogen oxides, ammonia, isocyanates, CO, CO_2
ACM	CO, CO_2, ethyl acrylate
Hydrocarbon rubbers	CO, CO_2, hydrocarbon fragments

Personnel fighting such fires must wear face masks and self-contained breathing apparatuses. All unprotected personnel must leave the area immediately.

Anyone exposed to fumes from the fire should be taken to fresh air at once and treated by a physician.

Anyone handling residues of elastomeric parts that have been involved in a fire must wear CR or PVC gloves to avoid skin contact with highly corrosive condensates, which may include hydrogen fluoride (section 13.4).

13.9 Disposal of Scrap and Waste Products

The disposal method must conform to national, state and local regulations. Landfill disposal is recommended. Burning is not recommended, unless conducted by an approved, licensed incineration agency.

13.10 Transport of Elastomeric Parts

Transport of elastomeric materials presents no known health hazards and hence particular measures related to safety are not required. However, other measures should be taken when elastomeric materials with poor cold resistance are transported in cold countries. As has been mentioned in sections 4.15 and 10.14, frozen elastomers can break under mechanical strain. Consequently, for transportation purposes, it is necessary to consider the brittleness point of the elastomeric materials and to take adequate precautions if the surrounding temperature is below the brittleness point.

References

1. M. Bowtell, "MRPRA Launches Study of Accelerators and Their Effect of Nitrosamine Levels," *Elastomers*, November 1990, pp. 8–9.
2. "Handling Precautions for Viton and Related Chemicals," Du Pont, VT-100.1, April 1987.
3. R. E. Tarney, "Viton Post-Cure Oven Fires," Du Pont, September 1987.

CHAPTER 14

How to Write a Material Specification

14.1 Introduction

Specifications are requirements, usually physical rather than chemical, imposed on a material or an end product. They dictate the tests to be made and lay down the allowable limits of the property data.

At one time, the engineer was content to specify his requirements on an engineering drawing in such broad terms as "black rubber," "oil-resistant rubber," "neoprene," "viton" and so on, leaving the supply of a suitable material to the manufacturer. As a result of serious problems in service, property requirements were laid down by the users in the form of specifications in order to ensure good performance of the elastomeric parts in service.

As the number of synthetic rubbers has increased and as new requirements imposed by developments in design engineering have been introduced, the number of specifications has grown. Today, rationalization of specifications is absolutely necessary.

Unfortunately, the current trend in specification writing is to require general quality indices such as tensile strength, elongation at break and tear resistance instead of requiring those properties which are important for the application. No wonder that approved compounds in terms of laboratory data fail frequently in service, whereas rejected ones may perform very well.

Current specifications may be divided into two groups:
1) standard specifications, based on standard classification systems, including ASTM D 2000, BS 5176, ISO 4632/1, ISO TR 8461 and DIN 78078; and
2) house specifications, written by large user organizations such as automobile manufacturers and government bodies.

This chapter shows that such specifications do not safeguard users against failure of elastomeric parts in service and outlines a method that ensures good performance.

14.2 ASTM D 2000

The well-known ASTM D 2000 (Standard Classification for Rubber Products in Automotive Applications) has been developed jointly by ASTM Committee D11 on Rubber and the Society of Automotive Engineers. It is intended for use in a wide range of industries and should not be regarded as limited to automotive applications.

The classification system is based on a "line call-out" arrangement of letters and code numbers in a specified order to be decoded into the property data of the rubber vulcanizate.

Table 14.1: Example of a "Line Call-out" Specification According to ASTM D 2000

M 2BG 710   B14 B34 EA14 EF11 EF21 EO14 EO34 F17

Basic Requirements   Suffix Requirements

Letter or Number	Meaning	Source (Table in ASTM D 2000)
M	The classification system is based on Si units	
2	Grade number expressing deviation from basic requirements (Grade 1 means no suffix requirements are permitted)	
B	Type (resistance to heat aging)	1
G	Class (resistance to swelling in ASTM oil No. 3)	2
7	Durometer hardness 70 (±5) points	6
10	Tensile strength (MPa) min.	6
B	Compression set	3
1	Test method D 395, 22 h, Method B, **solid**	4
4	Test temperature (100°C)	5
B	Compression set	3
3	Test method D 395, 22 h, Method B, **plied**	4
4	Test temperature (100°C)	5
EA	Fluid resistance (aqueous)	3
1	Test method, D 471, distilled water, 70 h	4
4	Test temperature (100°C)	5
EF	Fluid resistance (fuels)	3
1	Test method D 471, Reference fuel A, 70 h	4
1	Test temperature (23°C)	5
EF	Fluid resistance (fuels)	3
2	Test method D 471, Reference fuel B, 70 h	4
1	Test temperature (23°C)	5
EO	Fluid resistance (oils and lubricants)	3
1	Test method D 471, ASTM oil No. 1, 70 h	4
4	Test temperature (100°C)	5
EO	Fluid resistance (oils and lubricants)	3
3	Test method D 471, ASTM oil No. 3, 70 h	4
4	Test temperature (100°C)	5
F	Low-temperature resistance	3
1	Test method D 2137, Method A, 9.3.2	4
7	Test temperature (-40°C)	5

To briefly explain how ASTM D 2000 works, a typical example of a line call-out specification is given in **Table 14.1**. It indicates the basic and supplementary (suffix) requirements as specified in the six tables of the standard. These are:

Table 1: Basic Requirements for Establishing Type by Temperature
Table 2: Basic Requirements for Establishing Class by Volume Swell
Table 3: Meaning of Suffix Letters
Table 4: ASTM Test Methods
Table 5: Suffix Numbers to Indicate Temperature of Test
Table 6: Basic and Supplementary (Suffix) Requirements for Classification of Elastomeric Materials

14.2.1 Disadvantages of ASTM D 2000

It has always been recognized that ASTM D 2000 is not a perfect system. The main disadvantages are the following:

1) ASTM D 2000 uses the same letter designation for different polymer types, as shown in **Table 14.2** (which is a copy of **Table X1.1** of the appendix to ASTM D

Table 14.2 Table X1.1 of ASTM D 2000 Appendix

Polymers Most Often Used in Meeting Material Requirements	
ASTM D 2000-SAE J200 Material Designation (Type and Class)	Type of Polymer Most Often Used
AA	Natural rubber, reclaimed rubber, SBR, butyl, EP, polybutadiene, polyisoprene
AK	Polysulphides
BA	Ethylene propylene, high-temperature SBR and butyl compounds
BC	Chloroprene polymers (neoprene)
BE	Chloroprene polymers (neoprene)
BF	NBR polymers
BG	NBR polymers, urethanes
CA	Ethylene propylene
CE	Chlorosulphonated polyethylene (Hypalon)
CH	NBR polymers, epichlorohydrin polymers
DA	Ethylene propylene polymers
DF	Polyacrylic (butyl-acrylate type)
DH	Polyacrylic polymers
FC	Silicones (high-strength)
FE	Silicones
FK	Fluorinated silicones
GE	Silicones
HK	Fluorinated elastomers (Viton, Fluorel, etc.)

2000). This does not allow the engineer to know the basic rubber of the elastomeric material he or she is using. This can be misleading because the knowledge of the chemical structure of the polymer is indispensable for judging the suitability of an elastomeric material in service. The BA materials, for example, can be based on EPDM, high-temperature SBR or IIR. All of these would pass the short-term tests of ASTM D 2000, but they perform differently in service because they have different specific properties. EPDM, being a saturated polymer, will withstand continuous elevated temperatures and will perform for much longer service periods than SBR. On the other hand, SBR, being an unsaturated polymer, will have a shorter life span at elevated temperatures but will perform better at very low temperatures, below $-40\,^\circ$C. IIR has significantly lower gas permeability compared with EPDM or SBR. Difficulties can therefore arise if a user has had good experience with a certain BA material from a certain supplier and then, for economic or other reasons, uses another BA material from another supplier. He may later find out that the new material does not withstand high temperatures because the first was based on EPDM and the second on SBR. Higher gas permeability may also be expressed if IIR diaphragms are replaced by EPDM ones, because the gas permeability of EPDM is about ten times higher than that of IIR.

Similar difficulties can be experienced with BG materials, which can be based on NBR or AU/EU. Polyurethanes, as can be concluded from the chemical structure, will deteriorate in high humidity and hot water, whereas NBR elastomers are resistant.

Many users think that materials having the same ASTM D 2000 designation must have the same composition and service performance. It is rather difficult for the supplier to provide customers, using ASTM D 2000 as a specification, with the most suitable elastomeric material because the service conditions are usually not quoted. Further inquiries would mean delays and more costs.

2) ASTM D 2000 permits a very wide range of tolerances. An example is given in **Table 14.3**. It shows, for example, that the specification permits a volume change in ASTM oil No. 1 from -10 to $+5\%$, in ASTM oil No. 3 from 0 to $+25\%$ and in fuel B from 0 to $+40\%$. Therefore, it would not be surprising to find that oil-resistant elastomeric materials having the same ASTM D 2000 designation can show completely different swelling behavior in service oils or fuels, to the extent that the service performance could be seriously affected because of excessive shrinkage or excessive swelling.

3) ASTM D 2000 is a complicated and inflexible scheme. The letter designations and numbers are arbitrary. It is time-consuming for the user to code the specifications and for the supplier to decode them.

14.3 BS 5176

The classification system of vulcanized rubbers described in the British Standard 5176 is also based on vulcanizate properties without composition requirements. The code system follows closely ASTM D 2000 and has the same disadvantages.

Table 14.3 Properties of Two Qualities Having the ASTM D 2000 Designation:
M 2BG 710 B14 B34 EA14 EF11 EF21 EO14 EO34 F17

Properties	Spec. of ASTM D 2000	Test Results	
		Qual. A	Qual. B
Original properties:			
Durometer hardness, points	70 (±5)	66	74
Tensile strength, MPa min.	10	15.3	15.6
Ultimate elongation, %, min.	250	500	350
Properties after heat aging, ASTM D 573, 70 h at 100°C			
Change in tensile strength, %	±30	−6	+7
Change in ultimate elongation, %, max.	−50	−33	−23
Change in durometer hardness, points	±15	+8	+5
Suffix requirements:			
B14:			
Compression set, ASTM D 395, Method B, solid, 22 h at 100°C, % max.	25	23	16
B34:			
Compression set, ASTM D 395, Method B, plied, 22 h at 100°C, % max.	25	23	18
EA14:			
Water resistance, ASTM D 471, 70 h at 100°C			
Change in hardness, points	±10	+1	−1
Change in volume, %	±15	−1.0	+1.4
EF11:			
Fluid resistance, ASTM D 471, Reference fuel A, 70 h at 23°C			
Change in hardness, points	±10	+3	±0
Change in tensile strength, %, max.	−25	−13	−10
Change in ultimate elongation, %, max.	−25	−9	−3
Change in volume, %	−5 to +10	−1.0	+2.3
EF21:			
Fluid resistance, ASTM D 471, Reference fuel B, 70 h at 23°C			
Change in hardness, points	0 to −30	−14	−16
Change in tensile strength, %, max.	−60	−47	−31
Change in ultimate elongation, %, max.	−60	−35	−27
Change in volume, %	0 to +40	+22.4	+32

Table 14.3 (Cont.) Properties of Two Qualities Having the ASTM D 2000 Designation: M 2BG 710 B14 B34 EA14 EF11 EF21 EO14 EO34 F17

Properties	Spec. of ASTM D 2000	Test/Results Qual. A	Qual. B
EO14:			
Fluid resistance, ASTM D 471,			
ASTM oil No. 1, 70 h at 100 °C			
Change in hardness, points	−5 to +10	+9	+3
Change in tensile strength, %, max.	−25	−7	+3
Change in ultimate elongation, %, max.	−45	−32	−18
Change in volume, %	−10 to +5	−8.6	−1.6
EO34:			
Fluid resistance, ASTM D 471,			
ASTM oil No. 3, 70 h at 100 °C			
Change in hardness, points	−10 to +5	±0	−7
Change in tensile strength, %, max.	−45	−6	−6
Change in ultimate elongation, %, max.	−45	−24	−22
Change in volume, %	0 to +25	+3.1	+18.9
F17:			
Low-temperature brittleness,			
ASTM D 2137, Method A, 9.3.2	pass	pass	pass
Nonbrittle after 3 min at −40 °C			

14.4 ISO 4632/1 and ISO TR 8461

Work on the classification of vulcanized rubbers was carried out by Working Group 8 of Technical Committee ISO/TC 45 (Rubber and Rubber Products) for many years. This resulted in the circulation in 1980 of ISO/DIS 4632 (Rubber, Vulcanized-Classification System). This large document covered both the classification system and an extensive number of tables of elastomeric materials.

The comments on ISO/DIS 4632 were examined by WG 8 at its 1980 meeting. The comment that the document was too complicated for use by industry was accepted and it was resolved by TC 45 that ISO/DIS 4632 be divided into two parts:

Part 1: Description of the Classification System (ISO 4632/1)

Part 2: Rubber Materials, as a Technical Report (ISO/TR 8461)

The code system described in ISO 4631 differs from ASTM D 2000 and BS 5176. In brief, the designation begins with three letters describing the resistance to heat, oils and low temperatures. The code of basic properties consists of four figures describing the hardness in IRHD, tensile strength, elongation at break and compression set. Additional properties and test methods are indicated by suffix letters and suffix numbers, which can be combined to provide a line call-out designation.

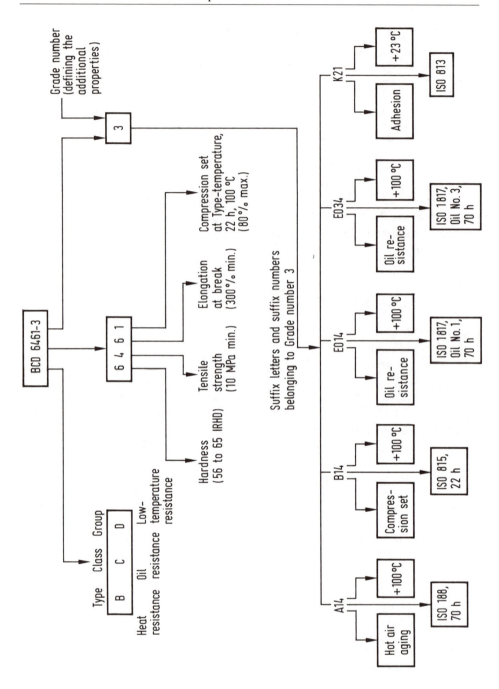

Fig. 14.1: Detailed Requirements for a Material Coded BCD 6461-3

In order to show how ISO 4632/1 works, the detailed requirements for a material coded BCD 6461-3 are illustrated in **Fig. 14.1**. It is evident that the code system of ISO 4632/1 is even more complicated than that of ASTM D 2000 and BS 5176.

14.5 DIN 78078

The German Standard DIN 78078 describes a classification and designation system for elastomeric materials that is also based on vulcanizate properties. The code system is technically equivalent to ISO 4632/1.

14.6 New Draft Classification System for Oil and Gas Industries

The Offshore Engineering Group of UK Plastics and Rubber Institute (PRI) have developed a draft classification system for elastomeric materials used in the oil and gas industries (1, 2, 3). The document is the result of discussions held over a four-year period with many PRI and American Petroleum Institute (API) committee members as well as representatives from seal users, manufacturers, raw material producers and research organizations. Earlier versions have been published at international conferences in Aberdeen, Scotland and Dallas, Texas, U.S.A. It is emphasized that this system is intended only for guidance and does not in any way set out to be a material specification. Thus, no pass/fail criteria are quoted and no claims are made concerning the suitability of any material for any particular application.

The objective of the document is to describe the overall performance properties of the material in a visually easy-to-read medium without the need to refer to several tables for interpretation. It is based on a line call-out designation system analogous to ASTM D 2000 but differs from it in the following points:
- The line call-out designation includes the designation of the basic rubber and the type of the vulcanization system. The basic rubbers are identified by abbreviations of their chemical composition in accordance with ISO 1629 and ASTM D 1418. A sulphur vulcanization system is identified by the letter S. Other curing agents as peroxides (P) or those not identified (X) are similarly indicated.
- The line call-out property designation is simple, clear and legible in contrast to ASTM D 2000, BS 5176, ISO 4632/1 and DIN 78078. This is because the letters used in the PRI document are abbreviations of words and the numbers are real values.
- The test periods are longer than those of ASTM D 2000 and related systems (at least 168 h compared with 22 and 70 h with ASTM D 2000).

The following example is a line call-out designation of a rubber compound:
1. **Chemical composition**
   NBR H/S
   Signifying:
   NBR   The elastomer is based on NBR
   H   High acrylonitrile content
   S   Curing agent is sulphur

2. Basic Physical Property Data

H90, TS15, EB310, M25 2.2, TR25, CS15, D1.38

Signifying:

H90	Hardness	= 90 IRHD
TS15	Tensile Strenght	= 15 MPa
EB310	Elongation at Break	= 310%
M25 2.2	Modulus at 25% Extension	= 2.2 MPA
TR25	Trouser Tear Resistance	= 25 N/mm
CS15	Compression Set	= 15%
D1.38	Density	= 1.38 g/cm^3

3. Temperature and Basic Fluid Data

T (−20/+100), CSH40, VC(A/+11)

Signifying:

T(−20/+100)	Temperature Range of Use	= −20°C to +100°C
CSH40	Compression Set at Higher Temperature	= 40%
VC(A/+11)	Volume Change in Fluid Type A	= +11%

4. Service Condition Data

EDR(E/2), ROFC, ER(B/2)

Signifying:

EDR(E/2)	Explosive Decompression Resistance in Fluid E	Rating: 2
ROFC	Resistance to Oil-field Chemicals	= Data from supplier
ER(B/2)	Extrusion Resistance Grade	= Method B, Rating: 2

Where certain data would not be available, or not be required by the user, then letters and values would be omitted from the line call-out, without leaving a space. Specific test conditions or environments should be identified by the use of notes (e.g., Z1, Z2).

All tests referred to are internationally accepted standard tests as published by ISO, ASTM and BS. However, in some cases there are no standard tests available capable of measuring the required properties. In those cases, the essential details of the test required are provided in the document.

14.7 House Specifications

The number of house or company specifications is almost indefinite. They are perhaps the most important standards, but frequently the most difficult to satisfy. Many of them require maximum values for too many properties, which have little or no influence on the serviceability. Consequently, approved compounds in terms of laboratory data may fail prematurely in service because other properties most relevant to the application have been overlooked. When mistakes of this sort occur, rubber products generally are condemned, although it is the specification writer who is to blame.

14.8 How to Ensure Good Performance of Elastomeric parts

It should be clear from the foregoing that standard and house specifications do not provide a guarantee for the efficiency of elastomeric components in service.

The problem of deciding which rubber compound to use for a particular application is often difficult and requires close cooperation between users and manufacturers.

The best way to safeguard users against failure of elastomeric parts in service is to adopt the following step-by-step procedure:

1) The user writes a performance specification listing all the operating conditions the elastomeric part will be expected to operate in (see section 14.9).
2) The user sends the performance specification to different specialized manufacturers, say manufacturer A, B and C.
3) Manufacturer A recommends rubber compound **x** and sends samples of finished parts to the user for testing.
4) The user runs a simulated service test with the received parts. If they pass the test, the next step is to establish a specification for the quality control of incoming parts (chapter 12). The user and manufacturer A assure the reproduceability of test results between their laboratories before they agree about the data limits of the control tests. When an agreement is reached, the resulting specification is valid only for the incoming parts in the qualified compound **x** supplied by manufacturer A.
5) Manufacturer B and C send samples of finished parts in compounds **y** and **z**, respectively. If these samples also pass the simulated service test, then the user follows the same procedure to establish two different specifications for the quality control of incoming parts in compounds **y** and **z** supplied by manufacturers B and C, respectively.

At the end, the user has three different compounds for the same application. The three compounds **x, y** and **z** may differ significantly in their mechanical properties and swelling behavior in ASTM oils and fuels, but they all pass the simulated service test. That means manufacturers **A, B** and **C** have found different ways to make a compound that performs well in the same application.

14.9 Performance Specifications

The almost indefinite number of standard and house specifications has resulted over the years in the manufacturing of a huge number of unremunerative rubber compounds. Most of these fall into the same elastomer group, but have slight differences in physical properties such as tensile strength and elongation at break. Due to economic pressure many rubber manufacturers offer a concise list of standard materials which cover most industrial requirements. If users write a performance specification (i.e., specify their service requirements and operating conditions), rubber manufacturers are able to offer the most suitable compound of their standard materials. When it has been proven satisfactory for application, the next step is to agree upon the data limits for the quality control of incoming parts (section 14.8).

A performance specification should include details of all operating conditions in which the elastomeric part will be expected to operate. The most important factors to be considered are:
– chemical resistance;
– temperature range and service period required;
– pressure applied and rate of pressure drop in gaseous environments; and
– type of performance (i.e., static or dynamic).

The first thing to be considered is the resistance of the elastomeric material to the media with which it will come in contact, including fluids, gases, air or any lubricant or cleaning agent occasionally used in the system (chapter 6). In some instances, it must be ensured that the elastomer remains resistant to used fluids that may change their chemical composition in service.

Consideration must also be given to the adverse effects of elastomers on materials with which they are in contact, such as metals, plastics, paints, refrigerants, insulating oils, food, explosives and so on (chapter 7).

The temperature limits in service are often overspecified. Actually, it is the temperature at the region of the elastomeric part that is decisive for the application and not the temperature elsewhere. The low-temperature limit depends on several factors, such as the nature of medium, pressure applied, design and other operating conditions. Such factors can favor or impair the low-temperature performance (section 10.14.1). The recommended maximum temperature may be exceeded in short-term applications (section 4.16).

Another important consideration when writing the performance specification is the pressure applied to the part. This is important for the choice of compound hardness, particularly when low temperatures are involved. For example, low pressures usually require soft seal materials that can be easily deformed as the temperature decreases. In gaseous environments the rate of pressure drop must be taken into account. A rapid rate of pressure drop can cause extensive damage to the elastomeric part if the rubber compound has poor resistance to explosive decompression (sections 4.10 and 10.12).

A very important aspect to be included in a specification for seal materials is the type of performance (i.e., static or dynamic). The most important property of a static seal is a good compression set resistance (sections 4.6 and 10.9). Dynamic applications, because of movement, are more complicated than static applications. The decisive factor that affects the life of a dynamic seal is its friction performance, which depends not only on the rubber compound but also on the seal geometry (sections 4.5 and 10.7). Friction, whether break-out or running, can cause excessive wear of the seal, which may result in premature leakage. Lubricants are commonly used to reduce friction, but there are systems in which lubricants introduce unacceptable contamination. This may require "internally lubricated" seal materials (internal lubrication means the incorporation of a friction-reducing ingredient in the rubber formula).

Another important factor to be carefully examined when considering dynamic seals is the fluid resistance; a volume increase of more than 10% results in a marked increase on friction, which may shorten the seal life to an unacceptable level. It should also be noted that the finish of the contiguous surface has a great influence on the life of dynamic seals.

14.10 Conclusion

Elastomers are complex materials that differ very considerably from other engineering materials. Consequently, the problem of deciding which rubber compound to use for a particular application is a subject best entrusted to rubber manufacturers who specialize in that field and have accumulated years of experience with successful compounds. The benifits for the users who accept this will include availability with minimum cost and less danger of mixup.

References

1. K. Nagdi, "Proposals for an ASTM D 2000 Type for Seals for Oil Related Duties," Proceedings of Polymers in Offshore Exploration Conference, PRI, June 1986.
2. "Guidelines: Properties Classification System for Elastomeric Materials Used in Oil and Gas Sealing Applications," Offshore Engineering Group, PRI.
3. M. Bowtell, "PRI Offshore Engineering Group Focuses on Seals for Oilfield Uses," *Elastomerics*, March 1991, pp. 11−12.

CHAPTER 15

General Chemical Resistance of Various Elastomers

15.1 Introduction

As discussed in chapter 6, elastomers can be degraded by the action of liquids or gases with which they come in contact. The best way to determine whether a rubber compound will be entirely satisfactory for a given application is to test it in actual service. If this is impractical, tests should be devised to simulate service conditions as closely as possible. In such test, attention should also be given to the possibility of the elastomer contaminating the liquid or gas (chapter 7).

Table 15.1, which should be used as a general guide only, rates the resistance of selected properly compounded elastomers to various chemicals such as gases, acids, alkalies, water solutions, oils, fuels and solvents. It should be noted that the rate and extent of chemical attack depends on several factors, including, for example:

– the grade of the rubber polymer;
– the nature of the compounding ingredients;
– the thickness of the elastomeric part and duration of contact;
– the temperature; and
– the chemical composition of the liquid or gas.

15.2 Effects of Rubber Polymer Grade

The elastomeric materials considered in Table 15.1 are based on the following rubber polymers: NR, IR, SBR, BR, IIR, EPDM, NBR, HNBR, CR, CSM, ECO, ACM, AEM, FPM, VMQ, FMQ, AU and T. As mentioned in chapter 8, there are normally many different grades of each rubber polymer, and this can have a significant effect on the chemical resistance of the elastomer.

Examples:

NBR: The amount of acrylonitrile (ACN), which can vary from about 18 to 48%, has a great effect on the swelling behavior of NBR elastomers in oils and solvents. The resistance to mineral oils and hydrocarbon (nonpolar) solvents will increase as the ACN content is increased, but the opposite effect can be observed with polar solvents (section 8.11).

CSM: The chlorine content, which can vary from about 24 to 43%, has a great effect on the swelling behavior of CSM elastomers in mineral oils and nonpolar solvents (section 8.15). The swelling in these liquids is reduced as the chlorine content increases.

FPM: The resistance of FPM elastomers to swelling in gasolines and gasohols depends primarily upon the fluorine level of the fluorocarbon rubber polymer, which can vary between approximately 65 and 70% (sections 6.21.1 and 8.19).

15.3. Effects of Compounding Ingredients

Compounding ingredients, particularly fillers, plasticizers, curing agents and age resistors, can have a great effect on the chemical resistance of the elastomer.

15.3.1 Fillers

The swelling of elastomers in oils and solvents is reduced by increasing the filler content, because it is the polymer that swells. However, the hardness will increase as the filler content increases, and a filler loading that is too high will result in poor mechanical properties.

15.3.2 Plasticizers

When the pasticizer content is high, which is the case in some NBR and EPDM compounds, a great amount of the plasticizer can be extracted by oils and solvents. This can result in excessive shrinkage of the material, which can cause trouble in the case of seals. Whenever possible, the elastomer should have only a small amount of extractable plasticizers.

15.3.3 Curing Agents

The curing agent can have an effect on the chemical resistance of the elastomer. For example, low-sulphur vulcanizing systems or peroxides produce vulcanizates that are more resistant to oxidation than those crosslinked with higher levels of elemental sulphur (section 2.5).

Furhtermore, the number of cross-links between the rubber molecules has a significant effect on swelling in oils, solvents and water. For example, hard rubbers (Fig. 2.1) based on NR, SBR and NBR show higher resistance to swelling in these liquids than with the corresponding soft materials.

When elastomeric materials based on CR, CSM and FPM are used in hot water or acids, the preferred curing system contains lead oxide. Other curing systems will produce higher swelling and greater deterioration in hot water, aqueous solutions and acids.

15.3.4 Age Resistors

Antioxidants are usually added to unsaturated rubbers such as NR, IR, SBR, CR and NBR to improve the resistance of their vulcanizates to oxidative aging (section 2.4). However, if the antioxidants are removed by extraction, a loss of aging resistance may result. This can be avoided by using antioxidants that are resistant to extraction by liquids. Special types of antioxidants may be required where the elastomer is to be exposed to chemicals containing certain metals such as copper, which might otherwise promote oxidation (section 5.8).

15.4 Effects of Part Thickness and Duration of Contact

The thickness of an elastomeric part has a major effect on its chemical resistance because the length of time of penetration of the swelling fluid depends on the part dimensions and surface-to-volume relationship. The bulk of a very thick part, for example, may remain almost unaffected during the projected service life. The duration of fluid contact should also be taken into account because it may be only partial or not continuous.

(Also note that parts under strain, such as O-rings, swell significantly less than in the free state).

15.5 Effects of Temperature

With the known exception of pure methanol (Table 6.16), high temperatures increase the effect of liquids and gases on elastomers. A rubber compound that performs very well at room temperature might fail miserably at elevated temperatures.

15.6 Effects of the Chemical Composition of Medium

The gases and liquids listed in Table 15.1 are technically pure chemicals. The same effect on elastomers may not necessarily apply to commercial chemicals because they may contain trace quantities of oxidizing agents or other impurities. It should also be noted that mineral oils and fuels vary appreciably in composition even when supplied according to a recognized specification. The action of acids, alkalis and oxidizing agents on elastomers increases with their concentration. For example, a rubber compound that deteriorates completely in a concentrated acid might perform very well in the same acid when diluted.

15.7 Rating System

The rating system used in Table 15.1 is based, for the most part, on laboratory tests published by various polymer suppliers and rubber manufacturers (see References at end of chapter). In cases where data were not available, the ratings were arrived at by theory and analogy. The author cannot guarantee their accuracy nor take responsibility for their use.

Unless the user has prior knowledge of or experience with the application, a selection based on the table should always be confirmed by functional tests on the selected compounds, using the actual part under the service conditions.

Following is an **explanation of the numerical rating** used in Table 15.1:

1 = Minor effect; recommended.

2 = Moderate effect; elastomeric parts probably stil useful in most applications.

3 = Severe effect; elastomeric parts (e.g., O-rings) might still function in static applications only but will fail in any dynamic application.

4 = Not recommended because of potential for deterioration or because of unsuitability for contact with potable water, other beverages and foodstuffs (e.g., polysulphide elastomers).

References

1. ISO/TR 7620, "Rubber Materials – Chemical Resistance."
2. *The General Chemical Resistance of Various Elastomers* (Los Angeles Rubber, Inc.).
3. SIS Handbook 131 (Sweden).
4. *Die Quellbeständigkeit von Vulkanisaten verschiedener Elastomere*, (Swell Resistance of Different Elastomers) Bayer, Leverkusen.
5. R.O. Menard, "Effect of Freon Fluorocarbons and other Halohydrocarbons on Elastomers," special report from Elastomer Chemicals Department, Du Pont.
7. "Fluid Compatibility Table," Parker-Prädifa GmbH, Germany.

Table 15.1.: General Chemical Resistance of Elastomer Types

Medium	Temp. (°C)	NR/IR	SBR/BR	IIR	EPDM	NBR	HNBR	CR	CSM	ECO	ACM	AEM	FPM	VMQ	FMQ	AU	T
Acetaldehyde	23	3	4	2	2	4	(4)	4	3	(4)	4	(4)	4	2	4	4	4
Acetamide	100	4	4	1	1	2	(2)	2	2	(2)	4	(4)	3	2	2	4	4
Acetic Acid, Aq.	23	4	4	3	3	4	(4)	4	3	(4)	4	(4)	4	3	4	4	4
Acetic Acid, Glacial	23	4	4	3	2	4	(4)	4	2	(4)	4	(4)	4	3	4	4	4
Acetic Anhydride	23	2	2	2	2	4	(4)	2	2	4	4	(4)	4	3	4	4	2
Acetone	23	2	2	1	1	4	(4)	3	3	4	4	4	4	3	4	4	2
Acetophenone	23	3	4	1	1	4	(4)	4	4	4	4	(4)	4	4	4	4	4
Acetyl Acetone	23	4	4	2	2	4	(4)	4	4	4	4	4	4	4	4	4	2
Acetyl Chloride	23	4	4	4	4	4	(4)	4	4	(4)	4	(4)	1	4	1	4	4
Acetylene	23	2	2	2	2	1	(1)	2	2	(1)	(1)	(1)	1	3	(1)	(1)	3
Acetylene Tetrabromide	23	4	4	4	4	4	(4)	(4)	(4)	(4)	(4)	(4)	1	4	2	(4)	(4)
Acrylonitrile	50	4	4	4	4	4	(4)	4	3	(4)	4	(4)	4	4	4	4	4
Adipic Acid, Aq.	50	1	1	1	1	1	(1)	1	1	2	4	(2)	1	1	1	4	(1)
Air	70	2	2	1	1	2	1	2	1	1	1	1	1	1	1	1	2
Air	100	4	4	1	1	4	1	4	1	1	1	1	1	1	1	2	4
Air	125	4	4	1	1	4	1	4	1	2	1	1	1	1	1	4	4
Air	150	4	4	2	1	4	2	4	4	4	1	1	1	1	1	4	4

Medium	°C														
Air	200	4	4	4	4	4	4	4	4	4	4	1	1	3	4	4
Aluminum Acetate, Aq.	23	2	1	1	2	(2)	2	1	3	4	(4)	4	3	4	4	4
Aluminum Chloride, Aq.	23	1	1	1	1	1	2	1	2	4	(4)	1	3	1	4	4
Aluminum Nitrate, Aq.	23	1	1	1	1	1	2	1	2	4	(4)	1	3	1	4	4
Aluminum Sulphate, Aq.	23	1	1	1	1	1	2	1	2	4	(4)	1	3	1	4	4
Ammonia Gas	23	4	1	1	1	1	1	1	(1)	(4)	(4)	4	1	4	(4)	1
Ammonia Gas	70	4	4	2	4	(4)	2	2	(4)	(4)	(4)	4	3	4	4	4
Ammonia Liquid	23	4	4	1	2	(2)	1	2	(4)	4	(4)	4	3	4	4	4
Ammonium Carbonate, Aq.	23	1	1	1	4	(4)	1	1	2	4	4	4	1	4	4	4
Ammonium Chloride, Aq.	23	1	1	1	1	(1)	1	1	2	4	4	4	1	4	4	4
Ammonium Hydroxide, Aq.	23	4	4	1	4	(4)	1	1	(2)	4	4	4	1	4	4	4
Ammonium Nitrate, Aq.	23	1	1	1	1	(1)	1	1	(2)	4	4	4	1	4	4	4
Ammonium Nitrite, Aq.	23	1	1	1	1	(1)	1	1	(2)	4	4	4	1	4	4	4
Ammonium Persulphate, Aq.	23	4	4	1	1	1	1	1	2	4	(4)	4	1	4	4	4
Ammonium Phosphate, Aq.	23	1	1	1	1	1	1	1	2	4	(4)	4	1	4	4	4
Ammonium Sulphate, Aq.	23	4	4	1	1	1	1	1	2	4	(4)	4	1	4	4	4
Ammonium Sulphide, Aq.	23	4	4	1	4	(3)	1	1	2	4	(4)	4	1	4	4	4
Amyl Acetate	23	4	4	2	4	(4)	4	4	4	4	(4)	4	4	4	4	3

RATINGS: 1 = Minor effect.   2 = Moderate effect.   3 = Severe effect.   4 = Not recommended.   ( ) = No data found; ratings based on theory and analogy.   Aq. = Aquesons sotions.

Medium	Temp. (°C)	NR/IR	SBR/BR	IIR	EPDM	NBR	HNBR	CR	CSM	ECO	ACM	AEM	FPM	VMQ	FMQ	AU	T
Amyl Alcohol	50	2	2	1	1	2	(2)	2	2	1	4	(3)	2	4	1	4	2
Aniline	50	4	4	2	2	4	4	4	4	(4)	4	(4)	3	2	3	4	4
Aniline Hydrochloride, Aq.	23	2	3	2	2	2	(2)	4	4	(3)	4	(4)	2	3	2	4	4
Aqua Regia	23	4	4	3	3	4	(4)	4	3	4	4	(4)	2	4	(4)	4	4
Argon	23	1	1	1	1	1	1	1	1	1	1	1	1	1	1	1	1
Arsenic Acid, Aq.	23	2	1	1	1	1	(1)	1	1	1	4	(4)	1	1	1	4	1
ASTM Fluid 101	100	4	4	4	4	3	(4)	4	4	3	4	(4)	1	4	1	4	4
ASTM Fuel A	50	4	4	4	4	1	1	2	2	1	1	2	1	4	2	1	1
ASTM Fuel B	50	4	4	4	4	3	4	4	4	3	4	4	1	4	2	2	1
ASTM Fuel C	50	4	4	4	4	4	4	4	4	4	4	4	1	4	2	4	2
ASTM Oil No. 1	70	4	4	4	4	1	1	1	1	1	1	1	1	1	1	1	1
ASTM Oil No. 1	100	4	4	4	4	1	1	1	1	1	1	1	1	1	1	2	4
ASTM Oil No. 1	125	4	4	4	4	4	1	4	2	1	1	1	1	1	1	4	4
ASTM Oil No. 2	70	4	4	4	4	1	1	2	2	1	1	2	1	1	1	1	1
ASTM Oil No. 2	100	4	4	4	4	1	1	3	3	1	1	3	1	2	1	2	4
ASTM Oil No. 2	125	4	4	4	4	4	1	4	4	1	1	4	1	3	1	4	4
ASTM Oil No. 3	70	4	4	4	4	2	2	3	3	1	1	3	1	3	1	2	1
ASTM Oil No. 3	100	4	4	4	4	2	3	4	4	1	1	4	1	4	1	3	4

Chemical	Temp (°C)																
ASTM Oil No. 3	125	4	4	1	4	1	4	2	1	4	4	3	4	4	4	4	4
Barium Chloride, Aq.	23	1	4	1	1	1	2	4	2	1	2	1	1	1	1	1	1
Barium Hydroxide, Aq.	23	1	4	1	1	1	2	4	2	1	2	1	1	1	1	1	1
Barium Sulphide, Aq.	23	1	4	1	1	1	2	4	2	1	2	1	1	1	1	1	1
Beer	23	1	4	1	1	1	1	4	2	1	2	1	1	1	1	1	4
Beet Sugar Liquors	23	1	4	2	1	1	4	4	2	1	1	2	2	1	1	1	4
Benzaldehyde	23	2	4	3	2	4	(4)	4	4	4	4	(4)	4	2	2	4	4
Benzene	23	4	4	2	4	1	4	4	4	4	4	4	4	4	3	4	4
Benzenesulphonic Acid, Aq.	23	4	1	2	4	1	(4)	4	(4)	1	2	(4)	4	2	3	4	4
Benzine	23	4	1	1	4	1	(3)	1	1	3	2	1	1	4	4	4	1
Benzoic Acid, Aq.	50	2	4	1	1	1	(4)	4	2	1	1	1	1	1	1	4	1
Benzophenone	50	2	4	1	(2)	1	(4)	4	(4)	(4)	(4)	(4)	(4)	2	2	4	2
Benzoyl Chloride	23	4	4	2	(4)	1	(4)	4	(4)	4	4	(4)	4	2	4	4	4
Benzyl Alcohol	23	2	4	2	(2)	1	(4)	4	(4)	2	2	(4)	2	2	2	4	4
Benzyl Benzoate	23	2	4	1	(3)	1	(4)	4	(4)	4	4	(4)	4	2	4	4	4
Benzyl Chloride	23	4	4	2	4	1	(4)	4	(4)	4	4	(4)	4	2	4	4	4
Biphenyl	70	4	4	2	4	1	(4)	4	(4)	4	4	(4)	4	4	4	4	4
Borax, Aq.	70	2	1	1	(2)	1	(2)	4	2	1	1	1	1	1	1	4	1

RATINGS: 1 = Minor effect.   2 = Moderate effect.   3 = Severe effect.   4 = Not recommended.   ( ) = No data found; ratings based on theory and analogy.   Aq. = Aquesons sotions.

Medium	Temp. (°C)	NR/IR	SBR/BR	IIR	EPDM	NBR	HNBR	CR	CSM	ECO	ACM	AEM	FPM	VMQ	FMQ	AU	T
Boric Acid, Aq.	70	2	1	1	1	1	1	1	1	2	4	(2)	1	1	1	4	1
Brake Fluids (Nonpetroleum)	70	1	1	1	1	4	(3)	1	1	4	4	(4)	4	1	4	4	1
Brake Fluids (Nonpetroleum)	100	4	2	1	1	4	(3)	2	2	4	4	(4)	4	1	4	4	4
Brake Fluids (Nonpetroleum)	150	4	4	1	1	4	(4)	4	4	(4)	4	(4)	4	(2)	4	4	4
Brine	23	1	1	1	1	1	1	1	1	2	4	(1)	1	1	1	4	4
Bromine, Dry	23	4	4	4	3	4	(4)	4	3	(4)	4	(4)	1	4	2	4	3
Bromine Trifluoride	23	4	4	4	4	4	(4)	4	4	(4)	4	(4)	4	4	4	4	4
Bromine Water	23	4	4	4	4	4	(4)	4	4	(4)	4	(4)	1	4	2	4	3
Bromobenzene	23	4	4	4	4	4	(4)	4	4	4	4	(4)	1	4	2	4	1
Butadiene	23	4	4	4	4	4	(4)	4	4	4	4	(4)	2	4	2	4	3
Butane	23	4	4	4	4	1	(1)	2	2	1	2	(3)	1	4	2	1	1
Butanol	50	1	1	1	1	2	(2)	1	1	4	4	4	1	3	2	4	1
Butene	23	4	4	4	4	2	(2)	3	4	(1)	4	(4)	1	4	2	4	2
Butter	50	4	4	3	3	1	(1)	3	3	1	4	4	1	1	1	4	4
Butyl Acetate	23	4	4	3	2	4	(4)	4	4	4	4	4	4	4	4	4	3
Butyl Acrylate	50	4	4	4	4	4	(4)	4	4	(4)	4	(4)	4	(4)	4	(4)	3
Butyl Alcohol	50	1	1	1	1	2	(2)	1	1	4	4	4	1	3	2	4	1
Butylamine	23	4	4	3	3	4	(4)	4	4	(4)	4	(4)	4	3	4	4	4

Chemical	°C															
Butyl Benzoate	23	4	4	1	1	4	(4)	4	4	4	(4)	4	1	4	1	4	4
Butylene	23	4	4	4	4	2	(2)	3	4	4	(1)	4	1	4	2	4	2
Butyl Oleate	23	4	4	2	2	4	(4)	4	4	(4)	(4)	(4)	1	(3)	2	(4)	(2)
Butyl Stearate	70	4	4	4	4	2	(2)	4	4	(4)	(2)	(4)	1	(3)	2	(4)	(3)
Butyraldehyde	23	4	4	2	2	4	(4)	4	4	4	(4)	4	4	4	4	4	3
Butyric Acid	23	(4)	(4)	2	2	4	(4)	4	4	4	(4)	4	2	(4)	(4)	(4)	(4)
Calcium Acetate, Aq.	23	2	2	1	3	3	(3)	2	2	3	3	4	4	3	4	4	4
Calcium Bisulphite, Aq.	23	4	4	2	4	4	(2)	2	2	(4)	(4)	4	1	3	2	4	4
Calcium Chloride, Aq.	23	1	1	1	1	1	1	1	1	2	2	4	1	1	1	4	1
Calcium Cyanide, Aq.	23	1	1	1	1	1	(1)	1	1	2	2	4	1	1	1	4	1
Calcium Hydroxide, Aq.	23	1	1	1	1	1	1	1	1	2	2	4	1	1	1	4	1
Calcium Hypochlorite, Aq.	23	4	4	3	3	4	(4)	3	2	4	(4)	4	1	4	2	4	4
Calcium Nitrate, Aq.	23	1	1	1	1	1	1	1	1	2	(2)	4	1	1	1	4	1
Calcium Thiosulphate, Aq.	23	1	1	1	1	1	1	1	1	2	(2)	4	1	1	1	4	1
Cane Sugar Liquors	23	1	1	1	1	2	2	1	1	2	4	4	1	1	2	4	4
Carbolic Acid	70	4	4	2	2	4	(4)	4	4	4	(4)	4	1	1	1	4	4
Carbon Dioxide, Dry	23	2	2	1	1	1	1	1	1	1	1	(2)	1	2	1	1	2
Carbon Disulphide	23	4	4	4	4	4	(4)	4	4	4	4	4	1	4	1	2	4

RATINGS: 1 = Minor effect. 2 = Moderate effect. 3 = Severe effect. 4 = Not recommended. ( ) = No data found; ratings based on theory and analogy. Aq. = Aqueous solutions.

Medium	Temp. (°C)	NR/IR	SBR/BR	IIR	EPDM	NBR	HNBR	CR	CSM	ECO	ACM	AEM	FPM	VMQ	FMQ	AU	T
Carbon Monoxide	23	2	2	1	1	1	(1)	2	2	1	(1)	(1)	1	1	2	1	(4)
Carbon Tetrachloride	23	4	4	4	4	4	4	4	4	4	4	4	1	4	2	4	3
Carbonic Acid	23	1	1	1	1	2	2	1	1	2	4	(1)	1	1	1	4	1
Castor Oil	23	1	1	2	2	1	1	1	2	(1)	1	(2)	1	1	1	1	4
Cellosolve	23	4	4	2	2	4	(4)	4	4	(4)	4	(4)	4	4	4	4	2
Cellosolve Acetate	23	4	4	2	2	4	(4)	4	4	(4)	4	(4)	4	4	4	4	2
Chlorine, Dry	23	4	4	4	3	4	4	4	3	(2)	4	4	1	4	2	4	4
Chlorine Dioxide	23	4	4	4	3	4	(4)	4	3	(4)	4	(4)	1	4	2	4	4
Chlorine Trifluoride	23	4	4	4	4	4	4	4	4	4	4	4	4	4	4	4	4
Chlorine Water	23	4	4	4	3	4	4	4	3	(3)	4	(4)	1	3	2	4	3
Chloroacetic Acid	23	4	4	2	1	4	(4)	4	1	(4)	4	(4)	4	(3)	4	4	4
Chloroacetone	23	4	4	2	1	4	(4)	3	3	(4)	4	(4)	4	4	4	4	4
Chlorobenzene	50	4	4	4	4	4	(4)	4	4	(4)	4	(4)	1	4	2	4	4
Chlorobromomethane	23	4	4	4	4	4	(4)	4	4	(4)	4	(4)	1	4	2	4	4
2-Chlorobutadiene	23	4	4	4	4	4	(4)	4	4	(4)	4	(4)	1	4	2	4	4
Chloroform	23	4	4	4	4	4	(4)	4	4	(4)	4	(4)	1	4	2	4	4
o-Chloronaphthalene	23	4	4	4	4	4	(4)	4	4	(4)	(4)	(4)	1	4	2	(4)	4
Chloroprene	23	4	4	4	4	4	(4)	4	4	(4)	4	(4)	1	4	2	4	4

Chemical	Temp. (°C)															
Chlorosulphonic Acid	23	4	4	4	4	(4)	4	4	(4)	4	4	4	(4)	4	4	4
Chlorotoluene	23	4	4	4	4	(4)	4	4	(4)	4	4	4	(4)	1	4	4
Chromic Acid, Aq.	23	4	4	2	2	(3)	3	2	(3)	4	2	4	(3)	1	4	4
Cinnamic Aldehyde	23	2	3	1	1	(4)	4	4	(4)	4	2	4	(4)	2	4	4
Citric Acid, Aq.	70	1	1	1	1	1	1	1	(1)	1	1	4	(2)	1	4	1
Cobalt Chloride, Aq.	23	4	2	1	1	1	1	1	(1)	1	1	4	(2)	1	4	1
Coconut Oil	60	4	4	3	3	(1)	2	2	(1)	1	3	1	(3)	1	2	4
Cod Liver Oil	23	4	4	2	2	(1)	2	2	(1)	1	3	1	(3)	1	1	4
Coffee	80	(4)	(4)	(3)	3	(4)	4	4	(4)	4	4	4	4	1	4	4
Copper Acetate, Aq.	23	4	2	1	1	4	2	2	3	2	2	4	(4)	4	4	4
Copper Chloride, Aq.	23	4	2	1	1	1	1	1	(2)	2	1	4	(2)	1	4	1
Copper Sulphate, Aq.	23	4	2	1	1	1	1	2	(2)	2	1	4	(2)	1	4	1
Corn Oil	70	4	4	3	3	(1)	3	3	1	1	3	1	(3)	1	1	4
Cottonseed Oil	70	4	4	3	3	(1)	3	3	1	1	3	1	(3)	1	1	4
o-Cresol	70	4	4	3	4	(4)	4	4	4	4	4	4	(4)	2	4	4
Cresylic Acids	70	4	4	3	4	(4)	4	4	(4)	4	4	4	(4)	2	4	4
Cumene	23	4	4	4	4	(4)	4	4	(4)	4	4	4	(4)	2	4	2
Cyclohexane	50	4	4	4	4	(2)	3	3	1	2	3	1	3	2	1	1

RATINGS: 1 = Minor effect.   2 = Moderate effect.   3 = Severe effect.   4 = Not recommended.   ( ) = No data found; ratings based on theory and analogy.   Aq. = Aqueous solutions.

Medium	Temp. (°C)	NR/IR	SBR/BR	IIR	EPDM	NBR	HNBR	CR	CSM	ECO	ACM	AEM	FPM	VMQ	FMQ	AU	T
Cyclohexanol	23	4	4	4	4	2	(2)	2	2	(4)	4	(4)	1	4	1	4	2
Cyclohexanone	23	4	4	4	4	4	(4)	4	4	4	4	4	4	3	4	4	4
p-Cymene	23	4	4	4	4	4	(4)	4	4	(4)	4	(4)	1	4	2	4	3
Decalin	23	4	4	4	4	4	(4)	4	4	(4)	(4)	(4)	1	4	1	(4)	2
Decane	23	4	4	4	4	1	(2)	3	3	(1)	1	(3)	1	2	1	2	1
Denatured Alcohol	23	1	1	1	1	2	2	1	1	(2)	4	(4)	1	1	1	4	1
Diacetone Alcohol	23	4	4	1	1	4	(4)	3	3	4	4	(4)	4	3	4	4	2
Dibenzyl Ether	23	4	4	2	2	4	(4)	4	4	4	4	(4)	1	2	(2)	4	4
Dibutylamine	23	4	4	4	4	4	(4)	3	4	(4)	4	(4)	4	3	4	4	4
Dibutyl Ether	23	4	4	4	4	2	(4)	4	3	4	4	(4)	1	4	(3)	1	1
Dibutyl Phtalate	23	3	4	1	1	4	(4)	4	4	4	4	4	1	1	(2)	4	2
Dibutyl Sebacate	23	4	4	2	2	4	(4)	4	4	3	4	(4)	2	2	2	4	2
o-Dichlorobenzene	23	4	4	4	4	4	(4)	4	4	4	4	(4)	1	4	2	4	3
Dicyclohexylamine	23	4	4	4	4	3	(3)	4	4	(4)	4	(4)	4	(4)	4	4	4
Diesel Oil	70	4	4	4	4	1	2	2	3	1	1	(3)	1	4	1	2	1
Diethylamine	23	4	4	4	4	4	(4)	4	4	(4)	4	(4)	4	4	(4)	4	4
Diethyl Ether	23	4	4	4	4	3	(4)	3	3	(4)	4	(4)	4	4	4	2	1
Diethylene Glycol	100	4	4	1	1	3	(2)	3	1	(3)	4	(4)	1	1	1	4	4

Chemical	°C														
Diisobutylene	23	4	4	4	2	(3)	4	4	(2)	4	(4)	1	4	3	4	1
Diisobutyl Ketone	23	4	2	2	4	(4)	4	4	(4)	4	(4)	4	4	4	4	3
Diisopropyl Benzene	23	4	4	4	4	(4)	4	4	(4)	(4)	(4)	1	(4)	2	(4)	2
Diisopropyl Ketone	23	4	2	2	4	(4)	4	4	(4)	4	(4)	4	4	4	4	3
Dimethylamine	23	(4)	(4)	4	4	(4)	4	4	(4)	(4)	(4)	4	(4)	(4)	(4)	(4)
Dimethyl Aniline	23	4	4	2	4	(4)	4	4	(4)	(4)	(4)	4	(4)	4	(4)	4
Dimethyl Formamide	23	4	2	2	2	(2)	3	3	(3)	(4)	(4)	4	2	4	4	4
Dimethyl Phthalate	23	2	1	1	4	(4)	3	2	(4)	4	(4)	2	1	(2)	1	1
Dioctyl Phthalate	23	4	2	2	2	(3)	4	3	(3)	2	(3)	1	1	(1)	1	1
Dioctyl Sebacate	23	4	2	2	4	(4)	4	4	3	4	(4)	2	3	3	2	3
Dioxane	23	4	3	2	4	(4)	4	4	(4)	4	(4)	4	3	(4)	4	4
Dioxolane	23	4	3	2	4	(4)	4	4	(4)	4	(4)	4	4	4	4	4
Dipentene	23	4	4	4	2	(3)	4	4	(4)	4	(4)	1	4	3	4	4
Diphenyl	70	4	4	4	4	(4)	4	4	(4)	4	(4)	1	3	2	3	3
Diphenylmethane 4,4'-Diisocyanate	70	4	4	4	4	(4)	4	4	(4)	4	(4)	1	2	(2)	2	4
Dry Cleaning Fluids	23	4	4	4	4	(4)	4	4	4	4	(4)	1	4	2	4	4
Epichlorohydrin	23	4	4	3	4	(4)	4	4	(4)	4	(4)	1	4	2	4	4
Ethane	23	4	4	4	1	(1)	2	2	(1)	1	(3)	1	4	(1)	2	1

RATINGS: 1 = Minor effect.   2 = Moderate effect.   3 = Severe effect.   4 = Not recommended.   ( ) = No data found; ratings based on theory and analogy.   Aq. = Aquesons sotions.

Medium	Temp. (°C)	NR/IR	SBR/BR	IIR	EPDM	NBR	HNBR	CR	CSM	ECO	ACM	AEM	FPM	VMQ	FMQ	AU	T
Ethanol	50	1	1	1	1	2	(2)	1	2	2	4	4	1	1	2	4	1
Ethanolamine	70	2	2	1	1	2	(2)	2	3	2	4	(4)	4	2	4	4	2
Ethyl Acetate	23	4	4	2	2	4	(4)	4	4	4	4	(4)	4	4	4	4	2
Ethyl Acetoacetate	23	3	3	2	2	4	(4)	3	4	4	4	(4)	4	2	4	4	2
Ethyl Acrylate	23	4	4	2	2	4	(4)	4	4	(4)	4	(4)	4	3	4	4	2
Ethyl Alcohol	50	1	1	1	1	2	(2)	1	2	2	4	4	1	1	2	4	1
Ethyl Benzene	23	4	4	4	4	4	(4)	4	4	4	4	(4)	1	4	1	4	3
Ethyl Benzoate	23	2	2	2	2	4	(4)	4	4	(4)	4	(4)	1	4	1	4	2
Ethyl Bromide	23	4	4	4	4	2	(2)	4	4	(2)	(4)	(4)	1	(4)	1	(3)	(4)
Ethyl Chloride	23	4	4	4	3	1	(2)	4	4	2	4	(4)	1	4	1	2	4
Ethyl Ether	23	4	4	4	4	3	(4)	3	3	(4)	4	(4)	4	4	4	2	1
Ethyl Formate	23	4	4	2	2	4	(4)	2	2	4	(4)	(4)	1	(4)	1	(4)	4
Ethyl Mercaptan	23	4	4	4	4	4	(4)	3	2	4	(4)	(4)	2	3	(3)	(4)	4
Ethyl Oxalate	23	1	1	1	1	4	(4)	3	4	4	4	(4)	1	4	2	(4)	1
Ethyl Silicate	23	2	2	1	1	1	(1)	1	2	1	(4)	(4)	1	(2)	1	(4)	2
Ethylene	23	3	3	2	2	1	(1)	3	(3)	(1)	(1)	(3)	1	(4)	1	(2)	(2)
Ethylene Chloride	23	4	4	3	3	4	(4)	4	4	4	4	(4)	1	4	3	4	4
Ethylene Chlorohydrin	23	2	2	2	2	4	(4)	2	2	(4)	4	(4)	1	3	2	4	2

Chemical	Temp																
Ethylene Diamine	23	1	2	1	1	1	1	1	2	1	(4)	4	1	4	4	4	4
Ethylene Dichloride	23	4	4	3	4	4	4	4	4	4	(4)	4	4	3	4	4	4
Ethylene Glycol	100	4	1	1	1	2	1	2	(2)	(3)	(3)	4	(1)	(1)	3	4	4
Ethylene Oxide	23	4	4	3	2	4	4	4	4	(4)	(4)	4	4	4	4	4	(4)
Ethylene Trichloride	23	4	4	4	4	4	4	4	4	4	(4)	4	(4)	4	4	4	4
Ferric Chloride, Aq.	23	4	2	1	1	1	1	2	1	(2)	(2)	4	1	1	1	4	1
Ferric Nitrate, Aq.	23	4	2	1	1	1	1	2	1	(2)	(2)	4	1	1	1	4	1
Ferric Sulphate, Aq.	23	4	2	1	1	1	1	2	1	(2)	(2)	4	1	1	1	4	1
Fish Oil	23	4	4	4	1	1	1	4	(1)	(3)	(1)	4	1	(1)	1	(2)	(4)
Fluorine	23	4	4	4	4	4	4	4	4	4	4	4	4	4	(2)	4	4
Fluorobenzene	23	4	4	4	4	4	4	4	(4)	(4)	(4)	4	4	4	2	4	(4)
Formaldehyde, Aq.	23	2	2	1	3	3	2	1	1	(4)	2	4	2	2	4	4	2
Formic Acid	23	3	2	1	3	3	1	1	1	(4)	2	4	3	2	3	4	4
Furan	23	4	4	4	4	4	4	4	(4)	(4)	(4)	4	(4)	(4)	(4)	(4)	2
Furfural	23	4	4	4	2	2	4	4	4	4	4	4	4	4	(4)	(4)	4
Furfuraldehyde	23	4	4	4	2	2	4	4	4	4	4	4	4	4	(4)	(4)	4
Furfuran	23	4	4	4	3	3	4	4	(4)	(4)	(4)	4	(4)	(4)	(4)	(4)	2
Furfuryl Alcohol	23	4	3	3	3	3	4	4	(4)	(4)	(4)	4	4	(4)	(4)	4	4

RATINGS: 1 = Minor effect. 2 = Moderate effect. 3 = Severe effect. 4 = Not recommended. ( ) = No data found; ratings based on theory and analogy. Aq. = Aquesons sotions.

Medium	Temp. (°C)	NR/IR	SBR/BR	IIR	EPDM	NBR	HNBR	CR	CSM	ECO	ACM	AEM	FPM	VMQ	FMQ	AU	T
Gasohol (section 6.21.1)	23	4	4	4	4	3	(4)	4	4	4	4	4	2	4	2	4	2
Gasoline (section 6.21.1)	23	4	4	4	4	3	4	4	3	4	4	4	1	4	2	3	2
Gelatin	40	1	1	1	1	1	1	1	1	3	4	(2)	1	(1)	(1)	4	4
Glucose, Aq.	80	1	1	1	1	1	(1)	1	1	1	4	(2)	1	1	1	4	4
Glyerol	100	4	1	1	1	1	1	1	1	1	4	(4)	1	1	1	4	4
Helium	23	1	1	1	1	1	1	1	1	1	1	1	1	1	1	1	1
n-Haptane	23	4	4	4	4	1	(2)	2	2	(1)	1	(3)	1	4	1	1	1
n-Hexaldehyde	23	4	4	2	1	4	(4)	1	3	(4)	(4)	(4)	4	2	4	3	2
n-Hexane	23	4	4	4	4	1	(2)	2	2	1	1	(3)	1	4	1	1	1
n-Hexanol	23	2	2	3	3	1	(2)	2	2	(2)	4	(4)	1	2	2	4	2
n-Hexene-1	23	4	4	4	4	2	(2)	2	2	(2)	1	(3)	1	4	1	2	1
n-Hexyl Alcohol	23	2	2	3	3	1	(2)	2	2	(2)	4	(4)	1	2	2	4	2
Hydrazine, Anhydrous	23	4	1	2	2	4	(4)	2	2	(4)	4	(4)	4	(3)	4	4	4
Hydrazine, Aq.	23	1	1	1	1	2	(2)	2	2	(2)	4	(4)	4	3	4	4	4
Hydrobromic Acid (40%)	23	3	3	1	1	4	(4)	2	1	(4)	4	4	1	4	3	4	4
Hydrochlorid Acid (37%)	23	4	4	2	2	4	4	4	4	(4)	4	4	2	4	3	4	4
Hydrocyanic Acid	23	2	2	1	1	2	(2)	2	1	(2)	4	(4)	1	3	2	(4)	4
Hydrofluoric Acid (65%)	23	4	4	3	3	4	(4)	4	2	(4)	4	(4)	1	4	4	4	4

Chemical	Temp (°C)																	
Hydrogen Fluoride, Anhydrous	23	4	4	2	2	4	4	4	2	4	2	4	4	4	4	4	4	4
Hydrogen Gas	23	1	1	1	1	1	1	1	1	1	1	1	1	1	1	3	3	1
Hydrogen Peroxide (10%)	23	2	2	1	1	2	1	1	1	1	1	(1)	4	(4)	1	1	1	4
Hydrogen Peroxide (90%)	23	4	4	3	(2)	4	4	4	2	4	2	(2)	4	(4)	1	2	2	4
Hydrogen Sulphide	23	4	4	1	1	4	(3)	2	2	2	2	2	(4)	(4)	4	3	3	4
Iodine Vapor	23	4	4	2	2	4	(2)	4	2	4	2	(2)	(4)	(4)	1	(3)	1	(4)
Iodine Pentafluoride	23	4	4	4	4	4	(4)	4	4	4	4	4	4	(4)	4	4	4	4
Isobutanol	23	2	2	1	1	1	(2)	1	1	1	1	(2)	4	(4)	1	1	2	4
Isobutyl Alcohol	23	2	2	1	1	2	(2)	1	1	1	1	(2)	4	(4)	1	1	2	4
Iso-Octane	23	4	4	4	4	1	1	2	2	2	2	1	1	2	1	4	2	1
Isophorone	23	4	4	2	2	4	(4)	4	4	4	4	(4)	4	(4)	4	4	4	4
Isopropanol	23	1	2	1	1	2	(2)	2	1	2	1	(2)	4	(4)	1	1	2	4
Isopropyl Acetate	23	4	4	2	2	4	(4)	4	4	4	4	(4)	4	(4)	4	4	4	4
Isopropyl Alcohol	23	2	2	1	1	2	(2)	2	1	2	1	(2)	4	(4)	1	1	2	4
Isopropyl Benzene	23	4	4	4	4	4	(4)	4	4	4	4	4	4	(4)	1	4	2	4
Isopropyl Chloride	23	4	4	4	4	4	(4)	4	4	4	4	(4)	(4)	(4)	1	4	2	4
Isopropyl Ether	23	4	4	4	4	3	(3)	4	4	4	4	(4)	(4)	(4)	4	4	4	3
Kerosene	70	4	4	4	4	1	(2)	3	3	3	3	1	2	3	1	4	1	1

RATINGS: 1 = Minor effect. 2 = Moderate effect. 3 = Severe effect. 4 = Not recommended. ( ) = No data found; ratings based on theory and analogy. Aq. = Aquesons sotions.

Medium	Temp. (°C)	NR/IR	SBR/BR	IIR	EPDM	NBR	HNBR	CR	CSM	ECO	ACM	AEM	FPM	VMQ	FMQ	AU	T
Lacquers	23	4	4	4	4	4	4	4	4	4	4	4	4	4	4	4	2
Lacquer Solvents	23	4	4	4	4	4	4	4	4	4	4	4	4	4	4	4	2
Lactic Acid	70	4	4	4	4	4	(4)	4	3	(4)	4	(4)	1	2	2	4	4
Lard	70	4	4	3	3	1	(1)	2	2	1	1	(3)	1	1	1	1	4
Lavender Oil	23	4	4	4	4	2	(3)	4	4	(3)	2	(4)	1	4	2	4	4
Lead Acetate, Aq.	23	2	2	1	1	4	4	2	2	3	4	(4)	4	3	4	4	4
Lead Nitrate, Aq.	23	1	1	1	1	1	1	1	1	2	4	(2)	1	1	1	4	1
Lead Tetraethyl	23	4	4	4	4	2	(2)	3	4	(2)	(4)	(4)	1	(4)	2	(4)	(4)
Ligroin	23	4	4	4	4	1	1	2	3	1	1	(3)	1	4	1	1	1
Linoleic Acid	70	4	4	4	4	2	(2)	4	4	(2)	(4)	(4)	2	2	(2)	4	4
Linseed Oil	23	4	4	3	3	1	(1)	2	3	1	1	3	1	1	1	2	4
Liquefied Petroleum Gas	23	4	4	4	4	1	(2)	2	2	1	3	(4)	1	4	3	1	1
Magnesium Chloride, Aq.	23	1	1	1	1	1	1	2	1	2	4	(2)	1	1	1	4	1
Magnesium Sulphate, Aq.	23	1	1	1	1	1	1	2	1	2	4	(2)	1	1	1	4	1
Mercury	23	1	1	1	1	1	1	1	1	1	(1)	(1)	1	(1)	(1)	1	1
Mesityl Oxide	23	4	4	2	2	4	(4)	4	4	(4)	4	(4)	4	4	4	4	2
Methane	23	4	4	4	4	1	(1)	2	2	1	(1)	(2)	1	4	2	2	1
Methanol (section 6.21.3)	60	1	1	1	1	2	2	1	1	2	4	(4)	3	2	2	4	1

Chemical	°C																			
Methyl Acetate	23	4	4	2	2	4	(4)	4	4	4	4	4	(4)	4	4	4	4	4	4	2
Methyl Acetoacetate	23	(4)	4	2	2	4	(4)	4	4	4	(4)	4	(4)	4	4	(4)	4	4	4	2
Methyl Acrylate	23	4	4	2	2	4	(4)	4	4	(4)	4	4	(4)	4	4	4	4	4	4	2
Methyl Alcohol	60	1	1	1	1	2	2	1	1	2	(4)	4	(4)	3	2	2	2	1	4	1
Methyl Benzoate	23	4	4	4	4	4	(4)	4	4	(4)	4	4	(4)	1	4	4	1	1	4	2
Methyl Bromide	23	4	4	4	4	4	(4)	4	4	(4)	4	(4)	(4)	1	1	(4)	1	1	(4)	(3)
Methyl Butyl Ketone	23	4	4	2	2	4	(4)	4	4	4	4	4	(4)	4	3	4	4	4	4	2
Methyl Cellosolve	23	4	4	2	2	3	(4)	4	(4)	4	(4)	4	(4)	4	4	4	4	4	4	(3)
Methyl Chloride	23	4	4	3	3	4	(4)	4	4	4	4	4	(4)	2	4	2	2	4	4	3
Methyl Cyclopentane	23	4	4	4	4	4	(4)	4	4	4	4	4	(4)	1	4	2	2	4	4	2
Methylene Chloride	23	4	4	4	4	4	(4)	4	4	4	4	4	(4)	2	4	2	2	4	4	4
Methyl Ether	23	2	2	1	1	1	(1)	3	(4)	4	(4)	4	(4)	1	1	1	1	1	(4)	2
Methyl Ethyl Ketone	23	3	3	1	1	4	(4)	4	4	4	4	4	(4)	4	4	4	4	4	4	3
Methyl Formate	23	4	4	2	2	4	(4)	4	2	2	4	2	4	2	4	2	2	4	(4)	3
Methyl Isobutyl Ketone	23	4	4	2	2	4	(4)	4	4	4	4	4	4	4	4	4	4	4	4	2
p-Methylisopropyl Benzene	23	4	4	2	2	4	(4)	4	4	(4)	4	4	(4)	1	4	2	2	4	4	3
Methyl Methacrylate	23	4	4	3	3	4	(4)	4	4	(4)	4	4	(4)	4	4	4	4	4	(4)	3
Methyl Oleate	23	4	4	2	2	4	(4)	4	4	4	(4)	4	(4)	1	2	(3)	2	2	(4)	(3)

RATINGS: 1 = Minor effect.   2 = Moderate effect.   3 = Severe effect.   4 = Not recommended.   ( ) = No data found; ratings based on theory and analogy.   Aq. = Aquesons sotions.

Medium	Temp. (°C)	NR/IR	SBR/BR	IIR	EPDM	NBR	HNBR	CR	CSM	ECO	ACM	AEM	FPM	VMQ	FMQ	AU	T
Methyl Salicylate	23	(4)	(4)	2	2	4	(4)	4	4	(4)	(4)	(4)	(4)	(3)	(4)	(4)	(2)
Milk	23	2	2	1	1	1	1	1	1	1	4	1	1	1	1	4	4
Mineral Oil	70	4	4	4	4	1	1	2	3	1	1	3	1	3	1	1	1
Monobromobenzene	23	4	4	4	4	4	(4)	4	4	(4)	4	(4)	1	4	2	4	1
Monochlorobenzene	50	4	4	4	4	4	(4)	4	4	(4)	4	(4)	1	4	2	4	4
Monoethanolamine	23	2	2	2	1	4	(4)	4	4	(4)	4	(4)	4	2	4	4	4
Monomethyl Aniline	23	4	4	2	2	4	(4)	4	4	4	4	(4)	2	(2)	(2)	4	4
Morpholine	23	(4)	(4)	2	2	4	(4)	2	2	(4)	(4)	(4)	4	(4)	(4)	(4)	(4)
Naphtha	23	4	4	4	4	2	(3)	3	4	1	2	(4)	1	4	2	2	2
Naphthalene	80	4	4	4	4	4	(4)	4	4	(4)	(4)	(4)	1	(4)	1	(4)	2
Naphthenic Acid	23	4	4	4	4	2	(3)	4	4	(2)	(4)	(4)	1	4	1	(4)	2
Natural Gas	23	4	4	4	4	1	(1)	2	2	1	(1)	(2)	1	4	2	2	1
Neatsfoot Oil	23	4	4	2	2	1	(1)	4	4	(1)	1	(3)	1	2	1	1	4
Neon	23	1	1	1	1	1	1	1	1	1	1	1	1	1	1	1	1
Nickel Acetate, Aq.	23	4	2	1	1	4	(4)	2	2	(3)	4	(4)	4	3	4	4	4
Nickel Chloride, Aq.	23	4	2	1	1	1	1	2	1	(2)	4	(2)	1	1	1	4	1
Nickel Sulphate, Aq.	23	4	2	1	1	1	1	2	1	(2)	4	(2)	1	1	1	4	1
Nitric Acid (10%)	23	4	4	2	2	4	(3)	3	1	(4)	4	(4)	1	4	3	4	4

Chemical	Temp																	
Nitric Acid (65%)	23	4	4	4	4	1	4	4	4	3	4	4	4	4	4	4	4	4
Nitric Acid, Red Fuming	23	4	4	4	4	4	4	4	4	4	4	4	4	4	4	4	4	2
Nitrobenzene	50	4	4	4	1	3	(4)	4	4	4	4	(4)	4	2	2	4	2	1
Nitroethane	23	(2)	4	4	4	4	(4)	4	(4)	2	2	(4)	4	2	2	4	2	1
Nitrogen	23	1	1	1	1	1	1	1	1	1	1	1	1	1	1	1	1	1
Nitrogen Tetraoxide	23	4	4	4	4	4	(4)	4	(4)	4	4	(4)	4	4	4	4	4	4
Nitromethane	23	(2)	4	4	4	4	(4)	4	(4)	3	3	(4)	4	2	2	3	2	2
1-Nitropropane	23	(2)	4	4	4	4	(4)	4	(4)	4	4	(4)	4	2	2	4	4	4
n-Octane	23	2	2	2	4	1	(4)	4	(2)	4	4	(2)	4	4	4	4	4	4
Octyl Alcohol	23	2	4	2	2	1	(4)	2	(2)	2	2	(2)	2	1	2	2	2	2
Oleic Acid	70	4	4	1	1	1	(4)	4	2	4	3	(4)	3	4	4	4	4	4
Olive Oil	50	4	1	(1)	1	1	(3)	1	1	2	2	(1)	1	3	2	4	2	4
Oxalic Acid, Aq.	70	4	4	1	2	2	(4)	4	3	2	2	(2)	2	1	1	3	1	3
Oxygen	23	1	1	1	1	2	1	1	1	1	1	1	1	1	1	1	1	1
Ozone (50 pphm)	40	1	1	1	1	4	1	1	1	1	1	1	4	1	1	4	4	4
Paint Thinner, Duco	23	2	4	4	4	4	4	4	4	4	4	4	4	4	4	4	4	4
Palmitic Acid	70	4	4	1	1	1	(4)	4	2	3	2	(2)	2	3	3	4	4	4
Paraffin Oil	70	1	1	1	1	1	1	1	1	1	1	1	1	4	4	4	4	4

RATINGS: 1 = Minor effect. 2 = Moderate effect. 3 = Severe effect. 4 = Not recommended. ( ) = No data found; ratings based on theory and analogy. Aq. = Aquesons sotions.

Medium	Temp. (°C)	NR/IR	SBR/BR	IIR	EPDM	NBR	HNBR	CR	CSM	ECO	ACM	AEM	FPM	VMQ	FMQ	AU	T
Peanut Oil	23	4	4	3	3	1	(1)	3	3	1	1	(3)	1	1	1	2	4
n-Pentane	23	4	4	4	4	1	(1)	2	2	1	2	(3)	1	4	2	1	1
Pentanol	50	2	2	1	1	2	(2)	2	2	1	4	(3)	2	4	1	4	2
Perchloroethylene	23	4	4	4	4	4	4	4	4	4	4	(4)	1	4	2	4	3
Petroleum Ether	23	4	4	4	4	1	1	2	3	1	1	(3)	1	4	1	1	1
Phenol	70	4	4	2	2	4	(4)	4	4	4	4	(4)	1	1	1	4	4
Phenylbenzene	70	4	4	4	4	4	(4)	4	4	(4)	4	(4)	1	4	2	4	4
Phenylethyl Ether	23	4	4	4	4	4	(4)	4	4	(4)	4	(4)	4	4	4	4	2
Phorone	30	4	4	2	2	4	(4)	4	4	(4)	4	(4)	4	4	4	4	4
Phosphoric Acid (20%)	23	2	2	1	1	2	(2)	2	1	(2)	4	(4)	1	2	2	4	4
Phosphoric Acid (45%)	23	3	3	1	1	4	(3)	2	2	(4)	4	(4)	1	3	2	4	4
Phosphorous Trichloride	23	4	4	1	1	4	(4)	4	4	(4)	(4)	(4)	1	(4)	1	(4)	(4)
Picric Acid, Aq.	23	2	2	1	1	2	(2)	2	1	(2)	4	(4)	1	4	2	4	4
Pinene	70	4	4	4	4	2	(2)	4	4	(2)	4	(4)	1	4	2	(3)	4
Pine Oil	70	4	4	4	4	4	(2)	4	4	(2)	(4)	(4)	1	4	1	(4)	4
Piperidene	23	4	4	4	4	4	(4)	4	4	(4)	4	(4)	4	4	4	4	4
Potassium Acetate, Aq.	23	2	2	1	1	4	(4)	2	2	3	4	(4)	4	3	4	4	4
Potassium Chloride, Aq.	23	1	1	1	1	1	1	1	1	(2)	4	(2)	1	1	1	4	1

Chemical	Temp.	1	2	3	4	5	6	7	8	9	10	11	12	13	14	15	16
Potassium Cuprocyanide, Aq.	23	1	4	1	1	1	(2)	4	(2)	1	1	(1)	1	1	1	1	1
Potassium Cyanide, Aq.	23	1	4	1	1	1	(2)	4	(2)	1	1	(1)	1	1	1	1	1
Potassium Dichromate, Aq.	23	1	4	1	1	1	(2)	4	(2)	1	1	1	1	1	1	1	1
Potassium Hydroxide (50%)	23	3	4	3	3	4	(4)	4	(2)	1	2	(2)	3	1	1	2	2
Potassium Iodide, Aq.	23	1	4	1	1	1	(2)	4	(2)	1	1	(1)	1	1	1	1	1
Potassium Nitrate, Aq.	23	1	4	1	1	1	2	4	2	1	2	(1)	1	1	1	1	1
Potassium Perchlorate, Aq.	23	(4)	4	1	1	1	2	4	2	1	2	(1)	2	1	1	3	3
Potassium Permanganate, Aq.	23	(4)	4	1	1	1	2	4	2	1	2	(1)	4	1	1	4	4
Potassium Persulphate, Aq.	23	(4)	4	1	1	1	(2)	4	(2)	1	2	(2)	4	1	1	4	4
Potassium Sulphate, Aq.	23	1	4	1	1	1	(2)	4	(2)	1	2	(1)	1	1	1	1	1
Potassium Sulphite, Aq.	23	(4)	4	1	1	1	2	4	2	1	2	(1)	2	1	1	2	2
Propane	23	1	1	2	4	1	1	1	1	3	2	1	1	4	4	4	4
Propanol	50	1	(4)	(1)	2	1	(4)	4	(2)	1	1	(2)	2	1	1	1	1
Propyl Acetate	23	2	4	4	4	4	4	4	4	4	4	4	4	2	2	4	4
n-Propyl Alcohol	50	1	(4)	(1)	2	1	(4)	4	(2)	1	1	(2)	2	1	1	1	1
Propylamine	23	4	4	4	4	4	(4)	4	(4)	4	4	(4)	4	4	4	4	4
Propylene	23	2	4	2	4	1	(4)	4	(4)	4	4	(4)	4	4	4	4	4
Propylene Oxide	23	4	4	4	4	4	(4)	4	(4)	4	4	(4)	4	2	2	4	4

RATINGS: 1 = Minor effect.   2 = Moderate effect.   3 = Severe effect.   4 = Not recommended.   ( ) = No data found; ratings based on theory and analogy.   Aq. = Aquesons sotions.

Medium	Temp. (°C)	NR/IR	SBR/BR	IIR	EPDM	NBR	HNBR	CR	CSM	ECO	ACM	AEM	FPM	VMQ	FMQ	AU	T
Propylnitrate	23	4	4	2	2	4	(4)	4	4	(4)	4	(4)	4	4	4	(4)	(2)
Pyridine	23	4	4	2	2	4	(4)	4	4	4	4	(4)	4	4	4	(4)	4
Pyrrole	23	3	3	4	3	4	(4)	4	4	(4)	4	(4)	4	3	4	(4)	4
Rapeseed Oil	70	4	4	3	3	1	1	3	3	1	1	(3)	1	1	1	2	4
Refrigerant 11 (section 6.22)	23	4	4	4	4	3	(3)	4	3	(3)	4	4	2	4	(4)	3	1
Refrigerant 12	23	3	3	3	3	1	(2)	1	1	1	4	(4)	3	4	4	2	1
Refrigerant 13	23	1	1	1	1	1	(1)	1	1	(1)	(1)	(1)	1	4	4	(1)	1
Refrigerant 14	23	1	1	1	1	1	(1)	1	1	(1)	(1)	(1)	1	4	4	(1)	(1)
Refrigerant 21	23	4	4	4	4	4	(4)	3	4	(3)	(4)	(4)	4	4	(4)	(4)	4
Refrigerant 22	23	2	1	1	1	4	(4)	1	1	(1)	(4)	(4)	4	4	4	4	1
Refrigerant 31	23	4	3	1	1	4	(4)	1	2	(3)	(4)	(4)	4	(4)	(4)	(4)	3
Refrigerant 32	23	1	1	1	1	1	(1)	1	(1)	(1)	(1)	(1)	4	(4)	(4)	(1)	1
Refrigerant 112	23	4	4	4	4	2	(3)	3	3	(3)	(4)	(4)	1	4	(4)	(4)	1
Refrigerant 113	23	4	3	4	4	1	(1)	1	1	1	(4)	4	3	4	4	2	1
Refrigerant 114	23	1	1	1	1	1	(1)	1	1	1	(1)	(1)	3	4	(4)	1	1
Refrigerant 115	23	1	1	1	1	1	(1)	1	1	(1)	(1)	(1)	2	(4)	(4)	(2)	1
Refrigerant 134a	23	(1)	(1)	(1)	1	1	1	1	(1)	(1)	(1)	(1)	(2)	(4)	(4)	(2)	(1)
Refrigerant 142b	23	2	1	1	1	1	(1)	1	1	(1)	(1)	(1)	4	(4)	(4)	(2)	1

Chemical	Temp (°C)															
Refrigerant 152a	23	1	1	1	1	(1)	1	3	(3)	1	1	4	(4)	(4)	(2)	1
Refrigerant 218	23	1	1	1	1	(1)	1	1	(1)	(1)	(1)	1	(4)	(4)	(2)	1
Refrigerant C 316	23	1	1	1	1	(1)	1	1	(1)	(1)	(1)	(2)	(4)	(4)	(2)	1
Refrigerant C 318	23	1	1	1	1	(1)	1	1	(1)	(1)	(1)	2	(4)	(4)	(2)	1
Refrigerant 13 B1	23	1	1	1	1	(1)	1	1	(1)	2	(2)	2	4	(4)	1	1
Refrigerant 114 B2	23	4	4	4	2	(2)	2	1	(2)	(3)	(3)	3	(4)	(4)	(3)	1
Refrigerant 502	23	1	1	1	2	(2)	1	1	(2)	(4)	(4)	3	(4)	(4)	(2)	1
Salicylic Acid, Aq.	50	2	1	1	1	1	1	1	(2)	4	(4)	1	1	1	4	1
Sea Water	23	1	1	1	1	1	2	1	2	4	1	1	1	1	4	1
Silicate Esters	70	4	4	4	2	(2)	1	(2)	(2)	(4)	(4)	1	4	1	(4)	(4)
Silicone Greases	70	1	1	1	1	1	1	1	1	1	1	1	4	1	1	1
Silicone Oils	70	1	1	1	1	1	1	1	1	1	1	1	4	1	1	1
Silver Nitrate, Aq.	23	1	1	1	1	1	1	1	2	4	(2)	1	1	1	4	4
Soap Solutions	23	1	1	1	1	1	1	1	2	4	2	1	1	1	4	4
Sodium Acetate, Aq.	23	2	1	1	4	4	2	2	3	4	(4)	4	3	4	4	4
Sodium Benzoate, Aq.	23	1	1	1	1	1	1	1	2	4	(2)	1	1	1	4	4
Sodium Bicarbonate, Aq.	23	1	1	1	1	1	1	1	2	4	(2)	1	1	1	4	1
Sodium Bisulphite, Aq.	23	4	1	1	4	(1)	1	1	2	4	(2)	1	1	1	4	1

RATINGS: 1 = Minor effect.   2 = Moderate effect.   3 = Severe effect.   4 = Not recommended.   ( ) = No data found; ratings based on theory and analogy.   Aq. = Aquesons sotions.

Medium	Temp. (°C)	NR/IR	SBR/BR	IIR	EPDM	NBR	HNBR	CR	CSM	ECO	ACM	AEM	FPM	VMQ	FMQ	AU	T
Sodium Borate, Aq.	23	1	1	1	1	1	1	1	1	2	4	(2)	1	1	1	4	1
Sodium Carbonate, Aq.	23	1	1	1	1	1	1	1	1	2	4	(2)	1	1	1	4	1
Sodium Chlorate, Aq.	23	3	3	1	1	2	(1)	1	1	2	4	(2)	1	1	1	4	1
Sodium Chloride, Aq.	23	1	1	1	1	1	1	1	1	(2)	4	(2)	1	1	1	4	1
Sodium Cyanide, Aq.	23	1	1	1	1	1	1	1	1	(2)	4	(2)	1	1	1	4	1
Sodium Dichromate, Aq.	23	1	1	1	1	1	1	1	1	(2)	4	(2)	1	1	1	4	1
Sodium Hydroxide (50%)	23	2	2	1	1	3	(2)	2	1	(2)	4	(4)	4	3	3	4	3
Sodium Hypochlorite, Aq.	23	4	4	2	1	3	(2)	2	1	(2)	4	(4)	1	2	2	4	2
Sodium Nitrate, Aq.	23	1	1	1	1	1	1	1	1	2	4	(2)	1	1	1	4	1
Sodium Nitrite, Aq.	23	1	1	1	1	1	1	1	1	2	4	(2)	1	1	1	4	1
Sodium Perborate, Aq.	23	3	3	1	1	2	(1)	1	1	2	4	(2)	1	1	1	4	1
Sodium Phosphate, Aq.	23	1	1	1	1	1	1	1	1	2	4	(2)	1	1	1	4	1
Sodium Silicate, Aq.	23	1	1	1	1	1	1	1	1	2	4	(2)	1	1	1	4	1
Sodium Stearate, Aq.	23	1	1	1	1	1	1	1	1	2	4	2	1	1	1	4	4
Sodium Sulphate, Aq.	23	1	1	1	1	1	1	1	1	2	4	(2)	1	1	1	4	1
Sodium Sulphide, Aq.	23	3	3	1	1	3	(2)	2	2	2	4	(4)	2	2	2	4	1
Sodium Thiosulphate, Aq.	23	1	1	1	1	1	1	1	1	1	4	(2)	1	1	1	4	1
Soft Drink Syrups	40	(1)	(1)	(1)	1	1	(1)	4	(4)	(4)	4	(4)	4	1	(4)	4	4

Chemical	Temp	1	2	3	4	5	6	7	8	9	10	11	12	13	14	15
Soyabean Oil	23	4	4	3	1	(1)	3	3	1	1	(3)	1	1	1	2	4
Stannic Chloride, Aq.	23	1	1	1	1	1	2	1	(2)	4	4	1	2	1	4	(2)
Stannous Chloride, Aq.	23	1	1	1	1	1	2	1	(2)	4	4	1	2	1	4	(2)
Steam (Section 6.25)	150	4	4	1	4	2	4	3	4	4	4	3	4	4	4	4
Steam	200	4	4	1	4	4	4	4	4	4	4	4	4	4	4	4
Stearic Acid	80	4	4	4	4	(4)	3	3	(3)	(4)	(4)	1	3	(2)	4	4
Styrene	23	4	4	4	4	4	4	4	4	4	4	2	4	3	4	4
Sucrose, Aq.	23	1	1	1	1	1	2	1	2	4	(2)	1	1	1	4	4
Sulphur Chloride, Aq.	23	4	4	4	4	4	4	4	4	4	4	1	3	2	4	4
Sulphur Dioxide, Dry	23	4	4	1	4	(2)	2	1	(3)	(4)	(4)	1	(2)	2	4	4
Sulphur Hexafluoride	23	4	4	1	2	(2)	1	2	(2)	4	(4)	1	2	2	(4)	3
Sulphur Trioxide, Dry	23	4	4	3	4	4	4	4	4	4	4	1	3	3	4	4
Sulphuric Acid (10%)	23	3	4	1	4	(3)	2	1	(2)	4	4	1	4	3	4	4
Sulphuric Acid (98%)	23	4	4	4	4	4	4	4	4	4	4	1	4	4	4	4
Tannic Acid, Aq.	23	1	2	1	1	(1)	2	2	(2)	4	(4)	1	2	(1)	4	(3)
Tartaric Acid, Aq.	100	2	1	1	1	1	2	1	2	4	(4)	1	1	1	4	4
Terpineol	23	4	4	3	2	(3)	4	4	(2)	(4)	(4)	1	(4)	1	2	1
Tertiary Butyl Alcohol	23	2	2	2	2	(2)	2	2	(2)	4	(4)	1	2	2	4	2

RATINGS: 1 = Minor effect.   2 = Moderate effect.   3 = Severe effect.   4 = Not recommended.   ( ) = No data found; ratings based on theory and analogy.   Aq. = Aquesons sotions.

Medium	Temp. (°C)	NR/IR	SBR/BR	IIR	EPDM	NBR	HNBR	CR	CSM	ECO	ACM	AEM	FPM	VMQ	FMQ	AU	T
Tetrabromoethane	23	4	4	4	4	4	(4)	(4)	(4)	(4)	(4)	(4)	1	4	2	(4)	(4)
Tetrabromomethane	23	4	4	4	4	4	(4)	4	4	(4)	(4)	(4)	1	4	2	4	4
Tetrachloroethane	23	4	4	4	4	4	(4)	4	4	4	4	(4)	1	4	2	4	4
Tetrachloroethylene	23	4	4	4	4	4	4	4	4	4	4	(4)	1	4	2	4	3
Tetraethyl Lead	23	4	4	4	4	2	(2)	3	4	(2)	(4)	(4)	1	(4)	2	(4)	(4)
Tetrahydrofuran	23	4	4	3	3	4	(4)	4	4	4	4	(4)	4	4	4	4	3
Tetralin	23	4	4	4	4	4	(4)	4	4	4	4	(4)	1	4	1	4	4
Thionyl Chloride	23	4	4	4	3	4	(4)	4	4	(4)	4	(4)	2	(4)	(4)	4	(4)
Titanium Tetrachloride	23	4	4	4	4	3	(3)	4	4	(4)	4	(4)	1	4	2	4	3
Toluene	23	4	4	4	4	4	4	4	4	4	4	4	1	4	2	4	3
2,4-Toluene Diisocyanate	70	4	4	2	2	4	(4)	4	4	(4)	4	(4)	4	4	4	4	4
Triacetin	23	1	1	1	1	2	(2)	1	1	(3)	4	(4)	4	1	(4)	4	2
Trialkyl Phosphates	100	4	4	2	2	4	4	4	4	4	4	4	4	4	4	4	4
Triaryl Phosphates	100	4	4	2	2	4	4	4	4	4	4	4	1	4	2	4	4
Trichloroacetic Acid, Aq.	23	3	3	2	2	2	(2)	4	4	(2)	4	(4)	3	(3)	3	4	(4)
Trichloroethane	23	4	4	4	4	4	4	4	4	4	4	4	1	4	2	4	4
Trichloroethylene	23	4	4	4	4	4	(4)	4	4	(4)	4	(4)	1	4	2	4	4
Tricresyl Phosphate	100	4	4	2	2	4	(4)	4	4	4	4	(4)	1	4	2	4	4

Chemical	°C																	
Triethanolamine	23	2	2	2	1	3	1	(3)	1	2	(3)	4	(4)	3	4	4	4	4
Triethylamine	23	4	4	4	4	3	4	(3)	4	4	(4)	(4)	(4)	3	4	(4)	(4)	2
Triisopropyl Benzene	23	4	4	4	2	2	4	(2)	4	4	(2)	2	(4)	1	4	(1)	1	1
Turpentine	23	4	4	4	1	1	4	(2)	4	4	1	2	(4)	1	4	2	4	2
Unsymmetrical Dimethyl Hydrazine	23	1	2	1	1	2	2	(2)	2	1	(2)	(4)	(4)	4	4	4	(4)	4
Vegetable Oils	70	4	4	3	3	1	2	1	2	3	1	1	3	1	2	1	2	4
Vinegar	23	4	4	2	2	3	3	3	2	2	3	4	4	4	3	4	4	4
Vinyl Chloride	23	4	4	4	4	4	4	(4)	4	4	(4)	4	(4)	1	1	(2)	4	(4)
Water (Section 6.25)	23	1	1	1	1	1	1	1	1	1	1	4	1	1	1	1	4	4
Water	70	2	1	1	1	1	1	1	1	2	2	4	1	1	1	1	4	4
Water	100	2	1	1	1	1	1	1	1	3	3	4	1	1	1	1	4	4
Xenon	23	1	1	1	1	1	1	1	1	1	1	1	1	1	1	1	1	1
Xylene	23	4	4	4	4	4	4	4	4	4	4	4	4	1	4	1	4	2
Zinc Acetate, Aq.	23	2	2	1	1	3	2	3	2	2	3	4	4	4	4	4	4	4
Zinc Chloride, Aq.	23	1	1	1	1	1	1	1	1	1	2	4	(2)	1	1	1	4	3
Zinc Sulphate, Aq.	23	1	1	1	1	1	1	1	1	1	2	4	(2)	1	1	1	4	3

RATINGS: 1 = Minor effect.   2 = Moderate effect.   3 = Severe effect.   4 = Not recommended.   ( ) = No data found; ratings based on theory and analogy.   Aq. = Aquesons sotions.

Appendix

Fundamentals of chemistry

A.1 Introduction

To the layman, the chemical processes, which are concerned with the composition, properties and changes of the different kinds of matter, might appear quite baffling and difficult to comprehend. This appendix will offer a useful introduction to the field of rubber chemistry for those readers who are not trained in chemistry. The terminology is greatly simplified for the sake of comprehension.

A.2 Elements

Elements are substances that cannot be resolved by ordinary chemical means into any simpler form of matter (section A.5). Approximately one hundred elements constitute the "basic building blocks" of the innumerable substances that make up our physical world.

Elements may be roughly classified into two groups:

1) **metals** (e.g., iron, copper, aluminum, magnesium, zinc, cobalt, nickel, platinum, gold, silver, lead, chromium, molybdenum, tungsten, mercury, sodium and so forth)
2) **nonmetals** (e.g., oxygen, nitrogen, hydrogen, carbon, silicon, sulphur, fluorine, chlorine, bromine, iodine and so on)

A.3 Compounds and Mixtures

It is important to distinguish between compounds and mixtures or blends. The main differences may be summarized as follows:

1) Compounds are substances produced by the chemical combination of elements. Their constituents are combined in a definite proportion and large amounts of heat are usually developed during the combination. Conversely, mixtures do not have constant composition and the constituents are simply mixed together and not combined chemically.
2) The properties of a compound are quite different from the properties of its constituents. For example, common salt (which is a compound of sodium and chlorine) has its own characteristic properties that are completely different from the properties of its constituents (sodium is a soft, silvery-white lustrous metal and chlorine is a very poisonous yellowish-green gas). Conversely, the properties of a mixture usually result from the properties of its constituents. For instance, a mixture of equal parts of white and black powder will be grey.
3) The constituents of a compound can be separated only by complicated chemical processes, whereas the constituents of a mixture can be separated usually by

mechanical or physical methods (e.g., by using a magnet, sieving, flotation, dissolution, distillation, liquidation or freezing).

4) All chemical compounds are homogeneous, whereas mixtures can be homogeneous or heterogeneous. For example, a solution of sugar in water is homogeneous and a mixture of limestone and sand is heterogeneous.

The best example by which to illustrate the differences between compounds and mixtures is given by a mixture of equal weights of finely powdered iron and sulphur. The color of such a mixture is intermediate between the color of iron and sulphur. The particles of iron and sulphur can be readily distinguished under the microscope. The iron particles can be removed by means of a magnet or by treating the mixture with carbon disulphide, which will dissolve sulphur and leave iron as a residue. If the solution is filtered and collected in a dish, the sulphur can be recovered by allowing the carbon disulphide to evaporate.

If a portion of the mixture indicated above is placed in a hard glass test tube and warmed over a Bunsen flame, the contents of the tube begin to glow and a kind of combustion spreads throughout the whole mass. If the test tube is broken after cooling, it will be found that the porous black mass formed during the reaction is quite different from the original mixture. Under the microscope the powdered mass is homogeneous, it is not magnetic like iron and it gives no sulphur when digested with carbon disulphide. These observations lead to the conclusion that there has been a chemical reaction between the sulphur and the iron. When a chemical combination occurs, the reacting constituents lose their identity more or less completely and each new substance that is formed has its own distinctive properties. It is important to note that a great deal of heat is developed during the combination of the iron and sulphur. The heat required to start the reaction does not account for the amount of heat developed during the reaction.

A.4 Organic and Inorganic Materials

In the past it was thought impossible to prepare any animal or vegetable product synthetically in the laboratory, because such products behave differently than mineral substances in that they are combustible. Consequently, all products, obtained directly or indirectly from living organisms, were called organic compounds and were classed separately from inorganic or mineral substances.

In the course of time, it was found that many organic substances could be prepared in the laboratory. Consequently, the term "organic" lost its original meaning. Nowadays, organic chemistry means the chemistry of carbon compounds, because the element carbon is the most important component of all animals and plants. However, some of the simpler compounds of carbon such as carbon monoxide, carbon dioxide and the carbonates (limestone, chalk, marble) are described in works on inorganic chemistry for the sake of convenience. Strictly speaking, they are organic compounds because they contain carbon.

The number of known carbon compounds (more than six million) is far in excess of the number of known compounds of all other elements taken together, and there are no signs as yet of any limit being reached. The enormous number and variety of carbon compounds are available because carbon atoms can combine with each other and form remarkably stable chains of great length and complexity. In addition, they form stable linkages with other elements, in particular with hydrogen, oxygen, nitrogen, sulphur and halogens.

A.5 Atoms

The atom is the smallest particle of all matter that cannot be subdivided by ordinary chemical processes. However, we know that atoms can be split apart with considerable energy release by means of nuclear fission processes and that they are made up of even smaller particles such as protons, electrons, neutrons and others. As these particles are the same in all kinds of atoms, the differences between atoms are explained by the different numbers and arrangements of these subatomic particles. There are as many different kinds of atoms as there are elements, that is, about one hundred.

A.6 Molecules

Molecules are aggregates of a definite number of atoms. In the case of elements, each molecule contains the same kind and number of atoms. For example, a molecule of hydrogen contains two hydrogen atoms. Conversely, the molecules of compounds consist of different kinds of atoms united in simple numerical proportions. A water molecule, for instance, is made up of two hydrogen atoms and one oxygen atom.

A.7 Atomic and Molecular Weights

The absolute weights of atoms are extremely small. A hydrogen atom, for instance, weighs 1.673×10^{-24} g, and a hydrogen molecule weighs twice as much. Therefore, it would be ridiculous to try to express the atomic or molecular weights in grams. For practical purposes, an arbitrary standard weight is used. This was at one time based on the hydrogen atom, whose weight was taken as 1. Today, the atom of carbon isotope ^{12}C is used as the standard weight and has been given the arbitrary value 12. Accordingly, the atomic weight of hydrogen is 1.0079 instead of 1. For practical purposes, however, the weight of a hydrogen atom can be taken as 1 and the atomic weight of any element can be considered as the number of times its atom is heavier than the hydrogen atom. The atomic weight of oxygen, for example, is found to be approximately 16 (exactly 15.9994), hence an oxygen atom is 16 times heavier than a hydrogen atom. The atomic weights of selected elements are listed in **Table A.1**.

The molecular weight of a compound is the sum of the atomic weights of its elements. It indicates the number of times its molecule is heavier than a hydrogen atom. For example, the molecular weight of water is calculated as follows:

2 × atomic weight of hydrogen + atomic weight of oxygen = $(2 \times 1) + 16 = 18$, which means that a water molecule is about 18 times heavier than a hydrogen atom.

Table A.1: Atomic Weights of Selected Elements Based on the Atomic Weight of Carbon Isotope ^{12}C

Element	Symbol	Atomic Weight	Element	Symbol	Atomic Weight
Aluminum	Al	26.98154	Mercury	Hg	200.59
Antimony	Sb	121.75	Neon	Ne	20.179
Argon	A	39.948	Nickel	Ni	58.70
Arsenic	As	74.9216	Nitrogen	N	14.0067
Barium	Ba	137.33	Oxygen	O	15.9994
Boron	B	10.81	Phosphorus	P	30.97376
Bromine	Br	79.904	Platinum	Pt	195.09
Cadmium	Cd	112.41	Potassium	K	39.0983
Calcium	Ca	40.08	Selenium	Se	78.96
Carbon	C	12.011	Silicon	Si	28.0855
Chlorine	Cl	35.453	Silver	Ag	107.868
Chromium	Cr	51.996	Sodium	Na	22.9877
Cobalt	Co	58.9332	Strontium	Sr	87.62
Copper	Cu	63.546	Sulphur	S	32.06
Fluorine	F	18.998403	Tellurium	Te	127.60
Gold	Au	196.9665	Tin	Sn	118.69
Helium	He	4.00260	Titanium	Ti	47.90
Hydrogen	H	1.0079	Tungsten	W	183.85
Iodine	I	126.9045	Uranium	U	238.029
Iron	Fe	55.847	Xenon	Xe	131.30
Lithium	Li	6.941	Zinc	Zn	65.38
Magnesium	Mg	24.305	Zirconium	Zr	91.22
Manganese	Mn	54.9380			

Source: *Römps Chemie-Lexikon*, Franckh'sche Verlagshandlung Stuttgart, 1979.

A.8 Chemical Symbols

In the past, alchemists represented different substances by figurative symbols. These symbols have all been abandoned because they are too cumbersome. Today, chemists use instead one or two letters from the recognized name of the element. Thus, H is the symbol for hydrogen, O for Oxygen, C for carbon, N for nitrogen, S for sulphur, F for fluorine, I for iodine, P for phosphorus and A for argon. A second letter is added in the case of elements that start with the same letter. Thus, Cl is used for chlorine, Ca for calcium, Cd for cadmium, Co for cobalt, Cr for chromium, Si for silicon, Br for bromine, He for helium, Ne for neon and Ni for nickel.

The symbols of certain elements are derived from their Latin names. Thus, Sb is the symbol for antimony (Latin *stibium*), Cu for copper *(cuprum)*, Au for gold *(aurum)*, Fe for iron *(ferrum)*, Pb for lead *(plumbum)*, K for potassium *(kalium)*, Na for sodium *(natrium)* and Sn for tin *(stannum)*.

A compound is symbolized by joining together the symbols of its elements. Thus, ZnO represents a molecule of zinc oxide, a compound of zinc and oxygen. If more than one atom of one element are present in the molecule, a small figure is appended to the bottom right-hand corner of the symbol representing that element to indicate the number of atoms present. Thus, H_2O represents a molecule of water, a compound containing two atoms of hydrogen and one atom of oxygen; Na_2CO_3 represents a molecule of sodium carbonate, a compound containing two atoms of sodium, one atom of carbon and three atoms of oxygen.

A.9 Valency

The valency, or atom-combining capacity, of an element is a number that expresses how many atoms of hydrogen, or of other atoms equivalent to hydrogen, can unite with one atom of the element in question. The following examples will illustrate this:

- A chlorine atom is never found to combine with more than one hydrogen atom, hence it is assigned a valency of one. The chlorine atom is said to be **univalent** and may be expressed by $Cl-$. In a similar manner, the univalent hydrogen atom may be represented by $H-$.
- An oxygen atom is capable of combining with two hydrogen atoms, hence it has a valency of two. The oxygen atom is then said to be **bivalent** and may be expressed by $O=$ or $-O-$.
- A nitrogen atom can combine with three hydrogen atoms, thus it is **trivalent** and may be expressed by $N\equiv$, $=N-$ or $-\overset{|}{N}-$.
- A carbon atom is **quadrivalent** or **tetravalent** because it can combine with four hydrogen atoms and may be expressed by $-C\equiv$, $=C=$ or $-\overset{|}{\underset{|}{C}}-$.
- A phosphorus atom is **pentavalent** because it can combine with five univalent chlorine atoms.
- A sulphur atom is capable of combining with three bivalent oxygen atoms, hence it is **hexavalent**.
- The valency of nobel or inert gases (e.g., helium, neon and argon) is supposed to be **zero** because these gases usually form no compounds, although the existence of few compounds has been reported.
- Some elements combine together in more than one proportion: that is, they have more than one valency. Sulphur, for example, can be bivalent (e.g., H_2S), quadrivalent (e.g., SO_2) or hexavalent (e.g., SO_3). Others have a valency of seven and are said to be **heptavalent**. The highest possible valency is eight.

A.10 Molecular and Structural Formulas

A molecular formula shows the kind and number of atoms present in one molecule, whereas a structural formula shows in addition how the atoms are bonded together. For example, a molecule of water that contains two atoms of hydrogen and one atom of oxygen is denoted by the molecular formula H_2O and by the structural formula $H-O-H$. The latter formula shows how one oxygen atom is bonded with two hydrogen atoms. Other examples of molecular and structural formulas are shown in **Fig. A.1**. It is understood that the structural formulas must satisfy the valency of all atoms involved (one for hydrogen, two for oxygen and four for carbon). For example, the structural formulas for ethanol shown in **Fig. A.2** are incorrect because they do not obey the valency rules. It is, therefore, very important to know the valency of each element involved in order to be able to write any structural formula.

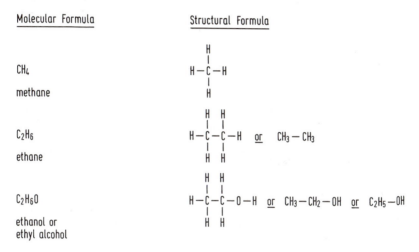

Fig. A.1: Molecular and Structural Formulas of Selected Compounds

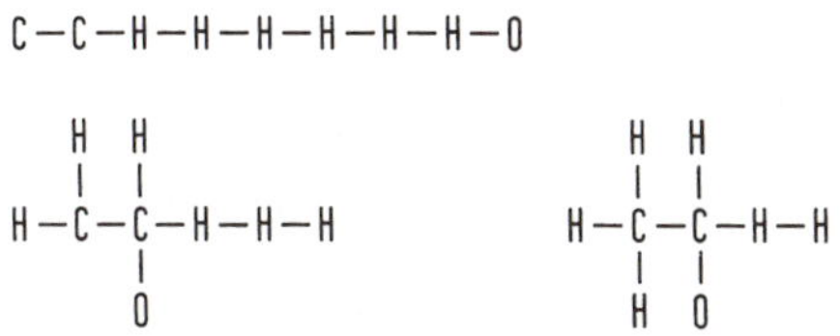

$$C-C-H-H-H-H-H-H-O$$

Fig. A.2: Incorrect Structural Formulas for Ethanol

A.11 Substitution Reactions

The term *substitution* is applied to chemical reactions in which certain atoms in a compound molecule are displaced by an equivalent number of other atoms without altering the arrangement of the rest of the atoms. The compounds formed, as the result of the change, are called substitution products. For example, methyl chloride (CH_3Cl) is a mono-substitution product and methylene dichloride (CH_2Cl_2) a di-substitution product of methane as presented by the following equations:

$$CH_4 + Cl_2 = CH_3Cl + HCl$$
$$CH_4 + 2\,Cl_2 = CH_2Cl_2 + 2\,HCl$$

A.12 Saturated and Unsaturated Compounds

Compounds in which the maximum valency of all the carbon atoms is exerted are termed saturated compounds. Such carbon atoms are joined to each other by single bonds. When the full combining capacity of two adjacent carbon atoms are not satisfied by atoms of other elements, the compound is said to be unsaturated. In this case the carbon atoms are considered to be joined to each other by more than one bond, double bond [as in ethylene ($CH_2 = CH_2$)] or triple bond [as in acetylene ($CH \equiv CH$)]. It must not be supposed that a double or triple bond has any mechanical significance, or that the two carbon atoms attract one another more strongly than when they are singly bonded. A double or triple bond between two carbon atoms is merely a convenient expression of the compound's capability of combining directly with a variety of other molecules such as those of hydrogen, halogens, sulphur, oxygen and ozone to form saturated compounds. This type of reaction is known as addition reaction and the resulting compounds are called *additive products*, in contradistinction to substitution products.

When an unsaturated compound reacts with another substance, the double bond is said to be broken and the two carbon atoms, previously represented as doubly bound, are then shown as being saturated. The reaction mechanism of ethylene with hydrogen, for example, is expressed graphically in **Fig. A.3**. Several double bonds or points of unsaturation may occur in a carbon compound. Butadiene, for example, contains two double bonds (section 1.3).

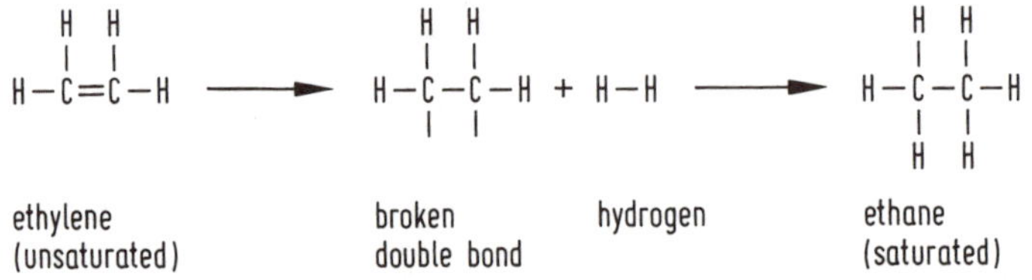

Fig. A.3: Mechanism of the Addition Reaction of Ethylene with Hydrogen

A.13 Aliphatic and Aromatic Compounds

Organic compounds are classed in two principal divisions:
1) fatty, or aliphatic; and
2) aromatic.

The term *fatty*, or *aliphatic*, which originally applied to some of the higher fatty acids such as stearic and oleic acids, is nowadays used to denote all compounds that may be regarded as derivative of methane **(Fig. A.1)**. Aromatic compounds, on the other hand, are those substances that are derived from benzene. The term **aromatic** was first applied to certain naturally occurring compounds because of their peculiar aromatic odor. These were afterwards proved to be benzene derivatives.

A.13.1 Structural Formula of Benzene

The aromatic compounds are comparatively richer in carbon than the corresponding aliphatic compounds. The simplest aromatic substance, benzene, has the molecular formula C_6H_6. It differs from aliphatic hydrocarbons (section A.17.1) very considerably in chemical behavior. This and many other observations, which were established during the investigation of benzene and its derivatives, led Kekulé (1865) to conclude that

1) the six carbon atoms in benzene form a closed chain or nucleus;
2) the molecule of benzene is symmetrical;
3) each carbon atom is united with one hydrogen atom; and
4) the three alternating double bonds may be in a state of constant oscillation between two possible structures. That is, the double bonds are distributed over the molecule as shown in **Fig. A.4**.

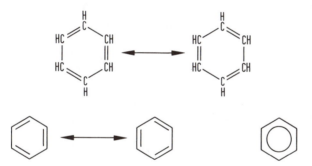

Fig. A.4: Different Expressions of the Benzene Formula

A.14 Radicals

Certain groups of atoms often remain unchanged during a whole series of chemical reactions. Methane (CH_4), for example, may be converted into methyl chloride (CH_3Cl), the latter may be transformed into methanol (CH_3OH) and this compound may be reconverted in methyl chloride:

$$CH_4 + Cl_2 = CH_3Cl + HCl$$
$$CH_3Cl + HOH = CH_3OH + HCl$$
$$CH_3OH + HCl = CH_3Cl + H_2O$$

It is evident that, during all these interactions, the group CH_3- remains unchanged and behaves as if it were a single atom. Such atom groups that act like single atoms and occur in a considerable number of compounds are termed radicals.

The collective name **alkyl** is given to all radicals that, theoretically, are obtained when one hydrogen atom is removed from the molecules of the paraffins methane, ethane, propane, butane and so on. The distinctive names of these radicals are derived from those of the paraffins (section A.17.1) by changing the ending **ane** to **yl**, as shown in **Table A.2**. The letter **R** is frequently employed to represent any alkyl radical. R−Br, for example, means any alkyl bromide. The symbols **Me**, **Et**, **Pr**, **Bu** and so on are also often used instead of CH_3-, C_2H_5-, C_3H_7- and C_4H_9, respectively.

Table A.2: Typical Alkyl Radicals

Paraffin	Radical
Methane (CH_4)	Methyl (CH_3-)
Ethane (C_2H_6)	Ethyl (C_2H_5-)
Propane (C_3H_8)	Propyl (C_3H_7-)
Butane (C_4H_{10})	Butyl (C_4H_9-)
Pentane (C_5H_{12})	Amyl ($C_5H_{11}-$)
Hexane (C_6H_{14})	Hexyl ($C_6H_{13}-$)
Heptane (C_7H_{16})	Heptyl ($C_7H_{15}-$)
Octane (C_8H_{18})	Octyl ($C_8H_{17}-$)
Nonane (C_9H_{20})	Nonyl ($C_9H_{19}-$)
Decane ($C_{10}H_{22}$)	Decyl ($C_{10}H_{21}-$)

The term **aryl** is given to all radicals derived from aromatic hydrocarbons, and the symbol **Ar** is frequently used to represent any aryl radical. The radical derived from benzene (C_6H_6) is called **phenyl** (C_6H_5-), not benzyl, and may be represented by the symbol **Ph**.

A.15 Functional Groups

In contrast to the alkyl and aryl radicals, the functional or polar groups are chemically reactive groups of atoms that behave independently of the rest of the molecule and change in composition after the reaction. The most common functional groups are listed in **Table A.3**.

A.16 Isomerism

Compounds that have the same molecular formula but different properties are said to be isomeric. The phenomenon is referred to as isomerism and the compounds themselves are called isomers or isomerides.

There are different types of isomerism, but only three of them will be considered below.

Table A.3: Typical Functional Groups

Name of Group	Formula		
Hydroxyl	$-O-H$	or	$-OH$
Hydrosulphide	$-S-H$		$-SH$
Carbonyl	$-\overset{\displaystyle \parallel}{\underset{\displaystyle O}{C}}-$		$-CO-$
Aldehyde	$-\overset{\displaystyle \parallel}{\underset{\displaystyle O}{C}}-H$		$-CHO$
Carboxyl	$-\overset{\displaystyle \parallel}{\underset{\displaystyle O}{C}}-O-H$		$-COOH$
Amino	$-N\begin{smallmatrix} H \\ \\ H \end{smallmatrix}$		$-NH_2$
Amide	$-\overset{\displaystyle \parallel}{\underset{\displaystyle O}{C}}-N\begin{smallmatrix} H \\ \\ H \end{smallmatrix}$		$-CO-NH_2$
Nitro	$-N\begin{smallmatrix} O \\ \\ O \end{smallmatrix}$		$-NO_2$
Nitrile or Cyanide	$-C \equiv N$		$-CN$
Isocyanate	$-N=C=O$		$-NCO$
Sulphonic	$-\overset{\displaystyle O}{\underset{\displaystyle O}{S}}-O-H$		$-SO_3H$

A.16.1 Structural Isomerism

Structural isomerism results from differences in the disposition of the atoms in the molecules. The molecular formula C_2H_6O, for example, represents two isomeric compounds with different properties: ethanol (CH_3-CH_2-OH) and dimethyl ether (CH_3-O-CH_3).

As the number of carbon atoms in the molecule increases, the number of possible isomers rapidly becomes larger, as shown in **Table A.4**.

Table A.4: Increase in Number of Isomers with Increase in Molecular Size

Molecular Formula	Possible Number of Isomers
CH_4	0
C_2H_6	0
C_3H_8	0
C_4H_{10}	2
C_5H_{12}	3
C_6H_{14}	5
C_7H_{16}	9
C_8H_{18}	18
C_9H_{20}	35
$C_{10}H_{22}$	75
$C_{15}H_{32}$	4347
$C_{20}H_{42}$	366319

A.16.2 Geometrical Isomerism

Geometrical isomerism is exhibited by certain structurally identical unsaturated compounds. The isomeric maleic acid and fumaric acid, for example, are both unsaturated compounds of the constitution COOH-CH=CH-COOH and yet they differ considerably in properties, both physical and chemical. Their isomerism is not structural but geometrical, and the two acids are referred to as the **cis-** and **trans**-isomerides, respectively. The configurations of the two acids are shown in **Fig. A.5**. In the cis-isomeride (maleic acid) the two hydrogen atoms are on the same side of the double bond, whereas in the trans-configuration they are on opposite sides. Another example of geometrical isomerism is shown in **Fig. 8.1**.

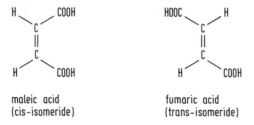

maleic acid
(cis-isomeride)

fumaric acid
(trans-isomeride)

Fig. A.5: Geometrical Isomerism

A.16.3 Substitution Isomerism

Substitution isomerism is exhibited by substitution products (section A.11) of benzene and its derivates. The examination of the substitution products of benzene has shown that when only one atom of hydrogen is displaced by any given atom or group, the same compound is always produced. That is, the mono-substitution products of benzene exist in one form only. When, for example, chlorobenzene (C_6H_5-Cl) is prepared, the same substance is always produced, indicating that all six hydrogen atoms are in similar positions relative to the rest of the molecule.

By the substitution of two univalent atoms or groups for two hydrogen atoms in the benzene molecule, only three isomerides are obtained. There are, for example, three dichlorobenzenes, three dibromobenzenes, three nitrobenzenes and so on. The isomeric forms are distinguished by the names **ortho** (1:2 position), **meta** (1:3 position) and **para** (1:4 position). The letters **o**, **m** and **p** are usually used to represent the ortho, meta and para isomers, respectively. **Fig. A.6** shows the structural formulas of **o**-, **m**- and **p**-dichlorobenzene.

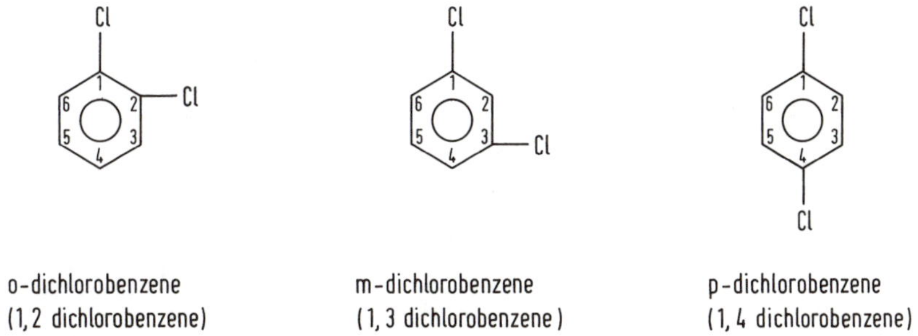

o–dichlorobenzene   m–dichlorobenzene   p–dichlorobenzene
(1,2 dichlorobenzene)   (1,3 dichlorobenzene)   (1,4 dichlorobenzene)

Fig. A.6: Substitution Isomerism of Dichlorobenzene

A.17 Hydrocarbons

It has already been noted that carbon differs from all other elements in forming an extraordinarily large number of compounds with hydrogen. Such compounds, composed of hydrogen and carbon only, are called hydrocarbons. They may be classed in two groups: aliphatic and aromatic hydrocarbons.

A.17.1 Aliphatic Hydrocarbons

As has been mentioned in section A.13, aliphatic hydrocarbons may be regarded as derivatives of methane. They may be subdivided into saturated and unsaturated hydrocarbons. The saturated hydrocarbons are remarkably inert and stable, whereas the unsaturated ones are reactive and capable of uniting with other elements.

The saturated hydrocarbons are called **paraffins**. Their names have the distinctive ending **ane**, and some have a prefix that denotes the number of carbon atoms in the molecule. They form a homologous series of compounds with the general formula C_nH_{2n+2}; that is, in any member containing n carbon atoms in the molecule there are 2n+2 hydrogen atoms. In propane (C_3H_8), for example, n = 3 and 2n+2 = 8. The first four members (methane, ethane, propane and butane) are gases, while those containing from 5 to 16 carbon atoms are liquids under ordinary conditions. The higher members of the series are solids.

All the above-mentioned paraffins have an open chain structure. However, there are other types of saturated hydrocarbons with closed chains, known as **cycloparaffins**. They have the general formula C_nH_{2n} (i.e., two hydrogen atoms less than in the general formula of open chain paraffins). The structural formulas of selected open chain paraffins and the corresponding cycloparaffins are shown in **Fig. A.7**.

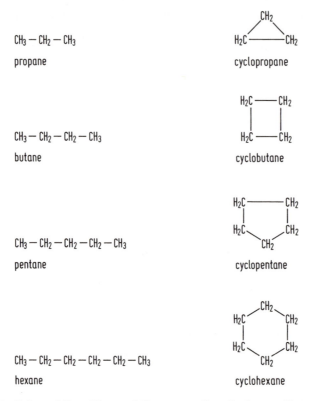

Fig. A.7: Selected Paraffins and Corresponding Cycloparaffins

The unsaturated hydrocarbons include those compounds containing double or triple bonds. Hydrocarbons with double bonds are called **olefins** and those with triple bonds are known as **acetylenes**.

The olefins form a homologous series with the general formula C_nH_{2n} (similar to that of cycloparaffins). Their names are derived from those of the paraffins by changing the ending **ane** to **ylene** or to **ene**. The simplest member of this series is ethylene, or ethene **(Fig. A.3)**. Very often the higher members are most conveniently regarded as derivatives of ethylene and named accordingly.

The acetylenes have the general formula C_nH_{2n-2}. They are capable of uniting (in two steps) with four univalent atoms of certain elements to form saturated products. Acetylene ($CH \equiv CH$), for example, combines with nacent hydrogen and is converted first into ethylene and then into ethane. Other important members of this series include allylene ($CH_3\text{-}C \equiv CH$) and crotonylene ($CH_3\text{-}C \equiv C\text{-}CH_3$).

A.17.2 Aromatic Hydrocarbons

Aromatic hydrocarbons are derived from benzene (section A.13.1) by substitution of alkyl or aryl radicals (section A.14) for the same number of hydrogen atoms. There are, however, other types of aromatic hydrocarbons based on condensed benzene nuclei, such as naphthalene, the parent substance of many aromatic compounds. The names and structural formulas of selected aromatic hydrocarbons are shown in **Fig. A.8**.

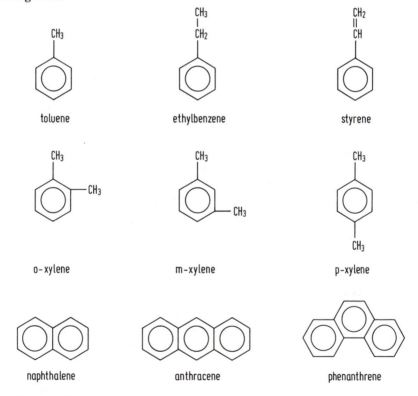

Fig. A.8: Selected Aromatic Hydrocarbons

A.18 Halogenated Hydrocarbons

The term **halogen** is used for any of the group of elements fluorine, chlorine, bromine and iodine. The halogenated hydrocarbons are formed by the displacement of one or more hydrogen atoms by the same number of halogen atoms. The names of most common halogen derivatives of aliphatic hydrocarbons and their structural formulas are given in **Table A.5**.

Table A.5: Typical Aliphatic Halogenated Hydrocarbons

Chemical Names	Structural Formulas
Methyl chloride or Chloromethane	CH_3Cl
Methyl bromide or bromomethane	CH_3Br
Ethyl chloride or chloroethane	C_2H_5Cl
Ethyl iodide or iodoethane	C_2H_5I
Methylene dichloride or dichloromethane	CH_2Cl_2
Chloroform or trichloromethane	$CHCl_3$
Iodoform or triiodomethane	CHI_3
Carbon tetrachloride	CCl_4
Trichloroethylene	$CHCl = CCl_2$
Tetrachloroethylene	$CCl_2 = CCl_2$
Hexachloroethane	$CCl_3 - CCl_3$
Tetrafluoroethylene	$CF_2 = CF_2$

In the case of aromatic hydrocarbons, the halogenation can take place in the nucleus or in the side chain, if there is any present. Aromatic hydrocarbons that have no side chains, such as benzene and naphthalene, yield halogen derivatives in which the halogen is united with carbon atoms of the nucleus. On the other hand, hydrocarbons with side chains, such as toluene, can give rise to halogen derivative of both types. **Fig. A.9** gives the names and structural formulas of selected halogen derivatives of aromatic hydrocarbons.

A.19 Alcohols

Alcohols are organic compounds that contain hydroxyl- (-OH) groups in their molecules. They can be monohydric, dihydric, trihydric or polyhydric, according to the number of hydroxyl groups they contain. However, distinction should be made among three kinds of compounds:
1) aliphatic alcohols;
2) aromatic alcohols; and
3) phenols.

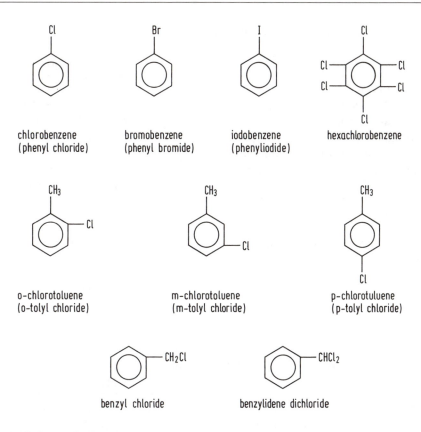

chlorobenzene
(phenyl chloride)

bromobenzene
(phenyl bromide)

iodobenzene
(phenyliodide)

hexachlorobenzene

o-chlorotoluene
(o-tolyl chloride)

m-chlorotoluene
(m-tolyl chloride)

p-chlorotoluene
(p-tolyl chloride)

benzyl chloride

benzylidene dichloride

Fig. A.9: Selected Halogenated Aromatic Compounds

A.19.1 Aliphatic Alcohols

The aliphatic monohydric alcohols form a homologous series of the general formula C_2H_{2n+1}-OH or R-OH. They may be regarded as derived from the paraffins (section A.17.1) by the substitution of the univalent hydroxyl group for one hydrogen atom. They are often named after the paraffin from which they are derived, using the ending **ol**, as in methanol, ethanol, propanol and so on.

Monohydric alcohols may be subdivided in primary, secondary and tertiary alcohols. The primary alcohols contain the group -CH_2-OH, the secondary alcohols the group $>$CH-OH and the tertiary alcohols the group $>$C-OH.

The dihydric alcohols or dihydroxy-derivatives of the paraffins are known as **glycols.** They form a homologous series with the general formula $C_nH_{2n}(OH)_2$. The simplest stable member of this series is ethylene glycol.

The trihydric alcohols are derived from those paraffins containing three or more carbon atoms. **Glycerol** or trihydroxypropane may be described as a typical trihydric alcohol. Examples of the different types of aliphatic alcohols are given in **Table A.6.**

Table A.6: Types of Aliphatic Alcohols

Chemical Names	Structural Formula
Primary Alcohols Methyl alcohol or methanol Ethyl alcohol or ethanol Normal propyl alcohol or 1-propanol Normal butyl alcohol or 1-butanol Normal amylalcohol or 1-pentanol Normal hexylalcohol or hexanol	CH_3OH $(H-CH_2-OH)$ CH_3-CH_2-OH $CH_3-CH_2-CH_2-OH$ $CH_3-(CH_2)_2-CH_2-OH$ $CH_3(CH_2)_3-CH_2-OH$ $CH_3-(CH_2)_4-CH_2-OH$
Secondary Alcohols Isopropyl alcohol or 2-propanol Isobutyl alcohol or 2-butanol	$\begin{array}{c}CH_3\\ \quad\ \ \diagdown\\ \qquad CH-OH\\ \quad\ \ \diagup\\ CH_3\end{array}$ $\begin{array}{c}CH_3-CH_2\\ \qquad\qquad\diagdown\\ \qquad\qquad CH-OH\\ \qquad\qquad\diagup\\ \qquad CH_3\end{array}$
Tertiary Alcohols Tertiary butyl alcohol or 2-methyl-2-propanol	$\begin{array}{c}CH_3\\ \quad\ \diagdown\\ CH_3-C-OH\\ \quad\ \diagup\\ CH_3\end{array}$
Dihydric Alcohols Ethylene glycol or 1:2 ethandiol	$\begin{array}{cc}CH_2-CH_2\\ |\quad\ \ |\\ OH\quad OH\end{array}$
Trihydric Alcohols Glycerol or 1,2,3-propantriol	$\begin{array}{ccc}CH_2-CH_2-CH_2\\ |\qquad |\qquad |\\ OH\quad OH\quad OH\end{array}$

A.19.2 Aromatic Alcohols and Phenols

Aromatic alcohols are those aromatic compounds in which the hydroxyl group is united with a carbon atom of the side chain. Compounds of this type are closely related to the aliphatic alcohols.

Phenols, on the other hand, are those aromatic compounds in which the hydroxyl group is united directly with a carbon atom of the nucleus. The names and structural formulas of most common aromatic alcohols and phenols are given in **Fig. A.10.**

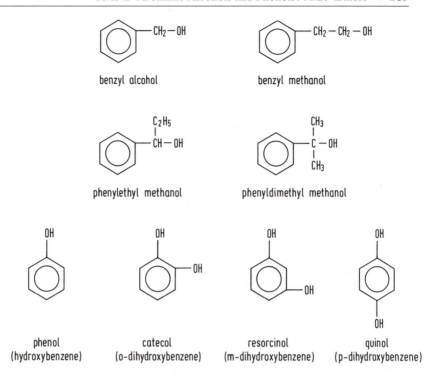

Fig. A.10: Selected Aromatic Alcohols and Phenols

A.20 Ethers

Ethers may be regarded as the oxides of alkyl or aryl radicals with the general formulas R-O-R, R-O-R', Ar-O-Ar, Ar-O-Ar' or Ar-O-R. The ethers containing two identical radicals are called simple ethers and those having two different radicals are known as mixed ethers. Examples of both types are given in **Fig. A.11**.

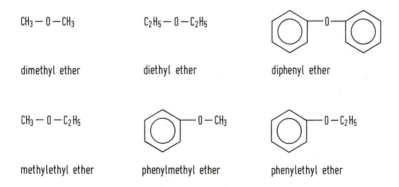

Fig. A.11: Selected Simple and Mixed Ethers

A.21 Aldehydes

Aldehydes are organic compounds containing the aldehyde- (-CHO) group in their molecules. They are derived from the primary alcohols (section A.19.1) by the removal of two hydrogen atoms from the -CH_2OH group. They may be classed as aliphatic or aromatic aldehydes.

A.21.1 Aliphatic Aldehydes

The aliphatic aldehydes form a homologous series of the general formula $C_nH_{2n}O$ or R-CHO. They may be regarded as derived from the paraffins (section A.17.1) by the substitution of one oxygen atom for two hydrogen atoms belonging to one of the -CH_3groups. The most important members of this series include

formaldehyde H-CHO;
acetaldehyde CH_3-CHO;
propaldehyde CH_3-CH_2-CHO;
butaldehyde CH_3-CH_2-CH_2-CHO; and
isobutaldehyde $(CH_3)_2$-CH-CHO.

A.21.2 Aromatic Aldehydes

Aromatic aldehydes, like those of the aliphatic series, are derived from aromatic primary alcohols by the removal of two hydrogen atoms from the -CH_2OH group. They have the general formula Ar-CHO. The aldehyde group is either directly united with a carbon atom in the nucleus, as in benzaldehyde (C_6H_5-CHO), or combined with a carbon atom of the side chain, as in the case of phenylacetaldehyde (C_6H_5-CH_2-CHO).

A.22 Ketones

Ketones are organic compounds containing the carbonyl- or ketonic(-CO-) group. They are derived from secondary alcohols (section A.19.1) by the removal of two hydrogen atoms from the $>$CH-OH group. They may be classed as aliphatic or aromatic ketones.

A.22.1 Aliphatic Ketones

The aliphatic ketones form a homologous series of the general formula $C_nH_{2n}O$ or R-CO-R'. They may be regarded as derived from the paraffins by the substitution of one oxygen atom for two hydrogen atoms belonging to a -CH_2- group.

When the alkyl radicals R and R' are identical, the compound is a simple ketone, but when R and R' are different, it is a mixed ketone. The most important aliphatic ketones include

acetone or dimethyl ketone (CH_3-CO-CH_3);
propione or diethyl ketone (C_2H_5-CO-C_2H_5); and
methyl ethyl ketone (CH_3-CO-C_2H_5).

A.22.2 Aromatic Ketones

The aromatic ketones have the general formula Ar-CO-Ar', where Ar and Ar' represent two different or identical aryl radicals. However, there are other types of ketones that contain one aryl and one alkyl radical (Ar-CO-R). The most important aromatic ketones include benzophenone or diphenylketone C_6H_5-CO-C_6H_5 and acetophenone or phenylmethylketone C_6H_5-CO-CH_3.

A.23 Carboxylic Acids

Carboxylic acids are organic compounds that contain one or more carboxyl- (-COOH) groups in their molecule. The acids can be monocarboxylic, dicarboxylic, tricarboxylic or polycarboxylic, according to the number of carboxylic groups they contain. They may be classed as fatty or aromatic acids.

A.23.1 Fatty Acids

The fatty monocarboxylic acids form a homologous series of the general formula C_nH_{2n+1}-COOH or R-COOH. The term *fatty* was given to this series because many of the higher members occur in the combined state in natural fats and resemble fats in physical properties.

With the exception of formic acid, the monocarboxylic fatty acids may be regarded as derived from paraffins (section A.17.1) by the substitution of the univalent carboxyl group for one hydrogen atom. The most important members of this homologous series include

formic acid (H-COOH);
acetic acid (CH_3-COOH);
propionic acid (CH_3-CH_2-COOH);
normal butyric acid (CH_3-CH_2-CH_2-COOH;
palmetic acid ($C_{15}H_{31}$-COOH); and
stearic acid ($C_{17}H_{35}$-COOH).

The dicarboxylic acids have the general formula C_nH_{2n}(COOH)$_2$. They may be considered as derived from the above-mentioned fatty acids by the substitution of a carboxyl-group for one hydrogen atom. The most important dicarboxylic acids include

oxalic acid (COOH-COOH);
malonic acid (COOH-CH_2-COOH); and
succinic acid (COOH-CH_2-CH_2-COOH).

A.23.2 Aromatic Acids

The carboxylic acids of the aromatic series are derived from the aromatic hydrocarbons (section A.17.2) by the substitution of one or more carboxyl groups for the same number of hydrogen atoms. Substitution can take place in the benzene nucleus or in the side chain, if there is any present. Benzene, for example, yields only acids of the first type such as benzoic acid and the three isomeric benzene dicarboxylic acids (known as phthalic acids). Aromatic hydrocarbons with side chains may give rise to derivatives of both kinds. Toluene, for example, yields phenylacetic acid and the three isomeric toluic acids **(Fig. A.12)**.

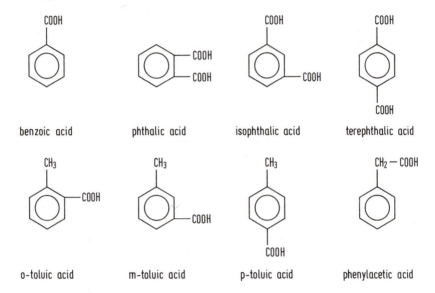

Fig. A.12: Selected Aromatic Acids

A.24 Esters

In some respect, the alcohols (section A.19) behave like metal hydroxides in that they react with organic and inorganic acids, forming esters and water according to the following general equation:

$$\text{alcohol} + \text{acid} \rightleftharpoons \text{ester} + \text{water}$$

The esters may be compared with mineral salts. They are named after the alcohol and acids from which they are formed. For example, the ester formed from ethyl alcohol and nitric acid is called ethyl nitrate; that from methyl alcohol and acetic acid, methyl acetate; that from benzyl alcohol and benzoic acid, benzyl benzoate; and so on.

The above general equation and those shown in **Fig. A.13** indicate that the reaction between alcohols and acids is reversible; that is, it takes place in either direction. The change proceeding from left to right is called **esterification** and the reverse process is known as **hydrolysis.** In the preparation of an ester, therefore, the water produced during the esterification must be removed (by adding dehydrating agents) so that the reaction proceeds in the desired direction.

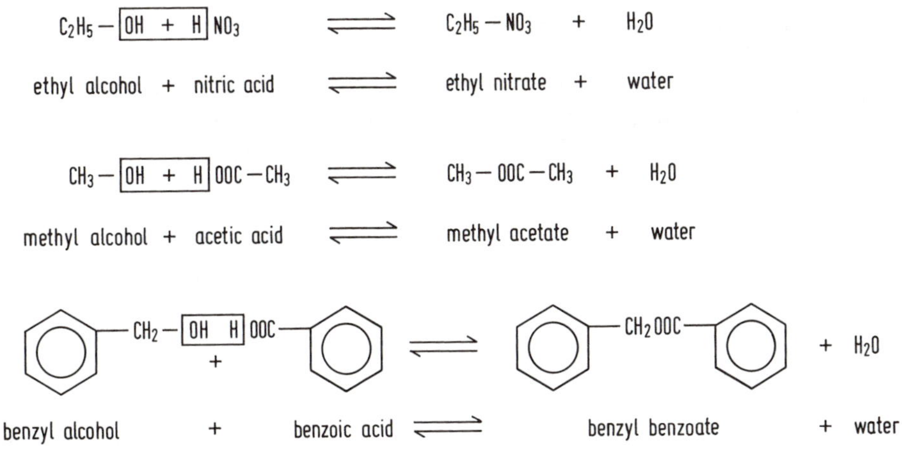

$$C_2H_5 - \boxed{OH \ + \ H} \ NO_3 \ \rightleftharpoons \ C_2H_5 - NO_3 \ + \ H_2O$$

ethyl alcohol + nitric acid $\rightleftharpoons$ ethyl nitrate + water

$$CH_3 - \boxed{OH \ + \ H} \ OOC - CH_3 \ \rightleftharpoons \ CH_3 - OOC - CH_3 \ + \ H_2O$$

methyl alcohol + acetic acid $\rightleftharpoons$ methyl acetate + water

benzyl alcohol   +   benzoic acid $\rightleftharpoons$ benzyl benzoate   + water

Fig. A.13: Formation of Esters

A.25 Natural Fats, Oils and Soaps

Animal fats and vegetable oils are esters formed from the trihydric alcohol, glycerol, and mixed fatty acids such as palmitic acid and stearic acid. These esters are collectively termed **glycerides** and, like all other esters, are hydrolyzed by hot water into glycerol and a mixture of fatty acids, as shown in **Fig. A.14**. When boiled with alkalis, the glycerides are decomposed much more rapidly than with hot water, and alkali salts of the fatty acids are formed together with glycerol. The alkali salts of fatty acids are called **soaps**.

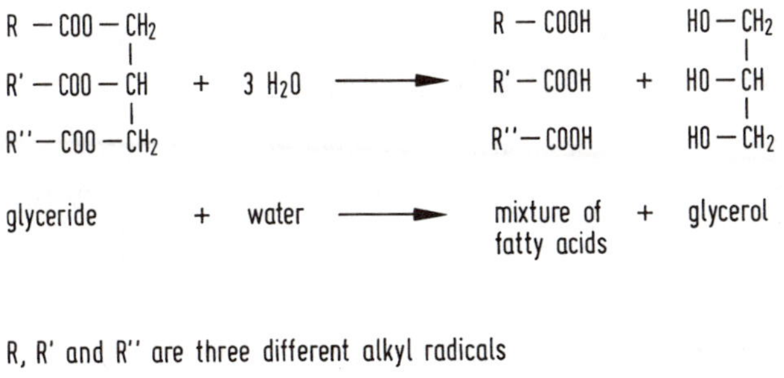

$$
\begin{array}{l}
R \ - COO - CH_2 \\
R' - COO - CH \quad + \ 3 \ H_2O \ \longrightarrow \\
R'' - COO - CH_2
\end{array}
\quad
\begin{array}{l}
R \ - COOH \\
R' - COOH \quad + \\
R'' - COOH
\end{array}
\quad
\begin{array}{l}
HO - CH_2 \\
HO - CH \\
HO - CH_2
\end{array}
$$

glyceride   +   water $\longrightarrow$ mixture of + glycerol
                                              fatty acids

R, R' and R'' are three different alkyl radicals

Fig. A.14: Hydrolysis of Glycerides

A.26 Amines

Amines are organic compounds derived from ammonia (NH_3) by the displacement of one, two or three hydrogen atoms by alkyl or aryl groups. In this way primary, secondary and tertiary aliphatic and aromatic amines are respectively produced with the following general formulas:

R-NH$_2$, R$_2$NH and R$_3$N for aliphatic amines and Ar-NH$_2$, Ar$_2$NH and Ar$_3$N for aromatic amines

The names and structural formulas of selected aliphatic and aromatic amines are given in **Fig. A.15**. The aromatic amines, in which the amino group is united with a carbon atom of the side chain (such as benzylamine), closely resemble the aliphatic amines in their chemical properties.

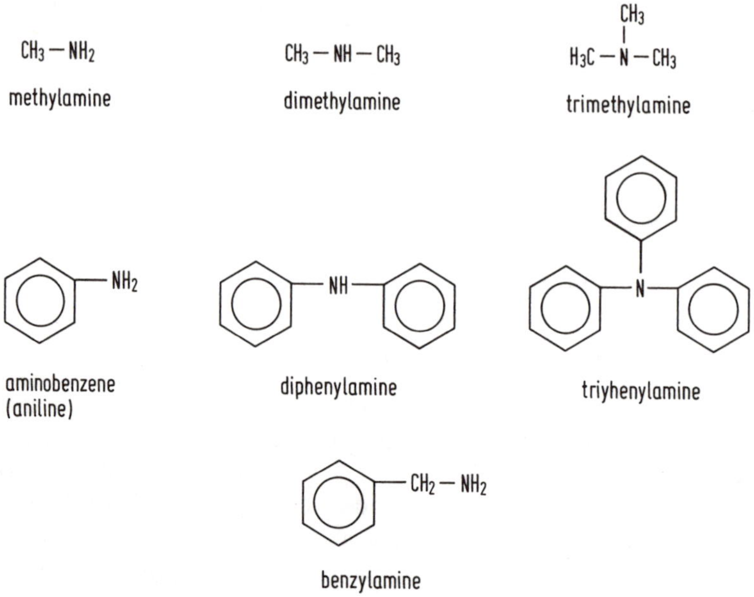

CH$_3$ — NH$_2$

methylamine

CH$_3$ — NH — CH$_3$

dimethylamine

H$_3$C — N — CH$_3$
    |
    CH$_3$

trimethylamine

aminobenzene
(aniline)

diphenylamine

triyhenylamine

benzylamine

Fig. A.15: Selected Aliphatic and Aromatic Amines

A.27 Nitro-Derivatives of Hydrocarbons

Nitro-derivatives of hydrocarbons are compounds that contain one or more nitro-(-NO$_2$) groups in their molecules. They may be classed in nitroparaffins and nitraded aromatic hydrocarbons.

The simplest nitroparaffins have the general formula R-NO$_2$ and are derived from paraffins (section A.17) by the substitution of a nitro group for one hydrogen atom. The lower members of this series include nitromethane (CH$_3$-NO$_2$) and nitroethane (C$_2$H$_5$-NO$_2$).

The nitro-derivatives of aromatic hydrocarbons are obtained by the substitution of one or more nitro groups for the same number of hydrogen atoms of the nucleus or side chain. The names and structural formulas of selected aromatic nitrocompounds are given in **Fig. A.16**.

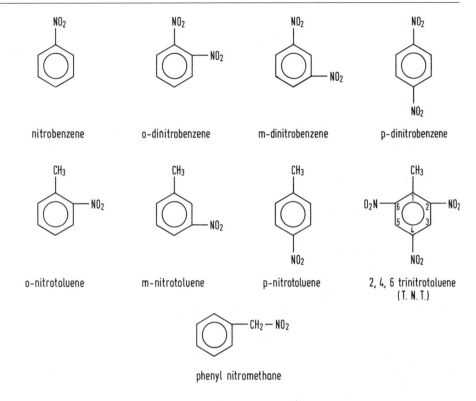

nitrobenzene   o-dinitrobenzene   m-dinitrobenzene   p-dinitrobenzene

o-nitrotoluene   m-nitrotoluene   p-nitrotoluene   2, 4, 6 trinitrotoluene
(T. N. T.)

phenyl nitromethane

Fig. A.16: Selected Aromatic Nitrocompounds

A.28 Amides

Amides are organic compounds that contain one or more amide- ($-CONH_2$) groups
in their molecules. They may be regarded as derived from carboxylic acids (section
A.23) by the displacement of an ($-OH$) group (of the carboxylic group) by a ($-NH_2$)
group. For this reason, the amides are named after the acids from which they are
derived. The lower members of this series of compounds include

formamide ($H-CONH_2$) from formic acid;
acetamide (CH_3-CONH_2) from acetic acid;
benzamide ($C_6H_5-CONH_2$) from benzoic acid;
oxamide ($H_2NCO-CONH_2$) from oxalic acid; and
succinamide ($H_2NCO-CH_2-CH_2-CONH_2$) from succinic acid.

A.29 Nitriles

Nitriles, or cyanides, are organic compounds that contain one or more nitrile-
($-CN$) groups in their molecules. They can be converted into carboxylic acids
(section A.23) when boiled with mineral acids or alkalis; that is, the ($-CN$) group is
converted into a ($-COOH$) group. For this reason, the nitriles are named after the

carboxylic acids that they yield on hydrolysis. Methyl nitrile (CH_3-CN), for example, is called acetonitrile; ethylnitrile (C_2H_5-CN), propionitrile; phenylnitrile (C_6H_5-CN), benzonitrile, and so on.

A.30 Isocyanates

Isocyanates are organic compounds that contain one or more isocyanate(-NCO) groups in their molecules. The simplest members of this series of compounds include methyl isocyanate (CH_3-NCO), ethyl isocyanate (C_2H_5-NCO) and phenyl isocyanate (C_6H_5-NCO).

Certain aromatic diisocyanates (with two isocyanate groups) are important materials for the production of polyurethanes (section 8.23.1).

A.31 Thioalcohols and Thioethers

There are two classes of organic compounds derived from hydrogen sulphide: thioalcohols and thioethers. Thioalcohols are hydrosulphides with the general formula R-SH. They are usually called mercaptans (e.g., ethylmercaptan, C_2H_5-SH) because of their property of reacting readily with mercuric oxides to form crystalline compounds.

The thioethers are organic sulphides with the general formula R-S-R such as diethyl sulphide (C_2H_5-S-C_2H_5). The mercaptans and thioethers are both characterized by having a highly unpleasant smell.

A.32 Sulphonic Acids

Sulphonic acids are organic compounds that contain one or more sulphonic-(-SO_3H) groups in their molecules. Generally speaking, they are very stable compounds capable of forming metallic salts. The most important member of this group is benzenesulphonic acid (C_6H_5-SO_3H).

Bibliography

General Books

Alliger, G., and I. J. Sjothun. *Vulcanization of Elastomers*. New York: Van Nostrand Reinhold, 1963.

Blackley, D. C. *Synthetic Rubbers: Their Chemistry and Technology*. London: Applied Science, 1983.

Brown, R. P. *Physical Testing of Rubbers*. London: Applied Science, 1979.

Brown, R. P. *Guide to Rubber and Plastics Test Equipment*. Shawbury: Rapra, 1979.

Braun, D. *Simple Methods for Identification of Plastics*. Brooklyn, N.Y.: Hanser, 1986.

Brydson, J. A. *Rubber Chemistry*. London: Applied Science, 1978.

Evans; C. W. *Developments in Rubber and rubber Composites*, vol. 1. London: Applied Science, 1980.

Hepburn, C., and Reynolds, R. J. W. *Elastomers: Criteria for Engineering Design*. London: Applied Science, 1979.

Legge, N. R., G. Holden, and H. E. Schroeder. *Thermoplastic Elastomers*. Brooklyn, N.Y.: Hanser, 1987.

Morton, M. *Rubber Technology*. New York: Van Nostrand Reinhold, 1987.

Scott, N., and V. Whalley. *Specialty and High Performance Rubbers*. Shawbury: Rapra Technology.

Seymour, R. B. *Polymers for Engineering Applications*. ASM International, 1987.

Thorn, A. D. *Thermoplastic Elastomers*. Shawbury: Rapra, 1980.

Warring, R. H. *Seals and Packings*. Morden, Surrey: Trade and Technical Press, 1967.

Whelan, A., and K. S. Lee. *Developments in Rubber Technology,* vols. 1–3. London: Applied Science, 1979.

Standard Guides

Annual Book of ASTM Standards, vols. 09.01 and 09.02: *Rubber.* Philadelphia: ASTM, 1991.

"BS 6716." *British Standard Guide to Properties and Types of rubbers*. London: British Standard Institution, 1986.

"The Language of Rubber." In *Elastomers Notebook*. Wilmington, Delware: Du Pont de Nemours International, 1991.

Parker O-Ring Handbook. Lexington, Mass.: Parker Seal Group, O-Ring Division, 1982.

The Vanderbilt Rubber Handbook. Norwalk, CT: R. T. Vanderbilt, 1978.

Index